Africa Now

Africa Now is published by Zed Books in association with the internationally respected Nordic Africa Institute. Featuring high-quality, cutting-edge research from leading academics, the series addresses the big issues confronting Africa today. Accessible but in-depth, and wide-ranging in its scope, Africa Now engages with the critical political, economic, sociological and development debates affecting the continent, shedding new light on pressing concerns.

Nordic Africa Institute

The Nordic Africa Institute (Nordiska Afrikainstitutet) is a centre for research, documentation and information on modern Africa. Based in Uppsala, Sweden, the Institute is dedicated to providing timely, critical and alternative research and analysis of Africa and to co-operation with African researchers. As a hub and a meeting place for a growing field of research and analysis the Institute strives to put knowledge of African issues within reach for scholars, policy makers, politicians, media, students and the general public.

www.nai.uu.se

Forthcoming titles

Atakilte Beyene (ed.), *Agricultural Transformation in Ethiopia*

Laura Stark and Annika Teppo (eds), *Power and Inequality in Urban Africa*

Titles already published

Fantu Cheru and Cyril Obi (eds), *The Rise of China and India in Africa*

Ilda Lindell (ed.), *Africa's Informal Workers*

Iman Hashim and Dorte Thorsen, *Child Migration in Africa*

Prosper B. Matondi, Kjell Havnevik and Atakilte Beyene (eds), *Biofuels, Land Grabbing and Food Security in Africa*

Cyril Obi and Siri Aas Rustad (eds), *Oil and Insurgency in the Niger Delta*

Mats Utas (ed.), *African Conflicts and Informal Power*

Prosper B. Matondi, *Zimbabwe's Fast Track Land Reform*

Maria Eriksson Baaz and Maria Stern, *Sexual Violence as a Weapon of War?*

Fantu Cheru and Renu Modi (eds), *Agricultural Development and Food Security in Africa*

Amanda Hammar (ed.), *Displacement Economies in Africa*

Mary Njeri Kinyanjui, *Women and the Informal Economy in Urban Africa*

Liisa Laakso and Petri Hautaniemi (eds), *Diasporas, Development and Peacemaking in the Horn of Africa*

Margaret Lee, *Africa's World Trade*

Godwin R. Murunga, Duncan Okello and Anders Sjögren (eds), *Kenya: The Struggle for a New Constitutional Order*

Lisa Åkesson and Maria Eriksson Baaz (eds), *Africa's Return Migrants*

Thiven Reddy, *South Africa: Settler Colonialism and the Failures of Liberal Democracy*

Cedric de Coning, Linnéa Gelot and John Karlsrud (eds), *The Future of African Peace Operations*

Tobias Hagmann and Filip Reyntjens (eds), *Aid and Authoritarianism in Africa*

Henning Melber, *The Rise of Africa's Middle Class*

Anders Themnér (ed.), *Warlord Democrats in Africa*

Paul Higate and Mats Utas (eds), *Private Security in Africa*

About the editors

Mimmi Söderberg Kovacs is Head of Research at the Folke Bernadotte Academy (FBA) and affiliated Senior Researcher with the Nordic Africa Institute (NAI) and the Department of Peace and Conflict Research at Uppsala University in Sweden. Her research focus is on non-state actors in civil wars, rebel-to-party transformations, conflict resolution, peace processes, and post-war democratisation.

Jesper Bjarnesen is Senior Researcher at the Nordic Africa Institute (NAI). His main research area is qualitative migration studies, with a focus on the overlaps between voluntary and involuntary movements; the dynamics of mobility in relation to armed conflict; and the micro-politics of inclusion and exclusion in urban contexts in West Africa.

Violence in African Elections

Between Democracy and Big Man Politics

edited by Mimmi Söderberg Kovacs and Jesper Bjarnesen

Nordiska Afrikainstitutet
The Nordic Africa Institute

ZED

Violence in African Elections: Between Democracy and Big Man Politics
was first published in association with the Nordic Africa Institute,
PO Box 1703, SE-751 47 Uppsala, Sweden in 2018 by Zed Books Ltd,
The Foundry, 17 Oval Way, London SE11 5RR, UK.

www.zedbooks.net
www.nai.uu.se

Editorial copyright © Mimmi Söderberg Kovacs and Jesper Bjarnesen 2018
Copyright in this collection © Zed Books 2018

The rights of Mimmi Söderberg Kovacs and Jesper Bjarnesen to be
identified as the editors of this work have been asserted by them in
accordance with the Copyright, Designs and Patents Act 1988.

Typeset in Minion Pro by seagulls.net
Index by John Barker
Cover design by Alice Marwick
Cover photo © Sven Torfinn/Panos

A catalogue record for this book is available from the British Library

ISBN   978-1-78699-229-1 hb
ISBN   978-1-78699-228-4 pb
ISBN   978-1-78699-230-7 pdf
ISBN   978-1-78699-231-4 epub
ISBN   978-1-78699-232-1 mobi

Contents

Abbreviations

AFRC	Armed Forces Revolutionary Council (Sierra Leone)
ANACOWA	All Nigerians Autobike Commercial Owners and Workers Association of Nigeria
APC	All People's Congress (Sierra Leone)
APC	All Progressives Congress (Nigeria)
CDC	Congress of Democratic Change (Liberia)
CENAP	Conflict Alert and Prevention Centre (Burundi)
CHRA	Combined Harare Residents' Association (Zimbabwe)
CNDD-FDD	National Council for the Defence of Democracy and the Forces for the Defence of Democracy (Burundi)
CNTB	National Commission on Land and Other Assets (Burundi)
CODEO	Coalition of Domestic Election Observers (Ghana)
CORD	Coalition for Reforms and Democracy (Kenya)
DCE	District Chief Executive (Ghana)
DDR	disarmament, demobilisation and reintegration
DDRR	disarmament, demobilisation, rehabilitation and reintegration
DP	Democratic Party (Kenya / Uganda)
ECOWAS	Economic Community of West African States
FDC	Forum for Democratic Change (Uganda)
FNL	National Forces of Liberation (Burundi)
FORD	Forum for the Restoration of Democracy (Kenya)
FPI	Ivorian Popular Front (Côte d'Ivoire)
FRODEBU	Front for Democracy in Burundi
GEMA	Gikuyu, Embu, Meru Association (Kenya)
GPA	global political agreement (Zimbabwe)
HRT	Harare Residents' Trust (Zimbabwe)
ICC	International Criminal Court
IEBC	Independent Electoral and Boundaries Commission (Kenya)
INPFL	Independent National Patriotic Front of Liberia
IOC	international oil company (Nigeria)
JIAM	Jesus Is Alive Ministries (Kenya)
KADU	Kenyan National Democratic Union
KAI	Kick Against Indiscipline (Nigeria)
KAMATUSA	Kalenjin, Maasai, Turkana, Samburu Association (Kenya)
KANU	Kenyan African National Union

KPM	Kono Progressive Movement (Sierra Leone)
KPU	Kenya People's Union
LNP	Liberian National Police
LURD	Liberians United for Reconciliation and Democracy
MAC-P	Military Aid to Civil Power (Sierra Leone)
MDC	Movement for Democratic Change (Zimbabwe)
MEND	Movement for the Emancipation of the Niger Delta (Nigeria)
MODEL	Movement for Democracy in Liberia
MP	member of parliament
MSD	Movement for Solidarity and Development (Burundi)
NARC	National Rainbow Coalition (Kenya)
NDC	National Democratic Congress (Ghana)
NDDC	Niger Delta Development Commission (Nigeria)
NDPL	National Democratic Party of Liberia
NDPVF	Niger Delta People's Volunteer Force (Nigeria)
NDV	Niger Delta Vigilante (Nigeria)
NEC	National Electoral Commission (Sierra Leone)
NIMASA	Nigerian Maritime Safety Agency
NNPC	Nigerian National Petroleum Company
NPC	National Peace Council (Ghana)
NPFL	National Patriotic Front of Liberia
NPN	National Party of Nigeria
NPP	New Patriotic Party (Ghana)
NPP	National Patriotic Party (Liberia)
NPRC	National Provisional Ruling Council (Sierra Leone)
NRA	National Resistance Army (Uganda)
NRM	National Resistance Movement (Uganda)
NTGL	National Transitional Government of Liberia
NUDP	National Union for Democratic Progress (Liberia)
NURTW	National Union of Road Transport Workers (Nigeria)
ONS	Office of National Security (Sierra Leone)
P4P	Partners for Peace (Nigeria)
PAP	Presidential Amnesty Programme (Nigeria)
PDP	People's Democratic Party (Nigeria)
PMDC	People's Movement for Democratic Change (Sierra Leone)
PNDC	Provisional National Defence Council (Ghana)
PNU	Party of National Unity (Kenya)
PPRC	Political Party Registration Commission (Sierra Leone)
RA	Reform Agenda (Uganda)
RFI	Radio France Internationale
RPA	Radio Publique Africaine (Burundi)
RUF	Revolutionary United Front (Sierra Leone)

SLPP	Sierra Leone People's Party
UN	United Nations
UNMIL	United Nations Mission in Liberia
UP	Unity Party (Liberia)
UPC	Uganda People's Congress
UPDF	Uganda Peoples Defence Forces
UPN	Unity Party of Nigeria
UPRONA	Union for National Progress (Burundi)
WANEP	West Africa Network for Peacebuilding
ZANU-PF	Zimbabwe African National Union Patriotic Front
ZAPU	Zimbabwe African People's Union
ZimPF	Zimbabwe People First

Acknowledgements

The first steps towards the writing of this book were taken in October 2015 with the organisation of a two-day writers' workshop at the Nordic Africa Institute (NAI) on this theme. During intense discussions, patterns and trends began to emerge across the different case studies of electoral violence in Africa that were presented, and many of the gaps that we try to address in this volume were identified. We owe a great deal to all those scholars who participated in the workshop but are not included in this book, notably Akin Iwilade, Ayokunle O. Omobowale, Azeez O. Olaniyan, Charly D. N. Tsafack, Felix Kumah-Abiwu, Johanna Riess, Michael N. Mbapndah, Olatokunbo O. Fayiga, Olusoji A. Odeyemi, Osita Odafi, Rodrick Henry and Surajudeen O. Mudasiro. We are also grateful to colleagues outside the author circle who provided insightful comments on some of the chapters, notably Anders Themnér, Angela Muvumba Sellström, Henrik Angerbrandt and Johan Broské. The Swedish Research Council financially supported the writers' workshop, as well as the production of this book, within the framework of a major research grant. Funding for the workshop was also generously provided by NAI, and we were able to benefit from much appreciated administrative assistance in the form of Annika Franklin's expertise. We are truly indebted to both institutions, without whose support this book project could not have been completed.

Several of the ideas expressed in this book also benefited from years of discussions and stimulating intellectual exchange with our research colleagues at NAI, not least in the dynamic research cluster on Conflict, Security and Democratic Transformation. Perhaps more than anyone, we would like to thank Mats Utas for first opening the door for us at NAI and successfully nurturing a space for productive interdisciplinary research on contemporary African studies. We would also like to extend our appreciation to former Director Carin Norberg for accepting to host the research grant at NAI in the first place, and to current Director Iina Soiri and Head of Research Victor Adetula for their continuous support. We are also grateful to NAI's former Head of Communications Elnaz Alizadeh for supporting our initial idea of an edited volume on this theme. During the writing of this volume, we have also relied on meticulous assistance from Henrik Persson at NAI and Sophia Wrede at the Folke Bernadotte Academy (FBA). We received insightful comments from Kristine Höglund at the Department of Peace and Conflict Research at Uppsala University on the introductory chapter, and several other colleagues and conference participants have provided useful input and advice on various parts of the book. We would also like to highlight the constructive and very useful comments provided by two anonymous reviewers. Their suggestions significantly helped us in strengthening our arguments and sharpening our contributions. We would also like to extend our appreciation to the team at Zed Books and especially to Ken Barlow, editor of the *Africa Now* series, for his enthusiasm and unwavering support. We have also benefited considerably from Judith Forshaw's perceptive copyediting of this text, and Henrik Alfredsson's tireless work in designing the maps for chapter 4.

Above all, we would like to say thank you to all the chapter authors, who took time out of busy schedules and demanding work piles to join us in this collaborative and interdisciplinary effort on violence in African elections.

Mimmi Söderberg Kovacs
Jesper Bjarnesen
Uppsala, December 2017

Introduction: The everyday politics of electoral violence in Africa

Mimmi Söderberg Kovacs

'*Ampa ampoh*,' yell the young men sitting on the back of the pickup truck that hastily enters the back gate of the State House building in downtown Freetown in Sierra Leone. It means 'It is over' in Temne, one of the local languages. It is late in the afternoon of Friday 24 November 2012, and the National Election Commission (NEC) has just held a press conference to announce the results of the presidential elections, ending days of intense speculation after the closing of the polls. According to the announcement, the sitting president Ernest Bai Koroma of the All People's Congress (APC) has secured a second term in power against Julius Maada Bio, the flag-bearer of the Sierra Leone People's Party (SLPP). Many hoped that this would be the end of a tense and occasionally violent election campaign. However, while APC supporters dressed in red (the party colour) danced in the streets of Freetown, cheering and singing amidst the ear-deafening sounds of car horns, whistle pipes and the banging of pots and pans, disgruntlement was mounting in the opposition camp. The following day, the SLPP accused the incumbent of electoral fraud, refusing to accept the results. The next few weeks saw several minor incidents of violence across the country, especially in traditional SLPP strongholds, as young party supporters took to the streets, clashed with the police and security personnel, and engaged in local fights against APC supporters. It was not until the SLPP leadership eventually conceded its electoral defeat a few weeks later that the violence finally subsided (Söderberg Kovacs 2012).

The example above reflects a larger trend that we have witnessed in sub-Saharan Africa since the (re-)introduction of multiparty democracy in the early 1990s. In a relatively short time period, democracy has formally been established as the dominant political system across the continent, and the holding of elections has emerged as the most important institutional mechanism for the distribution of political power. Other means and methods of political rule have grown increasingly difficult to motivate and sustain in the face of changing normative and institutional frameworks at both the global and the regional level. Yet, at the same time, we have witnessed a growing trend of electoral violence in many new democracies. According to Burchard (2015: 50), more than half of Africa's states, 55 per cent, have experienced electoral violence in the post-Cold War period. Importantly, beyond the relatively few cases of large-scale killings and widespread fear and insecurity that make it to the international headlines – such as in Kenya in 2007, Zimbabwe in 2008 and Côte d'Ivoire in 2010 – a more common scenario has been that of isolated violent events, harassment and coercive intimidation. Countries that have displayed such characteristics during election periods include, for example, Cameroon, the Democratic Republic of Congo, Liberia, Equatorial Guinea, the Gambia, Guinea, Madagascar, Sierra Leone, Senegal and Uganda (Straus and Taylor 2012).

In addition, and often forgotten both by the international media and by the scholarly community engaged in better understanding the phenomenon, a multitude of countries experience the kind of electoral violence that is low-scale but pervasive and typically occurs long before the elections, between electoral cycles, and in local elections far from the international limelight. MacGinty (2014) introduced the term 'everyday peace' to capture the routinised practices and norms deployed by individuals and groups to navigate their way through life in divided societies. This is a scholarly approach that emphasises bottom-up perspectives on a social phenomenon and takes seriously the notion of local agency (see also Autesserre 2010). We find this inspirational, and would like to evoke the expression of 'everyday politics of electoral violence' to characterise the overall perspective employed in this book. Most individuals and groups in Africa's electoral democracies are likely to find concepts such as 'competitive elections' and 'patronage politics' to be of little use for describing their everyday experiences. However, their everyday realities can assist us in better under-standing the specific and localised expressions of these theoretical concepts and contribute to a more deep-layered understanding of the phenomenon of electoral violence. Importantly, the 'bottom-up' perspective is not put in contrast or opposition to the 'top-down'. Instead, the two views inform each other, and we have deliberately put together a collection of contributions that together and jointly highlight both perspectives.

The example given above from the 2012 general elections in Sierra Leone is particularly interesting in this respect because it was generally considered a very successful election according to most traditional international criteria. For example, the national electoral institutions acknowledged only a handful of electoral irregularities. Very limited evidence of over-voting or ballot stuffing was discovered. The large number of international and domestic election observer teams all declared the elections free of systematic malpractice. Yet, at the same time, there is little doubt that the elections were conducted on an uneven playing field, where the incumbent was able to take significant advantage of his position in power, for example in terms of access to the media and to resources for campaigning. In addition, the heavy and visible presence of both the police and the military patrolling the streets during the election period did not always instil a sense of security among the population. Rather, for some it was a cause of provocation and a sign that the APC was conflating the party with the state (Söderberg Kovacs 2012). As if to further underscore this point, both the dominant public discourse and the language and terminology used by the parties were frequently cloaked in symbolism associated with battle and warfare. For example, Maada Bio was hailed as 'the Tormentor' by his supporters, in reference to his past as a military junta leader in the coup that overthrew the one-party APC regime at the beginning of the civil war in 1992 (Bangura and Söderberg Kovacs 2017). Maada Bio's transformation from wartime leader to political party representative running for office is not unique. A large number of post-war African states have witnessed the emergence of so-called 'warlord democrats': former military or political leaders of armed groups who subsequently participate in electoral politics (Themnér 2017). There are thus many good reasons for suggesting that elections have become 'the new battlegrounds' (Bøås and Utas 2014).

The threats associated with electoral violence are many. Beyond the immediate human, material and societal costs that such violence imposes on already impoverished and sometimes war-torn states, it also risks undermining the legitimacy of the electoral process and the democratic political system. Research shows that electoral violence is significantly related to individual assessments about willingness to vote, democratic satisfaction, support for democracy and trust in governing institutions (Burchard 2015). Violence and voter intimidation have also been found to reduce voter turnouts in some elections (Bratton 2008; Collier and Vicente 2008), although more recent research suggests that there are no such effects of violence on voter turnout more generally in African elections (Bekoe and Burchard 2017). Electoral violence also risks permeating cycles of revenge between political parties at the local level (Höglund and Piyarathne 2009). In countries where the winner literally takes all, the stakes of elections are high, and the costs of defeat devastating. Whether you are the flag-bearer of the party or an ex-soldier or ex-militia working behind the scenes as part of the security task force of a political party, a loss at the polls means another few years out in the cold, another few years of struggle for survival and for access to resources (Christensen and Utas 2016). In some exceptional cases, elections may even be an impetus for civil war, as the developments in Burundi in 2015 amply illustrated. Even if such instances are rare, when they do happen they can also affect neighbouring states through large-scale displacement of people, the creation of a humanitarian crisis, and the increasing circulation of arms in already volatile regions.

Following in the footsteps of this development, an emerging and fast-growing research agenda has developed that seeks to better understand the causes, dynamics and consequences of electoral violence. In this debate, several critical generic factors have been identified as explanations for why some countries are more likely than others to experience such violence (e.g. Fjelde and Höglund 2014; Hafner-Burton, Hyde and Jablonski 2013; Norris, Frank and Martinez i Coma 2015; Salehyan and Linebarger 2015). While such studies are important in identifying those countries most at risk, and while they can help us understand what characteristics of the political system in place generate the incentives for violence in the first place, they often fall short of explaining – and empirically demonstrating – exactly how and why these factors lead to specific incidents of violence. Also, this is not their primary purpose. Other studies persuasively capture the rich complexities of individual country cases or specific elections in more depth (e.g. Boone and Kriger 2012; Sisk 2012; Smith 2009). From such work, we can learn a lot about the relative importance of various factors in different empirical contexts. However, with some important exceptions (e.g. de Smedt 2009; Höglund and Piyarathne 2009; Klaus and Mitchell 2015), few previous studies have explored these issues on a subnational level, attempting to elucidate the patterns, dynamics and trends of such violence within states and why some areas and regions in a country are more likely than others to experience instances of election-related violence. In addition, we do not yet know enough about the micro-level factors and dynamics at work and the more intricate causal processes that link macro-level factors at the national level with the occurrences of violent events at the local level.

This book aims to address these identified gaps. The chapters all attempt to answer one or several of these pertinent questions at the front line of the research agenda: why are some regions, areas and towns within the same country more likely than others to see incidents of electoral violence? Why are some elections more violent than others within the same country? What is the relationship between the dynamics of national-level politics and incidents of electoral violence at the local level? Why are some actors more likely than others to engage in, or support, violent acts around election time? Why are some issues more likely than others to mobilise people for violence? The overall objective of this book is thus not only to explain when and why we see electoral violence in Africa's emerging democracies, but to empiri-cally trace the processes through which such events occur. By doing so, we hope that the findings from this book will be useful for policy makers and practitioners working in the field of election assistance and support, election observation, and the promotion of democracy, good governance and human rights, especially in new democracies in developing states.

The remainder of this introductory chapter is structured as follows. First, the phenomenon of electoral violence is discussed and problematised, building on previous contributions in the field. Second, the rationale for the empirical focus on the subnational level of analysis is explained, on the basis of scholarly work emphasising the need for increased analysis beyond the macro-level. Third, previous research on the causes and dynamics of election-related violence is considered, structuring the discussion around three main clusters: the structural conditions of holding elections in Africa's multi-ethnic states and patronage systems; the characteristics of multiparty elections, such as electoral competition and close electoral races; and the institutional framework of elections. The final section provides an introductory note on each of the chapters in this volume together with a few words on how they relate to the overall theme of the book.

The phenomenon of electoral violence

What is electoral violence? There is not yet an established definition in the academic literature and there is no strong consensus in previous research. As a point of departure for this book project, however, we began by defining electoral violence as *violent or coercive acts carried out for the purpose of affecting the process or results of an election.* This conceptual understanding is inspired by – yet also partly diverges from – previous developments in the field. This is discussed in more detail below. However, while agreeing on a joint platform to depart from and relate to in our individual chapters, we also believed that it was not necessary that all chapter authors remained loyal to this definition, and we have encouraged a broad approach to the concept in order to adapt the relevance of the theme to a range of different local contexts. After all, one of the objectives of this book is to build theory and to expand our empirical understanding of the phenomenon. As such, we believe that too narrow a definition might unnecessarily constrain the analysis and prevent new knowledge from being generated inductively.

Existing definitions usually highlight two criteria: motive and timing (Höglund 2009). Beginning with motive, we find, for example, that Laakso (2007: 227–8) argues that electoral violence by definition is 'an activity motivated by an attempt to affect the results of the elections – either by manipulating the electoral procedures and participation or by contesting the legitimacy of the results'. In other words, on an aggregated level, it makes sense to argue that the overall objective is to 'influence the electoral process' (Höglund 2009: 415). This emphasis on intent is critical not only in that it helps us to differentiate electoral violence from other forms of political violence, but also because it highlights the instrumentality of violence and the strategic motives involved. We find this aspect essential for understanding the causes and dynamics of electoral violence. Just as Bøås and Dunn (2007: 4) argue that African insurgencies 'are best understood as rational responses to the composition of African states and their policies', we believe that electoral violence is a rational response to the logic of elections in the context of African political systems. We discuss this in more detail in the next section. However, this emphasis on strategic motives aimed at influencing the electoral process does not exclude the fact that, behind and beyond this overarching picture, we find a range of additional motives. We are acutely aware of the potential risks associated with pursuing a framing of the problem that is too simplistic. As noted by Eriksson Baaz and Stern (2013), in the context of understanding the occurrence of sexual violence in war, the pursuit of a single narrative risks excluding and silencing additional and equally relevant motives, particularly at the micro-level of analysis. We therefore want to underline that the more precise motives of each actor involved in electoral violence may vary. Those motives may also shift over time. In addition, each actor might pursue a range of multiple motives when engaging in electoral violence. For example, several chapters in this book discuss the role that young people – mostly men – play as so-called 'foot soldiers' of electoral violence (Bob-Milliar 2014). These individuals are usually mobilised for violence by a range of different motives, such as access to short-term benefits, loyalty to a Big Man, and private score settling against rival groups. In some instances, they engage in violent activities without any prior contacts, encouragement or instructions from Big Men, hoping that their sacrifice will be noticed and rewarded (Christensen and Utas 2016). However, we argue that their violent behaviour cannot be understood outside the context of the instrumentality of electoral violence for the political elites. In doing so, we also take issue with attempts to draw a sharp differentiation between strategic and incidental electoral violence. Alston (2010: 5–6), for example, argues that some violence, particularly in connection with riots or protests, is not intended to influence or change electoral outcomes, but rather is motivated by 'indignation, anger and disappointment'. Burchard (2015: 12–13) echoes this message when she argues that some election-related violence lacks explicit intent, such as 'spontaneous' protests and killings by 'over-zealous security forces'. We believe that this interpretation ignores the overarching context in which these individual engagements in electoral violence take place. On this issue, we are inspired by Kalyvas, who argues that, in the context of civil wars, the decentralised and localised nature of conflict does not imply spontaneous and anarchical violence: such a perspective 'overlooks the political conflict in which [civil wars] occur' (Kalyvas 2003: 485).

When it comes to timing, the other definitional feature commonly identified in the literature (e.g. Bekoe 2012; Burchard 2015; Höglund 2009), this book deliberately avoids a definition that limits our analysis to violence 'directly tied to an impending electoral contest or an announced electoral result' (Straus and Taylor 2012: 19). While we agree that electoral violence can take place at all stages of the electoral process – notably before, during and after an election – it is close to impossible to pin down the exact time period this includes (and excludes) in the context of new and emerging democracies in developing states (see also Bekoe 2012: 2). The strategic electoral game is an ongoing process and an integral part of party politics itself. In addition, we believe that electoral violence is a phenomenon that is not limited to general and national elections, although these tend to generate the greatest attention.

Electoral violence is something that also takes place in connection with other elections, including, for example, local government elections, chiefdom elections, primaries and by-elections (see for example Höglund and Jarstad 2011). As discussed by Bangura and Söderberg Kovacs in Chapter 5 in the context of Sierra Leone, such in-between elections can sometimes generate more election-related violence than the often better monitored general elections.

Another aspect in the identification and delimitation of electoral violence concerns the relevant actors involved. The usual suspects, Höglund (2009: 416) argues, are the political parties in government and in opposition, although the exact line-up depends on the context. For example, in conflict or post-war societies, armed non-state actors as well as militias and paramilitary groups may play a significant role as violent instigators (ibid.; see also Höglund, Jarstad and Söderberg Kovacs 2009; Raleigh 2016). Most subsequent studies in the field have followed this lead and focus primarily on activities committed by the incumbent or the political opposition. As acknowledged by Straus and Taylor (2012: 20), however, there is usually a broad spectrum of actors who fall under these two umbrella categories. They employ a broad empirical operationalisation that includes activities by actors with both more explicit and more implicit or even clandestine ties to the political parties in question. For the purposes of this book, we agree with this broad perspective on potential perpetrators of electoral violence. We attempt to contribute to the scholarly debate precisely by examining some of these actors in more detail, such as youth party militias (Chapter 8) and ex-combatants linked to Big Men networks (Chapters 6 and 7). We study their characteristics, internal dynamics and incentives for engaging in acts of electoral violence. Through our largely inductive empirical approach, we also shed light on a number of additional actors that have rarely been the centre of attention in previous research on electoral violence but that play an instrumental role in our understanding of local trajectories of violence, notably traditional authorities in Sierra Leone (Chapter 5), transport unions in Nigeria (Chapter 10), and a criminal business network in Zimbabwe (Chapter 9). Given the analytical emphasis on patronage networks, several of the contributions also explicitly focus on the more intricate relationships between various actors, and how alliances, mutual dependencies and social networks around elections are shaped and formed.

A final aspect of relevance relates to the means and methods used. In other words, what kind of violence are we referring to? In the classic literature in the field of peace and conflict research, direct physical violence is usually considered a distinct phenomenon, separate from other forms of conflict behaviour (Galtung 1969). In his seminal work on the logic of violence in civil wars, Kalyvas (2006: 19) suggests that, at the most basic level, one can define violence as the deliberate infliction of harm on people. In other disciplinary fields, notably cultural anthropology, violence is commonly defined more broadly and stretched beyond physical violence to cover the infliction of suffering in a broader sense (see for example Nordstrom 1997). For the purpose of defining and studying electoral violence, the scholarly literature has usually settled on something of a middle road. According to Straus and Taylor (2012: 17–18), electoral violence, including direct physical violence in the form of targeted high-level assassinations or generalised killing in immediate connection to an electoral contest, occurs relatively rarely on the African continent. Such violence is much more likely to come in the form of 'harassment, intimidation, and disruption' (ibid. 24). Hence, although Straus and Taylor limit their focus to physical aspects of violence, they also include threats of physical violence, captured by the notion of coercive intimidation. Importantly, Fischer (2002: 8) informs us that the targets of electoral violence are not necessarily only people, but also institutions, facilities, materials and symbols associated with elections. As noted by Bekoe (2012: 3), however, victims can also be perpetrators, and Höglund and Piyarathne (2009) convincingly show that just as conflict begets conflict, electoral violence tends to result in cycles of revenge between the main political parties.

As the chapters in this book illustrate, the violent and coercive methods used to affect the process or results of an election are many and varied, being both direct and indirect, and both high-intensity and more subdued and subtle. Above all, the everyday kinds of electoral violence that take place behind the backs of international election observers are almost always intimately local in their expression. In Chapter 11 of this volume, Schmitz illustrates how violent language and verbal threats cloaked in coercive and derogatory references shape electoral outcomes in Ghana, one of the most prominent democratic success stories on the African continent.

On a final note, in this book we will use the terms 'electoral violence', 'election-related violence' and 'violence-induced elections' interchangeably. While these terms might imply different causal relationships between elections and violence, we believe that a more detailed understanding of the exact nature and characteristics of these relationships is something to be explored inductively in each chapter.

Looking beyond the national: shifting the level of analysis

In order to better understand the more specific patterns of variation across space and time, most chapters in this volume apply a subnational perspective that links macro-level events and processes at the level of national political leadership to dynamics at the local level: a sub-region, district, town or neighbourhood. Other contributions focus on particular aspects of these processes, primarily from the perspective of a specific actor: the incentives of the political elite in a country to mobilise votes along ethnic lines; a youth militia's quest for political inclusion, influence and power; or the rationale of individual ex-combatants to engage or not engage in acts of electoral violence on behalf of a Big Man. What binds the contributions in this book together is the identification and analysis of causal mechanisms at work in processes of election-related violence.

In this, we are inspired by scholars in the field of civil war literature who have stressed the importance of going beyond macro-level analyses to understand the dynamics of political violence and expose the causal mechanisms at work (e.g. Balcells 2017; Balcells and Justine 2014; Kalyvas 2003; Verwimp, Justino and Brück 2009). Kalyvas (2003) argues that, in order to understand how processes of political violence play out on the ground, attention must be paid to local dynamics. In his account, civil wars are complex processes that involve a range of actors and a mixture of motives and identities. The dynamics of violence can be driven as much by local and private motives on the periphery – individual rivalries and local power competition, unsettled disputes, and issues of revenge – as by political and collective incentives at the centre. Such local grievances are likely to have a substantial impact on the overall 'content, direction and intensity of violence' (ibid. 479). In her study of the Spanish civil war, Balcells (2017) similarly demonstrates the relevance of taking local dynamics of rivalry and revenge into account. Observations of election-related violence at the local level in various countries suggest similar dynamics at work (e.g. Dercon and Guiterrez-Romero 2012; Höglund and Piyarathne 2009; Kandeh 2008). This multi-layered reality of violence explains why it is usually difficult to pinpoint a single cause for the outbreak of violence at all levels of analysis. Sometimes local grievances are transformed and escalated into larger processes of violence over time, while at other times national political dynamics result in a specific divergence of interests on the ground in various localities. Most often, however, they coexist and converge at various moments in time, such as at the time of elections. According to Kalyvas (2003: 475), it is the convergence of various motives that endows civil wars with their particular and often puzzling character; together, they are responsible for the 'joint production' of political violence (ibid. 476).

Importantly for the purpose of this study and the research questions we pose in this book, it has been suggested that micro-level approaches advance our understanding of violent processes precisely because of their ability to account for important variations within one country or conflict (Verwimp, Justino and Brück 2009: 307). However, by looking at only the micro-level, we may miss out on the bigger picture and the possibility of drawing important general lessons from individual studies and local cases. Balcells and Justino (2014) hence call for greater attention to the linkages between micro-level conflict dynamics and the wider political, economic and social processes at work, and for research that attempts to bridge the gap between local dynamics of conflict and conflict processes and outcomes taking place in the macro arena. We believe that these are important insights that are equally relevant for the study of electoral violence. Following Balcells and Justino (ibid. 1345), we define the *macro-level* as the level of the state and national processes and the *micro-level* as the level of the individual, household or small group, such as an individual's ex-combatant network. In between the two, Balcells and Justino conceive of the *meso-level* as 'processes that take place at the community level or at the level of local social groups and organisations'. While these categories might be analytically distinct, they sometimes overlap empirically. For example, the national political elite in a country consists of a collection of individuals, and an in-depth analysis of their individual and collective behaviour simultaneously straddles both the macro- and the micro-level.

In this book, we have approached this turn beyond traditional macro-level analyses of electoral violence in different ways. A few contributions explicitly attempt to link national political dynamics with violent processes at the local level. Several other contributions address linkages between dynamics at different levels of analysis and strengthen our knowledge about the complex networks, alliances and allegiances in place beyond the façade of the unitary state. However, even in cases where the analysis is deeply embedded in the local context, we believe that there are important general lessons to be learned. For example, in Chapter 10, Agbiboa discusses electoral violence associated with the urban transportation sector in two areas of Lagos. From his detailed description of the interdependency and precarity between patrons and clients, he conveys a micro-cosmos as part of a much larger phenomenon in Nigeria, with important implications for our understanding of the dynamics of electoral violence in the country at large. At the other end of the spectrum, both Fjelde and Höglund (Chapter 1) and Sjögren (Chapter 2) discuss the strategies of national political elites while highlighting individual leadership experiences and learning processes. As such, all the contributions shed light on the micro-foundations of electoral violence in new and emerging democracies in developing states.

Between democracy and Big Man politics

At the beginning of this chapter, we highlighted a trend that at first glance might seem to be a paradox: while democratic elections are gaining ground on the African continent, we are simultaneously seeing a rise in election-related violence. In this book, we suggest that it is precisely because multiparty elections are gradually becoming more openly competitive and because the results of elections matter more that elections are also more contentious. In light of an increasingly narrow space for traditional means of electoral fraud and manipulation, contending political elites resort to coercive and intimidating tactics to influence the electoral process and outcome. The key problem is that, although the formal institutional mechanisms have changed, the underlying logics of politics have not. Power and resources are still largely concentrated at the centre, raising the stakes of electoral contests, and patronage politics is still the dominant mode of political mobilisation. In the next few sections, we will explore this statement further, discuss some key conceptual developments in the academic field, and set out the underlying theoretical assumptions that constitute our accumulated body of scholarly knowledge on electoral violence in Africa's electoral democracies.

'Stomach infrastructure', high stakes, and the struggle for power at the centre It is acknowledged that politics in many parts of the developing world is characterised by the pervasiveness of patronage politics, or what Utas (2012) and others refer to as Big Man politics (e.g. Médard 1992; Sahlins 1963). In situations of weak or absent state structures, alternative forms of informal governance structures usually thrive (Reno 1998). In Africa, the occurrence of hierarchical, informal networks of patron–client relations is known to be one of the most durable features of politics (Gyimah-Boadi 2007). As noted by Ohlson and Söderberg Kovacs (2002), this aspect of African politics has proved remarkably resilient and has survived all attempts at radical political reform in the postcolonial period, including the turn to multiparty democracy in the early 1990s. Hence, amid the enthusiasm shared by many scholars, policy makers and practitioners alike when the so-called third wave of democratisation (Huntington 1991) spread across a large number of African states in the early 1990s, some voices were raised to point out that this process of political change did not take place in an existing power vacuum. Nugent (1995) and Bratton and van de Walle (1997) argued that, instead of replacing or reforming existing patronage networks, the logic of patronage politics was likely to become incorporated as an integral part of the democratic political system in these states.

In the terminology used by Bratton and van de Walle (1997), this resulted in the establishment of 'neopatrimonial' regimes; these combine the institutions of the modern bureaucratic state, including competitive elections, with the informal reality of personalised, unaccountable power of patron–client relations. These relations, they argue, are organised in a hierarchical network, all the way from the executive office to the local level. Although there is a formal distinction between the private and the public, in practice the distinction is often distorted, and the informal practices of power generally overshadow the formal, as clients tend to be loyal to their patrons. Many other terms have also been used to describe these essentially hybrid political systems, including 'façade democracies' (Joseph 2003), 'semi-authoritarian states' (Ottaway 2003), 'illiberal democracies' (Zakaria 1997) and 'electoral autocracies' (Schedler 2006). As most of these terms aptly indicate, beyond the formal democratic outlook of these states, many are essentially autocratic in nature, with little resemblance to the workings of consolidated and liberal democracies. As pointed out by Chabal and Daloz (1999), this apparent disorder has often served the political elites in Africa well, and the incentives for governments to change this state of affairs are relatively low.

For the purposes of this book, the most important implication is that, beyond formal democratic institutions and processes, politics is often rooted in the informal sphere of power. As will be evident from the chapters that follow, beyond this generalised picture, there is also great diversity and heterogeneity across and within states, particularly as we move to the local level. In order to understand and explain the workings of individual Big Man networks we have to recognise that these informal structures are built on fluid, flexible and ever changing 'webs of power' (Utas 2012: 14). In conflict and post-war societies in particular, these networks are thus likely to be less stable than usually depicted. Each Big Man's network builds on temporary relationships that are constantly being revisited and renegotiated (ibid.). For example, Christensen and Utas (2008; 2016) have illuminated the many and complex ways in which ex-militia members engage with political Big Men around election time. Their studies reveal the fluidity of these social networks, characterised by mutual dependencies, shifting alliances, unfulfilled promises and unpaid debts.

Critical for understanding the phenomena of electoral violence is the aware-ness that electoral competition has generally tended to strengthen and reinforce rather than eradicate this hybrid political order (Lindberg 2003). In this context, patronage capacity easily becomes the most important factor in determining electoral outcomes (Gyimah-Boadi 2007). Voters choose among candidates less on the basis of public policy positions and political party programmes than on the candidates' assumed patronage capacity. In order to demonstrate their patronage potential, patrons thus need to distribute largesse to their followers. The clients are assured that their Big Men will attend to their needs – be it the provision of food, jobs, licences or contracts – in exchange for political loyalty transferred into votes at the time of the election (Diamond 2008: 145). Elections are thus costly affairs. Most often, the resources needed to win elections are extracted from the state, raising the stakes for political control over state resources (Lindberg 2003; Nugent 2001). The tendency of many African states to concentrate power and resources at the centre – effectively turning politics into a zero-sum game – further adds to this problem (Diamond 2008). The winner thus literally takes all, as alluded to in the title of Chapter 7 by Bjarnesen, and losers are left struggling at the margins. What is at stake is more than just the state coffers. If you are the biggest man in a system based on Big Man networks, the seat of executive power can also be used to control appointments in key state institutions, procurement processes and the distribution of business contracts, and ensure immunity from criminal prosecution, sometimes for life (Collier 2010). This is why elections in these contexts are often referred to as 'do-or-die' affairs.

In Chapter 10, Agbiboa illustrates the logic of Big Men politics within the empirical confines of the urban transport system in the mega-city of Lagos. As discussed in his chapter, it was in Nigeria that the concept of 'stomach infrastructure' was first born, particularly in relation to the re-election campaign by Governor Ayo Fayose in the gubernatorial elections in Ekiti State in 2014, although the practice itself is neither new nor specific to Nigeria. So-called 'stomach items', such as food, funds, and other gifts and goods, are widely distributed to voters in order to ensure their support at the ballot box. Several of the contributions in this book stress the complex power relations and multi-layered functions hidden in this practice, which appear at first glance to be unidirectional in nature. For the Big Men, the distribution of largesse is conceived as a form of welfare system in which they fulfil their duty by securing the well-being of their people. For the voters, elections are also an opportunity to exercise power and influence. As noticed by Utas (2007), the electorate has learned how to squeeze the most out of this practice and is sometimes able to play a double game: people pretend to be loyal to one party while voting for another. Hence, most politicians have learned that carrots without sticks are not sufficient to win an election. Successful candidates also need to silence the opposition through alliances and co-optation (Bøås and Utas 2014: 55). A number of other studies have pointed to the intricate relationship between vote buying, fraud and violence in connection with competitive elections, suggesting that political elites strategically deploy different illicit strategies in different locations depending on how successful those strategies are deemed to be in delivering favourable election results (e.g. Bratton 2008; Collier and Vicente 2008; 2011).

In sum, the underlying logic of the distribution of power in most states in sub-Saharan Africa is still essentially based on Big Man politics in spite of the introduction of multiparty democracy, with power and resources still largely concentrated at the centre, raising the stakes of elections. What is new in many countries, however, is the emergence of real political competition for power, while a range of traditional methods for keeping potential challengers in check are being constrained by democratic norms. Next, we turn to this debate.

Competition, ethno-regional politics and close races Competitive elections are by their very nature conflictual processes aimed at mobilising divergent interests in society and stimulating political competition between political actors. In the scholarly debate on the overarching relationship between elections and violent conflict in societies that are either in transition to democracy from authoritarian rule or in transition from civil war to democracy, it is acknowledged that the competitive nature of democratic elections may cause violence or even war (e.g. Mansfield and Snyder 2005; Snyder 2000). In societies where the non-violent norms associated with consolidated democracies are not widespread and political tolerance more generally is low, there is a risk that the electoral contest will contribute to intensifying and polarising existing socio-economic cleavages and other divisions in society. According to Collier (2010), the world's poorest democracies are more likely than others to see instances of political violence, as they generally lack the key conflict-mitigating mechanisms of consolidated and wealthier democracies: accountability and legitimacy. The added challenges of holding competitive elections in war-ravaged societies have also been well documented (e.g. Kumar 1998; Lyons 2005).

What does electoral competition look like in Africa's new democracies? Because patron–client networks are commonly organised along ethnic lines or regional constellations, elections are frequently characterised by the direct or indirect mobilisation of ethnic or regional votes (Arriola 2009; Bates 1983; Gyimah-Boadi 2007; Posner 2007). In Chapter 1, Fjelde and Höglund provide an in-depth account of how and why ethnic divisions emerged as a powerful tool for violent electoral mobilisation in the context of Kenya after the introduction of multiparty democracy. They show how elite strategies used during the era of single-party rule for the purpose of securing political and economic resources and keeping competitors at bay later paved the way for exclusionary identity formations and ethnic voting. However, they argue, the historical legacy of exclusionary identity politics does not predetermine the occurrence of election-related violence along ethnic lines; it merely provides the structural conditions for the political elite to utilise an electoral strategy based on this narrative.

The likelihood that the political elite will resort to electoral strategies that increase the risk of violence also depends on the challenge they face. This reasoning is supported by insights from previous works on electoral violence, where close races (Norris, Frank and Martinez i Coma 2015) and the incumbent's fear of losing an election (Hafner-Burton, Hyde and Jablonski 2013) have been identified as important explanatory factors. For example, Wilkinson's (2004) study of ethnic riots in India shows that in situations of close electoral competition at the community level, party elites have incentives to polarise the population along ethnic lines through the instigation of violent incidents for the purpose of securing electoral support from pivotal swing voters within their own ethnic community or intimidate their ethnic opponents. Wilkinson's study is particularly important as it can help explain not only why but also when and where we are likely to see incidents of electoral violence on the subnational level. Hence, the risk of electoral violence may be higher precisely in situations where there is real political competition between parties and genuine possibilities to change existing power relations. In Chapter 2 of this volume, Sjögren demonstrates that the degree of government-sponsored violence linked to national elections in Uganda has been strongly influenced by the intensity of the competition.

As democracy is slowly becoming more entrenched, and electoral competition grows stronger, the risk of election-related violence may thus increase. As long as the electoral stakes remain high, competition and uncertainty about the outcome may come at a high price. As argued by Höglund, Jarstad and Söderberg Kovacs (2009) not only are there significant benefits to be gained from control over the executive office, there are also often high costs associated with an electoral loss. Some costs may even have increased as democracy has gained ground. In Burundi during the 2015 demonstrations, it was widely speculated that one of the reasons why Nkurunziza wanted to run for a third term was the fear associated with having to face legal accountability for human rights abuses committed during his time in power if he were to step down (Söderberg Kovacs 2015). As a consequence, politicians resort to illicit electoral strategies such as violent attacks, harassment and intimidation of both party candidates and potential voters, sometimes long before election day. Party rallies and campaign events are violently interrupted, often by party supporters who are strategically and purposefully transported to various events. Party offices and party symbols are destroyed and vandalised, and people, facilities and materials associated with the electoral administration are attacked or sabotaged. In their quest to increase their chances of winning the election or strengthening their post-election bargaining position, politicians often enter into precarious relationships with militant youth wings, militias or the state security forces. The chapters in this book all explore such violent strategies in greater detail in different empirical settings, and take a closer look at some of the actors involved in the production of violence.

Institutional (dis)incentives and constraints on violence In societies where the structural conditions of elections create major incentives for violence, the institutional and administrative arrangements in place for regulating the electoral contest can play an important role in either mitigating or instigating electoral violence. This question has received considerable attention in the somewhat broader field of institutional design in divided or war-torn societies, where a large number of scholarly contributions have focused on how the design of elections or the conditions in which elections are held may influence the relative success or failure of the electoral experience (e.g. Horowitz 2000; Lijphart 1977; Reilly 2001; Reilly and Reynolds 1999). For example, it has been suggested that electoral systems that encourage broad-based and inclusive strategies for mobilising voters across existing cleavages in society are more likely to alleviate the risk of political polarisation. Conversely, systems that are more exclusive, such as the first-past-the-post system, encourage a winner-takes-all logic and are hence more likely to encourage violence in already divided and polarised societies (Reilly and Reynolds 1999).

Some of these findings are echoed in the literature on electoral violence. For example, Fjelde and Höglund (2014) find that electoral violence is indeed more likely in countries employing majoritarian voting rules, especially in societies characterised by great socio-economic cleavages. Other studies have found that considerations of the timing of elections in high-risk structural conditions may reduce the likelihood of electoral violence (Brancati and Snyder 2013; Flores and Nooruddin 2012). The electoral administrative system – for example, a politically independent electoral commission – may also influence the efficacy, transparency and political integrity of the elections, contributing to a decrease in the risk of violence due to perceptions of fraud and manipulation (Höglund 2009: 420–3).

However, alleviating uncertainties about illicit manipulation is not sufficient. In fact, the documentation of such irregularities may even increase the risk of violence. Daxecker (2012) demonstrates that the presence of international election observers in African elections may add to the potential for post-election violence precisely because of their ability to detect and publicise serious irregularities in a credible manner. The monitoring of fraudulent elections by international election observers draws attention to unfair electoral processes, reduces uncertainty over whether fraud was indeed committed or not, and provides the impetus for such constituencies to take action. Monitoring therefore may contribute to violent contestation after manipulated elections, Daxecker argues (ibid.). Election observation may also produce other unintended results. Daxecker (2014) shows that, although the presence of international observers has been proven to reduce the likelihood of violence on election day in African elections, it has contributed to an increase in violence in the pre-election period, suggesting a temporal adjustment in the use of violent strategies, not their disappearance. Asunka et al. (2017), based on a study of domestic election observation in the 2012 elections in Ghana, point to a similar pattern of adjustment across space in local constituencies. They argue that although observers were successful in reducing both fraud and violence at the polling stations which they monitored, such strategies were simply relocated to polling stations without election observers. Election observation may also have different effects on different actors. Smidt (2016), for example, finds that while the presence of international observation missions can deter violence by governments, it tends to have the opposite effect on opposition groups.

While the oversight function of electoral institutions may thus produce mixed results, these are not the only institutions of relevance. Hafner-Burton, Hyde and Jablonski (2013) find that electoral violence is more likely to occur when there are few or weak institutional constraints on the executive power – such as constitutional checks and balances, and functioning and independent judiciaries. Such institutional constraints limit the risk that the incumbent uses the power at his or her disposal to steer the outcome in a favourable direction through coercive means, they argue. Mueller (2011), however, cautions against believing too strongly in the ability to improve institutions to address the problems associated with electoral violence. Based on a study of Kenya, she argues that in the absence of incentives to adhere to the rule of law and the integrity and legitimacy of institutions, there is always the risk that these institutions will be 'bypassed, undermined and not accepted by the political elite or the public' (ibid. 100–1).

This suggests that, in order to understand the occurrence of electoral violence in a particular empirical setting, we should examine a range of explanatory factors at different levels of analysis. In addition to the structural conditions that provide the underlying incentives for political actors to engage in violent acts – some of which are generic to the political system at large and some more immediately associated with competitive multiparty arrangements – we should pay attention to the details of the electoral system and the institutional framework in place, which may serve either to reinforce or to mitigate the risk of electoral violence. However, we still have only a relatively limited understanding of the more intricate details of these causal processes at work and how these macro-level factors lead to the outcome of interest, particularly at the local level. For this, we turn to the individual chapters in this volume.

Chapter outline

Following this introduction, the book proceeds with eleven empirically oriented chapters by authors with extensive experience of the cases they discuss. Their analytical and methodological approaches vary, as do their levels of analysis, but they all address the micro-foundations at work in processes of electoral violence and thereby attempt to move the scholarly debate on the causes and dynamics of electoral violence forward.

Chapters 1 and 2 retain the primary focus on the macro-level, but contribute to strengthening our knowledge about the processes at work by explicitly linking identified structural causes and historical conditions to elite incentives and behaviour during election time. By doing so, they are able to explain important variations across time and space in the countries under study. In Chapter 1, Hanne Fjelde and Kristine Höglund provide a thorough consideration of Kenya's 1992 elections complemented by an analysis of subsequent elections. The authors trace the dynamics of electoral violence in this inaugural vote to underlying continuities in terms of exclusionary ethnic identity formations and ethnic outbidding strategies used by the elite under single-party rule in order to control patronage resources. The legacies of injustice and victimisation created through these informal institutions subsequently shaped the pattern of elite competition and mass electoral support once the country returned to competitive party politics. The authors are thus able to explain how and why ethnic divisions have become a powerful tool for violent electoral mobilisation in Kenya. However, they are also able to show that the degree to which the political elite is willing and able to exploit or evoke such historical narratives for electoral purposes is also dependent on the ways in which particular reforms, policies and leadership make ethnic themes more or less salient. In Chapter 2, Anders Sjögren provides additional depth to the conceptual sensibility towards temporality in the study of electoral violence. He argues that Ugandan electoral politics under the thirty-year reign of Yoweri Museveni must be understood sequentially rather than in isolation, and that the experiences and lessons drawn from past elections shape the political elite's expectations, calculations and adaptations for subsequent ones. Sjögren examines the changing levels of state violence against the opposition across time and over five presidential elections, with an emphasis on the 2011 and 2016 elections. He finds that the degree of government-sponsored violence is strongly shaped by both the intensity of the electoral competition and the presence or absence of institutional constraints on the use of force. The closer the race, the more likely that the government will engage in strategically deployed violence for the purpose of controlling the electoral process and outcome. However, this is mediated by a number of deterring factors, in particular the incumbent's assessment of the risks and rewards associated with deploying violence.

Chapters 3, 4 and 5 all focus on important subnational variations in the countries studied. The authors of these chapters explicitly attempt to link macro-level processes and events to the occurrences of violence at the local level. Chapter 3 considers a central theme in African politics, namely the importance of land conflict dynamics in fuelling electoral violence. Through an analysis of Côte d'Ivoire's famously troubled western cocoa regions, which saw high levels of electoral violence both in the decade leading up to the 2010–11 post-electoral crisis and during the crisis itself, Matthew Mitchell explains the conditions under which local land conflict dynamics served to fuel such violence. The key argument is that political entrepreneurs seeking power at the centre strategically revive historically grounded discourses of belonging and exclusionary narratives over land claims as a form of patronage in order to secure the electoral support of local constituencies in the periphery. Local actors, for their part, ally with national elites and reinforce such processes when they view such promises as both legitimate and feasible. In Chapter 4, Willy Nindorera and Jesper Bjarnesen analyse the geographical distribution of violence in connection with the 2015 elections in Burundi, where initially peaceful protests against incumbent president Pierre Nkurunziza's candidacy for a third term later turned into violent confrontations and armed conflict. Importantly, the violence that followed displayed a distinct spatial pattern, with concentration in some neighbourhoods in the capital. Nindorera and Bjarnesen tie this specific pattern of violence to a longer history of ethno-political divisions and armed conflict. They also show how historical grievances were gradually reactivated by the Nkurunziza regime as a deliberate strategy to divide the opposition and support its claims that the public protests were in fact a 'Tutsi rebellion'. In Chapter 5, Ibrahim Bangura and Mimmi Söderberg Kovacs explain why the eastern district of Kono in Sierra Leone has been the scene of unusually high levels of violence for decades. They argue that the key explanation is to be found in the district's unique position as an electoral swing district. Whatever party wins elections in Kono is likely to also gain the upper hand nationally, which means that Kono is a highly courted district by all political parties, and contributes to raising the stakes of even minor elections. In order to carry out violence locally, national political elites enter into mutually dependent relationships with both local chiefs and organised youth gangs.

The next set of chapters examines specific actors involved in the dynamics of electoral violence and their embeddedness in patronage networks that stretch all the way from the local level to national political dynamics. Chapters 6 and 7 both explore the role of ex-militants and their involvement in processes of electoral violence, but from different analytical and methodological perspectives. Their findings speak to the importance of paying close attention to the contextual realities that shape the choices of groups, networks and individuals. In Chapter 6, Tarila Marclint Ebiede follows the trajectories of former militia combatants in electoral politics in Nigeria's Niger Delta, with particular focus on the 2015 general elections. His study demonstrates how ex-militant fighters who had previously gone through the regional disarmament, demobilisation and reintegration (DDR) programme were re-mobilised during the elections through their former commanders. In the quest to maintain or gain access to patronage networks or political power at the governmental level, these leaders mobilise their ex-fighters to carry out electoral violence aimed at increasing the electoral chances of their preferred political candidates. In Chapter 7, Mariam Bjarnesen takes us beyond this general analysis of ex-combatant remobilisation and examines important variations at the micro-level of individual ex-fighters. Through the narratives of two former commanders who found themselves on opposing sides in the second post-war elections in Liberia in 2011, the chapter illustrates the diverse trajectories of networks associated with electoral winners and with losing candidates. In addition, while Bjarnesen, much like Ebiede, shows that former rebel structures often survive in spite of DDR programmes and are sometimes used by the elite for political purposes, she is also able to demonstrate how ex-combatants use elections as an opportunity to renegotiate leverage and power through their wartime links.

The violent potentials and practices of non-state actors with alleged ties to national political elites are further explored in the two subsequent chapters. In Chapter 8, Jacob Rasmussen returns our attention to the context of electoral politics in Kenya, but this time from the perspective of the Mungiki movement, one of the key actors associated with the perpetration of electoral violence in the country, not least in connection with the 2007 elections. Over the years, the movement has assumed many different roles and forms, ranging from a youth-dominated social movement and an ethnic militia to a political party, a religious organisation and a criminal network. By analysing the movement's elusive nature, its foundational symbolism and its ties with Kenya's political elite, Rasmussen frames the politics of patronage played out between the political elite and the Mungiki leadership as a 'parasitic politics'. While some-times an effective tool in the hands of opportunistic politicians who want to access power by any means, the movement's potential for violence is also a powerful resource that allows it to retain its influence over the country's political agenda, even when this potential is not realised. In Chapter 9, Tariro Mutongwize discusses an equally elusive and violent non-state actor that plays an important role as a mobiliser of electoral violence: the Chipangano move-ment in Zimbabwe, a business entity and criminal network operating primarily in the high-density southern suburb of Mbare in the capital of Harare. While the government denies the existence of Chipangano and any alleged affiliation to the group, evidence suggests that the movement is supported by members of the ruling party, the Zimbabwe African National Union – Patriotic Front (ZANU-PF). Mutongwize argues that Chipangano's pattern of disappearance and re-emergence can be ascribed to the nature of electoral cycles, during which the political leadership's demand for potentially violent actors to secure victory at the polls spurs the reactivation of the movement's violent potential. In exchange, Chipangano's allegiance with political Big Men allows it to control space and daily business activity in Mbare.

In Chapter 10, we shift the perspective to micro-foundations of election-related violence through an in-depth study of the intricacies of patronage politics in transit places (motor parks, bus stops and junctions) in two major local government areas in the city of Lagos in the post-1999 period. Electoral violence has become a fundamental aspect of political competition in the city and elsewhere in Nigeria, and Daniel Agbiboa contributes to our understanding of the dynamics of such processes at the local level through a study of the roles played by the city's transportation trade unions and their standing army of the sector's middlemen, the *agberos*, whose responsibility it is to ensure that the minibus drivers honour their dues to the unions. During election periods, the *agberos* are recruited by Big Men for the purpose of attacking rival political candidates, coercing members of the public, rigging elections and providing security to their patrons. Agbiboa provides us with a deepened knowledge of the precarious nature of such patronage politics. Elections are times of uncertainties that highlight the precariousness of both Big Men and Small Men who struggle to remain relevant and influential.

In Chapter 11, Afra Schmitz considers an aspect of electoral violence rarely discussed: the effects of violent speech acts during electoral campaigns in Ghana, a country with largely peaceful elections. Her contribution provides insights into the ways in which talking about violence is strategically used and communicated by political actors in an environment that is shaped by existing stereotypes, structural challenges and local conflict dynamics. Even in the absence of physical violence, such discourses can still be used as a mobilising force during campaigning. Schmitz's study shows how supra-ethnic cleavages have developed around the binary opposition of 'northerners' and 'southerners', with people in the northern regions of the country being stereotyped nationally as a remote and primitive people with a violent nature. In the context of competitive and closely contested elections, these prevailing discursive practices feed into the campaign speeches of both the major political parties.

In the last and concluding chapter, the editors of this volume draw some general conclusions from the findings presented in these chapters, and suggest some avenues for theoretical refinements, future research and policy thinking.

References

Alston, P. (2010) *Report of the Special Rapporteur on Extrajudicial, Summary or Arbitrary Executions: Addendum on Election-related Violence and Killings.* Geneva: Office of the United Nations High Commissioner for Human Rights.

Arriola, L. (2009) 'Patronage and Political Stability in Africa', *Comparative Political Studies* 42 (10): 1339–62.

Asunka, J., S. Brierley, M. Golden, E. Kramon and G. Ofosu (2017) 'Electoral Fraud or Violence: The Effect of Observers on Party Manipulation Strategies', *British Journal of Political Science.* Available at https://doi.org/10.1017/S0007123416000491.

Autesserre, S. (2010) *The Trouble with the Congo: Local Violence and the Failure of International Peacebuilding.* Cambridge and New York NY: Cambridge University Press.

Balcells, L. and P. Justino (2014) 'Bridging Micro and Macro Approaches on Civil War and Political Violence: Issues, Challenges, and the Way Forward', *Journal of Conflict Resolution* 58 (8): 1343–59.

Bangura, I. and M. Söderberg Kovacs (2017) 'Shape Shifters in the Struggle for Survival: Warlord Democrats in Sierra Leone' in A. Themnér (ed.), *Warlord Democrats in Africa*, London: Zed Books.

Bates, R. H. (1983) 'Modernization, Ethnic Competition and the Rationality of Politics in Contemporary Africa' in D. Rothchild and V. Olorunsola (eds), *State Versus Ethnic Claims: African Policy Dilemmas.* Boulder CO: Westview Press.

Bekoe, D. A. (ed.) (2012) *Voting in Fear: Electoral Violence in Sub-Saharan Africa.* Washington DC: United States Institute for Peace Press.

Bekoe, D. A. and S. Burchard (2017) 'The Contradictions of Pre-election Violence: The Effects of Violence on Voter Turnout in Sub-Saharan Africa', *African Studies Review* 60 (29): 73–92.

Bøås, M. and K. Dunn (2007) *African Guerrillas: Raging against the Machine.* Boulder CO and London: Lynne Rienner.

Bøås, M. and M. Utas (2014) 'The Political Landscape of Postwar Liberia:

Reflections on National Reconciliation and Elections', *Africa Today* 60 (4): 47–65.

Bob-Milliar, G. M. (2014) 'Party Youth Activities and Low-intensity Electoral Violence in Ghana: A Qualitative Study of Party Foot Soldiers' Activism', *African Studies Quarterly* 15 (1): 125–52.

Boone, C. and N. Kriger (2012) 'Land Patronage and Elections: Winners and Losers in Zimbabwe and Côte d'Ivoire' in D. A. Bekoe (ed.), *Voting in Fear: Electoral Violence in Sub-Saharan Africa*. Washington DC: United States Institute for Peace Press.

Brancati, D. and J. Snyder (2013) 'Time to Kill: The Impact of Election Timing on Post-conflict Stability', *Journal of Conflict Resolution* 57 (5): 822–53.

Bratton, M. (2008) 'Vote Buying and Violence in Nigerian Election Campaigns', Electoral Studies 27 (4): 621–32.

Bratton, M. and N. van de Walle (1997) *Democratic Experiments in Africa: Regime Transitions in Comparative Perspective*. Cambridge: Cambridge University Press.

Burchard, S. M. (2015) *Electoral Violence in Sub-Saharan Africa: Causes and Consequences*. Boulder CO and London: First Forum Press.

Chabal, P. and J.-P. Daloz (1999) *Africa Works: Disorder as Political Instrument*. Oxford and Bloomington IN: James Currey and Indiana University Press.

Christensen, M. M. and M. Utas (2008) 'Mercenaries of Democracy: The "Politricks" of Remobilized Combatants in the 2007 General Elections, Sierra Leone', *African Affairs* 107 (429): 515–39.

Christensen, M. and M. Utas (2016) 'Ex-militias and Ambiguous Debt Relations during Post-war Elections in Sierra Leone', *African Conflict and Peacebuilding Review* 6 (2): 23–47.

Collier, P. (2010) *Wars, Guns and Votes: Democracy in Dangerous Places*. New York NY: Harper Perennial.

Collier, P. and P. Vicente (2008) 'Voters and Violence: Evidence from a Field Experiment in Nigeria', CSAE WPS 16. Oxford: Centre for the Study of African Economies, University of Oxford.

Collier, P. and P. Vicente (2011) 'Violence, Bribery, and Fraud: The Political Economy of Elections in Sub-Saharan Africa', *Public Choice* 153 (1–2): 117–47.

Daxecker, U. E. (2012) 'The Cost of Exposing Cheating: International Election Monitoring, Fraud and Post-election Violence in Africa', *Journal of Peace Research* 49 (4): 503–16.

Daxecker, U. E. (2014) 'All Quiet on Election Day? International Election Observation and Incentives for Pre-election Violence in African Elections', *Electoral Studies* 34: 232–43.

Dercon, S. and R. Guiterrez-Romero (2012) 'Triggers and Characteristics of the 2007 Kenyan Electoral Violence', *World Development* 40 (4): 731–44.

de Smedt, J. (2009) '"No Raila, No Peace!" Big Man Politics and Election Violence at the Kibera Grassroots', *African Affairs* 108 (433): 581–98.

Diamond, L. (2008) 'The Rule of Law versus Big Man', *Journal of Democracy* 19 (2): 138–49.

Eriksson Baaz, M. and M. Stern (2013) *Sexual Violence as a Weapon of War?: Perceptions, Prescriptions, Problems in the Congo and Beyond*. London and New York NY: Zed Books.

Fischer, J. (2002) 'Electoral Conflict and Violence: A Strategy for Study and Prevention'. IFES White Paper 2002-01. Arlington VA: International Foundation for Electoral Systems (IFES). Available at www.ciaonet.org/attachments/10188/uploads.

Fjelde, H. and K. Höglund (2014) 'Electoral Institutions and Electoral Violence in Sub-Saharan Africa', *British Journal of Political Science* 46 (2): 297–320.

Flores, T. E. and I. Nooruddin (2012) 'The Effect of Elections on Post-conflict Peace and Reconstruction', *Journal of Politics* 73 (2): 558–70.

Galtung, J. (1969) 'Violence, Peace, and Peace Research', *Journal of Peace Research* 6 (3): 167–91.

Gyimah-Boadi, E. (2007) 'Political Parties, Elections and Patronage: Random Thoughts on Neo-patrimonialism and African Democratization' in M. Basedau, G. Erdmann and A. Mehler (eds), *Votes, Money and Violence: Political Parties in Sub-Saharan Africa*. Uppsala: Nordic Africa Institute.

Hafner-Burton, E. M., S. D. Hyde and R. S. Jablonski (2013) 'When Do Governments Resort to Election Violence?', *British Journal of Political Science* 44 (1): 149–79.

Höglund, K. (2009) 'Electoral Violence in Conflict-ridden Societies: Concepts, Causes, and Consequences', *Terrorism and Political Violence* 21 (3): 412–27.

Höglund, K. and A. K. Jarstad (2011) 'Towards Electoral Security: Experiences from KwaZulu-Natal', *Africa Spectrum* 46 (1): 33–59.

Höglund, K. and A. Piyarathne (2009) 'Paying the Prize for Patronage: Electoral Violence in Sri Lanka', *Commonwealth and Comparative Politics* 47 (3): 289–307.

Höglund, K., A. Jarstad and M. Söderberg Kovacs (2009) 'The Predicament of Elections in War-torn Societies', *Democratization* 16 (3): 530–57.

Horowitz, D. L. (2000) *Ethnic Groups in Conflict*. Berkeley CA: University of California Press.

Huntington, S. (1991) *The Third Wave: Democratization in the Late Twentieth Century*. Norman OK: University of Oklahoma Press.

Joseph, R. (2003) 'Africa: States in Crisis', *Journal of Democracy* 14 (3): 159–70.

Kalyvas, S. N. (2003) 'The Ontology of "Political Violence": Action and Identity in Civil Wars', *Perspectives on Politics* 1 (3): 475–94.

Kalyvas, S. N. (2006) *The Logic of Violence in Civil Wars*. Cambridge: Cambridge University Press.

Kandeh, J. D. (2008) 'Rouge Incumbents, Donor Assistance and Sierra Leone's Second Post-conflict Elections of 2007', *Journal of Modern African Studies* 46 (4): 603–35.

Klaus, K and M. I. Mitchell (2015) 'Land Grievance and the Mobilization of Electoral Violence: Evidence from Côte d'Ivoire and Kenya', *Journal of Peace Research* 52 (5): 622–35.

Kumar, K. (ed.) (1998) *Postconflict Elections, Democratization, and International Assistance*. Boulder CO: Lynne Rienner.

Laakso, L. (2007) 'Insights into Electoral Violence in Africa' in M. Basedau, G. Erdmann and A. Mehler (eds), *Votes, Money and Violence: Political Parties in Sub-Saharan Africa*. Uppsala: Nordic Africa Institute.

Lijphart, A. (1977) *Democracy in Plural Societies: A Comparative Exploration*. New Haven CT: Yale University Press.

Lindberg, S. I. (2003) '"It's Our Time to 'Chop'": Do Elections in Africa Feed Neo-patrimonialism rather than Counteract it?', *Democratization* 10 (2): 121–40.

Lyons, T. (2005) *Demilitarizing Politics: Elections on the Uncertain Road to Peace*. Boulder CO: Lynne Rienner.

MacGinty, R. (2014) 'Everyday Peace: Bottom-up and Local Agency in Conflict-affected Societies', *Security Dialogue* 45 (6): 548–64.

Mansfield, E. D. and J. Snyder (2005) *Electing to Fight: Why Emerging Democracies Go to War*. Cambridge MA: MIT Press.

Médard, J.-F. (1992) 'Le "big man" en Afrique: esquisse d'analyse du politician entrepreneur', *L'Année Sociologique* 42: 167–92.

Mueller, S. D. (2011) 'Dying to Win: Elections, Political Violence, and Institutional Decay in Kenya', *Journal of Contemporary African Studies* 29 (1): 99–117.

Nordstrom, C. (1997) *A Different Kind of War Story*. Philadelphia PA: University of Pennsylvania Press.

Norris, P., R. W. Frank and F. Martinez

i Coma (2015) *Contentious Elections: From Ballots to Barricades*. New York NY: Routledge.

Nugent, P. (1995) *Big Men, Small Boys and Politics in Ghana*. London: Pinter.

Nugent, P. (2001) 'Winners, Losers and Also Rans: Money, Moral Authority and Voting Patterns in the Ghana 2000 Election', *African Affairs* 100 (400): 405–28.

Ohlson, T. and M. Söderberg Kovacs (2002) 'From Intra-state War to Democratic Peace in Weak States'. Uppsala Peace Research Paper 5. Uppsala: Department of Peace and Conflict Research, Uppsala University.

Ottaway, M. (2003) *Democracy Challenged: The Rise of Semi-authoritarianism*. Washington DC: Carnegie Endowment for International Peace.

Posner, D. N. (2007) 'Regime Change and Ethnic Cleavages in Africa', *Comparative Political Studies* 40 (11): 1302–27.

Raleigh, C. (2016) 'Pragmatic and Promiscuous: Explaining the Rise of Competitive Political Militias across Africa', *Journal of Conflict Resolution* 60 (2): 283–310.

Reilly, B. (2001) *Democracy in Divided Societies: Electoral Engineering for Conflict Management*. Cambridge: Cambridge University Press.

Reilly, B. and A. Reynolds (1999) *Electoral Systems and Conflict in Divided Societies*. Washington DC: National Academy Press.

Reno, W. (1998) *Warlord Politics and African States*. Boulder CO: Lynne Rienner.

Sahlins, M. D. (1963) 'Poor Man, Rich Man, Big-man, Chief: Political Types in Melanesia and Polynesia', *Comparative Studies in Society and History* 5: 285–303.

Salehyan, I. and C. Linebarger (2015) 'Elections and Social Conflict in Africa, 1990–2009', *Studies in Comparative International Development* 50 (1): 23–49.

Schedler, A. (ed.) (2006) *Electoral Authoritarianism: The Dynamics of Unfree Competition*. Boulder CO: Lynne Rienner.

Sisk, T. D. (2012) 'Evaluating Election-related Violence: Nigeria and Sudan in Comparative Perspective' in D. A. Bekoe (ed.), *Voting in Fear: Electoral Violence in Sub-Saharan Africa*. Washington DC: United States Institute for Peace Press.

Smidt, H. (2016) 'From a Perpetrator's Perspective: International Election Observers and Post-electoral Violence', *Journal of Peace Research* 53 (2): 226–41.

Smith, L. (2009) 'Explaining Violence after Recent Elections in Ethiopia and Kenya', *Democratization* 16 (5): 867–97.

Snyder, J. (2000) *From Voting to Violence: Democratization and Nationalist Conflict*. New York NY and London: W. W. Norton & Company.

Söderberg Kovacs, M. (2012) '"Ampa Ampoh!": Sierra Leone after the Announcement of the 2012 Election Results', Mats Utas blog, 30 November. Available at https://matsutas.wordpress.com/2012/11/30/ampa-ampoh-sierra-leone-after-the-announcement-of-the-2012-election-results-guest-post-by-mimmi-soderberg-kovacs/ (accessed 19 August 2017).

Söderberg Kovacs, M. (2015) 'Brinkmanship in Bujumbura: A Struggle for Power at All Costs?', Mats Utas blog, 6 May. Available at https://matsutas.wordpress.com/2015/05/06/brinkmanship-in-bujumbura-a-struggle-for-power-at-all-costs-by-mimmi-soderberg-kovacs/ (accessed 19 August 2017).

Straus, S. and C. Taylor (2012) 'Democratization and Electoral Violence in Sub-Saharan Africa 1990–2008' in D. A. Bekoe (ed.), *Voting in Fear: Electoral Violence in Sub-Saharan Africa*. Washington DC: United States Institute for Peace Press.

Themnér, A. (2017) *Warlord Democrats in Africa: Ex-military Leaders and*

Electoral Politics. London and New York NY: Zed Books.

Utas, M. (2007) 'Watermelon Politics in Sierra Leone: Hope amidst Vote Buying and Remobilized Militias', *African Renaissance* 4 (3–4): 62–6.

Utas, M. (ed.) (2012) *African Conflicts and Informal Power: Big Men and Networks*. London and New York NY: Zed Books.

Verwimp, P., P. Justino and T. Brück (2009) 'The Analysis of Conflict: A Micro-level Perspective', *Journal of Peace Research* 46 (3): 307–14.

Wilkinson, S. I. (2004) *Votes and Violence: Electoral Competition and Ethnic Riots in India*. Cambridge: Cambridge University Press.

Zakaria, F. (1997) 'The Rise of Illiberal Democracy', *Foreign Affairs* 76 (6): 22–43.

1 | Ethnic politics and elite competition: the roots of electoral violence in Kenya

Hanne Fjelde and Kristine Höglund

Introduction[1]

In the early 1990s, Kenyan president Daniel arap Moi succumbed to domestic and international pressure to democratise after a long period of single-party rule. In the face of multiparty elections, Moi 'repeatedly argued that the legalization of opposition parties would usher in tribal conflict and destroy national unity' (Barkan 1993: 90). Indeed, the 1992 elections were fraught with violence resulting in the death of at least 1,500 people, orchestrated by Moi in order to disenfranchise opposition supporters. Moreover, violence and displacements at varying levels have accompanied all elections in Kenya since the reintroduction of multiparty elections in the 1990s, and there has been violent and repressive action by the government against political opponents.

The literature on electoral violence in Africa generally, and Kenya specifically, provides important insights to understand the prevalence of such violence. Studies have highlighted, for example, how the precariousness of the institutional framework surrounding elections and the stakes of the electoral contest may precipitate violent manipulation of electoral competition (cf. Höglund 2009; Salehyan and Linebarger 2015). The existing scholarship on Kenya has also emphasised the role of powerful elite incentives for mobilising on divisive ethnic issues. While some studies place ethnicity at the very core of an explanation of Kenya's violent electoral history (e.g. Burchard 2015), others claim that ethnicity is not the key factor in determining violent electoral outcomes, but rather it interacts with powerful influences such as perceptions of a flawed electoral process (e.g. Dercon and Gutiérrez-Romero 2012) or resource scarcity (e.g. Kahl 1998). Our analysis links up with these perspectives to provide a more historically rooted approach to understanding how and why ethnic divisions have become a powerful tool for violent electoral mobilisation in Kenya. We thereby build on the rich scholarship on Kenyan politics that points to the importance of the ethnicisation of politics, especially as it is linked to historical patterns of unequal land distribution (Anderson and Lochery 2008; Boone 2011; 2012), and the use of extra-legal force during a period of authoritarianism (Kagwanja 2003; Mueller 2014). We complement these studies by focusing specifically on the political dimensions

27

of elite interaction and political mobilisation in the era of authoritarian rule. Our focus is on the ways in which these dynamics created political legacies that made Kenya vulnerable to electoral violence during the transition to multiparty competitive elections.

In this chapter, we trace how elite strategies to mobilise divisive ethnic issues in order to secure political and economic resources during the era of single-party rule paved the way for exclusionary identity formation and ethnic voting. Focusing on the elections in 1992, together with an analysis of subsequent elections, we show how these historical patterns shaped the incentive structures and opportunities for the political elites in the transition to multiparty rule and came to underpin elite competition, as well as mass electoral conduct. In short, we suggest that these historical legacies increased the stakes of the electoral contest and precipitated the use of violent electoral strategies as more open and competitive political processes were introduced. Moreover, the patterns of violence across elections in Kenya also underscore the fact that the historical legacies relating to ethnic animosities need to be exploited or evoked continuously by political leaders to become decisive in mobilisation for electoral violence.

Our analysis highlights the importance of the linkages between structural factors and more agency-based explanations, and proposes a theoretical perspective that provides a link between seemingly disparate explanations of electoral violence in the existing literature. We argue that historical patterns of elite interaction and political mobilisation under authoritarian rule may put in place informal institutions that influence the dynamics of political competition even when the formal institutions are reformed. The historical roots of ethnic politics imply that ethnic divides can be evoked or exploited by political elites. The focus on historical legacies thus helps us identify countries that are vulnerable to violent electoral mobilisation under circumstances in which elites have incentives to rely on violent, rather than peaceful, electoral campaign strategies. Moreover, the focus on the importance of both structure and individual elite agency suggests that the significance of historically rooted informal institutions may shift over time in the post-democratisation state, depending on how particular reforms, policies and leadership make ethnic themes more or less salient. The historical perspective also provides insights for understanding spatial variations in the occurrence of electoral violence within the same country – for example, why violence has been particularly prevalent in Kenya's Rift Valley – variations that may not be apparent from studying only present-day politics. We therefore propose the historical turn as a complement to the existing literature that has tended to address electoral violence from a short-term perspective and that does not recognise the way in which institutional and political legacies are driving factors in the risk of violence. For this reason, we place ethnic politics in a historical context in order to understand elite strategies and elite–voter interaction around elections (see, e.g., LeBas 2011; Mueller 2014; Riedl 2014).

We proceed by presenting some theoretical points of departure relating to ethnic politics and electoral violence. The empirical analysis first outlines the nature of electoral competition in Kenya's 1992 election, and then we trace the origins of the political action and ethnic politics that influenced the violent electoral outcome and address some additional explanations. Next, we contrast the 1992 election to subsequent elections. In the concluding section, we discuss some avenues for future research and suggest a few implications for policy.

Ethnic politics, identity formation and electoral violence

In many places, the introduction of more open and democratic institutions has been accompanied by the rise of interethnic violence and armed conflict. Several studies point to a heightened risk of violence during periods of democratic transition, particularly in countries where institutions are weak (cf. Höglund, Jarstad and Söderberg Kovacs 2009; Brancati and Snyder 2013; Cederman, Gleditsch and Hug 2013). Snyder (2000) links the risk of ethnic violence during democratisation to elite incentives to foment exclusionary identities. Extremist nationalist rhetoric and ethnic outbidding are used by leaders to foster political support, build large voter coalitions and retain their hold on power when political competition renders their positions insecure (see also Rabushka and Shepsle 1972; Mann 2005). Rather than resulting from ethnic animosities and deep-seated group rivalries that precede the introduction of democratic institutions, Snyder (2000) links the upsurge in ethnic violence to reckless elite manipulation in the early phases of electoral democracy.

We do not take issue with this argument directly, but we contend that the reliance on exclusionary ethnic rhetoric and the strategic manipulation of in-group and out-group sentiments for political survival do not necessarily surface with the introduction of multiparty elections. Many authoritarian leaders in Africa have politicised ethnicity to foment political support and to prevent challenges to their rule. The exclusionary rhetoric and violence along ethnic lines that are expressed in the transition to multiparty politics may thus have deeper historical roots. More specifically, the prominence of ethnicity in the political organisation of postcolonial neopatrimonial states in Africa laid the groundwork for the salience of ethnicity with the introduction of multiparty elections. Yet, not all postcolonial African states were alike: there were substantial variations in the ways in which non-democratic political leaders chose to meet the challenge of building and maintaining political coalitions of support across ethnically heterogeneous societies in Africa. Elite strategies to mobilise people on divisive ethnic issues in order to secure political and economic resources in the pre-democratic era pave the way for violent political mobilisation when competitive multiparty elections are instituted. The political legacy shapes the strategies available to elites and contributes to making some of these transitions more prone to electoral violence than others.

Across various authoritarian regime types, ethnicity is and has been a key political asset around which political leaders have built support to consolidate power; much of the political struggle in Africa since independence has centred on the control of patronage resources by ethnically defined coalitions (Bates 1983). The postcolonial state combined the modern bureaucratic state with influential informal institutions based on personalised and unconstrained power and pervasive patron–client relationships that were organised along ethnic or sub-ethnic lines (cf. Bratton and van de Walle 1994). Whereas the personalist authoritarian regimes, dominated by a single strongman, can be seen as the embodiment of exclusionary clientelist rule, other regime types also relied on the selective distribution of state patronage to forge political support among ethnic elites (Bayart 1993; Bratton and van de Walle 1994). Horowitz (2000) notes how bans on electoral contest and the institutionalisation of single-party rule shifted the bargaining between ethnically defined factions into a forum where transparency and accountability regarding ethnic representation were weaker (see also Huntington 1970). As a result, some single-party regimes became dominated by a hegemonic ethnic group (or a small number of groups) and displayed highly exclusionary practices in the distribution of state resources, such as jobs in the civil sector and public transfers, underpinned by a highly coercive state apparatus.

In the next sections we explore how historical patterns of political organisation in Kenya – specifically the narrow ethnic base under single-party rule – have encouraged the formation of exclusionary ethnic identities, which served to raise the stakes of elections and ethnically based electoral mobilisation during the transition period, and which contributed to the violent outcome of the 1992 elections.

Kenya's violent transition

The 1992 elections in Kenya marked a return to multiparty politics. Why were the elections preceded by large-scale election-related violence? We are particularly interested in the ways in which ethnic politics at the time of the transition structured political competition and how this created incentives and opportunities for the incumbent to use violence as a means to win elections. First, we present the basic features and dynamics of the 1992 election. Second, we outline the main ethnic cleavages in Kenya and discuss the importance of ethnicity in political mobilisation. Third, we analyse the formation of exclusionary ethnic identities in Kenya and the policies and leadership that made ethnic themes particularly salient in the pre-democratic era, and how these two features help explain the violent 1992 elections. In addition, we discuss how other factors, such as the importance of land, also add to our understanding of the violent electoral outcome.

The 1992 elections From 1970 until 1992, the Kenyan African National Union (KANU) was the sole political party running the Kenyan state. First president Jomo Kenyatta established de facto one-party rule that was extended after his death in 1978 when Daniel arap Moi took over power. In 1982, constitutional amendments made Kenya de jure a one-party state. The shift to multiparty politics in 1991 clearly changed the formal rules of the political game (Mueller 2014). Yet, by the time the election was held on 29 December 1992, thousands of Kenyans had been deprived of their right to vote due to displacement and destruction caused by state-sponsored attacks. In the violence, which took place over a period of almost two years, it is estimated that at least 1,500 people were killed and 300,000 displaced (Africa Watch 1993: 1).

The transition to multiparty politics has its origin in a combination of factors. Kenyans were suffering from mounting inflation and food shortages. The Moi regime had become increasingly authoritarian and depended on support from Moi's own Kalenjin group and a few other minority tribes. The Forum for the Restoration of Democracy (FORD) was formed in August 1991, representing a broad coalition of opposition groups, clergy and lawyers, but the arrest of several FORD leaders resulted in the suspension of foreign aid by key donors until the government initiated political and economic reforms (Kirschke 2000). Moi reacted swiftly and finalised the legalisation of multiparty politics in December 1991. The opposition suffered from pervasive factionalism from the outset and its political leaders were divided by the essential factor of ethnicity, as well as by personal conflicts (Mueller 2014). These divisions quickly transformed the opposition into networks of rival alliances that all fought to nominate their own presidential candidate.

The 1992 elections were accompanied by large-scale violence and displacement. While repressive measures had been used during previous elections, both under Kenya's first president, Jomo Kenyatta, and during Moi's tenure, the means and locus of repression changed in 1991. Previously monopolised by the state, violence was now committed by gangs. This was a major shift, with clear in- and out-groups being created and violence targeting whole communities (Kirschke 2000; Mueller 2014). The Moi regime had previously warned about the consequences of the return of multiparty politics in Kenya's volatile ethnic landscape and portrayed the clashes as a result of prevailing conflicts over land, fanned by a heated election campaign (Barkan 1993: 90; Throup 1993: 390). However, there is irrefutable evidence that the government was involved in sparking the violence for its own purposes and did not engage in adequate measures to prevent it. High-ranking government officials supported and coordinated the training and arming of young men predominantly drawn from Moi's own ethnic group, the Kalenjin (Africa Watch 1993; NCCK 1992). The police seemed unwilling to arrest the majority of the attackers and it was reported that the security forces were restrained by orders 'from above' (Throup and Hornsby 1998: 64). To a significantly lesser extent, there were retaliatory attacks against the Kalenjin communities in the affected areas, but these were less organised in character (Africa Watch 1993: 2).

The violence had the dual purpose of guaranteeing promised resources for KANU-supporting communities and of punishing the opposition voters. The violence was designed to establish an exclusive 'KANU zone' in the entire Rift Valley, by expelling all other ethnic groups from the land that had been occupied by the Kalenjin before the colonial era. The introduction of a 25 per cent rule (a constitutional amendment in August 1991) made it necessary for any presidential candidate to obtain at least 25 per cent of the vote cast in at least five of the country's eight provinces, in addition to winning a (relative) majority of the total national vote. The clashes, therefore, were meant to guarantee that none of the other candidates would obtain 25 per cent of the presidential vote in the Rift Valley (Throup and Hornsby 1998: 196).

The first sporadic clashes erupted in Nandi district in November 1991 and grew in intensity in mid-January. In April 1992 the clashes entered a new, even more violent phase as the frequency of incidents rose and the number of displaced and killed people increased significantly (Throup and Hornsby 1998: 195). During the registration process of political candidates in November and December, there were various assaults, kidnappings and attacks on opposition candidates. There were some violent incidents on the polling day of 29 December; however, widespread violence did not occur. After the election, the volatile situation was largely defused, but clashes between Kalenjin and Kikuyu continued in several areas (ibid. 541–2).

KANU also used its control over the state machine to its advantage in the electoral game. For instance, KANU manipulated the voter registration process and made it difficult for the opposition to organise politically by denying permits to hold rallies or open local offices (Barkan 1993: 93). Additional measures included the manipulation of the electoral commission, gerrymandering, and the delayed registration of opposition parties.

KANU emerged as the sole winner in the December 1992 election. Moi won the presidential election with 36 per cent of the vote and KANU gained 108 out of 188 seats in parliament. However, it remains questionable whether KANU actually secured an overall majority, given the various irregularities (Throup and Hornsby 1998: 517). Under pressure from supporters, the important churches and Western governments, the Democratic Party (DP) and FORD-Kenya eventually decided to take up their seats in parliament. Predictions of an uprising by the marginalised Kikuyu in the case of an electoral defeat did not materialise (ibid. 525). However, quite substantial violence continued, especially against Kikuyu seeking to return to their land, and was supported by KANU politicians (Steeves 1997: 37).

To a large extent the victory of KANU can be explained by the failure of the opposition to unite. This fragmentation was due to both ethnic divisions and personal conflicts, and has remained a feature of Kenyan politics since 1992 (LeBas 2011: 250; Mueller 2014). Moreover, the destructive influence of state-sponsored violence on opposition campaigning played a critical role in explaining KANU's electoral success.

Exclusionary ethnic identity and victimisation Ethnicity plays an important role in political mobilisation in Kenya: ethnic affiliation is considered to be a critical source of patronage and has influenced voting patterns both in contemporary politics and during single-party rule (Bratton and Kimenyi 2008; Hydén and Leys 1972; Haugerud 1995; Oyugi 1997; Posner 2005).[2] National politics are largely perceived as a competition between Kikuyu, Luo, Kalenjin, Luhya and Coastal people, but at the local level each of these groups is constituted of numerous ethnic communities (Posner 2005: 260). Ethnic identification is therefore diverse, and in a local setting other ethnic or tribal identities may be of greater significance.[3] Ethnic and tribal groups in rural areas live relatively segregated geographically, dominating a specific region and with their own ideas of specific rural homelands.[4]

While ethnic identity is politically salient in many African societies, Kenya's ethnic politics have become formulated around exclusion and victimisation to a large extent, which has precipitated the use of violence. Many ethnic identities in Kenya are what have been labelled 'exclusionary ethnicities': a form of identification that offers guidance not only as to which group has a legitimate right to access power, but also about which groups should be denied state power (Lynch 2011: 9; Mueller 2008). This form of ethnic identity formation has been shaped by violence and repression, which has led to a sense of victimisation and injustice among several groups. The dynamics around the violent struggle for independence – the Mau Mau uprising – and the transition to independence are illustrative in this regard. Kenya was a settler economy that suffered particularly severe repression from the colonisers. The British response to the violent challenge involved gross massacres. Although the Mau Mau movement included numerous ethnic groups, it was primarily constituted of elements from the Kikuyu community. The Kikuyu, which is the largest ethnic group today (21 per cent of the total population), interacted extensively with the colonisers, but the relationship also had a conflictual dimension. Resistance against the colonisers was, for instance, spurred by a process of repatriation of 'undesired' Kikuyu wage workers from the 'white' settlements; this created illegal squatter camps, in the Rift Valley and around Nairobi, where the squatters lived in harsh conditions. Unrest led to a state of emergency, which further increased a sense of grievance among the Kikuyu and formed the basis of the Mau Mau uprising. During the violence, the Kikuyu community was severely divided (Throup 1993). However, people of Kikuyu origin faced detention whether or not they were part of the uprising. When released, many of them could not return to the native reserves in the Central Province, but had to settle in illegal squatter camps in the Rift Valley.

Kikuyus suffered the most during Kenya's struggle to become independent and therefore expected that independence would produce particular benefits for the community. When Jomo Kenyatta – of Kikuyu origin – came to power in 1963, expectations were that the Kikuyu who had been forced to leave their land would get it back. However, Kenyatta supported only a small elite group, although it also included several other ethnic communities. Members of the Kikuyu community came to dominate the civil service, and the Central Province (particularly its small coffee and tea growers) was economically favoured by state policies (Barkan 1993: 87). Kenyatta's programme to buy land from departing settlers benefitted mainly the already privileged, who had enough resources to secure land. However, this group included a Kikuyu elite that financed land buying, which resulted in many Kikuyu farmers leaving the Central Province for land in the Rift Valley. In its attempts to consolidate power, the Kenyatta regime also turned against the Luo community, which comes from Nyanza Province in the west (van Stapele 2010).

The development of exclusionary ethnic identities in Kenya was also tied to the way in which political leaders sought to build political support after independence. In a context without a dominant ethnic group, a leader cannot rely solely on a core group; rather, they need the support of other groups to build a sufficiently strong base.

In Kenya, there was an initial attempt at building a broad-based ethnic coalition after independence, but politics soon became exclusionary. Although other groups were included, Kikuyu came to dominate single-party rule under Kenyatta (Horowitz 2000: 435).[5] KANU won the first free elections in 1963 and initially managed to unite all ethnic groups by co-opting key members of the Kenyan National Democratic Union (KADU) with promises of patronage. KADU merged with KANU in 1964 (Barkan 1993). The two parties had similar political agendas but drew support from different ethnic and social groups. KANU's support base was primarily found in the Kikuyu community (Central Province and part of Rift Valley), and among the Embu and Meru of the Eastern Province. In addition, support also came from the Luo in Nyanza Province in the west, and – to a more limited extent – from the Kamba (Eastern Province) and Kisii (Nyanza Province). KADU's ethnic base was among the Luhya (Western Province), the Kalenjin and associated groups (Rift Valley) and the Mijikenda (Coast Province), along with nomadic groups from the Northeastern Province and the arid and semiarid areas of Rift Valley (Barkan 1993).

One interpretation of Kenyatta's co-opting of KADU was that it was an interethnic elite 'pact', where 'in exchange for political power KADU dropped its opposition to settlement schemes in the Rift Valley. These schemes were meant, in part, to deal with the landlessness and the political unrest associated with it' (Klopp 2001: 477). Thus, during the Kenyatta era, support for power at the centre was based on a coalition of several ethnic groups, and depended locally on the ethnic makeup of the area (Throup 1993: 377). However, members from the Kikuyu community dominated the civil service (Barkan 1993: 87), which is central in accessing state-controlled resources such as land, jobs and government contracts, particularly during periods of authoritarian politics. Ethnic divisions were further entrenched when Kenyatta fell out with his vice president Oginga Odinga. While initially viewed as an ideological dispute, the conflict took an ethnic dimension since Odinga came from the Luo community. The ruling regime delegitimised the Luo leadership through smear campaigns and by classifying Luo as second-rank citizens (van Stapele 2010: 114–15). For instance, the ruling party insisted in public that Odinga's newly formed party – Kenya People's Union (KPU) – was exclusively a Luo party; such accusations were very difficult for KPU to counter due to the regime's strict control over information. As an example, the opposition was prevented from holding meetings and KPU was eventually banned in 1969, which led to de facto one-party rule (Mueller 1984: 409–13).[6] During this era, the formation of ethnic identity based on victimisation continued and state policies 'were responsible for narrowing the range of political identities that Kenyans could choose' (LeBas 2011: 101).[7]

Daniel arap Moi took power after the death of Kenyatta in 1978. Up until 1991, Moi's tenure was characterised by unaccountable, personal, paranoid and kleptocratic rule (Barkan 1993: 87–8; Throup 1993: 385). Moreover, the political support base for the regime became even narrower from an ethnic and geographical perspective. Moi's main support base was in the Rift Valley. He began favouring formerly 'disadvantaged groups', particularly his own Kalenjin and allied tribes, at the expense of Kikuyu, who were forced out of the civil service (Kahl 1998: 113). Public investments, which had been directed primarily to the Central Province, were reoriented to other parts of Kenya, especially the Rift Valley. This resulted in a more narrow support base for Moi's government. In addition, critics were dealt with harshly. In 1982, constitutional amendments made Kenya a de jure one-party state. In the aftermath of a coup attempt, the regime became even more repressive (Barkan 1993). While Moi's policies did not benefit all Kalenjin equally, a perception of 'Kalenjinisation' became widespread in Kenya and the Kalenjin became associated with the repressive measures taken by the Moi regime (Lynch 2011: 140). 'Over time, through reorganizing national alliances and patronage networks to ensure patrimonial control, KANU alienated many within Kikuyu and Luo constituencies ...

particularly over irregular allocations of land, which proceeded apace under the Moi regime' (Klopp 2001: 477). This marginalisation of certain groups can partly be explained by deteriorating economic conditions, which eroded the basis for more inclusive governance based on patronage (Mueller 2008; Throup 1993: 383). At the same time, the Kikuyu remained the most prominent group economically, which 'contributed to Moi's sense of isolation and political vulnerability' (Holmquist and Ford 1995: 177).

Ethnic political mobilisation Exclusionary ethnic identity formation and narrow interethnic elite co-optation/coalition building laid the foundations for the type of political mobilisation that transpired when multiparty elections were introduced. During the colonial period, national-level political organisation was not allowed, so when parties began operating in the post-independence era they largely became 'federated ethnic loyalties grouped around individuals' (Okoth-Ogendo 1972: 13). Political competition during single-party rule mainly involved group mobilisation according to locally defined ethnic identities. However, the type of cleavages that were the most politically salient changed with the reintroduction of multiparty politics in the 1990s. While the main parties in the electoral contest had an 'ethnic appeal', the 'politicians' local ethnic backgrounds were trumped by the regional ethnic orientations suggested by their party affiliations' (Posner 2007: 1318). This was also seen in the voting patterns in 1992, which showed a very high regional concentration of votes (Throup 1993: 391). Moreover, in contrast to some other African societies, there is little evidence to suggest that there exist cross-cutting ethnic identities that serve to bridge ethnic divides (Horowitz 2016: 330).

The violence that occurred prior to the 1992 election can be seen as a form of ethnic outbidding, which included an exclusionary ethnic rhetoric that served to mobilise support for violence. The violence during the election cannot be understood without reference to the Kenyan concept of '*majimbo*', which is essentially a federal political system based on ethnicity (Anderson 2008). The first constitution in 1962 introduced this idea by dividing the country into seven semi-autonomous regions, each with its own regional assembly. *Majimbo* resurfaced in 1991, with destructive consequences. Moi's KANU, representing the relatively small Kalenjin group, was in favour of *majimbo* as a means to mobilise support and eventually undermine political liberalisation. Its connection to violence was direct: 'ethnic' violence began shortly after high-ranking KANU officials in favour of *majimbo* organised a series of rallies in the Rift Valley as a direct challenge to multiparty campaigners. These politicians demanded the expulsion of all 'aliens' and 'foreigners' (mostly Kikuyu) from land that had been in the possession of the 'native' pastoralist groups (Kalenjin, Maasai, Turkana and Samburu) before colonial times (Africa

Watch 1993: 18). The latter communities were led to believe that they would be driven out themselves if Moi and KANU lost power, and that the only solution would be a 'pure' Rift Valley with semi-autonomy. Although this incitement was most prominent in the Rift Valley Province, the rhetoric of intimidation and violence occurred in all *majimbo* meetings held by KANU officials (Kahl 1998: 109). For many Kenyans, *majimbo* became synonymous with antagonistic neighbours and the necessity of ethnic violence.

One of the main objectives of the KANU-supported violence in 1991 and 1992 was to unite the Kalenjin community, especially in the crucial areas of Nandi and Kipsigis, and to spark mass support for Moi. Since the Rift Valley Province had the largest number of parliamentary seats, such support was crucial (Kahl 1998: 111–12). In several locations land registration was ongoing and individual titles were replacing communal deeds (Throup and Hornsby 1998: 198). The 'ethnic clashes' helped reunite the Kalenjin groups against 'foreigners'. If settlers from other ethnic groups – mainly Kikuyu, Gusii and Luo – could be forced to leave the western border areas of the Rift Valley before the registration procedures were terminated, the former owners would lose all their claims and the Kalenjin could take over. Through these actions, members of the Kalenjin were enticed to support Moi and his ruling clique. This strategy was essentially rooted in intra-group struggles that constituted a serious threat to KANU's electoral performance in its very own ethnic heartland. Certain Nandi and Kipsigis elites had remained opposed to Moi, and there was a risk that many voters from these groups would vote for the opposition (ibid. 199). The rhetoric around violent ethnic mobilisation therefore had a clear connection to ideas about historical injustices, victimisation and ethnic division, and Moi played on these to garner political support.[8]

The absence of a tradition of inclusive elite negotiations created conditions under which the instigation of violent ethnic mobilisation became a viable option for Moi in advance of the 1992 election. The opposition emerged outside Moi's circle of power and did not have the same ethnic support base; in fact, many joined the opposition because they had been excluded from power and resources based on ethnic or regional affiliation. The way in which political support was secured – via state-based patronage and 'ethnic brokerage' – made it difficult for the opposition to unite and mobilise cross-ethnic support (LeBas 2011). Also, without an inclusive elite pact, 'there were no basic guarantees which could limit the risks which the transition posed' (Kirschke 2000: 396).

This ethnicity-focused account of violent electoral competition contributes to an understanding of the ways in which elite considerations are linked to ethnic identity formation emanating from historical developments, such as past injustices and legacies from colonialism and single-party rule. Yet several additional factors came into play. First, while the opposition was clearly fragmented in Kenya, Moi's power base was diminishing with the distribution of patronage to maintain support becoming narrower due to economic decline. Moi must have perceived a real threat to his continued rule, and this factored into his decision to use violence. This is in line with previous research that has highlighted several issues relating to incumbent–opposition dynamics as crucial in understanding election-related violence (e.g. Hafner-Burton, Hyde and Jablonski 2014; Salehyan and Linebarger 2015; Sisk 2012; Wilkinson 2004).

A second issue relates to long-standing land grievances present in Kenya that have underpinned electoral competition in different ways. Patterns of land ownership and exchanges in Kenya – from colonial times onwards – have resulted in very uneven land distribution in rural areas (Boone 2012). These historical developments clearly serve to explain the geography of violence and the specific tendency to violence in the Rift Valley, and they played a key role in the violence prior to the 1992 elections. For instance, the areas in which Kikuyu migrants had established farms under Kenyatta were also the locus of violence in 1991 (Kahl 1998; Boone 2011). These insights, however, do not contradict our analysis of Kenya's vulnerability to election-related violence, but rather serve to reinforce an understanding of how ethnic mobilisation ties in with real and perceived historical grievances.

Third, the electoral system in place in Kenya in 1992 may have encouraged electoral violence. Kenya was operating under majoritarian electoral institutions, and research has shown that these raise the risk of electoral violence by augmenting winner-takes-all dynamics (e.g. Fjelde and Höglund 2016; Reilly and Reynolds 2000). In addition, the introduction of the 25 per cent rule – which made it necessary for presidential candidates to win at least 25 per cent of the votes in at least five provinces – gave Moi a clear electoral advantage (Kahl 2008: 203). At the same time, it failed to provide the opposition with enough incentive to unite across ethnic divisions.

Finally, international attention and monitors were unable to discourage electoral violence in Kenya in 1992. Electoral fraud was rampant. Although international monitors were on-site, they could not prevent irregularities. It is particularly interesting to note, as suggested by previous research, that international attention to the elections may have shaped the timing and forms of violence (Daxecker 2014). The decision of the donor community to stop financial aid at the end of 1991 was a major reason why the Moi regime was willing to reintroduce party pluralism. International support remained conditional on democratic progress, which limited government possibilities to directly engage in open conflicts with opposition supporters. Instead, KANU resorted to subtle tactics of extra-legal intimidation and violence to disempower its critics. Although the widespread attacks caused substantial casualties and raised considerable concern among donor countries, the government could portray these attacks as 'ethnic clashes' over land (Africa Watch 1993: 15; see also Kirschke 2000). The strategy, therefore, must be viewed as a deliberate move to influence the electoral game while avoiding international censure and loss of aid.

Electoral violence beyond 1992

Violence has remained a pervasive feature of electoral politics in Kenya. It has 'become a routine aspect of Kenyan politics, and "ethnic clashes" are now part of the elite bargaining process' (Klopp 2001: 503). Yet, it is important to recognise that not all elections have been equally violent and, among violent elections, dynamics have varied. In 1997, as in 1992, the violence occurred primarily before the election, orchestrated by the regime to swing the election. But there were also considerable polling-day conflicts and continued clashes in some constituencies of the Rift Valley involving militia groups of young men, predominantly Kalenjin but also from other tribes. Internal opposition and defections also led to significant intra-KANU violence (Rutten, Mazrui and Grignon 2002; Laakso 2007). The elections were held against a backdrop of instability in the political arena and a civil movement calling for reforms. To win the elections, KANU sought to split the opposition, co-opt opposition politicians and render protesters irrelevant with harassment and disenfranchisement. Moi and KANU were able to win the elections although their parliamentary victory was particularly small.

The violence following the December 2007 election garnered the most attention by far. Although there were instances of pre-electoral violence, it was the post-electoral eruption that resulted in a high number of casualties: approximately 1,500 deaths and more than half a million displaced people (Kagwanja and Southall 2010). The first wave of violence hit the area in and around Eldoret in North Rift Valley, where well-organised Kalenjin militias attacked supporters of the Party of National Unity (PNU), mainly their Kikuyu neighbours but also Kisii communities. In a second wave, the violence spilled over to Naivasha and Nakuru in South Rift, with major confrontations as Kikuyu groups started retaliatory attacks against Kalenjin and Luo. Similar patterns of attacks and counter-attacks took place in Nairobi's slums between Luo and Kikuyu, and in Kisumu, where the police responded forcefully to protests and looting. It is important to note that the violence was not equally severe throughout Kenya. The main share of the violence was a response to what was seen as an unjust election result. Prior to the election, there had been widespread hope of victory for the opposition candidate – Raila Odinga – and his message of change. Over the years, a sense of political and economic marginalisation among non-Kikuyu groups had grown and had combined with deep resentments against Kikuyu. The centralisation of power around the president had also peaked, political institutions were weak, and political violence had become normalised and institutionalised (Mueller 2008). When it was announced that the incumbent Mwai Kibaki had won the election, violence escalated and diffused quickly and did not come to a halt until elite-level negotiations resulted in a power-sharing agreement and the leaders called for the violence to stop.

In contrast to 1992, 1997 and 2007–08, the elections in 2002 and 2013 were significantly more peaceful. Why? In 2002, the violence that took place was predominantly pre-electoral, occurring during the nomination period. In addition, there were isolated events in highly competitive constituencies in Rift Valley and Nyanza. Compared with previous elections, this presidential contest was between two Kikuyu candidates – Moi's designated successor Uhuru Kenyatta, and Kibaki, who represented a broad, united and interethnically based opposition front under the National Rainbow Coalition (NARC). As expected, NARC won the election, and many KANU leaders seemed to accept that popular sentiments had finally turned against the old regime. Thus, while underlying issues of land and equality remained unresolved, these disputes were not activated by the political leadership. However, there were reasons for concern due to the ongoing latent diffusion of informal violence, especially originating from the Mungiki movement, blurring the lines between criminal and political violence (Kagwanja 2003, see also Rasmussen, Chapter 8 in this volume). State responses to this violence contributed to a further institutionalisation of extra-legal state violence during the Kibaki regime, which in turn contributed to the popular discontent that played into the explosive aftermath of the 2007 elections.

The 2013 elections were held under a new constitution and saw the creation of the Jubilee Alliance, which brought together Uhuru Kenyatta and William Ruto, representing ethnic groups across the 2008 conflict lines and making this particular divide less salient during the election. The opposition was led by Raila Odinga, who again lost – by a narrow margin and amid accusations of electoral malpractice. A major difference this time was that the opposition challenged the result through constitutional means, rather than street protest. While generally considered relatively peaceful, localised violence connected to the election did occur, especially in North Rift Valley, the Coast and in Northeastern Province (Cheeseman, Lynch and Willis 2014; Long et al. 2013).

The August 2017 elections were again held amid fears of violent mobilisation and escalation. More than a year ahead of the elections, the opposition criticised the Independent Electoral and Boundaries Commission (IEBC) for being partial, and this distrust persisted throughout and beyond election day. Communal tensions arose in several areas, and only a few days before the election, a high-profile IEBC member was killed. The immediate aftermath of the election saw some limited protest by the disappointed opposition supporters, but this was heavily suppressed by the government (Cheeseman, Lynch and Willis 2017). However, the opposition refused to accept defeat and challenged the election results in court, resulting in a ruling by the Supreme Court in favour of new presidential elections. The trajectory of the electoral process illustrates how electoral conflict can be resolved via the formal institutions that exist, but also shows the contentious nature of elections in Kenya.

Conclusions

In many societies, political elites view ethnic kin as their most reliable political supporters, and ethnic identity can be used as a tool to facilitate low-cost collective action and to mobilise significant electoral constituencies (Arriola 2009; Chandra 2004; Posner 2007). Yet not all societies with politicised ethnic identities face electoral violence. Kenya's violent electoral history gives some clues as to why some societies become particularly vulnerable to political violence. Our analysis suggests that the violent political mobilisation prior to the 1992 election must be understood against the background of very strongly politicised and polarised ethnic identities, linked to perceived inequality and exclusion, which also had historical roots. In places where ethnic distinctions serve as a basis for claims to state power, the stakes of elections are elevated. Moreover, when ethnic mobilisation also leads to ethnic voting – as is the case in Kenya (Bratton and Kimenyi 2008) – several mechanisms may encourage election-related violence. For instance, Kuhn (2015: 93) discusses why we would expect electoral violence to be more common where ethnic voting is high. In essence, when an election basically becomes an ethnic census, many standard campaign strategies – including promises of patronage – will prove ineffective for political candidates to mobilise voters. In such situations, violence becomes a means (or even a last resort) to discourage opposition voters and also to suppress undecided voters.

In many countries that are subject to electoral and ethnically based violence, constitutional reform has been a means to curb violence, address underlying grievances and create incentives for cross-ethnic cooperation. In Kenya, the 2010 constitution was partially a direct response to the 2007 electoral violence. However, the outcome of the reform process remains inconclusive and the impact of different dimensions of the reform package can be interpreted in different ways. For instance, on the one hand, the restructuring of political institutions may have helped reduce the stakes in the 2013 election: 'the crea-tion of a new constitution with 47 new county governments in which many Odinga supporters were able to secure county-level seats, meant that, while the Coalition for Reforms and Democracy (CORD) lost nationally, they often won locally, softening the blow of the controversial presidential elections' (Cheeseman, Lynch and Willis 2014: 4). On the other hand, and as seen in other cases, there are signs that devolution of power and control over resources to local government has elevated the importance of local-level politics, and this has served to displace conflict from the national level to the local level rather than solving it (ICG 2016; see also Angerbrandt 2011). The implication is that reform to address election-related violence through constitutional reform may have unintended and counterproductive effects.

This analysis of Kenya's vulnerability to electoral violence is not intended to be deterministic in its approach. Rather, the varying outcomes across electoral contests in Kenya show how a mix of circumstances are necessary for electoral violence to happen (see Sjögren, Chapter 2 in this volume for a similar argument). Yet, we argue that in explaining electoral violence, it may be important to know where ethnic divisions came from and why they have endured, especially when violence itself shapes the identities that gain salience (Fearon and Laitin 2000: 850). This also implies that efforts to reduce the risk of electoral violence – for example through institutional reform or active democracy support – must recognise ethnic distinctions without reinforcing them. While our analysis focuses on top-down strategies that deliberately or inadvertently serve to uphold ethnic saliency, other studies have focused on the ways in which local narratives of ethnic 'others' interact with elite manipulations. For instance, several studies highlight the 'immigrant metaphor' and 'son of the soil' dynamics as rationales behind the persistence of ethicised land conflict in Kenya (Jenkins 2012; Klaus and Mitchell 2015). Combined, these factors explain how violence can become a widespread phenomenon driven from both above and below. Policies to reduce the risk of electoral violence must therefore strive to mitigate elite incentives to resort to divisive electoral strategies, while also recognising how political, social and economic inequalities across the population makes such strategies viable.

Notes

1 This study was funded by the Swedish Research Council 421-2010-1515 and Riksbankens Jubileumsfond, grant P16-0124:1.

2 Bratton and Kimenyi (2008: 276), in a survey from 2007, find that:

Although Kenyans downplay ethnicity when portraying themselves, they are less charitable in their assessments of fellow citizens ... Kenyans do not easily trust co-nationals who hail from ethnic groups other than their own. They also think that political conflict is all too common among people of different ethnic backgrounds, especially in the national political arena. Finally, they worry that their co-nationals are prone to organize politically along exclusive ethnic

lines and to govern in discriminatory fashion.

They also find that, overall, 'voting in Kenya is ... defensively and fundamentally an ethnic census' (ibid. 287).

3 For instance, the Kalenjin community subsumes many smaller tribes, including Nandi, Sabaot, Pokot and Marakwet (Lynch 2011).

4 'Prior to independence, the British assisted the Kenyans in creating administrative districts that were drawn around existing ethnic settlements' (Burchard 2015: 58).

5 The coalitions that have formed have adopted different ethnic constellations, pointing to the strategic nature of the leadership's use of ethnicity in politics (Burchard 2015: 57; Lynch

2008). Consider, for instance, the politics of William Ruto, a prominent Kalenjin politician, who supported Raila Odinga from the Luo community in the 2007 election, and who sided with Uhuru Kenyatta from the Kikuyu community in 2013 (Lynch 2008).

6 A further polarising event was the assassination of Tom Mboya in 1969.

7 LeBas argues that, pre-independence, 'organised labor served as a mobilizing structure independent from ethnicity' (2011: 101). For instance, Tom Mboya (Luo), who was a prominent trade unionist leader and held important positions within KANU and the government, drew support from several ethnic groups.

8 Lower levels of group identity in urban areas help explain why the 1991–92 violence in Kenya remained largely contained in rural areas and did not escalate further (Kahl 1998: 117).

References

Africa Watch (1993) 'Divide and Rule: State-sponsored Ethnic Violence in Kenya'. New York NY: Human Rights Watch.

Anderson, D. (2008) 'Majimboism: The Troubled History of an Idea' in D. Branch and N. Cheeseman (eds), *Our Turn to Eat! Politics in Kenya since 1950*. Berlin: Lit Verlag.

Anderson, D. and E. Lochery (2008) 'Violence and Exodus in Kenya's Rift Valley, 2008: Predictable and Preventable?', *Journal of Eastern African Studies* 2 (2): 328–43.

Angerbrandt, H. (2011) 'Political Decentralisation and Conflict: The Sharia Crisis in Kaduna, Nigeria', *Journal of Contemporary African Studies* 29 (1): 15–31.

Arriola, L. (2009) 'Patronage and Political Stability in Africa', *Comparative Political Studies* 42 (10): 1339–62.

Barkan, J. D. (1993) 'Kenya: Lessons from a Flawed Election,' *Journal of Democracy* 4 (3): 85–99.

Bates, R. H. (1983) 'Modernization, Ethnic Competition and the Rationality of Politics in Contemporary Africa' in D. Rothchild and V. Olorunsola (eds), *State Versus Ethnic Claims: African Policy Dilemmas*. Boulder CO: Westview Press.

Bayart, J.-F. (1993) *The State in Africa: The Politics of the Belly*. New York NY: Longman.

Boone, C. (2011) 'Politically Allocated Land Rights and the Geography of Electoral Violence: The Case of Kenya in the 1990s', *Comparative Political Studies* 44 (10): 1311–42.

Boone. C. (2012) 'Land Conflict and Distributive Politics in Kenya', *African Studies Review* 55 (1): 75–103.

Brancati, D. and J. Snyder (2013) 'Time to Kill: The Impact of Election Timing on Post-conflict Stability', *Journal of Conflict Resolution* 57 (5): 822–53.

Bratton, M. and M. S. Kimenyi (2008) 'Voting in Kenya: Putting Ethnicity in Perspective', *Journal of Eastern African Studies* 2 (2): 272–89.

Bratton, M. and N. van de Walle (1994) 'Neopatrimonial Regimes and Political Transitions in Africa', *World Politics* 46 (4): 453–89.

Burchard, S. M. (2015) *Electoral Violence in Sub-Saharan Africa: Causes and Consequences*. Boulder CO: Lynne Rienner.

Cederman, L., K. Gleditsch and S. Hug (2013) 'Elections and Ethnic Civil War', *Comparative Political Studies* 46 (3): 387–417.

Chandra, K. (2004) *Why Do Ethnic Parties Succeed? Patronage and Ethnic Head Counts in India*. New York NY: Cambridge University Press.

Cheeseman, N., G. Lynch and J. Willis (2014) 'Democracy and its Discontent: Understanding Kenya's 2013 Elections', *Journal of Eastern African Studies* 8 (1): 2–24.

Cheeseman, N., G. Lynch and J. Willis (2017) 'Voting for the Devil You Know: Kenya's 2017 Election', *Review of African Political Economy* blog. Available at http://roape. net/2017/08/14/voting-devil-know-kenyas-2017-election/ (accessed 26 November 2017).

Daxecker, U. E. (2014) 'All Quiet on Election Day? International Election Observation and Incentives for Pre-election Violence in African Elections', *Electoral Studies* 34: 232–43.

Dercon, S. and R. Gutiérrez-Romero (2012) 'Triggers and Characteristics of the 2007 Kenyan Electoral Violence', *World Development* 40 (4): 731–44.

Fearon, J. D. and D. D. Laitin (2000) 'Violence and the Social Construction of Ethnic Identity', *International Organization* 54 (4): 845–77.

Fjelde, H. and K. Höglund (2016) 'Electoral Institutions and Electoral Violence in Sub-Saharan Africa', *British Journal of Political Science* 46 (2): 297–320.

Hafner-Burton, E. M., S. D. Hyde and R. S. Jablonski (2014) 'When Do Governments Resort to Election Violence?', *British Journal of Political Science* 44 (1): 149–79.

Haugerud, A. (1995) *The Culture of Politics in Modern Kenya*. Cambridge: Cambridge University Press.

Höglund, K. (2009) 'Electoral Violence in Conflict-ridden Societies: Concepts, Causes, and Consequences', *Terrorism and Political Violence* 21 (3): 412–27.

Höglund, K., A. Jarstad and M. Söderberg Kovacs (2009) 'The Predicament of Elections in War-torn Societies', *Democratization* 16 (3): 530–57.

Holmquist, F. and M. Ford (1995) 'Stalling Political Change: Moi's Way in Kenya', *Current History* 94 (591): 177–81.

Horowitz, D. L. (2000) *Ethnic Groups in Conflict*. Berkeley CA: University of California Press.

Horowitz, J. (2016) 'The Ethnic Logic of Campaign Strategy in Diverse Societies: Theory and Evidence from Kenya', *Comparative Political Studies* 49 (3): 324–56.

Huntington, S. (1970) 'Social and Institutional Dynamics of One-party Systems' in S. Huntington and C. P. Moore (eds), *Authoritarian Politics in Modern Societies*. New York NY: Basic Books.

Hydén, G. and C. Leys (1972) 'Elections and Politics in Single-party Systems: The Case of Kenya and Tanzania', *British Journal of Political Science* 2 (4): 389–420.

ICG (2016) 'Commentary: Kenya: Development, County Governments and the Risk of 2017 Election Violence'. Brussels: International Crisis Group (ICG). Available at www. crisisgroup.org/africa/horn-africa/kenya/kenya-development-county-governments-and-risk-2017-election-violence (accessed 16 December 2016).

Jenkins, S. (2012) 'Ethnicity, Violence and the Migrant-guest Metaphor in Kenya', *African Affairs* 111 (445): 576–96.

Kagwanja, P. M. (2003) 'Facing Mount Kenya or Facing Mecca? The Mungiki, Ethnic Violence and the Politics of the Moi Succession in Kenya, 1987–2002', *African Affairs* 102 (406): 25–49.

Kagwanja, P. M. and R. Southall (2010) 'Kenya's Uncertain Democracy: The Electoral Crisis of 2008', *Journal of Contemporary African Studies* 27 (3): 259–77.

Kahl, C. H. (1998) 'Population Growth, Environmental Degradation, and State-sponsored Violence: The Case of Kenya', *International Security* 23 (2): 80–119.

Kahl, C. H. (2008) *States, Scarcity, and Civil Strife in the Developing World*. Princeton NJ: Princeton University Press.

Kirschke, L. (2000) 'Informal Repression, Zero-sum Politics and Late Third Wave Transitions', *Journal of Modern African Studies* 38 (3): 383–405.

Klaus, K. and M. I. Mitchell (2015) 'Land Grievance and the Mobilization of Electoral Violence: Evidence from Côte d'Ivoire and Kenya', *Journal of Peace Research* 52 (5): 622–35.

Klopp, J. M. (2001) '"Ethnic Clashes" and Winning Elections: The Case of Kenya's Electoral Despotism', *Canadian Journal of African Studies* 35 (5): 473–517.

Kuhn, P. M. (2015) 'Do Contentious Elections Trigger Violence?' in P. Norris, R. W. Frank and F. Martínez i Coma (eds), *Contentious Elections: From Ballots to Barricades*. New York NY: Routledge.

Laakso, L. (2007) 'Insights into Electoral Violence in Africa' in M. Basedau, G. Erdmann and A. Mehler (eds), *Votes, Money and Violence: Political Parties in Sub-Saharan Africa*. Uppsala: Nordic Africa Institute.

LeBas, A. (2011) *From Protest to Parties: Party-building and Democratization in Africa*. Oxford: Oxford University Press.

Long, J. D., K. Kanyinga, K. E. Ferree and C. Gibson (2013) 'Kenya's 2013 Election: Choosing Peace over Democracy', *Journal of Democracy* 24 (3): 140–55.

Lynch, G. (2008) 'Courting the Kalenjin: The Failure of Dynasticism and the Strength of the ODM Wave in Kenya's Rift Valley Province', *African Affairs* 107 (429): 541–68.

Lynch, G. (2011) *I Say to You: Ethnic Politics and the Kalenjin in Kenya*. Chicago IL: University of Chicago Press.

Mann, M. (2005) *The Dark Side of Democracy: Explaining Ethnic Cleansing*. Cambridge: Cambridge University Press.

Mueller, S. D. (1984) 'Government and Opposition in Kenya, 1966–9', *Journal of Modern African Studies* 22 (3): 399–427.

Mueller, S. D. (2008) 'The Political Economy of Kenya's Crisis', *Journal of Eastern African Studies* 2 (2): 185–210.

Mueller, S. D. (2014) 'The Resilience of the Past: Government and Opposition in Kenya', *Canadian Journal of African Studies* 48 (2): 333–52.

NCCK (1992) *The Cursed Arrow: Contemporary Report on the Politicised Land Clashes in Rift Valley, Nyanza and Western Provinces*. Nairobi: National Council of Churches of Kenya (NCCK).

Okoth-Ogendo, H. W. O. (1972) 'The Politics of Constitutional Change in Kenya since Independence, 1963–69', *African Affairs* 71 (282): 9–34.

Oyugi, W. O. (1997) 'Ethnicity in the Electoral Process: The 1992 General Elections in Kenya', *African Journal of Political Science* 2 (1): 41–69.

Posner, D. N. (2005) *Institutions and Ethnic Politics in Africa*. Cambridge: Cambridge University Press.

Posner, D. N. (2007) 'Regime Change and Ethnic Cleavages in Africa', *Comparative Political Studies* 40 (11): 1302–27.

Rabushka, A. and K. A. Shepsle (1972) *Politics in Plural Societies: A Theory of Democratic Instability*. Columbus OH: Merrill.

Reilly, B. and A. Reynolds (2000) 'Electoral Systems and Conflict in Divided Societies' in P. C. Stern and D. Druckman (eds), *Conflict Resolution after the Cold War*. Washington DC: National Academy Press.

Riedl, R. B. (2014) *Authoritarian Origins of Democratic Party Systems in Africa*. New York NY: Cambridge University Press.

Rutten, M., A. Mazrui and F. Grignon (eds) (2001) *Out for the Count: The 1997 General Elections and Prospects for Democracy in Kenya*. Kampala: Fountain Publishers.

Salehyan, I. and C. Linebarger (2015) 'Elections and Social Conflict in Africa, 1990–2009', *Studies in Comparative International Development* 50 (1): 23–49.

Sisk, T. D. (2012) 'Evaluating Election-related Violence: Nigeria and Sudan in Comparative Perspective' in D. A. Bekoe (ed.), *Voting in Fear: Electoral Violence in Sub-Saharan Africa*. Washington DC: United States Institute for Peace Press.

Snyder, J. (2000) *From Voting to Violence: Democratization and Nationalist*

Conflict. New York NY and London: W. W. Norton & Company.

Steeves, J. S. (1997) 'Re-democratisation in Kenya: "Unbounded Politics" and the Political Trajectory towards National Elections', *Commonwealth and Comparative Politics* 35 (3): 27–52.

Throup, D. (1993) 'Elections and Political Legitimacy in Kenya', *Africa* 63 (3): 371–96.

Throup, D. and C. Hornsby (1998) *Multiparty Politics in Kenya*. Oxford: James Currey.

van Stapele, N. (2010) 'Maisha Bora, Kwa Nani? A Cool Life, for Whom? Mediations of Masculinity, Ethnicity, and Violence in a Nairobi Slum' in L. Kapteijns and A. Richters (eds), *Mediations of Violence in Africa*. Boston MA: Brill.

Wilkinson, S. I. (2004) *Votes and Violence: Electoral Competition and Ethnic Riots in India*. Cambridge: Cambridge University Press.

2 | Wielding the stick again: the rise and fall and rise of state violence during presidential elections in Uganda

Anders Sjögren

Introduction

In four consecutive elections, Uganda's president Yoweri Museveni has faced the opposition leader Kizza Besigye as his main challenger for the presidency. All these presidential contests have been charged, but to different degrees and expressed in different ways. The 2001 and 2006 elections were marred by various forms of violence, not exclusively but mainly exercised or sanctioned by the state or by the ruling party, the National Resistance Movement (NRM), targeting opposition politicians or supporters. The presence of the government security apparatus loomed large over these campaigns: a sizeable number of people on the opposition side were injured and threatened, and during the 2006 campaign Besigye was arrested and charged with treason, leading to major riots. By contrast, the elections of 2011, though underpinned by tension between Museveni and Besigye, were more peaceful (as were the 1996 elections) and instead characterised by the large amount of money spent by the government side during the campaigns. The 2016 elections, however, were again marked by a higher degree of outright violence or threats of violence.

This chapter, drawing on official documents, media material and reports by election observers, examines the changing levels of state-executed or state-sanctioned violence against the opposition over the five most recent presidential elections, with an emphasis on the 2011 and 2016 elections. The earlier three elections, which have received previous treatment in the literature, are used as an illuminating backdrop. How can this variation be explained? While shifting levels of electoral violence within countries over time is common, this is as yet an understudied topic relative to research on electoral violence that compares different countries. This chapter situates the research problem in the context of research on the use of state-organised violence as one mechanism among others to influence the outcome of elections, and builds on existing arguments which hold that the degree of government-sponsored violence is shaped by the intensity of the competition and institutional constraints that may limit the use of force (Bhasin and Gandhi 2013; Hafner-Burton, Hyde and Jablonski 2014). It goes beyond existing research by emphasising the sequential aspect of elections and the significance of the ways in which experiences and lessons drawn from past elections shape expectations, calculations and adaptations for subsequent ones. The findings lend support to this: the lower degree of competition in combination with a particular set of deterring factors – such as interventions by the international justice system – that emerged from elections in other countries, as well as from other political events such as popular uprisings, made violence a less desirable government strategy in 2011. In 2001, 2006 and 2016, competition was fiercer and the deterrence factors were less significant. It should be stressed that government violence has been used in all these elections; this chapter analyses the degrees of such violence.

Following this introduction, the first section presents the main contributions to research about incumbents' use of violence in the context of elections and then develops theoretical arguments, drawing and elaborating on this body of research. The chapter proceeds by outlining the context of the study: the history of electoral violence in Uganda and the character of electoral politics under the NRM government. The following section first describes the 1996, 2001 and 2006 Ugandan presidential elections before examining in greater depth the 2011 and 2016 elections. The chapter concludes by summarising the findings and relating them to the theoretical arguments, and then closes with a discussion of policy implications. Although elections for the presidency and the parliament have been held simultaneously since 2006, the study is limited to violence in relation to the presidential elections, by far the most significant in Uganda's presidential system, especially in deciding the government's propensity for using violence.[1]

Previous research on government-sponsored violence

The rapidly expanding field of electoral violence has undergone conceptual, theoretical and empirical developments over the last decade – for overviews, see Höglund (2009a), Staniland (2014) and Straus and Taylor (2012). This chapter examines variations over time of one important – and the most common (Straus and Taylor 2012) – variant of electoral violence: state-organised violence. In line with existing literature, the chapter approaches state-organised violence as one instrument among others – such as public financial resources, control over information and the utilisation of legal-administrative measures – deployed strategically in order to manipulate elections in electoral autocracies (Bhasin and Gandhi 2013; Fjelde and Höglund 2016; Gandhi and Lust-Okar 2009; Hafner-Burton, Hyde and Jablonski 2014; Schedler 2013: 93; Staniland 2014: 107–12). In such contexts autocratic governments exercise power within nominally democratic institutions and face the challenge of balancing credibility and control (Bhasin and Gandhi 2013: 622). Competitive elections are held, but the playing field – the balance between the opposition and the incumbent with regard to access to resources, media and the law (Helle 2016) – is uneven, and incumbents are to varying degrees able and willing to distort the electoral process. Borrowing from Hafner-Burton, Hyde and Jablonski, I define state-organised electoral violence as 'events in which incumbent leaders and ruling party agents employ or threaten violence against the political opposition and potential voters before, during or after elections' (2014: 150). Such violence may be executed, sponsored or tolerated by state agencies, who in the latter case delegate it or turn a blind eye to its exercise (Schedler 2013: 93; Staniland 2014: 109–10). It may come in the shape of full-scale and sustained attacks, but more often it tends to be low-intensity, selective and intermittent (Schedler 2013: 92).

When do governments make use of violence during elections? While much cross-country work has been done, relatively little attention has been paid to variations in the level of violence in the same political entity over time.[2] As structural and institutional factors are often constant in such cases, these factors may explain a general propensity for violence rather than its variation, for which contest-specific factors appear to be more relevant. Existing research suggests that the most significant factors in structuring violence are the level of the electoral threat and the nature of institutionalised constraints on incumbents – both in overall terms (Hafner-Burton, Hyde and Jablonski 2014) and with regard to shaping the timing and targeting of violence (Bhasin and Gandhi 2013).[3] It is posited here that these aspects are significant as well as sensitive to contest-specific situations and will be utilised in the present study, but that they need to be elaborated and complemented. First, instead of institutional constraints, this study refers to rewards and sanctions in order to capture a broader scope of incentives, both enabling and constraining, and whether or not they are formally institutionalised. Second, this study contributes to existing research by emphasising the sequential aspect of elections and that learning experiences need to be considered when explaining variations in government-sponsored violence over time.

Framework and argument: competition, rewards, sanctions and experiences

Drawing on the findings from previous research noted above, this chapter proposes that the degree of government-sponsored violence is shaped by incentive structures that include the intensity of the electoral challenge and the possible rewards and sanctions for using or abstaining from violence, and that such calculations are critically informed by experiences from prior elections and other political events, both within the country in question and elsewhere. It is posited that, all things being equal, the more competitive high-stakes elections are, the higher the propensity for government-sponsored violence. This is mediated by governments' assessments of the balance between the risks and rewards involved in deploying violence, shaped by experience. With reference to democratisation, similar incentive structures have been framed by Lindberg (2009: 320) – drawing on Dahl's famous formulation – as rulers' assessments of the costs of oppression weighed against the costs of toleration. The study investigates these dimensions for the Ugandan 1996, 2001, 2006, 2011 and 2016 presidential elections, with an emphasis on the last two. Starting with the electoral threat, the literature suggests that incumbents may be tempted to make use of violence in order to supress registration or turnout, or both, among assumed opposition supporters when they face electoral loss[4] or a close race – or, it should be added, when they run the risk of not achieving a sufficiently wide margin of victory for purposes of prestige or instrumentality, for instance when they need to reach or stay above important thresholds, such as parliamentary absolute majorities or supermajorities (Bhasin and Gandhi 2013: 622).[5] The electoral challenge may vary geographically, and thus shape strategies for spatially targeted violence.

Incentive structures also involve the potential rewards and sanctions or risks associated with deploying or avoiding violence, domestically as well as in relation to external actors. Some of the rewards have been alluded to above: in many cases, government-sponsored violence is exercised in order to disenfranchise constituencies. Again, such violence may be executed sporadically and intermittently, and by proxy, so that governments can reduce the risk of attention and condemnation. Violence may also be targeted towards selected groups or actors, with the expectation that such victimisation of dissent will produce indirect intimidation effects on opposition supporters, swing voters and moderate government supporters (Bhasin and Gandhi 2013: 623).[6] It should be noted that there may be other beneficial effects for governments in exercising overt or covert violence that are not immediately tied to the shaping of the electoral outcome, but which are easily displayed during elections. Such rewards could include a more general signalling of armed strength to actors within the state, as well as to political supporters and opponents in order to enforce cohesion (Schedler and Hoffmann 2016). This is likely to be an important consideration in the case of the NRM government, whose power rests on coercive state institutions to a large degree. In relation to possible risks associated with violence that might deter governments from using it, Hafner-Burton, Hyde and Jablonski (2014: 158) point to credible threats by contending actors of using political or judicial accountability mechanisms to punish perpetrators. These mechanisms could be domestic or international, such as sanctions, withdrawn international development assistance or charges in international courts or tribunals. As far as domestic mechanisms are concerned, this chapter argues that impunity is part and parcel of electoral autocracies, albeit to varying degrees, and that therefore domestic accountability mechanisms can be expected to be weak. This is particularly probable in cases such as Uganda where violence has previously been exercised with impunity. Violence might also be deployed to a lesser degree, or by intimidation rather than direct force, if incumbents estimate it to be less efficient than other means of manipulation (Collier and Vicente 2012).[7]

It is important to appreciate the complex role and significance of experiences and expectations in influencing the behaviour of governments, opposition parties, citizens and external actors and in shaping continuity and change in state-organised violence. While elections can usefully be compared for certain purposes, they are not entirely discrete events; they are also and fundamentally parts of historical trajectories, where conditions for one particular election builds on experiences from prior ones. The actors are often the same over time and draw lessons from previous elections, and such experiences shape both incentive structures and calculations at later stages.[8] These actors can also be expected to learn from elections as well as from other political events elsewhere. Furthermore, electoral challenges and perceived rewards and sanctions in relation to the use of violence often evolve dynamically over an electoral cycle or campaign. Electoral strategies crafted in particular circumstances may reshape not only the level of competition – as they are always intended to do – but also the incentive structures for using – or not using – violence. Following on from this argument, we would expect that the 2011 elections were characterised by a more modest electoral challenge and/or a particular set of perceived rewards and sanctions that reduced the deployment of high levels of violence.

Electoral authoritarianism and the ebb and flow of state-organised violence in Uganda

During the first decades after independence in 1962, Ugandan politics was characterised by violent political conflict, turmoil and authoritarian rule. The country has experienced two military *coups d'état*, several inter-state and civil wars and a large number of armed insurgencies. None of the country's seven heads of state has left power as a result of a peaceful election, and no national elections were held between independence and 1980. Following the political crisis of 1966 – when a falling out between the Uganda People's Congress (UPC) government and Buganda kingdom led the central government to abolish all kingdoms and semi-federal units, and to use the military to enforce its decisions – the general elections scheduled for 1967 were postponed until 1971; because of the military takeover that year, however, they were never held. The general elections of 1980, which brought Milton Obote and the UPC to power, were broadly regarded as rigged (Carbone 2008: 19); this was the stated reason for Yoweri Museveni, whose party came a distant third in the elections, to wage a guerrilla war against the government.

After a five-year war, Museveni's National Resistance Army (NRA) took power in 1986 and imposed a ban on party political activity in the name of national unity, as parties were alleged by the new government to have been based on and to have promoted ethnic and religious sectarianism. Uganda was declared to be ruled under a no-party system (renamed the Movement system in the 1995 constitution), in which elections to political assemblies at all levels, from the very local to the national, were contested on the basis of individual merit. New avenues for local-level participation and (restricted) competition were opened up by the introduction of councils, and, following the enactment of a new constitution in 1995, elections to the National Assembly and the presidency were held in 1996 and again in 2001 (Carbone 2008). From the mid-1990s, both the old political parties and the emerging opposition within the NRM increasingly protested against what they regarded as the imposition of a one-party state and demanded the return of multiparty politics. Museveni finally conceded to the demands in 2003, and the change was confirmed through a referendum on the matter in 2005. In the process, however, presidential term limits were abolished, and Museveni was accordingly able to retain his grip over Ugandan politics (Makara, Rakner and Svåsand 2009). While control of the opposition under the no-party system was ensured by law, domination in the new dispensation has been conducted using a combination of means, and has been reproduced through elections every five years. The concentration of power in the presidency is considerable; the NRM has enjoyed strong majorities in parliament throughout; party and state functions have become increasingly fused; and Museveni's power ultimately rests on his firm control of the security apparatus – the police, the military and the intelligence services (Sjögren 2013; Tripp 2010).

While in overall terms Uganda has been more stable under Museveni than under past regimes – and, during the last ten years, more peaceful – certain structural factors create a high general propensity for election-related violence. These include sharp divides between government and opposition and bitterly fought elections; weak and partisan regulatory institutions, including the electoral management body, the police and the judiciary; pronounced political involvement by the military; and perceived political victimisation and exclusion of opposition politicians and supporters. These features, along with all other important structural and institutional factors, except the transition from no-party to multiparty politics in 2005, have not changed during the period under study; it can therefore be assumed that the differences between elections in terms of the degree of violence are caused by dynamics specific to the respective contests.[9] This again underlines the importance of analysing variations in electoral violence over time, and doing so by relating historically created patterns to incentive structures particular to each electoral contest (for a similar perspective, see Fjelde and Höglund, Chapter 1 in this volume).

1996–2006: from consent to challenge and crackdown While elections under the Movement system did not allow for formal party affiliation, Museveni's contenders in 1996 and 2001 were nevertheless associated with political parties or pressure groups distinct from the NRM. In 1996, Museveni's main opponent was Paul Ssemogerere, leader of the Democratic Party (DP), and Museveni secured a landslide victory with around 75 per cent of the votes. Evidently, the sitting president enjoyed all the advantages of incumbency, and it appears above all that he made use of monetary resources and the administrative functions of the Movement state (Muhumuza 1997). However, the level of state-sponsored violence was low; this would be consistent with the theoretical expectations, as the electoral threat to Museveni was very limited. While there were a few incidents of threats and outright violence targeted at Ssemogerere's campaigns, particularly in Rukungiri in the south-west (Tukahebwa 2003: 187), and while some of Museveni's campaign messages sought to intimidate the electorate by suggesting a return to chaos and war in the event of an opposition victory (Makara 2003: 20), the 1996 election has to be considered as peaceful by and large.

The 2001 presidential election, on the other hand, was anything but violence-free. For the first time Museveni faced a strong challenge from within the NRM. A retired army colonel, Kizza Besigye, became the voice of the growing dissatisfaction with corruption and political intolerance that had developed within sections of the NRM, and he stood against Museveni for the presidency as an independent, linked to the pressure group Reform Agenda (RA). In the end, Museveni won by a big margin – gaining 69 per cent against Besigye's 28 per cent – but Besigye's bid presented a serious challenge to Museveni on three fronts: within the NRM; within south-western Uganda, the home region of both men; and within the military. Besigye filed a petition to nullify the election, and while the Supreme Court ruling upheld the election result by three votes to two, the judgment agreed with the petitioner that the election had indeed been marred by serious irregularities, including vote buying, fraudulent administration and state-sanctioned violence, mainly exercised by the military.

The unprecedented level of electoral violence in 2001 prompted a parliamentary select committee report on the matter. The report documented widespread, systematic harassment of opposition supporters and activists orchestrated and conducted by a wide range of state security agencies, including the Uganda Peoples Defence Forces (UPDF), intelligence organs and various unofficial but state-sanctioned militia groupings, particularly in areas where RA and other opposition candidates constituted a threat (Uganda Parliament Select Committee 2002: Chapter 7). A great number of people were threatened, beaten, abducted and detained and seventeen people lost their lives. The strength of Besigye's electoral challenge appears to have come as a surprise to the government, and therefore violence was used alongside other means in order to influence the electoral outcome and to prevent the divisions within the NRM to widen and deepen.

In the longer run, such divisions could not be prevented, and multiparty politics was reintroduced in 2005. Besigye had escaped into exile after the 2001 elections, but he returned to Uganda in October 2005 in order to be the flag-bearer of the Forum for Democratic Change (FDC). Soon afterwards, he was arrested and charged with treason, concealment of treason and rape. Although he was eventually freed of all accusations, his presidential campaign was disrupted. Besigye's arrest triggered widespread riots, which met heavy-handed treatment from the state security organs; on one occasion the High Court in Kampala was surrounded by a previously unknown security force. Throughout the campaigns, the presence of the security apparatus, including the UPDF, was highly visible and its conduct partisan (Human Rights Watch 2006), although Kibandama (2008: 147) argues that there was a shift in emphasis from the overt violence in 2001 to more indirect and structural forms of violence, such as intimidation, in 2006. The overall violent character of the 2006 election needs to be seen against the backdrop of a general pattern of increasingly coercive political rule and the militarisation of the state apparatus (Human Rights Watch 2006; Sjögren 2013; Tripp 2010). The political challenge to the NRM grew in strength, as reflected in the results of the presidential election, in which Museveni received 59 per cent and Besigye 37 per cent. Again Besigye appealed, again the Supreme Court validated many of the grounds of the petition – and again it still upheld the results (Murison 2013).

2011: toleration outweighing repression The unanimous view among analysts is that the 2011 polls witnessed substantially less open state-organised violence than the two general elections that preceded it (Gibb 2012: 460; Izama and Wilkerson 2011: 70–1; Perrot, Lafargue and Makara 2014: 30–2). This relative change does not mean that the elections were entirely peaceful. Lower-level opposition activists were targeted, a government-friendly paramilitary group occasionally attacked opposition supporters (Makara 2014: 132–3), and, around election day, the country witnessed heavy military and police deployment (Izama and Wilkerson 2011: 69). However, while the impact of such a demonstration of force should not be neglected, the presence of the security forces remained at the level of a silent threat, and the government strategy throughout the campaigns did not revolve around intense harassment of the opposition of the kind that had marked previous elections.

To what extent did this reflect the effect of a less even electoral playing field, one where the government was more confident about the prospects for electoral victory? With hindsight, the outcome would suggest that it did: the result was a major triumph for Museveni and the NRM. In the presidential election, Museveni increased his margin of victory, gaining 68 per cent to Besigye's 26 per cent, and NRM candidates claimed 70 per cent of the parliamentary seats. Even when these results are treated with a degree of caution, as warranted by the critique voiced by the opposition and observers of the Electoral Commission's lack of competence and neutrality (COG 2011; EU-EOM 2011; Makara 2014), they imply that the opposition failed to challenge the government in a serious manner.

This was not immediately obvious when the campaigns began in October 2010. Opposition parties had been able to prepare for elections for five years, and would seemingly be able to capitalise on government weaknesses, the most visible of which were a series of corruption scandals and the deteriorating relations with the influential Buganda kingdom (Izama and Wilkerson 2011: 66). The opposition found it difficult, however, to translate potential advantages to real competitive strength. For a start, it was divided, with splits occurring both among and within opposition parties, and a proposed electoral alliance never materialised effectively. Furthermore, it was not easy to mobilise Buganda as a vote bloc, as the many sources of widespread disquiet with the central government caused divisions within the region, and because the Buganda kingdom representatives themselves needed to tread carefully on political matters (Gay 2014).

At the same time, the NRM reached out to regions such as Acholi (where the end of the war had improved the government's electoral prospects) and Teso, which had been opposition strongholds in 2006; in this they had some success, as the results later showed. The NRM had also reactivated its presence throughout the country with a huge membership drive in 2010, a strategy that lay the groundwork for its campaign networks. And while internal competition for electoral positions increased within the party, leading to many independent candidates, this did not result in any serious factional fallout benefiting the opposition. When campaigns began, the government used resources of such a magnitude that the expenses contributed to rising inflation in the post-election period (Helle and Rakner 2014). There is a debate over the extent to which this financial extravagance contributed to Museveni's victory (Conroy-Krutz and Logan 2012; Helle and Rakner 2014; Izama and Wilkerson 2011), but it is agreed that the level was unprecedented. In summary, the opposition initially posed a potential electoral challenge, but the campaigns produced a divided opposition and an energised and resource-rich NRM – a reminder that the level of electoral threat may shift during campaigns.

Electoral threat is not only a changing phenomenon; it is relative in another sense too, although this is more difficult to capture. The playing field for Ugandan elections under a Museveni government is not likely to be level. Key institutions, such as the Electoral Commission, the military and the police, have long been and are likely to remain partisan, something the Ugandan electorate is well aware of. It could be argued that, at least to some extent, Museveni had already won the 2011 elections with the Supreme Court ruling on the electoral petition in 2006, a ruling that contributed to diminished faith in electoral politics among opposition supporters. Some indications that this might have been the case include the lower figures for Besigye compared with the 2006 results; a lower turnout (59 per cent, down from 69 per cent in 2006), especially in opposition strongholds; and the fact that Museveni and the NRM were able to make inroads into and (re)capture some regions.

With regard to the use of violence, however, the main difference compared with 2006 lay in the changing structures of potential rewards and sanctions. Starting with the advantages of refraining from violence, the NRM needed to counter the possible loss of support in Buganda by seeking to capture new constituencies in the north, and by recapturing parts of the east. A combination of factors favoured a rewards- and resource-based strategy in these areas. The northern parts of the country, and especially Acholi, were among the poorest and had suffered from rebellions, wars and coercive government behaviour. In order to win over that segment of the electorate, the NRM invested heavily in government development programmes in the region. Furthermore, such expenditures had become easier to justify following the discovery of oil in western Uganda and the prospects of massive future revenue, and promises of immediate and future financial rewards constituted the core of the NRM campaign throughout the country (Helle and Rakner 2014).

Turning to the constraining factors, Museveni and the NRM are likely to have drawn lessons from events following the flawed elections in Kenya in 2007, Zimbabwe in 2008 and Côte d'Ivoire in 2010, when state-organised violence and violent protests in different combinations resulted in international interventions, political agreements and coalition governments in Kenya and Zimbabwe, and civil war (and the eventual overthrow of the government) in Côte d'Ivoire. Other deterring examples came from North Africa, where popular protests had ousted sitting presidents in several countries. These examples are likely to have contributed to a more restrictive approach to excessive violence for two reasons: one was the uncertainty linked to uprisings, and the other was the fact that political leaders in Kenya had been charged with crimes against humanity before the International Criminal Court (ICC) in the Hague. One opposition presidential candidate, Olara Otunnu, threatened Museveni with a similar fate should he use coercive state power against the population (Izama and Wilkerson 2011: 70). While Museveni made repeated public reference to these examples, warning the opposition against emulating them (ibid. 69), he had to weigh the necessity of preventing insurgencies against the risks of being held accountable for state-organised violence. The balancing act resulted in a politics of signalling the threat: indicating rather than exercising military power, and doing so with more skilful timing, targeting and fine-tuning than in 2001 and 2006.

Before turning to the 2016 elections, it is useful to provide a brief discussion of the 'walk to work' protests and the heavy deployment of state violence in response to these – even though this was not strictly election-related – as this episode conditioned future potential electoral protests and state violence. Two months after the elections, the opposition launched the 'walk to work' campaign. The stated target of these protest marches was the rising cost of living in general and the high cost of transport in particular – an effect of post-election inflation – but they also offered an opening for political grievances more broadly (Goodfellow 2013). Museveni had clearly stated that popular protests of the kind then recently witnessed in North Africa would not be tolerated in Uganda, and the police clamped down hard. Many protestors were arrested, dozens injured, and one person shot dead. Besigye was arrested three times within a few weeks; the third time he was manhandled so badly that he had to seek medical care abroad. When news of the brutal treatment of Besigye reached the public, violent riots erupted in Kampala and in many other urban centres around the country. The government, in contrast to the strategic constraint that had characterised the campaigns, appeared to be caught unaware and responded to the challenge with a return to its old ways: a massive and heavy-handed deployment of its security agencies (Izama and Wilkerson 2011: 77).

To conclude, both the more limited electoral threat and a new set of structures of potential rewards and sanctions contributed to limit state-organised violence in the 2011 elections. Furthermore, these factors were dynamically linked. While the initial electoral challenge to Museveni was not negligible, it was not overwhelming either. The incentive structures that discouraged the heavy use of overt violence on the one hand and encouraged the use of state-based resources and rewards for electoral support on the other turned the government strategy towards greater moderation. The opposition had relatively more freedom to campaign – but at the same time it could not mobilise support around resistance to government repression as credibly as in past elections. The opposition also displayed its own disunity and weaknesses more clearly, and thus lost some of its competitive edge.

2016: repression outweighing toleration again The 2016 general elections were tightly and intensely fought and displayed slightly more overt violence and considerably higher levels of state intimidation than the 2011 elections, expressed most visibly as repeated harassment and arrests of opposition politicians and supporters (Abrahamsen and Bareebe 2016: 753–5; FHRI 2016; Human Rights Network Uganda 2016: 57–8). The tense competition was not reflected in the official results: the Electoral Commission declared Museveni the winner of the presidential election with 61 per cent against Besigye's 35 per cent, while the other supposed main opposition candidate, Amama Mbabazi, got a paltry 1.4 per cent. It is probably wise to treat the results with caution, as there are strong reasons to suspect that the 2016 elections were more fraudulent than those of 2011. Indeed, this was one of the reasons why Mbabazi challenged the election results in the Supreme Court, which ruled to uphold them.

There had been early signs of state-organised electoral violence. For at least a year prior to the elections, and possibly longer, the government had recruited so-called crime preventers with the stated objective of engaging in community policing; the government's target was to recruit more than 1.5 million crime preventers across the country. In reality, and following a long-standing tradition of government-sponsored vigilante groups, they functioned as a semi-formal NRM militia, who in many cases intimidated, extorted and assaulted opposition members and supporters (Human Rights Watch 2016b). Various agents representing the formal state apparatus were also active in suppressing the opposition. The regular police frequently broke up opposition rallies and kept opposition leaders, including Mbabazi and Besigye, under 'preventive arrest' (Amnesty International 2015: 11), and representatives of the state and the ruling party threatened potential protestors against election results with the ultimate consequence: death (Kirunda 2016; Wesonga 2016). State repression against Besigye accelerated as the elections approached (Sserunjogi and Kafeero 2016). During the last week of the campaigns, he was arrested four times, and following the election on 18 February he was detained in his home (*Daily Monitor* 2016b) for six weeks.

A number of events that occurred after the 2011 elections were significant in shaping the electoral threat and the structures of potential rewards and sanctions for the government in the elections of 2016. While on one level the 'walk to work' protests were a victory for Besigye, transforming him from electoral loser to internationally recognised victim of government repression, the extra-parliamentary opposition strategy did not result in any substantive concession from the government. Instead, the main pattern of events over the next few years ran in the other direction. In 2013, parliament passed – and the president soon signed – the Public Order Management Bill. This legislation serves to restrict public gatherings: in order for more than three persons to meet and discuss issues of a political nature in public places, the police must be notified in writing seven days in advance and they have the right to refuse such applications and break up meetings (Kagoro 2016: 167).[10]

Two months after the end of the 'walk to work' protests, Besigye declared that he would step down as party leader of the FDC. When, in 2012, Mugisha Muntu beat Nandala Mafabi in the struggle for party leadership, this was widely regarded as a victory for the more moderate faction of the FDC and a departure from Besigye's confrontational leadership style. The NRM on its part also witnessed a leadership struggle. Long-standing rumours about the presidential ambitions of the Prime Minister, Amama Mbabazi, culminated in the removal of the latter from his cabinet position in September 2014. A year later, Mbabazi finally declared his intention to run for president. Meanwhile, in a surprise move Besigye offered himself as the FDC flag-bearer once again, and in September 2015 was elected as the party's presidential candidate. However, neither opposition demands for electoral reforms nor its efforts to create a united electoral alliance resulted in the intended outcome. Thus, Besigye and Mbabazi both ran as candidates in an unreformed electoral setting.

At the outset of the campaigns in November 2015, Museveni seemed to face a stronger electoral threat than in 2011. While the opposition alliance had failed to reconcile Besigye and Mbabazi – who was formally still in the NRM but ran as an independent candidate backed by the Democratic Alliance – there was a general understanding that, in the event of a run-off, something that Museveni would probably want to avoid, the remaining candidate would get the backing of the others against Museveni.[11] The electoral challenge to the incumbent was of two kinds. Mbabazi was a dark horse. His electoral strength was untested, but rumours abounded of vast resources, strong networks within and beyond the NRM and deep inside knowledge of Museveni's electoral strategies.[12] Prior to and at the beginning of the campaigns, Mbabazi appeared to be the main target of government harassment. His meetings – and Besigye's –were blocked by the police, who referred to the Public Order Management Act (Amnesty International 2015); both Mbabazi and his supporters were repeatedly arrested; and in December 2015 there were several serious skirmishes between Museveni and Mbabazi supporters (Kigambo 2016).

Once the campaigns took off, however, Besigye gradually proved to be the main challenger to Museveni. Not only was he far ahead of Mbabazi in all opinion polls and in terms of attendance at rallies, the emotional intensity of the support he received also suggested that he would put up a stronger performance than in 2011. To some extent, his relatively recent return to national politics offered an energising surprise effect to his campaign, similar to what had occurred in 2001 and 2006. Consequently, government attention increasingly turned to Besigye, who was detained repeatedly and treated with considerable brutality towards the end of the campaigns. The assertion that Besigye posed a real electoral challenge – one that grew in strength as the campaigns evolved – finds statistical support. While some opinion polls indicated a first-round victory for Museveni, a least one poll pointed to a potential run-off (*Daily Monitor* 2016a).

The electoral threat to Museveni was thus greater. The incentive structures of potential rewards and sanctions also differed from those in 2011, and were less conducive to restraints on state-organised violence. The campaigns obviously displayed extensive use of other types of resources, too; the NRM did not abandon its campaign strategies from 2011. The money spent by contenders during the campaigns – by far the greatest part of it by NRM candidates – dwarfed even the expensive 2011 campaigns (ACFIM 2016). However, oil extraction has not begun yet, and with the current low world market prices, future revenue from this seems uncertain. The political significance of this is that promises of future development programmes based on oil revenue were likely to appear less convincing than in 2011. The government also attempted to control information flows (Human Rights Watch 2016a) and made use of administration and law in order to prevent the opposition from reaching out to the electorate. The more widespread use of intimidation and overt violence compared with the 2011 elections would suggest, however, that these measures were deemed to be insufficient.

The temptation to make use of violence was thus stronger. The deterrence mechanisms that had been significant five years before were also weaker in 2016. While it was always likely that the Ugandan security forces would be able to contain riots by the use of force, at least in the longer run, the political costs of doing so seemed to be lower in 2016. Constraints could also be imposed by important international actors. Experiences from the military takeover in Egypt in 2013, however, suggested that while the United States and other important external actors might voice protests, they would have no choice but to continue cooperating with an important regional ally such as Uganda. Furthermore, events at the ICC showed that Uhuru Kenyatta, after becoming president of Kenya, had been able to manoeuvre his way out of the trial against him, while Laurent Gbagbo found himself still in court after having lost power in Côte d'Ivoire. It is possible that Museveni concluded that these trajectories underlined the importance of retaining power. In summary, the urge for the government to make use of violence was stronger in 2016 than in 2011 due to more intense competition, and the risks involved were probably perceived as smaller following diminishing sanctions.

Conclusions

This chapter has examined changes in levels of state-organised violence against the opposition in Uganda between 1996 and 2016, focusing on why previous high levels of violence fell in the 2011 elections but increased again in 2016. The findings give support to the argument that the level of government-sponsored violence is shaped by incentive structures that include the intensity of the competition and the rewards and sanctions for using or abstaining from violence, and that these are informed by experiences drawn from previous elections and other significant political events that pose serious challenges to the government. With regard to the electoral challenge, the chapter demonstrates that in 2011 President Museveni faced a more divided opposition and a slightly weaker main contender than in 2001, 2006 and again in 2016. More importantly, the structures of potential rewards and sanctions were different: in 2011, Museveni was more constrained in using violence than in previous and subsequent elections. In view of the aftermath of the Kenyan post-election violence in 2008, when leaders were charged before the ICC, the civil war in Côte d'Ivoire following the 2010 elections, and the ongoing uprisings and ousting of governments in North Africa, the government was keen to avoid not only popular protests but also violent crackdowns with uncertain outcomes. In addition, it was now in command of anticipated oil revenue, which opened up the possibility of an election strategy more geared towards the distribution of monetary resources. In both 2006 and 2016, after factions broke away from the ruling party, the challenge from the opposition was perceived as more serious, and the constraining factors that were significant in 2011 had become less important five years later. As stated above, it is difficult to determine with precision whether different mechanisms of government-organised electoral manipulation substitute or mutually reinforce each other, but an overall assessment suggests that they were complementary in the 2016 Ugandan elections. There was a higher level of violence than in 2011, more money was spent than ever before, and the administrative measures taken to influence the outcome were cruder.

In examining the potential incentive structures that inform decision making about the use of violence, the chapter demonstrates that learning processes matter, and that the contextual dimensions of particular elections are heavily shaped by lessons drawn from past elections, both in the same country and elsewhere. Whereas violence (or other forms of electoral manipulation) is not necessarily cumulative in the sense of a linear progression, such experiences are critical in shaping the incentive structures for behaviour in the present as well as expectations of the future. Violence and other forms of manipulation exercised during past elections – or between them – have lingering and complex effects on all significant actors, including the governments themselves, opposition parties, citizens and external actors. In exploring this argument beyond the Ugandan case, comparative sequential analyses (see Falleti and Mahoney 2015) of electoral violence over time would appear to be a fruitful approach.

The policy dimensions that arise from the Ugandan experience of state-organised electoral violence and election rigging are easy to decipher but difficult to act upon. The role of international actors in the construction of the NRM state has been considerable. From the early 1990s to the mid-2000s, the Ugandan government was in the good books of most important international actors, who allocated to Uganda substantial amounts of development assistance and political support. The attitude towards the Museveni government changed from enthusiastic embrace to reluctant acceptance among most external actors, but the latter found themselves with rather limited scope for exercising real influence with regard to urging respect for civil and political rights, if indeed that were ever considered a priority (Anderson and Fisher 2016; Fisher 2013; Sjögren 2013). While many foreign governments have repeatedly voiced their concerns, and most foreign election observers have in various assessments stated that Ugandan elections over the last decade have not been fair by international standards (COG 2006; 2011; 2016; EU-EOM 2006; 2011; 2016), such pronouncements are unlikely to persuade the Ugandan government to level the electoral playing field. As long as the stakes of presidential elections are high, the opposition relatively competitive, and past impunity effectively rewarded rather than accounted for, the temptation to seek to manipulate electoral outcomes using various means, including violence, will remain strong.

Acknowledgements

The author wishes to thank Jesper Bjarnesen, Johan Brosché, Hanne Fjelde, Kristine Höglund, Mimmi Söderberg Kovacs, Anders Themnér, Maria Wendt and the anonymous reviewers for insightful comments on earlier versions.

Notes

1 This is not to suggest that parliamentary elections (or party primary elections) in Uganda are peaceful affairs. The level of violence in the NRM primaries and the parliamentary elections in 2016 was high.

2 For exceptions, see the case studies of Ethiopia (Smith 2012) and Sri Lanka (Höglund 2009b).

3 These factors may explain not only electoral violence, but also whether, when, how and to what extent governments embark on election rigging in general. An investigation into the precise composition of the various methods of manipulation in different elections in Uganda falls outside the scope of the chapter. Similarly, the chapter will not systematically examine possible changes in the overall level of electoral manipulation over time; however, brief reflections on the latter will be offered in the concluding remarks.

4 Unless forthcoming defeat seems inevitable, in which case incumbents may choose to accept it.

5 Another possibility is that opposition violence comes first, and that government-sponsored violence is best explained as a response to this. In Uganda, this has not been the case. The riots in November 2005 in the run-up to the 2006 elections following the arrest of Kizza Besigye are an example of the opposite: how state repression triggered riots by opposition supporters – which led to more state repression.

6 Other means of repression not captured by the definition of electoral violence noted above, such as actual or threatened economic or social victimisation, may be deployed to achieve the same goal (Schedler 2013: 93).

7 However, it is difficult to determine whether violence substitutes for or complements the use of money or administrative fraud, let alone the precise degree to which this might be the case; according to Schedler (2013: 201) no law-like hierarchy of preferred manipulation mechanisms can be established. They might combine in different ways, depending to a large extent on the character of the perceived threat and the incentive structure in a particular election. This may affect the timing and targeting not only of violence, but also of the use of money, information control and administrative and legal regulation in relation to groups and regions.

8 For discussions on the learning processes of authoritarian governments, see Bank and Edel (2015) and Heydemann and Leenders (2014).

9 The shift in political regime does not explain the difference in the level of violence, as there have been peaceful as well as violent elections under both the no-party and the multiparty dispensation.

10 It should be noted that, since the appointment in 2005 of the new Inspector General, former military officer Kale Kayihura, the Uganda Police Force had been transformed in a distinctly militarised direction, and in the public perception it had emerged as a key vehicle for preserving not only law and order but also the government's political control.

11 The rules stipulate that if none of the presidential candidates obtains an absolute majority in the first round, there is a second round between the two front runners.

12 The way in which the campaigns evolved suggests that Mbabazi's assets in this regard may initially have been overrated, or at least were made difficult to utilise.

References

Abrahamsen, R. and G. Bareebe (2016) 'Uganda's 2016 Elections: Not Even Faking It Anymore', *African Affairs* 115 (461): 751–65.

ACFIM (2016) *Analytical Case Study on Flow of Budget Funds and Expenditure during the Election Period. Final Report.* Kampala: Alliance for Campaign Finance Monitoring (ACFIM).

Amnesty International (2015) '*We Come in and Disperse Them.' Violations of the Right to Freedom of Assembly by the Ugandan Police.* London: Amnesty International.

Anderson, D. M. and J. Fisher (2016) 'Authoritarianism and the Securitization of Development in Uganda' in T. Hagmann and F. Reyntjens (eds), *Aid and Authoritarianism in Africa: Development without Democracy.* London: Zed Books.

Bank, A. and M. Edel (2015) 'Authoritarian Regime Learning: Comparative Insights from the Arab Uprisings'. GIGA Working Paper 274. Hamburg: German Institute of Global and Area Studies (GIGA).

Bhasin, T. and J. Gandhi (2013) 'Timing and Targeting of State Repression in Authoritarian Elections', *Electoral Studies* 32 (4): 620–31.

Carbone, G. (2008) *No-Party Democracy? Ugandan Politics in Comparative Perspective.* Boulder CO: Lynne Rienner.

COG (2006) *Uganda Presidential and Parliamentary Elections, 23 February 2006.* London: Commonwealth Observer Group (COG), Commonwealth Secretariat.

COG (2011) *Uganda Presidential and Parliamentary Elections, 18 February 2011.* London: Commonwealth Observer Group (COG), Commonwealth Secretariat.

COG (2016) *Uganda General Elections, 18 February 2016.* London: Commonwealth Observer Group (COG), Commonwealth Secretariat.

Conroy-Krutz, J. and C. Logan (2012) 'Museveni and the 2011 Ugandan Election: Did the Money Matter?', *Journal of Modern African Studies* 50 (4): 625–55.

Daily Monitor (2016a) 'Museveni Lead Drops to 51 Per Cent in New Poll', *Daily Monitor*, 21 January.

Daily Monitor (2016b) 'One Month Later: What Next for Besigye?', *Daily Monitor*, 20 March.

EU-EOM (2006) *Uganda: Presidential and Parliamentary Elections 23 February 2006.* Brussels: European Union Election Observation Mission (EU-EOM).

EU-EOM (2011) *Uganda: Final Report General Elections 18 February 2011.* Brussels: European Union Election Observation Mission (EU-EOM).

EU-EOM (2016) *Uganda: Final Report Presidential, Parliamentary and Local Council Elections 18 February 2016.* Brussels: European Union Election Observation Mission (EU-EOM).

Falleti, T. G. and J. Mahoney (2015) 'The Comparative Sequential Method' in J. Mahoney and K. Thelen (eds), *Advances in Comparative-Historical Analysis: Resilience, Diversity and Change.* Cambridge: Cambridge University Press.

Fisher, J. (2013) 'The Limits – and Limiters – of External Influence: Donors, the Ugandan Electoral Commission and the 2011 Elections', *Journal of Eastern African Studies* 7 (3): 471–91.

Fjelde, H. and K. Höglund (2016) 'Electoral Institutions and Electoral Violence in Sub-Saharan Africa', *British Journal of Political Science* 46 (2): 297–320.

FHRI (2016) *Human Rights and Elections in Uganda (2016): A Call for Action.* Kampala: Foundation for Human Rights Initiative (FHRI).

Gay, L. (2014) 'A "Hot Cake": The Land Issue in the Buganda Kingdom during Uganda's 2011 Elections' in S. Perrot, S. Makara, J. Lafargue and M.-A. Fouéré (eds), *Elections in a Hybrid Regime: Revisiting the 2011 Ugandan Polls.* Kampala: Fountain Publishers.

Gandhi, J. and E. Lust-Okar (2009) 'Elections Under Authoritarianism', *Annual Review of Political Science* 12: 403–22.

Gibb, R. (2012) 'Presidential and Parliamentary Elections in Uganda, February 18, 2011', *Electoral Studies* 31 (2): 458–61.

Goodfellow, T. (2013) 'The Institutionalisation of "Noise" and "Silence" in Urban Politics: Riots and Compliance in Uganda and Rwanda', *Oxford Development Studies* 41 (4): 436–54.

Hafner-Burton, E. M., S. D. Hyde and R. S. Jablonski (2014) 'When Do Governments Resort to Election Violence?', *British Journal of Political Science* 44 (1): 149–79.

Helle, S.-E. (2016) 'Defining the Playing Field: A Framework for Analysing Fairness in Access to Resources, Media and the Law', *Zeitschrift für Vergleichende Politikwissenschaft* 10 (1): 47–78.

Helle, S.-E. and L. Rakner (2014) 'Grabbing an Election: Abuse of State Resources in the 2011 Elections in Uganda' in T. Søreide and A. Williams (eds), *Corruption, Grabbing and Development: Real World Challenges.* Cheltenham and Northampton MA: Edward Elgar Publishing.

Heydemann, S. and R. Leenders (2014) 'Authoritarian Learning and Counterrevolution' in M. Lynch (ed.), *The Arab Uprisings Explained: New Contentious Politics in the Middle East.* New York NY: Columbia University Press.

Höglund, K. (2009a) 'Electoral Violence in Conflict-ridden Societies: Concepts, Causes, and Consequences', Terrorism and Political Violence 21 (3): 412–27.

Höglund, K. (2009b) 'Elections and Violence in Sri Lanka: Understanding Variation across Three Parliamentary Elections' in A. Swain, R. Amer and J. Öjendahl (eds), The Democratization Project: Opportunities and Challenges. London: Anthem Press

Human Rights Network Uganda (2016) *Election Observation Report 2016 General Elections: Examining the Role of Security in the Electoral Process.* Kampala: Human Rights Network Uganda (HURINET-U).

Human Rights Watch (2006) *In Hope and Fear: Uganda's Presidential and Parliamentary Polls.* New York NY: Human Rights Watch.

Human Rights Watch (2016a) *'Keep the People Uninformed': Pre-election Threats to Free Expression and Association in Uganda.* New York NY: Human Rights Watch.

Human Rights Watch (2016b) *Uganda: Suspend 'Crime Preventers'.* New York NY: Human Rights Watch.

Izama, A. and M. Wilkerson (2011) 'Uganda: Museveni's Triumph and Weakness', *Journal of Democracy* 22 (3): 64–78.

Kagoro, J. (2016) 'Competitive Authoritarianism in Uganda: The Not So Hidden Hand of the Military', *Zeitschrift für Vergleichende Politikwissenschaft* 10 (1): 155–72.

Kibandama, A. (2008) 'The Security Question in the 2006 Presidential and Parliamentary Elections' in J. Kizza, S. Makara and L. Rakner (eds), *Electoral Democracy in Uganda: Understanding the Institutional Processes and Outcomes of the 2006 Multiparty Elections*. Kampala: Fountain Publishers.

Kigambo, G. (2016) 'Violence Looms Large in Uganda Campaigns', *The East African*, 2 January.

Kirunda, A. (2016) 'Election Saboteurs Will Be Shot Dead – Jinja RDC', *The Daily Monitor*, 2 February.

Lindberg, S. I. (2009) 'A Theory of Elections as a Mode of Transition' in S. I. Lindberg (ed.), *Democratization by Elections: A New Mode of Transition*. Baltimore MD: Johns Hopkins University Press.

Makara, S. (2003) 'Voting for Democracy in Uganda: Issues in Recent Elections, 1996–2001' in S. Makara, G. B. Tukahebwa and F. E. Byarygaba (eds), *Voting for Democracy in Uganda: Issues in Recent Elections*. Kampala: LDC Publishers.

Makara, S. (2014) 'Managing Elections in a Multiparty Political Dispensation: The Role of the Electoral Commission in Uganda's 2011 Elections' in S. Perrot, S. Makara, J. Lafargue and A.-M. Fouéré (eds), *Elections in a Hybrid Regime: Revisiting the 2011 Ugandan Polls*. Kampala: Fountain Publishers.

Makara, S., L. Rakner and L. Svåsand (2009) 'Turnaround: The National Resistance Movement and the Reintroduction of a Multiparty System in Uganda', *International Political Science Review* 30 (2): 185–204.

Muhumuza, W. (1997) 'Money and Power in Uganda's 1996 Elections', *African Journal of Political Science* 2 (1): 168–79.

Murison, J. (2013) 'Judicial Politics: Election Petitions and Electoral Fraud in Uganda', *Journal of Eastern African Studies* 7 (3): 492–508.

Perrot, S., J. Lafargue and S. Makara (2014) 'Introduction: Looking Back at the 2011 Multiparty Elections in Uganda' in S. Perrot, S. Makara, J. Lafargue and M.-A. Fouéré (eds), *Elections in a Hybrid Regime: Revisiting the 2011 Ugandan Polls*. Kampala: Fountain Publishers.

Schedler, A. (2013) *The Politics of Uncertainty: Sustaining and Subverting Electoral Authoritarianism*. Oxford: Oxford University Press.

Schedler, A. and B. Hoffmann (2016) 'Communicating Authoritarian Elite Cohesion', *Democratization* 23 (1): 93–117.

Sjögren, A. (2013) *Between Militarism and Technocratic Governance: State Formation in Contemporary Uganda*. Kampala: Fountain Publishers.

Smith, L. (2012) 'A Disturbance or a Massacre? The Consequences of Electoral Violence in Ethiopia' in D. A. Bekoe (ed.), *Voting in Fear: Electoral Violence in Sub-Saharan Africa*. Washington DC: United States Institute for Peace Press.

Sserunjogi, E. M. and S. Kafeero (2016) 'Police Block Besigye Rally as One is Killed, Scores Injured', *The Daily Monitor*, 16 February.

Staniland, P. (2014) 'Violence and Democracy', *Comparative Politics* 47 (1): 99–118.

Straus, S. and C. Taylor (2012) 'Democratization and Electoral Violence in Sub-Saharan Africa, 1990–2008' in D. A. Bekoe (ed.), *Voting in Fear: Electoral Violence in Sub-Saharan Africa*. Washington DC: United States Institute for Peace Press.

Tripp, A. M. (2010) *Museveni's Uganda: Paradoxes of Power in a Hybrid Regime*. Boulder CO: Lynne Rienner.

Tukahebwa, G. B. (2003) '"Block Voting" in South Western Uganda: The Case of the 1996 Elections in Rukungiri District' in S. Makara, G. B. Tukahebwa and F. E. Byarugaba (eds), *Voting for Democracy in Uganda: Issues in Recent Elections.* Kampala: LDC Publishers.

Uganda Parliament Select Committee (2002) *Report of the Parliamentary Committee on Election Violence.* Kampala: Parliament of Uganda.

Wesonga, N. (2016) 'Lumumba Shoot-to-kill Threat Sparks Outrage', *The Daily Monitor*, 1 February.

3 | Land conflict and electoral violence in Côte d'Ivoire: a micro-level analysis

Matthew I. Mitchell

Introduction

In recent years Africa has been beset by an upsurge of electoral violence. Although rare during the era of one-party regimes of the 1970s and 1980s, the reintroduction of multiparty elections in the 1990s has led to outbreaks of electoral violence in a wide range of countries including Democratic Republic of Congo, Ethiopia, Kenya, Madagascar, Nigeria, Senegal, Uganda and Zimbabwe. However, one of the worst instances of such violence undoubtedly took place during the 2010–11 post-election crisis in Côte d'Ivoire, in which over 3,000 people were killed and 500,000 were displaced (UNHRC 2011). While there are a number of factors that triggered this violence, central among them is the explosive issue of unresolved land conflicts that have plagued the country since the late 1990s (McGovern 2011; Mitchell 2012a; Straus 2011).[1]

Yet notwithstanding the growing recognition of the importance of land conflict dynamics in fuelling electoral violence (cf. Straus 2012), there is little systematic research that theorises the interconnections between the contentious politics around land and electoral violence.[2] Moreover, most attempts to analyse electoral violence have adopted a macro-level perspective when examining this phenomenon (e.g. Basedau, Erdmann and Mehler 2007; Goldsmith 2015; Höglund 2009; Rapoport and Weinberg 2001). Consequently, there is little work that explores the micro-level dynamics and causes of electoral violence, and this prevents us from understanding the local cleavages and contextual factors that help explain instances of land conflict (Berry 2009; Derman, Odgaard and Sjaastad 2007). In short, while we know relatively little about the causal dynamics underlying electoral violence in Africa, we know even less about the relationship between land conflict and electoral violence.

This chapter addresses an important gap by theorising the relationship between land conflict and electoral violence. In so doing, it provides a micro-level analysis to explain how land conflict dynamics can serve to fuel electoral violence. Building on the work of Kalyvas (2003: 476), the core argument is that actors seeking power at the centre use resources and symbols in order to ally themselves with actors on the periphery who are fighting local conflicts, which results in the 'joint production of action'. As such, the ontology of land-related electoral violence has both a material and a symbolic dimension given the multiple meanings and values attributed to land. Actors seeking power at the centre strategically use the land card as a form of patronage to secure the support of actors in the periphery. The use of nativist discourses of belonging has proven to be a particularly useful strategy for politicians during elections (cf. Geschiere 2009), as electoral promises to redistribute land play upon the idea of land as both a resource and a symbol. Local actors, for their part, ally with elites when they view such promises to restore or secure their rights or claims to land as both legitimate and feasible (cf. Klaus and Mitchell 2015).

For land conflicts to become electorally charged issues, however, conditions must be fertile on the ground. The presence of competing narratives over contested claims to land can provide a powerful vehicle for violent collective action when they involve competing groups' rights to land. More specifically, such conflicts tend to pit insiders (i.e. natives, indigenes and autochthons)[3] against outsiders (i.e. migrants, strangers or aliens). While land conflicts obviously exist and occur outside the channels of electoral competition, they can provide political entrepreneurs (including national and local electoral candidates, political parties and party activists) with an instrumental electoral strategy to secure the support of local constituents. The force of exclusionary narratives is magnified during electoral periods since elections tend to heighten debates over belonging and raise the stakes of land as they provide windows of opportunity to revisit and/or redistribute groups' access and rights to land. Land conflicts that boil over during electoral moments are thus the result of a joint production of action. Such forms of conflict ultimately challenge the conventional wisdom that privileges national over local dynamics in explaining the outbreak of electoral violence, as it highlights the key role of micro-level dynamics that also motivate violent conflict (cf. Autesserre 2010).

In theorising the relationship between land conflict and electoral violence, the chapter focuses on the history of land conflict and electoral violence in Côte d'Ivoire. Notwithstanding the unparalleled levels of violence during the 2010–11 post-election crisis, Côte d'Ivoire has a long and troubled history of land conflict and electoral violence. As such, the chapter proposes to examine the causal mechanisms linking contested claims over land with electoral violence from both a historical and a more contemporary perspective. In so doing, it focuses its analytical lens on the country's far west cocoa regions, where land conflict and electoral violence have been most pronounced both in the decade leading up to the 2010–11 post-electoral crisis and during the crisis itself.

The arguments developed here are informed by in-depth fieldwork conducted in 2012 in Côte d'Ivoire. The field research sheds light on the more neglected and localised micro-level dynamics linking land conflict and electoral violence.

To garner insights from a wide variety of actors on the ground, the chapter draws upon interviews that were conducted with a range of stakeholders, such as government officials, landowners, local residents (migrants and autochthons), NGOs, politicians, security officials, and traditional authorities. To quote Kalyvas (2003: 481), the micro-level insights garnered from fieldwork provide 'fascinating empirical possibilities for exploring the various paths, trajectories, modalities, and combinations of central and local cleavages, as well as their consequences'.

The chapter is organised as follows: the next section provides a brief historical overview of the contentious politics around land and elections in Côte d'Ivoire. It then narrows the analysis to shed light on the land conflict dynamics that characterise the country's far west cocoa regions – dynamics that in turn feed into the explosiveness of electoral politics. In the penultimate section, the chapter connects land conflict with electoral violence to theorise the ways in which land conflicts and electoral violence become intertwined processes that engage actors and logics at both the national and local levels. Finally, the chapter concludes with a brief analysis of the 2015 presidential elections and discusses the policy implications related to the land question in Côte d'Ivoire and beyond.

Contentious politics around land and elections in Côte d'Ivoire

The contentious politics around land and elections in contemporary Côte d'Ivoire have their origins in colonial and postcolonial migration into the country's cocoa regions. As early as the 1920s, both internal and foreign migrants descended upon the south-eastern regions of Côte d'Ivoire to work in the burgeoning cocoa sector. As land became scarcer in these regions, the cocoa frontier shifted westward, eventually arriving in the south-western parts of the country in the lead-up to independence in 1960. While some of the first migrants worked for wages and entered into sharecropping arrangements, a transformation in land–labour relations occurred when migrants received land of their own to clear and farm. This transformation was spearheaded by Côte d'Ivoire's founding president, Félix Houphouët-Boigny, who implemented a controversial land tenure policy in 1963 that stated that the land belongs to those who make it productive. Although such a policy contradicted colonial-inherited legal arrangements governing land ownership, it rapidly transformed the social, political, economic and demographic landscapes of Côte d'Ivoire (Chauveau 2000: 105). As we shall see, the socio-political implications of these migration flows and land tenure policies would fundamentally serve to alter relations between hosts and migrants in the cocoa regions and provide fuel for future land conflicts and electoral violence.

The liberal immigration and land tenure policies espoused by Houphouët-Boigny facilitated the rapid expansion of the cocoa sector, which in turn gave rise to a period of impressive economic growth and political stability during the 1960s and 1970s known as the 'Ivorian miracle'. However, with the downward spiral of the economy in the mid- to late 1980s, cracks began to appear in the Ivorian model of growth. Along with the economic uncertainties of the day, the end of the Ivorian miracle ushered in a new era of political uncertainty. Facing pressure from the international community and an increasingly economically (and politically) disgruntled citizenry, the ailing Houphouët-Boigny agreed to hold the country's first multiparty elections in 1990. While Houphouët-Boigny easily defeated his main rival candidate in the elections, garnering over 80 per cent of the vote, the main opposition party at the time – the Front Populaire Ivoirien under Laurent Gbagbo – attempted to build an electoral campaign by 'arousing an Ivorian xenophobic nationalism' that took aim at the ruling party's historical favouritism of foreigners (Crook 1997: 222–3). As a member of the Bété ethnic group, with origins in the central-west cocoa regions, Gbagbo was able to mobilise support among the disgruntled autochthonous peoples by playing upon the contentious issues of migration and land tenure arrangements, which in some places had rendered them minorities in their own home regions (McGovern 2011).

The contentious politics around land and belonging would reach new levels after the death of Houphouët-Boigny in 1993. In order to eliminate his political rival, Alassane Ouattara, President Henri Konan Bédié took a page out of Gbagbo's political playbook and adopted the exclusionary policy of Ivorian nationalism embodied in the slogan of *ivoirité* – or Ivorianess. This nationalist policy was institutionalised through a new electoral code, which prevented Ouattara from competing in presidential elections in 1995 and 2000 on the grounds that he was not eligible based on the supposedly foreign origins of his parentage.

The politics of *ivoirité* and the ethnicisation of electoral politics during the post-Houphouët-Boigny years clearly heightened tensions between the predominantly Muslim northern and the Christian southern regions, as the former came to view Ouattara's exclusion as their own, given his Muslim and northern origins. Such divisions would be further exacerbated by President Gbagbo's embrace of ethnonational politics, divisions that would eventually culminate in the outbreak of civil war in 2002. Although the civil war pitted the north against the south, the most acute violence in the early years of the conflict was in the western cocoa zones, where tensions between ethnic groups over land ownership, control of property and *ivoirité* exploded, and resulted in mass expulsions and the exodus of tens of thousands of migrants.[4] The mass displacement caused by the civil war further complicated the explosive and unresolved issues over land in the western cocoa regions. As McCallin and Montemurro (2009: 5) note: 'While people were displaced, many of the plots they had planted were sold or leased by others, so depriving IDPs of their principal means of subsistence on their return and fuelling inter-community tensions.'

The outbreak of violence in these regions and the protracted nature of the conflict served to further radicalise discourses around autochthony and belonging. As Banégas and Marshall-Fratani (2007: 85) explain, the discourse of autochthony took 'a resolutely xenophobic and ultranationalist form, designating foreigners and northerners as the "enemies" of Côte d'Ivoire'. In sum, the underlying root causes of the conflict – contested rights over land and belonging – became increasingly politicised as a result of the massive displacement and exclusionary rhetoric by political elites.

Despite a lull in violence during the late 2000s, the political and security climate took a turn for the worse when both candidates (Gbagbo and Ouattara) claimed victory after the second round of the 2010 presidential elections. Notwithstanding countless efforts by international actors and the Ouattara camp to end the stalemate through political channels, the crisis was finally resolved through military means when, on 11 April 2011, Gbagbo was arrested after a ten-day siege of the presidential palace (Mitchell 2012b). Suffice it to say, it should not have come as a surprise that the land question would play a prominent role in the run-up to the elections and during the post-electoral crisis. As the chapter will show, the unresolved land conflicts described above would play a key underlying causal role in the post-election violence that is estimated to have resulted in the death of over 3,000 people (UNHRC 2011). As such, while the causal forces behind the 2010–11 post-electoral violence have complex political, military and economic dimensions (cf. Straus 2011), the contentious politics around land served to fuel the terrible levels of electoral violence.

Land conflict in the western cocoa regions: a micro-level perspective

As the introduction to this chapter argues, for exclusionary and anti-immigrant rhetoric to resonate among local populations, large sections of society must be receptive. This was indeed the case in the Ivorian cocoa regions, where the ability of political elites to mobilise supporters through the use of autochthony discourses was greatly facilitated by the fractured state of relations between autochthons and migrant communities in these regions. The contemporary state of these relations has been fundamentally shaped by deep-rooted historical processes of state building in the Ivorian countryside (Boone 2003). As alluded to above, the changing political economy of migration and land–labour relations helps to explain the shifting political power relations at the local level: namely, the wresting of power away from local elites and the centralisation of political authority. In this sense, this provides the critical subtext for understanding the contemporary dynamics described below. The far west cocoa regions are not apolitical spaces; rather, they are deeply politicised places, albeit where grievances are more often mobilised as a result of national historical and political processes.

In writing about autochthons' perceptions of migrant populations during the Ivorian crisis, Chauveau and Colin (2010: 94–5) provide a detailed summary of autochthons' grievances against allochthons (i.e. native Ivorians who are not original inhabitants of the soil):

> the strangers have become richer and richer, whereas local families are struggling; they invest at home the money they earn locally; they show no interest in village affairs; they no longer respect their duty of gratitude towards the local community; the Ivorian strangers do not vote for the autochthons' candidates and their numerical importance gives them a political advantage.

Echoing these insights, I draw upon findings from the field to argue that four interrelated factors provided key ingredients for the explosive nature of land-related conflict and electoral violence in the western cocoa regions. These factors, in essence, created fertile conditions for elites to instrumentalise the land question in Côte d'Ivoire. As we shall see in the following section, the joint production of action was made possible given the salience of land conflicts at the local level, which in turn would incentivise disgruntled autochthons (in particular) to ally with key actors in the centre. But before we can turn to this analysis, we must first consider the following critically important enabling conditions: (1) the lack of integration of migrant populations; (2) autochthons' loss of land; (3) the disputed nature of land sales; and (4) the weakening of chieftaincies.

Lack of integration of migrant populations In addition to being both outnumbered and outperformed, many autochthons cite the pervasive unwillingness of migrant populations to integrate into the local community as a major source of resentment. The lack of integration of migrants throughout the cocoa regions can be physically observed in many towns and villages by the simple fact that autochthons and migrants often live on opposite sides of the roads that divide these communities. However, it is the nature of the *campements* system – whereby thousands of migrant-inhabited communities have developed in the forests, often many kilometres from local autochthonous villages – that is perhaps an even greater source of autochthons' frustration vis-à-vis migrants. While expressing concerns about the Baoulé invasion of his community, one autochthon chief stated: 'The Baoulés don't come and settle down in the village, they create their own *campements*!'[5] This critique of Baoulé migrants was echoed by a senior figure in President Ouattara's Rassemblement des Républicains party, who suggested that 'quite often the Baoulé, when they arrive, they stay in their own plantations, in their own villages, and they don't participate in community life, and I believe this contributed a great deal to the friction between these populations'.[6]

This lack of integration has recently taken both generational and symbolic dimensions, as observed by one local chief who lamented the behaviour of the offspring of the original migrants. According to the chief:

> Until recently, relations had always been good. Those who came from elsewhere respected those that received them. In recent years, the children of the descendants of those who came first, they have adopted different behaviour from their fathers. They are less respectful; they are less considerate of those who received them … For example, when the first migrants came, when our parents gave them land, often at the end of the year during the holiday period, they brought goods, fish, or even money to thank their *tuteurs*, to say because of you I was able to have land. The first migrants did this. Nowadays, the youth no longer do this. They no longer come to thank their *tuteurs*.[7]

This break with tradition represents yet another manifestation of the lack of integration of migrant populations in local communities, and, consequently, is an additional source of friction that created fertile conditions for the joint production of electoral violence.

Autochthons' loss of land In writing about the acrimonious nature of host–stranger relations in the south-western cocoa regions, McGovern highlights another underlying cause: namely, the extent to which autochthons have witnessed the loss of their lands. Whereas, in certain areas, migrants (notably Burkinabè) worked as labourers who were paid from the harvest resulting from their work, in other regions (notably those that are home to the Guéré and Bété ethnic groups) land was often sold outright. Consequently, tensions over the status of these lands are ubiquitous (McGovern 2011). As such, the frequency of the outright sale of lands by autochthons to migrants has been a major factor in contributing to the violent conflict in the cocoa regions. When asked to explain the root of the violence in these regions, most interviewees cited the loss of land as a key ingredient in the broader conflict narrative in Côte d'Ivoire. For example, one journalist stated: 'A lot of it has to do with the relation people have with their land and whether they're using the land themselves, or using migrant labour … Most of the conflict is when the ownership is no longer with the autochthons.'[8] The interviewee further noted:

> I think a lot of it has to do with a loss of status in their own land, in their own area, in their own zone, by giving away this land they're watching these outsiders, whether they be from other parts of Ivory Coast or from other parts of West Africa, they're watching them become successful, and some

73

are getting quite rich, and you know, there's the whole problem of village jealousies and things like that.[9]

The sense of autochthons' loss of land has been further compounded not only by the fact that they have lost control of their lands, but also owing to the bitter reality that migrants have surpassed them economically by exploiting these lands. As one president of the local youth association argued:

> Because you are a *tuteur* and you give a parcel of land, after five years the migrant has made himself because he has farmed, and because you are lazy you have not, and so there are jealousies; because those who received the land quickly progressed whereas the others have remained in poverty.[10]

The sense of autochthons' loss would become most pronounced when many autochthon youth returned to their home towns during Côte d'Ivoire's economic crisis. In the words of one local autochthon chief: 'The youth who returned from school, who could not get jobs in the city, returned to find a situation in which all of the lands that belonged to their parents are now occupied by others. So the youth ask, where will we stay? How will we live?'[11] These questions would trigger fierce electoral debates over citizenship and belonging, and serve to fracture the social contracts that had bound autochthon and migrant populations for decades.[12]

The disputed nature of land sales On a related point, a third source of conflict between autochthons and migrants revolves around the disputed nature of land sales. The unresolved and seemingly irreconcilable positions surrounding the ownership of land are at the heart of the enduring tensions between these groups. While the vast majority of autochthons boldly claim that the land was never sold and that it was merely leased, rented or lent to migrant populations, migrants overwhelmingly reject these declarations, stating that their ancestors – and, more recently, themselves – purchased the land outright. Consequently, it is not simply autochthons' sense of loss of land that fuels tensions in the cocoa regions; rather, the disputed nature of land transactions poses a major obstacle to resolving these protracted conflicts.

A sample set of responses from both autochthons and migrants over the perceived nature of land sales in the far west cocoa regions provides striking evidence of the contested claims to land. Autochthons, for their part, consistently declare that: 'The land cannot be sold, it can only be allocated, we lease it to you, we rent it [to] you; the land is a property for decades and decades, an individual cannot sell it, he can rent it.'[13] They add that: 'We only leased the land – the word "sold", we do not know it.'[14] As the following quotation highlights, autochthons generally reject the premise that lands were sold outright:

Do they constitute sales? What we recognise is not that they purchased the land, because you cannot purchase land. A bottle of gin or liquor that you offer a local community that accepts to give you 20 hectares of forest is not the price for 20 hectares! But you claim that you have paid for it, which is not true![15]

Meanwhile, migrant responses capture the fundamentally different interpretation of the nature of these land transactions. They state that 'This is false, everyone has a paper. We cannot purchase something without receiving a receipt,'[16] or '"Let you use" is not a term that exists. People often make distinctions between leasing and selling. Listen, it's the same term. So when they say lease a portion of land, it means a purchase.'[17] As one respondent provocatively noted: 'Nobody here received a free piece of land from a Guéré. First of all, Guérés don't like to give freely. Guérés don't like to share.'[18]

The above comments are indicative of the polarised perspectives of autochthon and migrant claims over land. The ambiguity around land ownership further underscores why electoral promises to redistribute or consolidate groups' claims to land help shore up political support. One dangerous implication is that this ambiguity provides a signal to local populations that violent resistance or pre-emptive attacks may be required to fend off opponents' efforts to reclaim contested land.

The uncertainty surrounding land sales and ownership were further heightened by the introduction of a new land law (Loi 98–759) in 1998 (cf. Mitchell 2014). In concrete terms, the new land law aimed to identify, recognise and protect rights acquired through customary transfers while excluding foreigners from land ownership (Chauveau and Colin 2010: 86). As Chauveau and Colin (ibid. 86) note, the law 'bolstered the claims put forward by autochthons that they are the only legitimate holders of property rights', as the new policy 'gives priority to customary rights in the process of identifying and certifying land rights prior to their registration'. Despite some potential improvements proposed by the new law, it was particularly controversial in the far west cocoa regions. By making national citizenship a prerequisite for land ownership and by establishing customary rights as the essential source of land rights, the new land policy established 'a legal foundation for expropriation of non-indigènes' acquired land rights in the forest zone' (Boone 2007: 75). The law served to undermine Ivorian migrants' land rights, as it required them to renegotiate their agreement with their autochthonous *tuteur*. Thus, notwithstanding its purported objectives of reducing insecurity and providing greater clarity around land ownership, the 1998 land law instead exacerbated the land problems. This, combined with the disputed nature of land sales, provided fertile ground for the political instrumentalisation of the land question.

The weakening of chieftaincies The final factor that has served to further strain host–migrant relations in the far west region is the weakening of chieftaincies. In writing about the implications of the absence of a neo-traditional chiefly elite in the region, Crook et al. (2007: 12) note that land relations 'have relied more on social bargaining and informal arrangements which were often overridden by the state', and that such conditions have 'provoked politicised ethnic conflict and perceptions of dispossession amongst host communities'. In recent decades, the Ivorian crisis has further weakened chieftaincies throughout these regions to the point where local authorities in the Ivorian south rarely occupy positions of notable power. As one head of a leading NGO suggested: 'because the chiefs have been weakened, they are weakened in their ability to play a leading role in their capacity to resolve conflicts. This, in turn, weakens their credibility in the eyes of the locals.'[19] While the interviewee noted that the weakening of chieftaincies is not the root cause of the violence in these regions, he argued that it nevertheless facilitates such violence.[20]

While the absence of strong traditional authorities may serve to undermine the ability of local communities to resolve their own disputes over land, the question that remains is which factors contributed to the recent deterioration of local authorities. In answering this question, one respondent provided a particularly insightful account of the downfall and complexities of chieftaincy rule in the cocoa regions. According to the interviewee:

> This started if you go back to the 1990s and you had the *cadres* coming back from the city who no longer respected traditional chiefs and started already eating away at their power, but [it] has been made much worse by the conflicts. You have a chief who dies and then there's a struggle for power. In every community you have the chief of the autochthons, you have the chief of the *allogènes*, you have the chief of the allochthons, then you have the chief of the *campements* who responds to the *chef de village*, and it's very, very unclear in every community where the real power lies. And that makes a big difference. If you still have strong traditional leaders who are respected then they are able to solve conflicts more easily.[21]

Thus, while traditional chiefs continue to occupy important roles in local communities, their weakened ability to resolve local disputes over land (and other issues) enables political elites from the centre to more easily manipulate the land question. If chiefs had the capacity to peacefully manage and resolve land conflicts within their jurisdiction, political elites would presumably have less fodder for their attempts to mobilise supporters on the basis of electoral promises to revisit groups' rights and claims to land. Instead, a weakened chieftaincy further enables the use of divisive politics around land as a potent electoral strategy.

In sum, the weakening of chieftaincies coupled with the lack of integration of migrant populations, autochthons' loss of their lands, and the disputed nature of land sales constitute four interrelated factors that help explain the contentious politics surrounding land among autochthons and migrants in the far west cocoa regions. As the following section reveals, these land conflicts provide a key ingredient for the possibility of the joint production of land-related electoral violence when local and national interests and motives collide.

Land conflict and electoral violence: the 'joint production of action'

The Ivorian case provides a particularly striking example of the dangerous consequences of national interventions in local dynamics. McGovern (2011: 69–70) notes that: 'What sets Côte d'Ivoire apart from its neighbours is the way in which national politicians have recuperated these local tensions in their attempts to turn the politics of resentment to their electoral advantage, and to encourage the use of violence to accede and hold on to power.' In the pursuit of political power at the national level, political elites harnessed autochthons' grievances by employing a strategic approach – arming autochthons with a political ideology that promised to restore the balance of power in their favour and return their lands. The insidious role of political elites in this process is illustrated in the findings from recent fieldwork in the far west region. Many interviewees consistently emphasised the deleterious ways in which political elites instrumentalised local land grievances, and, in so doing, provided the spark for numerous rounds of host–migrant conflict.

According to one local autochthon chief: 'Life between the communities was good in the beginning. When politics invaded the area, everything deteriorated. Politics destroyed everything!'[22] This sentiment was shared by an autochthonous youth president from a neighbouring region, who stated: 'It's especially politics that brought all these disagreements. The population was manipulated by politicians who preached hatred.'[23] Such interpretations are corroborated by allochthons, members of NGOs and journalists. In the words of an allochthon village chief:

> This is when things were exacerbated, when they came to power, when Gbagbo came to power he put into his compatriots' heads that the Dioulas, the Malinkés, we will chase them away, we will give you their lands. They're Chinese, they're invaders. So these are the seeds of the conflict, because they are the ones that put these ideas into people's heads as otherwise we lived in harmony.[24]

The alliance between local and national actors is illustrated through the comments of a head of an international NGO: 'The entirety of these conflicts, of the political manipulations and tensions at the national level, all reverberated to the local level where they were amplified. If there had only been the land disputes, the country would have remained stable. We would have far fewer problems.'[25] This account was echoed by a renowned Ivorian journalist, who stated:

> Before 1990, a lot of the problems were resolved within the communities … these conflicts existed before, but they were resolved within a local system where the village chief and the autochthons or allochthons discussed matters and came to agreements. But since 1990, politicians exacerbated these problems and said that strangers had to leave the land … and the local politicians pushed or encouraged the youth to expropriate allochthons who had legally or justly acquired the lands by buying the land with gin or a little bit of money … so the principal source of the conflict was due to the political instrumentalisation.[26]

In sum, the interaction between local grievances and national politics proved to be politically explosive.

While elites at the centre and actors on the ground engaged in the joint production of violence throughout much of the 2000–10 period of political turmoil in Côte d'Ivoire, the events of 2010–11 clearly capture the interconnections between existing land conflicts and electoral logics. As Kalyvas (2003: 486) explains, the concept of alliance 'entails a transaction between supralocal and local actors, whereby the former supply the latter with external muscle, thus allowing them to win decisive local advantage; in exchange the former rely on local conflicts to recruit and motivate supporters and obtain local control, resources, and information'. The notion of alliance has important implications for understanding the land conflict–electoral violence nexus in the far west region. Given the electoral geography of the elections[27] – characterised by both ethnic cleavages and close regional electoral races – candidates at the national level strategically used the land issue to try to mobilise support. The tactical decision to use the land card has deep roots. As Bassett (2011: 471–2) writes, 'Gbagbo's popularity in these forest region departments mainly revolves around his ethno-nationalist politics regarding land ownership and citizenship … Gbagbo's Ivorian Popular Front (FPI) party has consistently supported local peoples over "foreigners" in forest region land disputes.' Yet while the far west has historically been a relative electoral stronghold for Gbagbo, the region is home to large numbers of pro-Ouattara migrant populations. Writing before the 2010 elections, one leading correspondent presciently noted: 'The battle in the West will be very heated' (Airault 2010).

Understandably, then, Gbagbo strategically used the electoral promise of land as both a resource and a symbol to build an alliance with actors on the periphery – in this case, local autochthonous populations in the far west – in their efforts to seek electoral power at the centre. In this sense, the transaction between supralocal (i.e. political elites) and local (autochthons) involved implicit – and sometimes even explicit – promises to strengthen autochthons' access and rights to land in exchange for their crucial electoral support. Echoing Kalyvas (2003), this enabled the joint production of action as local communities were given incentives to mobilise and engage in violent acts in both the pre- and post-electoral periods.

Evidence of the instrumentalisation of local land grievances during the 2010–11 post-electoral crisis has been well documented elsewhere. A United Nations report on violations of human rights and international humanitarian law in the far west region notes how, during the lead-up to the elections, pro-Gbagbo media outlets bombarded both radio listeners and television viewers with hate messages aimed at migrants. The report similarly documents the distribution of xenophobic leaflets in the early days of the post-electoral crisis. Ominously titled 'The hour has come for ultimate vengeance', the leaflets urged the autochthonous sons and daughters of the far west to chase away and kill both Ivorian and foreign migrants (ONUCI 2011: 4–6). Moreover, additional accounts highlight how autochthons threatened to expropriate migrants' land in the event that Gbagbo were to lose the elections (Airault 2010).

These examples are by no means isolated incidents of local actors engaging in opportunistic ploys to secure increased access to and control over land. Instead, they are the product of strategies employed by political actors at the highest echelons of government, who have consistently embraced the exclusionary language of autochthony to divide populations in their pursuit of electoral power. As one news source reported, in the run-up to the elections even Gbagbo himself was quoted on countless occasions as saying that there were 'two types of candidates ... a candidate for Côte d'Ivoire and a candidate for foreigners' (*Jeune Afrique* 2010). Such comments have deep connections with the enduring tensions surrounding land, as they were ultimately employed to signal Gbagbo's commitment to support autochthons' efforts to regain their control over land from allochthons (i.e. non-indigenous people). The condoning – and even encouragement – of the use of violence by Gbagbo was on full display in the days after the first round of elections. Speaking again about his rival, Alassane Ouattara, he declared that 'the snake is not yet dead; you must not put down your stick' (ibid.).

The precarious nature of host–migrant relations and the explosiveness of the land question provide a critical background for understanding why the far west region experienced such high levels of violence at the height of the post-electoral crisis. While Abidjan was in many respects the epicentre of the violence, the western parts of Côte d'Ivoire experienced similarly high levels of violence – by one estimate accounting for nearly half of those killed during the crisis (CNE 2012). What, then, is the connection between electoral violence along the macro-level cleavages of the post-electoral crisis and the ubiquitous conflicts over land? Certainly, a multiplicity of political, military and strategic factors helps explain the more direct or proximate causes of the electoral violence in the far west region (Straus 2011).[28] And yet below the surface the contentious politics around land in the far west and the use of exclusionary and hostile discourses by the country's political elites served to create fertile conditions for the eruption of electoral violence at the micro-level. In this way, to paraphrase Kalyvas (2003), the interaction between local and master cleavages proved to be particularly explosive in Côte d'Ivoire's far west region, given the overlapping interests and motives of actors at the centre and the periphery. In short, the ontology of electoral violence here cannot be understood without integrating the land dynamics and electoral logics unique to the far west region.

While the case of Côte d'Ivoire sheds light on the explosive ways in which land grievances can be mobilised during elections (cf. Klaus and Mitchell 2015), it further underscores the perils of employing nativist discourses as an electoral strategy. The use of the concept of autochthony represents an alarming trend as it provides a powerful weapon in the arsenal of political entrepreneurs. While scholars have noted the slippery and fluid nature of this identity category (e.g. Geschiere 2009), the basic essence of autochthony is that one is either from the soil or *not* of the soil. As such, the autochthony category is particularly amenable to political mobilisation as it can serve to entrench notions of groups' status as strangers to the land. This in turn can give rise to burning questions about their rightful place in the country's polity. As the troubled electoral history of Côte d'Ivoire reveals, the use of this concept has been a central motif in the political and electoral tactics of the country's elites for decades. To what extent, then, have this concept and the enduring challenges regarding land continued to undermine prospects for peace in Côte d'Ivoire?

Conclusions: the politics of land in the 2015 elections and beyond

On 25 October 2015, Ivorians voted in the first presidential elections since the post-electoral crisis of 2010–11. With nearly 84 per cent of the overall vote, the incumbent Alassane Ouattara easily secured the presidency. The sizeable margin of victory was in no small measure due to the divided and dysfunctional nature of the opposition, and the impressive economic recovery that the country has experienced over the last few years under the tenure of President Ouattara (World Bank 2015).

To what extent (if any) did the land question play a role in destabilising the presidential vote? While pre-electoral protests in the months leading up to the elections resulted in the loss of lives and injury, such protests hinged more on the lingering debates surrounding the incumbent's eligibility as a presidential candidate (Broadhurst 2015). The short answer is that the politics of land failed to emerge as a major electoral cleavage issue.[29] Given the fractured state of the opposition and the lack of electoral incentive on the part of Ouattara to play the land card, the absence of large-scale land-related electoral violence should not come as a surprise. The overwhelming victory of the Ouattara side undoubtedly provided a further disincentive to the incumbent's political opponents to attempt to instrumentalise the issue of land for electoral purposes. Simply put, why run the risk of trying to mobilise violence around the land issue when the likelihood of successfully contesting the electoral outcome is so low (cf. Klaus and Mitchell 2015)? Such a conclusion echoes earlier work on the triggers of electoral violence which argue that violence is much less likely to occur in the absence of close elections with narrow vote margins (Wilkinson 2004).

The joint production of action therefore did not materialise, as there was a lack of political appetite to try to harness the power of land. In the current political context, actors on the periphery in the far west region were equally unlikely to resort to violence, as the non-indigenous population retains the balance of power in the region (Côté and Mitchell 2016). Given the security stranglehold of the incumbent in the area (cf. Human Rights Watch 2015) and the contemporary electoral dynamics in the country, it was not politically expedient – and possibly even dangerous – for Ouattara's (autochthonous) opponents to vocalise their grievances over land through electoral channels. In short, the unresolved land conflicts at the local level thus failed to emerge as a master cleavage among the country's competing political elites and failed to mobilise actors at the local level.

Beyond the 2015 elections, this could prove to be a different story. Numerous reports have highlighted the enduring challenges for resolving the land question (Human Rights Watch 2013; ICG 2014; Mitchell 2014). Despite the recent changes to the highly controversial land tenure and nationality laws, there have as yet been no meaningful efforts to implement and enforce such reforms. As Pritchard (2016: 271–3) highlights, there is a multiplicity of practical challenges facing the application and adoption of the country's land law. One such challenge relates to the lack of awareness of the legal framework governing land tenure. The following quotation is illustrative of this challenge. When asked by a reporter whether the land conflicts have been resolved, the Special Representative and Head of the United Nations Operation in Côte d'Ivoire stated: 'No. The conflicts linked with land continue, but I think that the law of 1998 modified in 2014 provides conditions for resolving them. The problem is that it has not been sufficiently explained so that populations know how to act when they are confronted with these sorts of problems' (Duhem 2015).[30]

The slow progress on the implementation of the new land reforms has been further complicated by the problem of displacement (Pritchard 2016). The huge numbers of the displaced during the civil war of the early 2000s were compounded by the renewed hostilities of 2010–11. While there has been some progress in allowing some people to return to their lands, a recent estimate suggests that there may be as many as 300,000 who are still displaced (Internal Displacement Monitoring Centre 2015). It is therefore hard to imagine how the contentious politics around land can be meaningfully resolved given the state of flux surrounding groups' access to and control over land.

In sum, until the land question is resolved, it will continue to pose a serious threat for future rounds of elections. A different electoral context – one in which Ouattara (or his successor) and his supporters no longer enjoy such a fragmented political opposition – could incite political elites to once again instrumentalise the issue of land.[31] If or when this occurs, the joint production of action could again unite elites at the centre and actors on the periphery in their quest to pursue their objectives, whether they be motivated by the desire to seek greater private gains or to rectify perceived injustices of the past. As Côte d'Ivoire's history has shown, under this scenario the instrumentalisation of land could once again be a trigger for electoral violence.

What policy implications can be drawn from this micro-level analysis of the links between land conflict and electoral violence? Balcells and Justino (2014: 1346) underscore the need to establish a better theoretical understanding of the link between macro-level political processes and local conflict dynamics, as they rightly note that such an understanding is critical for the development of policies designed to break vicious cycles of violence, war and underdevelopment. Yet despite the centrality and causal significance of the micro-foundations of conflict, 'most programmes of conflict resolution, prevention and mediation are typically driven by regional, national and international perspectives' (Verwimp, Justino and Brück 2009: 308). This echoes the core finding in this chapter: namely, that any approach to mitigate future land-related electoral violence must consider the ways in which national and local forces and factors collide to produce the joint production of action. In so doing, we must therefore 'explore the social production of violent conflict, and how land becomes part of larger patterns of violent contestation' – notably in the context of elections (Van Leeuwen and Van der Haar 2016: 95).

In concrete terms, it is clear that more needs to be done to support and strengthen the development of reforms aimed at improving the governance of land. As recent research shows, the insecure and unenforceable nature of property rights regimes is a leading contributory factor to host–migrant conflicts over land (Côté and Mitchell 2017). Given the propensity of political elites at both the national and the local level to try to mobilise electoral violence by using the land card, one obvious safeguard against this is to create more certainty and enforcement in the area of property rights. While this may prove to be a tall order in places such as Côte d'Ivoire, the stakes are high as land-related electoral violence shows no sign of abating.

Notes

1 The CNE (2012) report provides a detailed account and a geographical breakdown of the different forms of violence committed during the electoral period. As the report shows, there was a wide range of causes of death, such as executions committed for political or ethnic reasons by both security forces and citizens, torture, and violent acts committed during detention.

2 Recent exceptions include Boone (2014), Boone and Kriger (2012), Côté and Mitchell (2016) and Klaus and Mitchell (2015).

3 'Autochthons' refers to those who, literally, emerged directly from the soil. See Geschiere (2009) for a detailed analysis of the concept of autochthony.

4 According to one estimate, Côte d'Ivoire's civil war resulted in the internal displacement of more than 1 million people, with approximately 80 per cent of these taking up residence in Abidjan (see Chirot 2006: 72).

5 Author interview, local autochthon village chief in Haut Sassandra Region, 5 May 2012. Note that all interviews were conducted in French and translated by the author unless otherwise stated.

6 Author interview, senior figure in Rassemblement des Républicains party in Abidjan, 2 May 2012. Although northerners (both Ivorian and foreigners) have been the target of more violence than the Baoulé (who are originally from central Côte d'Ivoire), the latter seem to receive greater criticism for their lack of integration.

7 Author interview, local autochthon village chief in Bas Sassandra Region, 12 May 2012. The term 'tuteur' can be translated as 'guardian'. The tutorat system is an informal institution for regulating relations between first-comers (i.e. guardians) and newcomers (i.e. tuteurs).

8 Author interview (in English), foreign journalist in Abidjan, 2 May 2012.

9 Ibid.

10 Author interview, autochthon president of local youth association in Moyen Cavally Region, 9 May 2012.

11 Author interview, local autochthon village chief in Bas Sassandra Region, 12 May 2012.

12 On the role of youth in fuelling autochthony discourses, see Chauveau and Bobo (2003) and Marshall-Fratani (2006).

13 Author interview, local autochthon chief of lands in Moyen Cavally Region, 9 May 2012.

14 Author interview, local autochthon village chief in Haut Sassandra Region, 5 May 2012.

15 Author interview, local autochthon village chief in Bas Sassandra Region, 12 May 2012.

16 Author interview, assistant leader of local dozo contingent in Moyen Cavally Region, 8 May 2012.

17 Author interview, Burkinabè cocoa farmer in Moyen Cavally Region, 9 May 2012.

18 Author interview, spokesperson of allochthon and allogène communities in Moyen Cavally Region, 10 May 2012.

19 Author interview, head of leading NGO in Abidjan, 24 April 2012.

20 In Chapter 5 of this volume, Bangura and Söderberg Kovacs provide an alternative analysis on the role of chiefs. They argue that, in the case of Sierra Leone, traditional chiefs played a more active role in contributing to local instances of violence.

21 Author interview (in English), head of leading NGO in Abidjan, 1 May 2012. Once again, the autochthons are those viewed as the original inhabitants of the soil whereas allochthons refers to native Ivorians who are migrants to the host community. Meanwhile, allogènes refers to non-Ivorian migrants.

22 Author interview, local autochthon village chief in Haut Sassandra Region, 5 May 2012.

23 Author interview, local autochthon community youth president in Moyen Cavally Region, 9 May 2012.

24 Author interview, allochthon

village chief in Haut Sassandra Region, 4 May 2012.

25 Author interview, head of international NGO in Abidjan, 24 April 2012.

26 Author interview, Ivorian journalist in Abidjan, 2 May 2012.

27 See Bassett (2011) for an analysis of the electoral geography of the 2010 presidential elections.

28 For a more detailed overview of the electoral violence dynamics in the far west, see CNE (2012), ICG (2014) and ONUCI (2011).

29 Piccolino (2016: 102–3) notes that the pre-electoral and electoral campaigns focused more on issues relating to the fate of Laurent Gbagbo, the fairness of electoral institutions, the state of the economy, and broader themes linked to transitional justice and democracy.

30 Author's translation from French.

31 Piccolino (2016: 106) argues that the selection of a successor to Ouattara may prove to be a particularly destabilising process.

References

Airault, P. (2010) 'Présidentielle: La bataille de l'Ouest n'est pas gagnée par Laurent Gbagbo', *Jeune Afrique*, 27 October. Available at www.jeuneafrique.com/Article/ ARTJAJA2597p038-039.xml0/ (accessed 27 October 2010).

Autesserre, S. (2010) *The Trouble with the Congo: Local Violence and the Failure of International Peacekeeping.* Cambridge and New York NY: Cambridge University Press.

Balcells, L. and P. Justino (2014) 'Bridging Micro and Macro Approaches on Civil Wars and Political Violence: Issues, Challenges, and the Way Forward', *Journal of Conflict Resolution* 58 (8): 1343–59.

Banégas, R. and R. Marshall-Fratani (2007) 'Côte d'Ivoire: Negotiating Identity and Citizenship' in M. Bøås and K. C. Dunn (eds), *African Guerrillas: Raging against the Machine.* Boulder CO: Lynne Rienner.

Basedau, M., G. Erdmann and A. Mehler (eds) (2007) *Votes, Money and Violence: Political Parties and Sub-Saharan Africa.* Uppsala: Nordic Africa Institute.

Bassett, T. J. (2011) 'Winning Coalition, Sore Loser: Côte d'Ivoire's 2010 Presidential Elections', *African Affairs* 110 (440): 469–79.

Berry, S. (2009) 'Property, Authority and Citizenship: Land Claims, Politics and the Dynamics of Social Division in West Africa', *Development and Change* 40 (1): 23–45.

Boone, C. (2003) *Political Topographies of the African State: Territorial Authority and Institutional Choice.* New York NY: Cambridge University Press.

Boone, C. (2007) 'Africa's New Territorial Politics: Regionalism and the Open Economy in Côte d'Ivoire', *African Studies Review* 50 (1): 59–81.

Boone, C. (2014) *Property and Political Order: Land Rights and the Structure of Conflict in Africa.* New York NY: Cambridge University Press.

Boone, C. and N. Kriger (2012) 'Land Patronage and Elections: Winners and Losers in Zimbabwe and Côte d'Ivoire' in D. A. Bekoe (ed.), *Voting in Fear: Electoral Violence in Sub-Saharan Africa.* Washington DC: United States Institute for Peace Press.

Broadhurst, C. (2015) 'Fear of Further Clashes with Upcoming Elections in Cote d'Ivoire', *RFI English*, 11 September. Available at www.english. rfi.fr/africa/20150911-fear-further-clashes-upcoming-elections-cote-divoire (accessed 17 October 2015).

Chauveau, J.-P. (2000) 'Question Foncière et Construction Nationale en Côte d'Ivoire: Les Enjeux Silencieux d'un Coup d'État', *Politique Africaine* 78: 94–125.

Chauveau, J.-P. and K. S. Bobo (2003) 'La Situation de Guerre dans l'Arène Villageoise: Un Exemple dans le

Centre-Ouest Ivoirien', *Politique Africaine* 89: 12–32.

Chauveau, J.-P. and J.-P. Colin (2010) 'Customary Transfers and Land Sales in Côte d'Ivoire: Revisiting the Embeddedness Issue', *Africa* 80 (1): 81–103.

Chirot, D. (2006) 'The Debacle in Côte d'Ivoire', *Journal of Democracy* 17 (2): 63–77.

CNE (2012) *Rapport d'enquête sur les violations des droits de l'homme et du droit international humanitaire survenues dans la période du 31 octobre 2010 au 15 mai 2011*. Abidjan: Commission Nationale d'Enquête (CNE), République de Côte d'Ivoire.

Côté, I. and M. I. Mitchell (2016) 'Elections and "Sons of the Soil" Conflict Dynamics in Africa and Asia', *Democratization* 23 (4): 657–77.

Côté, I. and M. I. Mitchell (2017) 'Deciphering "Sons of the Soil" Conflict: A Critical Review of the Literature', *Ethnopolitics* 16 (4): 333–51.

Crook, R. C. (1997) 'Winning Coalitions and Ethno-regional Politics: The Failure of the Opposition in the 1990 and 1995 Elections in Côte d'Ivoire', *African Affairs* 96 (383): 222–3.

Crook, R. C. et al. (2007) *The Law, Legal Institutions and the Protection of Land Rights in Ghana and Côte d'Ivoire: Developing a More Effective and Equitable System*. Brighton: Institute of Development Studies.

Derman, B., R. Odgaard and E. Sjaastad (2007) 'Introduction' in B. Derman, R. Odgaard and E. Sjaastad (eds), *Conflicts over Land and Water in Africa*. East Lansing MI: Michigan State University Press.

Duhem, V. (2015) 'La présidentielle ivoirienne doit permettre d'exorciser la crise de 2010–2011', *Jeune Afrique*, 10 June. Available at www.jeuneafrique. com/234375/politique/la-presidentielle-ivoirienne-doit-permettre-dexorciser-la-crise-de-2010-2011/ (accessed 18 July 2017).

Geschiere, P. (2009) *The Perils of Belonging: Autochthony, Citizenship, and Exclusion in Africa and Europe*. Chicago IL: University of Chicago Press.

Goldsmith, A. (2015) 'Elections and Civil Violence in New Multiparty Regimes: Evidence from Africa', *Journal of Peace Research* 52 (5): 607–21.

Höglund, K. (2009) 'Electoral Violence in Conflict-ridden Societies: Concepts, Causes, and Consequences', *Terrorism and Political Violence* 21 (3): 412–27.

Human Rights Watch (2013) '"That Land is My Family's Wealth": Addressing Land Dispossession after Côte d'Ivoire's Post-Election Conflict'. New York NY: Human Rights Watch.

Human Rights Watch (2015) 'Côte d'Ivoire: Extortion by Security Forces'. New York NY: Human Rights Watch.

ICG (2014) 'Côte d'Ivoire's Great West: Key to Reconciliation'. Africa Report No. 212. Brussels: International Crisis Group (ICG).

Internal Displacement Monitoring Centre (2015) 'Côte d'Ivoire: New Commitments Signal Hope for 300,000 Still Internally Displaced', IDMC, 26 February. Available at www.internal-displacement.org/sub-saharan-africa/cote-divoire/2015/cote-divoire-new-commitments-signal-hope-for-300000-still-internally-displaced (accessed 17 October 2015).

Jeune Afrique (2010) 'Rhétorique de combat pour Gbagbo et Ouattara', *Jeune Afrique*, 24 November. Available at www.jeuneafrique.com/Article/ARTJAWEB20101124083654/ (accessed 24 November 2010).

Kalyvas, S. N. (2003) 'The Ontology of "Political Violence": Action and Identity in Civil Wars', *Perspectives on Politics* 1 (3): 475–94.

Klaus, K. and M. I. Mitchell (2015) 'Land Grievances and the Mobilization of Electoral Violence: Evidence from Côte d'Ivoire and Kenya', *Journal of Peace Research* 52 (5): 622–35.

Marshall-Fratani, R. (2006) 'The War of "Who is Who": Autochthony,

Nationalism and Citizenship in the Ivoirian Crisis', *African Studies Review* 49 (2): 9–43.

McCallin, B. and M. Montemurro (2009) 'Whose Land Is This?: Land Disputes and Forced Displacement in the Western Forest Area of Côte d'Ivoire. Report for the Norwegian Refugee Council'. Geneva: Internal Displacement Monitoring Centre and Norwegian Refugee Council.

McGovern, M. (2011) *Making War in Côte d'Ivoire*. Chicago IL: University of Chicago Press.

Mitchell, M. I. (2012a) 'Migration, Citizenship and Autochthony: Strategies and Challenges for State-building in Côte d'Ivoire', *Journal of Contemporary African Studies* 30 (2): 267–87.

Mitchell, M. I. (2012b) 'Power-sharing and Peace in Côte d'Ivoire: Past Examples and Future Prospects', *Conflict, Security and Development* 12 (2): 171–91.

Mitchell, M. I. (2014) 'Land Tenure Reform and Politics in Post-conflict Côte d'Ivoire: A Precarious Peace in the Western Cocoa Regions', *Canadian Journal of African Studies* 48 (2): 203–21.

ONUCI (2011) 'Rapport sur les violations des droits de l'homme et du droit international humanitaire commises à l'ouest de la Côte d'Ivoire'. Abidjan: Division des Droits de l'Homme, Opération des Nations Unies en Côte d'Ivoire (ONUCI).

Piccolino, G. (2016) 'One Step Forward, Two Steps Back? Côte d'Ivoire's 2015 Presidential Polls', *Africa Spectrum* 51 (1): 97–110.

Pritchard, M. F. (2016) 'Contesting Land Rights in a Post-conflict Environment: Tenure Reform and Dispute Resolution in the Centre-West Region of Côte d'Ivoire', *Land Use Policy* 54: 264–75.

Rapoport, D. C. and L. Weinberg (2001) 'Elections and Violence' in D. C. Rapoport and L. Weinberg (eds), *The Democratic Experience and Political Violence*. London: Frank Cass.

Straus, S. (2011) '"It's Sheer Horror Here": Patterns of Violence during the First Four Months of Côte d'Ivoire's Post-electoral Crisis', *African Affairs* 110 (440): 481–9.

Straus, S. (2012) 'Wars Do End! Changing Patterns of Political Violence in Sub-Saharan Africa', *African Affairs* 111 (443): 179–201.

UNHRC (2011) 'Report of the Independent International Commission of Inquiry on Côte d'Ivoire'. New York NY: United Nations Human Rights Council (UNHCR).

Van Leeuwen, M. and G. Van der Haar (2016) 'Theorizing the Land–Violent Conflict Nexus', *World Development* 78: 94–104.

Verwimp, P., P. Justino and T. Brück (2009) 'The Analysis of Conflict: A Micro-level Perspective', *Journal of Peace Research* 46 (3): 307–14.

Wilkinson, S. I. (2004) *Votes and Violence: Electoral Competition and Ethnic Riots in India*. Cambridge: Cambridge University Press.

World Bank (2015) 'Côte d'Ivoire'. Available at www.worldbank.org/en/country/cotedivoire (accessed 17 October 2015).

4 | The geography of violence in Burundi's 2015 elections

Willy Nindorera and Jesper Bjarnesen

Introduction

In the span of less than a year, Burundi's strides towards a sustainable peace following its civil war were marred by an escalation of electoral violence and a rapid descent into outright authoritarianism. At the end of April 2015, the proclamation of incumbent president Pierre Nkurunziza's candidacy for a third term led to a major crisis against a backdrop of violent clashes, mainly in the capital of Bujumbura, between civilian protestors opposed to this candidature and the security forces, supported by the ruling party youth wing, the Imbonerakure.[1] Violence was limited, however, to specific neighbourhoods in the capital and to certain districts in the provinces. The aim of this chapter is to decipher the geography of this violence: what factors explain the concentration of electoral violence in the city of Bujumbura? Why were particular neighbourhoods in the capital the locus of electoral violence, while others were left relatively untouched? What explains the delimitation of electoral violence in rural areas to specific municipalities?

In line with what seems to be a general tendency across African states and in other parts of the world (Goldsmith 2015; Reilly 2011; Taylor, Pevehouse and Straus 2013), electoral violence relating to Burundi's 2015 elections seems to have been driven primarily by the quest for government survival. In a context of intense frustration, especially among urban youths, over high unemployment rates, poverty, lack of prospects and civic rights, the Nkurunziza regime resorted to a strategy of intimidation and repression in order to discourage opposition, both armed and peaceful. This chapter suggests that the specific geography of these forms of electoral violence is central for understanding the social divisions and post-conflict political stratifications that have shaped Burundi's current conflict landscape.

This chapter contributes to the micro-level exploration of the dynamics of electoral violence, as called for in the introduction to this volume, and more specifically to an understanding of how these subnational dynamics came to be unequally distributed geographically, within the capital as well as across the Burundian territory, during the turbulent months following the April 2015 protests. This analysis of Burundi's geography of violence thus explores empirically the interplay between electoral politics and public protests (McAdam and Tarrow 2010), providing some explanations for the recent observation that 'protests across Africa seem unable to effect substantive reforms in national politics despite their success in bringing tens of thousands of people into the streets' (Branch and Mampilly 2015: 6). Given the current interest in public protests among scholars and policy makers, as well as political activists across the African continent and beyond (cf. Arnould, Tor and Vervaeke 2016), the chapter presents a sobering account of how popular mobilisation may play out in an increasingly authoritarian state (Schedler 2013: 389).

Given the concentration of electoral violence in the city of Bujumbura, the Burundian capital will be the main geographical area under scrutiny, and our analysis will largely be limited to the period from the end of April 2015 until April 2016. This period covers the bulk of violence in Bujumbura, while the following months were marked by a de-escalation of violence. The chapter is based on literature research (press articles, studies and reports by NGOs and United Nations organisations, academic research, etc.); statistical surveys that explain the geographical distribution of violence; and the maps, graphs and statistical data produced by various NGOs that provide a clear visualisation of the geography of violence during the period. It is also based on interviews with people who witnessed the violence first-hand. A focus group was also organised with young academics living in two of the neighbourhoods affected by the violence, who thus observed the dynamics that motivated the violence and its repercussions on the lives of the inhabitants. These methodological choices were made in light of a security situation in which more systematic empirical data collection was deemed too dangerous for both the researchers and the informants. The chapter's analysis should be read with an awareness of the limitations that this selection of material has implied.

The chapter first summarises Burundi's history of electoral violence from its independence in 1962 until the most recent crisis, and continues with a more detailed consideration of the run-up to and aftermath of the 2015 elections. The bulk of the chapter then analyses the specific geography of electoral violence during the period under consideration, emphasising three patterns and suggesting some explanations for their occurrence. Firstly, we explore the reasons for the centrality of the city of Bujumbura in the confrontation between protestors and security forces, emphasising the demographic particularities of the capital in relation to the rest of the country. Secondly, we consider the uneven distribution of violence within the capital, drawing links to the roles of specific neighbourhoods during the country's recent civil war. Finally, we discuss the occurrence and distribution of violence outside the capital, documenting aspects of the electoral crisis that have been largely overlooked in news reporting and subsequent debates outside Burundi.

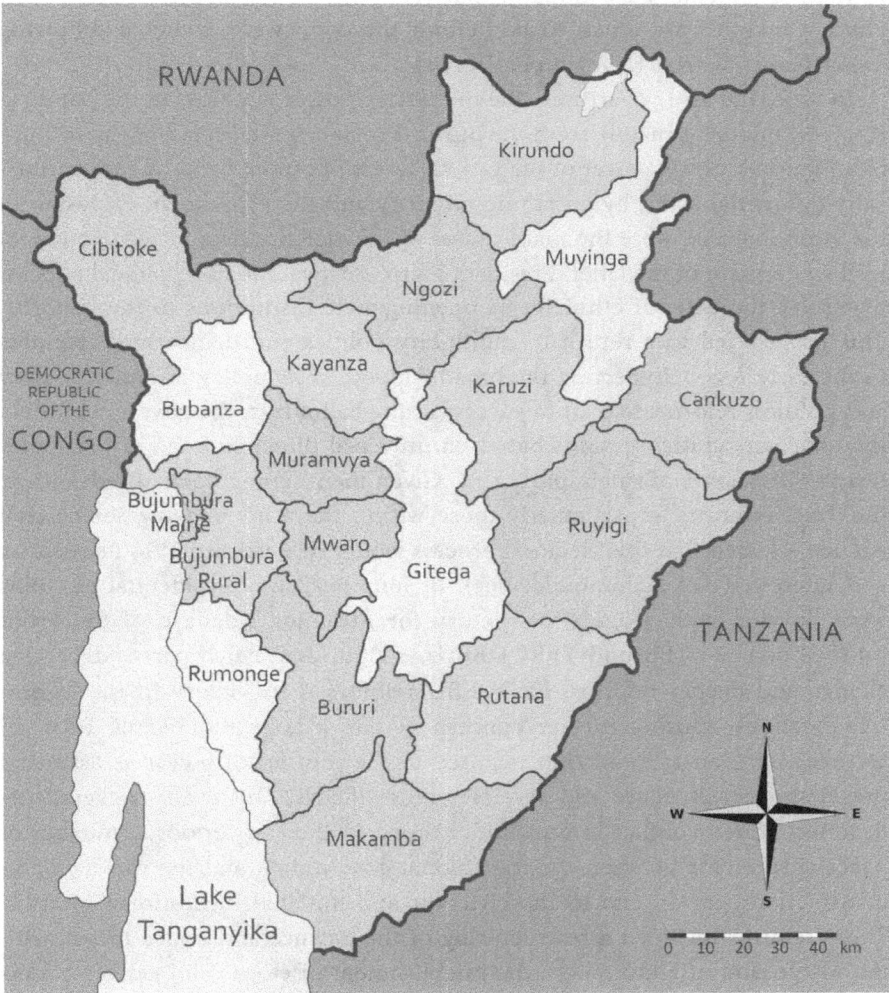

Figure 1: Map of Burundi, designed by Henrik Alfredsson

Electoral violence in Burundi

Burundi has a troubled contemporary history marked by cycles of violence, most often of an ethno-political nature. Burundi's first postcolonial crisis in 1965 was the result of an attempted coup, accompanied by ethnic massacres led by Hutus (the ethnic majority) in the armed forces frustrated by the defeat of the Hutu candidates of the Union for National Progress (UPRONA) in the parliamentary elections of that year. The coup failed and about sixty Hutu who were presumed to be behind the coup were executed following a controversial trial (Ngayimpenda 1998).

In 1966, the army overthrew the monarchy. Power was now in the hands of the Tutsi minority, mainly from the Bururi Province in the south of the country (see Figure 1). The takeover of the various levers of power, including the historically influential army, by an ethnic minority and the subsequent exclusion of the Hutu majority were the main causes of the violent crises in 1972 and 1988. In the aftermath of the latter, President Pierre Buyoya initiated political reforms to resolve the issue of ethnicity by opening state institutions to the majority. This process led to a return to multiparty politics and democratic openness in the early 1990s. Expecting the broad support of its policy of national unity and political reforms to lead to success at the ballot box, the government held the first democratic elections based on universal direct suffrage in 1993, after nearly thirty years of single-party rule. Given their demographic disadvantage, the Tutsi minority – particularly those within the army and the senior civil service – feared that this electoral process would be detrimental to its security and interests (Ben Hammouda 1995). In June 1993, the presidential elections were decided with a landslide victory for Melchior Ndadaye of the Front for Democracy in Burundi (FRODEBU), a Hutu-dominated party advocating change and deeper reforms. FRODEBU reinforced its victory in the legislative elections, causing further concern among a large number of Tutsi. In October 1993, an army faction opposed to the transfer of power assassinated president-elect Ndadaye and several senior officials. This event triggered the deadliest armed conflict in Burundi's history. In the early 2000s, a number of peace agreements between the transitional government and the various Hutu insurrections put an end to the civil war and initiated institutional reforms. These reforms included a restructuring of the defence and police forces, with the integration of Hutu rebels; the establishment of ethnic and gender quotas in most state institutions; and the periodic organisation of pluralistic elections based on universal suffrage. The most influential agreement was the Arusha Peace and Reconciliation Agreement for Burundi, brokered by Nelson Mandela and Julius Nyerere, which was signed on 28 August 2000.[2] The Arusha Accords contain numerous provisions including a number of institutional reforms that would later be incorporated into the 2005 constitution, which is still in force at the time of writing.[3]

The 1993 crisis and subsequent civil war caused socio-political trauma in Burundian society (Nimubona 2004). When elections were held in 2005, many Burundians were afraid that their country would relapse into armed conflict, as a large part of the population now perceived the electoral process as a source of tension and potential violence, as one rebel group – the National Forces of Liberation (FNL) – still refused to disarm and remained underground (ICG 2005). Moreover, the political scene saw the arrival of several formations originating in former rebel groups, including the National Council for the Defence of Democracy and the Forces for the Defence of Democracy (CNDD-FDD). The CNDD-FDD gained popularity in rural areas, relying on their image as a movement consisting primarily of young rural Hutu, which was already articulated in populist rhetoric during the civil war. Its political platform emphasised the reform of the defence and police forces, one of the main issues of the peace negotiations and the main demand of the Hutu majority. But its underground discourse and propaganda aimed at the Hutu electorate, which the party perceived as its potential electoral base, also played strongly on fear and intimidation (ibid.). For an electorate primarily concerned with peace and security, and wary of the risks of a return to war in the event of a CNDD-FDD defeat, the choice was clear – or, indeed, was not much of a choice at all. Thus, the 2005 elections resulted in a large victory for the CNDD-FDD,[4] and although the electoral process was tense and subject to some violence, it did not lead to a new crisis. A more enduring outcome of these elections, furthermore, was a shift in the principal political dividing lines from the interethnic divisions that characterised the postcolonial period to increasing intra-ethnic tensions, primarily between the main Hutu-dominated political parties.

The CNDD-FDD's first term, owing to popular social reforms, was welcomed by large parts of the population. At the same time, however, the ruling party displayed a propensity for authoritarianism, which led to a series of political crises during its first five years in power, as well as serious human rights violations and an increase in corruption. Not surprisingly, popular perceptions of the party's performance in government varied significantly from the outset, the city being less appreciative than the countryside, where people were more concerned about their basic needs, as discussed below. Preparations for the 2010 elections took place in a tense climate characterised, among other things, by the restriction of civil liberties and the instrumentalisation of the judiciary, the defence and the police, attesting to the ruling party's increasingly authoritarian governing practices (ICG 2010). The CNDD-FDD thereby controlled the direction of the electoral process and mobilised all means and resources at its disposal to remain in power. Tensions were also exacerbated by new circumstances. The Hutu rebels of the FNL, led by Agathon Rwasa, who had not participated in the previous elections, had by now demobilised

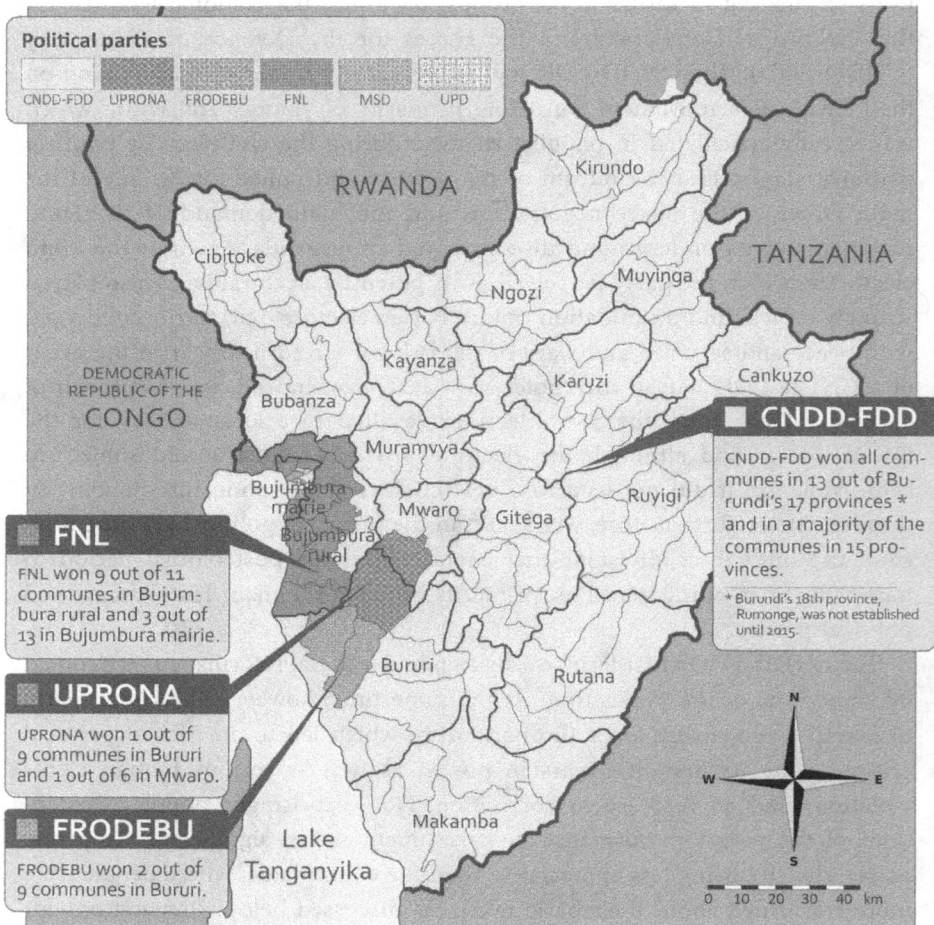

Political parties

CNDD-FDD   UPRONA   FRODEBU   FNL   MSD   UPD

RWANDA

Kirundo

TANZANIA

Cibitoke

Muyinga

Ngozi

DEMOCRATIC
REPUBLIC OF THE
CONGO

Kayanza

Karuzi

Cankuzo

Bubanza

Muramvya

CNDD-FDD

CNDD-FDD won all com-
munes in 13 out of Bu-
rundi's 17 provinces *
and in a majority of the
communes in 15 pro-
vinces.

Bujumbura
mairie

Mwaro   Gitega

Ruyigi

FNL

FNL won 9 out of 11
communes in Bujum-
bura rural and 3 out of
13 in Bujumbura mairie.

Bujumbura
rural

* Burundi's 18th province,
Rumonge, was not established
until 2015.

UPRONA

UPRONA won 1 out of
9 communes in Bururi
and 1 out of 6 in Mwaro.

Bururi

Rutana

N

W   E

S

FRODEBU

FRODEBU won 2 out of
9 communes in Bururi.

Lake
Tanganyika

Makamba

0   10   20   30   40 km

Figure 2: National distribution of votes in 2010 municipal elections. Map by
Henrik Alfredsson, based on results announced by the National Independet
Electoral Commmission (CENI).

and transformed into a political party, running for the first time in the 2010 elections. This was perceived as a serious threat by the CNDD-FDD. Secondly, in keeping with the Arusha Accords, the president had been elected by indirect vote in 2005, but was now to be elected by universal direct suffrage. Finally, the ruling party had been mobilising its youth wing, the Imbonerakure, for a campaign of intimidation for some time (Human Rights Watch 2010). This intimidation, in turn, incited the formation of youth movements connected to the main opposition parties and led to violent confrontations between these groups (ICG 2010). The first municipal elections were, once again, won by the CNDD-FDD, with a considerable margin in all parts of the country, except for Bujumbura and some parts of Bururi and Mwaro (see Figure 2). While this first ballot was deemed legitimate by election observers, however, it was rejected by the opposition, who denounced the climate of fear and intimidation that had marred the electoral process. For the same reasons, the opposition decided to boycott the following elections. Faced with threats to their safety, the main opposition leaders went into exile. The 2010 elections therefore initiated a new political crisis that was marked by numerous extrajudicial executions, among other things (UN Security Council 2011). Between the 2010 and 2015 electoral cycles, the authoritarian tendencies of the CNDD-FDD regime became increasingly evident. This period was characterised by the deliberate obstruc-tion of the activities of opposition parties outside the capital; the instrumental transformation of the justice system and the national security forces to serve regime interests; the arrest of some opposition figureheads as a show of force; and the appointment of regime loyalists to central positions within the institu-tions safeguarding democracy and the rule of law, such as the national electoral and human rights commissions. These worrying changes, however, should still be understood against the backdrop of the Arusha Agreement, which remained in effect, despite being increasingly challenged by the CNDD-FDD hardliners.

Burundi's history of electoral violence prior to the 2015 elections, there-fore, is not a straightforward example of 'electoral authoritarianism', which Schedler characterises as 'institutional façades of democracy, including regular multiparty elections for the chief executive, in order to conceal (and repro-duce) harsh realities of authoritarian governance' (Schedler 2006: 1), since genuinely democratic reforms have been introduced since the end of the civil war. However, the CNDD-FDD government's record consistently points in an authoritarian direction, perhaps a testimony to the complicated transition of a former rebel movement into a political party (cf. Söderberg Kovacs and Hatz 2016), and its chair, Pierre Nkurunziza, from a military to a civilian leader (Burihabwa 2017). As has been well documented elsewhere, these transitions often entail the persistence of a military ethos and operationality, rendering elected leaders into military-civilian hybrids, or what Themnér describes as 'warlord democrats' (2017).

The build-up to the 2015 elections

The 2015 electoral process generated tensions early on. As early as 2014, there were unmistakable indications of CNDD-FDD's desire to win by any means necessary. The tightening of laws on civil liberties, irregularities in the early stages of the electoral process, increased pressure on and harassment of the media and civil society, inopportune interference in the functioning of opposition parties, the reinforcement of the Imbonerakure and their massive deployment across the country, and their formation as militia units[5] – these were all indicators of the CNDD-FDD's intentions. As such, the record of its ten years in power was largely poor, and many expectations were dashed, particularly from a socio-economic perspective. A 2014 Afrobarometer survey of the general perceptions of the population in the social, political and economic spheres reveals high levels of dissatisfaction in rural communities, and even higher levels in urban areas, especially regarding living conditions and government performance on development issues. For example, 57 per cent of respondents across urban and rural populations gave a negative assessment of their overall living conditions, and 72 per cent of urban respondents estimated that overall economic conditions had declined during the last year, while 51 per cent of rural respondents provided similar answers. Finally, 78 per cent of urban respondents provided a negative assessment of the overall economic situation, as did 51 per cent of rural respondents. In short, frustration had risen by the end of the government's second term, especially among urban populations. The lack of prospects for young people, who were increasingly faced with unemployment, underemployment and poverty, and the determination of certain opposition parties not to accept authoritarian rule heightened the risk of renewed violence and instability (UNDP and MFPDE 2014).

The CNDD-FDD was the manifestation of a rebel movement whose transformation into a political party proved to be flawed. The party's propensity to resort to force and confrontation, to the detriment of dialogue and compromise, had been a constant since its arrival on the scene largely due to the vestiges of its wartime past and the strong influence of its former military wing. Indeed, as already implied, the former rebel movement never truly departed from the violent culture it had developed during its underground years (see also Rufyikiri 2016). Moreover, despite having more contact and forming alliances with the outside world, it tended to inflate certain potential threats and even to fabricate them, such as the frequently raised danger of a Tutsi resurgence to its colonial and postcolonial dominance, especially when the party was confronted with internal difficulties and in need of scapegoats. This inflammatory political rhetoric by the authorities framed those who opposed Nkurunziza's candidacy for a third term as the same people responsible for the assassination of Melchior Ndadaye in the aftermath of the 1993 elections

(Madirisha 2015), or, more bluntly, it associated them with a Tutsi menace that needed to be eliminated (Bensimon 2015).

The CNDD-FDD deployed this rhetoric as a response to virtually any line of criticism, in an attempt to garner the support of an electorate that it knew was growing increasingly disillusioned and frustrated (ICG 2016). At the same time, the ruling party was gradually being destabilised by internal tensions linked in part to its neopatrimonial administration and the dominance of a quartet of corrupt generals (Impunity Watch 2015). Against this backdrop of an already tense political climate, the question of the third term was the spark that ignited the violence of 2015, and exacerbated tensions within the ruling party.

The controversy over Pierre Nkurunziza's candidacy The Arusha Agreement clearly states that the president of the republic may hold no more than two terms in office. The Burundian constitution is more ambiguous on this subject. It states in one of its articles that the head of state is elected by universal direct suffrage for a five-year term renewable only once, while another provision stipulates that, as an exception, the first president of the post-transition republic can be elected by the National Assembly and the Senate meeting in congress, by a two-thirds majority of their members. Conscious of the forthcoming challenges in the event of a third term, Pierre Nkurunziza, in office since 2005, wanted to circumvent this obstacle by proposing a constitutional amendment at the beginning of 2014. This amendment would have effectively offset the two-term limit, but the proposal failed to pass by a single vote.[6] If Nkurunziza's ambitions in this regard were still somewhat hidden, the public speeches of the leaders of the ruling party, in contrast, were unequivocal. Faced with the increasing likelihood of Nkurunziza's candidacy in the 2015 presidential elections, hundreds of civil society organisations formed a coalition in early 2015 called 'Stop the Third Term' and vowed to call upon the people to take to the streets. The opposition actively prepared to mobilise against the third term and threatened to do the same. Conversely, the CNDD-FDD was already organising demonstrations across the country to support Nkurunziza's candidacy, in which the mobilised Imbonerakure would shout menacing slogans at opponents of the candidacy. For its part, the international community, wary of the risk of a violent crisis caused by the prospect of a third term, dispatched several high-level missions to Bujumbura to dissuade Nkurunziza from running for office out of respect for the Arusha Agreement and the constitution (Reyntjens, Vandeginste and Verpoorten 2016).

The first months of 2015 were extremely tense. In March 2015, several senior CNDD-FDD officials signed a letter opposing the third term. This movement, however, was quickly supressed. When a CNDD-FDD party congress was announced for the end of April, the capital was already in turmoil (Reyntjens, Vandeginste and Verpoorten 2016).

Understanding Burundi's geography of violence

On 25 April 2015, the CNDD-FDD party congress proclaimed the president's candidacy for the presidency at the general elections scheduled for May to August 2015. The following day, residents from several neighbourhoods of the capital initiated peaceful demonstrations to protest against Nkurunziza's candidacy. The first casualty occurred on the very first day of the protests. Despite the initially peaceful nature of the demonstrations, the police forces responded brutally, blocking the protestors' path towards Place de l'Indépendence in the city centre (see Figure 3) and employing tear gas, batons and rubber bullets to keep them back. In some neighbourhoods, the police were already using live bullets at this early stage of the protests. The regime thus used disproportionate repression to discourage further demonstrations. When protests persisted, the authorities turned to unrestrained violence with the aim of spreading fear before resorting to a campaign of terror in the districts involved in early May, mobilising mainly the Imbonerakure and special units of the police and the national intelligence service. This repression was organised through a parallel chain of command within the police forces and, to a lesser extent, in the army, based on past allegiances, the infiltration of several police units by the Imbonerakure and the use of ethnic loyalty as a political strategy. In this regard, the ethnic discourse of some authorities, who called for the annihilation of the protesting neighbourhoods in exchange for material gains, was deeply worrying to the international community (Ba and Muhorakeye 2015).

In the space of a few months, peaceful protests had turned into an armed insurrection, and, to stifle any further opposition, the authorities deployed every means possible. These methods included mass arrests, public beatings, live ammunition aimed at unarmed demonstrators or fired blindly into protesting neighbourhoods, torture, kidnappings, often followed by extrajudicial executions with the bodies subsequently found in the main opposition strongholds, and rape committed in households in these same neighbourhoods (UNCAT 2016). This diverse toolbox of brutality, in other words, amounted to a deliberate strategy to create fear and submission, the main targets of which were protestors in the neighbourhoods of Musaga, Nyakabiga, Jabe, Mutakura, Cibitoke and Ngagara, and, to a lesser extent, Kanyosha and Bwiza (see Figure 3). Furthermore, the ruling party also used the unfolding violence to settle scores within its own ranks, blaming the opposition parties for the killings. For example, after a police commissioner in Kamenge was killed in early May, the police spokesperson – once he had deserted and gone into exile – revealed that the assassination had been carried out on the orders of his superiors. Such targeted assassinations may account for the more sporadic instances of violence in the neighbourhoods of Kamenge, Kinama and Buterere together with the occasional shifting of front lines to the periphery or to the interior of these areas. The violence reached its peak on 11 December 2015, when the police and the army effectively locked down the entire metropolitan area. All the protesting districts were surrounded and some of them were besieged by elements of the various armed forces assisted by the Imbonerakure, who engaged in mass killings and mass arrests (Malagardis 2015). The international community now feared the worst (*Le Monde* 2016). In a communiqué published in mid-January 2016, the United Nations High Commissioner for Human Rights expressed concern that '[a]ll the alarm signals, including the increasing ethnic dimension of the crisis, are flashing red' (OHCHR 2016).

Overall, the excessive use of force by police and the Imbonerakure, most often against unarmed demonstrators, was a clear indication that the regime would try to keep the outgoing president in power at all costs. In response, a gradual militarisation of factions within the major opposition parties, facilitated by the presence of former rebel fighters and deserters from within the armed forces, led the protests to take a violent turn. The youth of the neighbourhoods in which confrontations were most intense justified the use of arms by claiming self-defence and the need to protect their local areas from the murderous incursions of the police and the Imbonerakure. Among the protestors who came to support certain neighbourhoods during the demonstrations were FNL ex-combatants, who played an active role in the nocturnal clashes in several of the neighbourhoods involved and assisted in training other youths in the same areas in the use of weapons.[7] Ex-combatants would help in the nightly defence of these neighbourhoods, setting up rotas for patrols and even ambushing the police. The armed groups in these neighbourhoods often consisted of people from outside the area, who came to organise an armed struggle. Some actors from the political opposition also played an active role in the organisation of the armed insurrection, supplying logistics, weapons and ammunition to the protestors. In early 2016, the armed insurrection seemed to have been considerably weakened by the overwhelming force of the regime, and essentially packed up and left for an unknown destination.

Why the capital was the primary site of violence The initial violence was thus mainly enacted by the police forces and the Imbonerakure youth militias. It was only later that this one-sided aggression escalated into an armed confrontation between protestors and security forces in several neighbourhoods of the capital. In general, the violence observed in the months that followed this escalation was mainly limited to the neighbourhoods in which demonstrations against the president's third term had taken place. The violent confrontations affected certain areas adjacent to these neighbourhoods, including Rohero and Bwiza, mainly because of the mobility of some protestors. During this time, the interior of the country was less affected. The rural districts of Mukike, Mugon-gomanga (both in Bujumbura Rural province), Rusaka (Mwaro province) and Mugamba (Bururi province) were the main areas affected by violence (see Figure 1), although not with the same intensity as in the capital. This section analyses the particular geography of violence in the months following the initial protests against Nkurunziza's third term.

Despite the presence of some pockets of protest in certain parts of the Bujumbura Rural province, the capital was the undisputed centre of the demonstrations and, consequently, of the violence that accompanied them. In fact, like most other African capitals, Bujumbura is the main location in which protest against those in power emerges (Raleigh 2015). All available studies on the demands and concerns of the population as reflected in opinion surveys reflect a marked discrepancy in general perceptions between rural and urban areas (Ministry of the Presidency 2008; Afrobarometer 2012; 2014; CENAP 2014). Bujumbura shows greater dissatisfaction on issues related to governance, justice, security and the performance of government authorities and services. As early as May 2008, the diagnostic survey on governance in Burundi (Ministry of the Presidency 2008) revealed very different expectations among the respondent groups. When asked what they perceived to be their main concerns, the surveyed households, predominantly located in rural areas, cited in ascending order of priority increasing unemployment, poverty and access to land, whereas civil servants, entrepreneurs and NGOs, mainly based in the capital, identified insecurity/crime, impunity and corruption. At the end of 2012, an Afrobarometer survey, particularly on attitudes towards democracy, highlighted a marked contrast between the city and the countryside regarding trust in institutions, with urban communities expressing a 20 per cent lower level of satisfaction than people in the countryside. A survey conducted by the same organisation in 2014 (Afrobarometer 2014) showed the same contrasts, notably on the question of the limitation of presidential terms, in answer to which city residents expressed a markedly more pronounced opposition to a third term (82 per cent against in the urban areas compared with 59 per cent in the rural areas). The same survey highlighted city dwellers' much more critical opinions on the level of corruption and the will to combat it. In the same year, an opinion poll conducted by the Conflict Alert and Prevention Centre (CENAP) on perceptions of security needs led to contrasting results on the question of the performance of the Burundi police and of the national intelligence service depending on the respondents' location, the city being once again much less lenient than the countryside (CENAP 2014).

Clearly, the view of city dwellers is generally much more unfavourable towards issues relating to governance. This is due to different factors. First, the level of education of the urban population is significantly higher than in rural areas. Indeed, a large amount of educational and academic infrastructure is concentrated in the capital, whereas access to education outside Bujumbura has always been problematic despite improvements in recent decades. For example, Bujumbura is host to more than 75 per cent of the thirty-three accredited universities and higher institutes in Burundi (Ministry of Higher Education and Scientific Research 2015). Secondly, the greater part of the civil service, state-owned enterprises, the private sector, services and businesses, NGOs, the UN system and all the embassies are concentrated in the capital. As a result, the vast majority of highly educated people are based in Bujumbura. Put simply, the capital concentrates access to knowledge, and these demographics are more likely to be critical of a government that is condemned for its corrupt practices, its authoritarianism and its poor economic performance. In addition, as the centre of all major opinion makers, including political parties as well as civil society, the capital is also the centre of activity for these actors in terms of public involvement and outreach. The urban population is thus more immediately able to access the discourses of political leaders and other critical voices, who in turn tend to adapt their messages to appeal to this particular segment of the population. The relative success of the political opposition party Movement for Solidarity and Development (MSD) is a case in point.[8]

Moreover, independent media – radios in particular – are popular in Bujumbura and have contributed to an increased awareness of civic rights and have encouraged urban populations to take a more critical look at the public authorities in view of the numerous human rights abuses and economic embezzlement reported by the press. Increased access to the internet and the availability of international television channels in the capital and the consequent access to images of developments elsewhere in the world have also contributed to the outlook of many urbanites. In particular, news of popular revolts against autocracies elsewhere on the continent inspired a belief among urban youths that the mobilisation in the streets of Burundi could lead to similar changes (RFI 2015). For example, it is clear that civil society movements such as the *Balai Citoyen* (literally 'Citizen Broom') movement in Burkina Faso had some influence on the winds of protest that blew over Bujumbura. Similarly, the strong presence of civil society organisations in the capital – namely, those working in the fields of governance and human rights – also encouraged this civic awareness and culture, particularly through campaigns for the protection and promotion of rights and liberties.[9] These factors were emphasised by a young protestor interviewed by Radio France Internationale (RFI):

> In fact, young people have woken up because democracy has started to be practised a little, because there are civil societies, there is the media, there

is all this that raises young people's awareness. They try to show them how they can defend their rights peacefully. That's what is happening right here. (RFI 2015)

For all these reasons, Bujumbura had been the main stronghold of the opposition for several years prior to the 2015 elections, as evidenced by the results obtained by the opposition in the capital during the 2010 municipal elections (see Figure 4). Although the CNDD-FDD won the elections with 28 per cent of the votes, this victory was primarily the result of a divided opposition, with six opposition parties (if UPRONA is included, as its electoral base is opposed to the ruling party) sharing more than 69 per cent of the vote. Compared with the national results, in which the CNDD-FDD carried 64 per cent of the vote (see Figure 2), Bujumbura was clearly far less favourable to the ruling party.

Following the 2010 elections, the attitude of the authorities towards the population of the capital became markedly apprehensive. Many young people in Bujumbura were increasingly appalled by the personalisation of power and the cases of embezzlement and misappropriation by a small group at the head of government, as reported by the media, in an environment characterised by widespread corruption, clientelism and nepotism.[10] Moreover, favouritism shown towards members of the CNDD-FDD for access to employment and even certain basic services, together with discrimination against members and alleged supporters of the opposition, created a sense of exclusion felt by the majority of young people in the capital. In this regard, the measures taken in Bujumbura by the National Commission on Land and Other Assets (CNTB), an institution perceived as being controlled by the ruling party, to systematically dispossess owners of houses whose ownership was claimed by former refugees, regardless of how that ownership was acquired, also contributed to turning a large part of the youth in the neighbourhoods affected by these measures against the government.[11] Notably, the case of Justin Nyakabeto and his family, who were evicted from their house in Ngagara, lead to the arrest and conviction of ten youths who were part of the group of protestors who rallied to oppose these measures (Reyntjens, Vandeginste and Verpoorten 2015). The government's neopatrimonial practices and the feelings of exclusion and marginalisation among the young people from the protesting neighbourhoods coupled with their increased civic awareness and, in many cases, their politicisation were decisive factors in the capital's strong mobilisation against the president's third term, which was seen as tantamount to keeping the CNDD-FDD in power.

By comparing Figures 3 and 4, one can see that the neighbourhoods in which demonstrations were mobilised during the 2015 protests – most importantly Cibitoke (which included Mutakura), Musaga, Ngagara and Nyakabiga – voted for the opposition by a very large majority in 2010. The MSD opposition party, in fact, was the leading party in all these neighbourhoods (*Le Visionnaire* 2010). The dominance of the opposition parties, and particularly the MSD, in these areas greatly influenced the mapping of the 2015 protests and hence their geography of violence.

The identity factor also played a role in the protests. The decisions of the CNTB essentially favoured former Hutu refugees at the expense of Tutsi families. This policy resulted in a sense of victimisation among many Tutsi, in a context where the minority ethnic group already felt that they were discriminated against (Afrobarometer 2012). Indeed, despite the easing of the ethnic divide in Burundian society, the concerns of the Tutsi community increased during Nkurunziza's second term for the reasons mentioned above. In addition, another important element in the mobilisation of Tutsi youth was the often expressed willingness of some CNDD-FDD officials to challenge some of the achievements of the Arusha Agreement, including ethnic quotas, which had been perceived as a guarantee of the collective security of the Tutsi, at the very least with regard to the equal representation in the defence and police forces. Finally, the increasingly radical discourse of certain leaders in the ruling party on the ethnic issue and the Imbonerakure's threatening (albeit indirect) slogans against the Tutsi minority during demonstrations were also factors that contributed to a rising awareness among Tutsi urbanites of the dangers that they could face if President Nkurunziza remained in power.

The main centres of protest and violence in Bujumbura were neighbourhoods with a large population of young people with low incomes. Musaga, Nyakabiga, Cibitoke, Mutakura, Ngagara and Jabe were all home to civil servants and workers from the private and informal sectors.[12] Poverty was undoubtedly another factor behind the mobilisation, since the living conditions of people in these neighbourhoods had not improved during the CNDD-FDD's decade in power; in fact, conditions deteriorated for most of the inhabitants in these neighbourhoods.[13] Not only were these populations poor, but the young people in these neighbourhoods often lacked employment opportunities.

Unemployment, underemployment and, above all, the lack of prospects for young people were major sources of frustration for the people of the protesting neighbourhoods. When they were employed, they tended to have precarious jobs that did not correspond to their level of qualification and for which they received inadequate wages that hardly covered their basic needs. A survey conducted on households' living conditions in 2013–14 put the unemployment rate in urban areas at 14.7 per cent (ISTEEBU 2015). The same survey highlighted that, in the city, 30.1 per cent of respondents who were declared active were in fact underemployed. Young people from the northern neighbourhoods of Bujumbura interviewed during a focus group, mostly students and youths in search of employment, said that most young people in their respective neighbourhoods were unemployed. Poverty and unemployment,

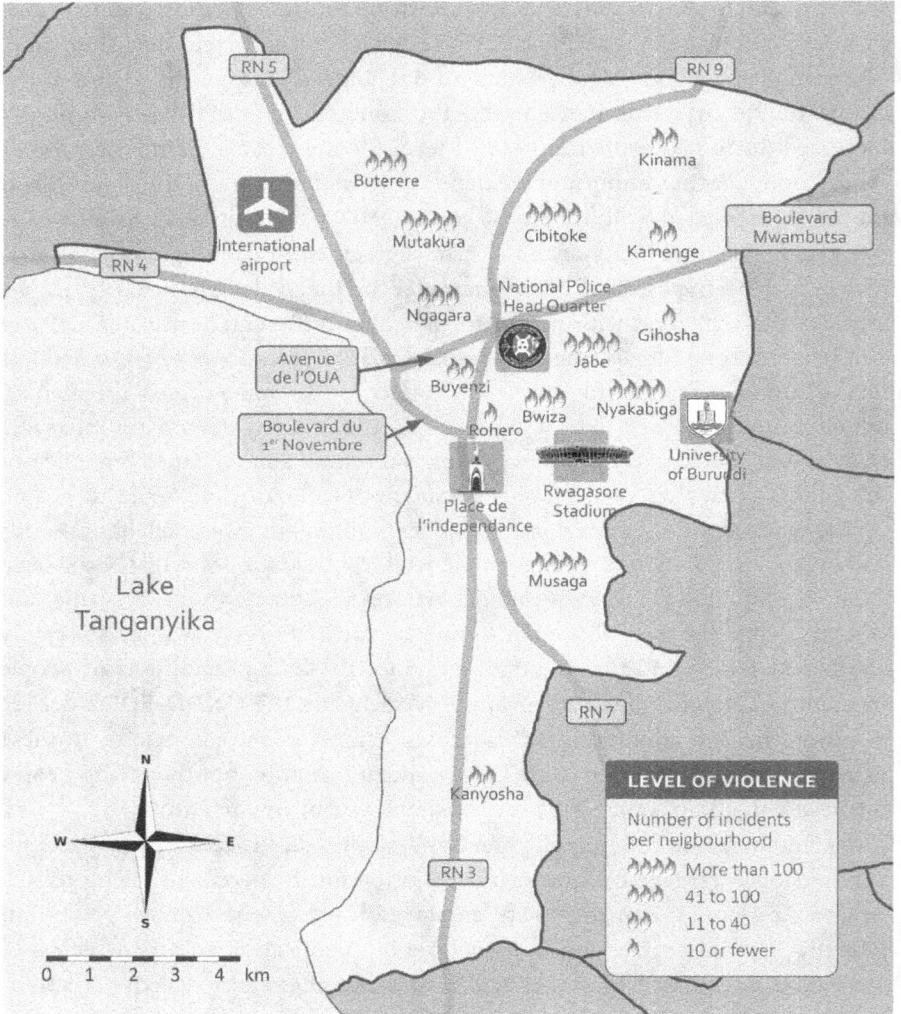

Figure 3: Distribution of violent incidents within Bujumbura city, April–November 2015
Map by Henrik Alfredsson, based on data provided by ACLED.

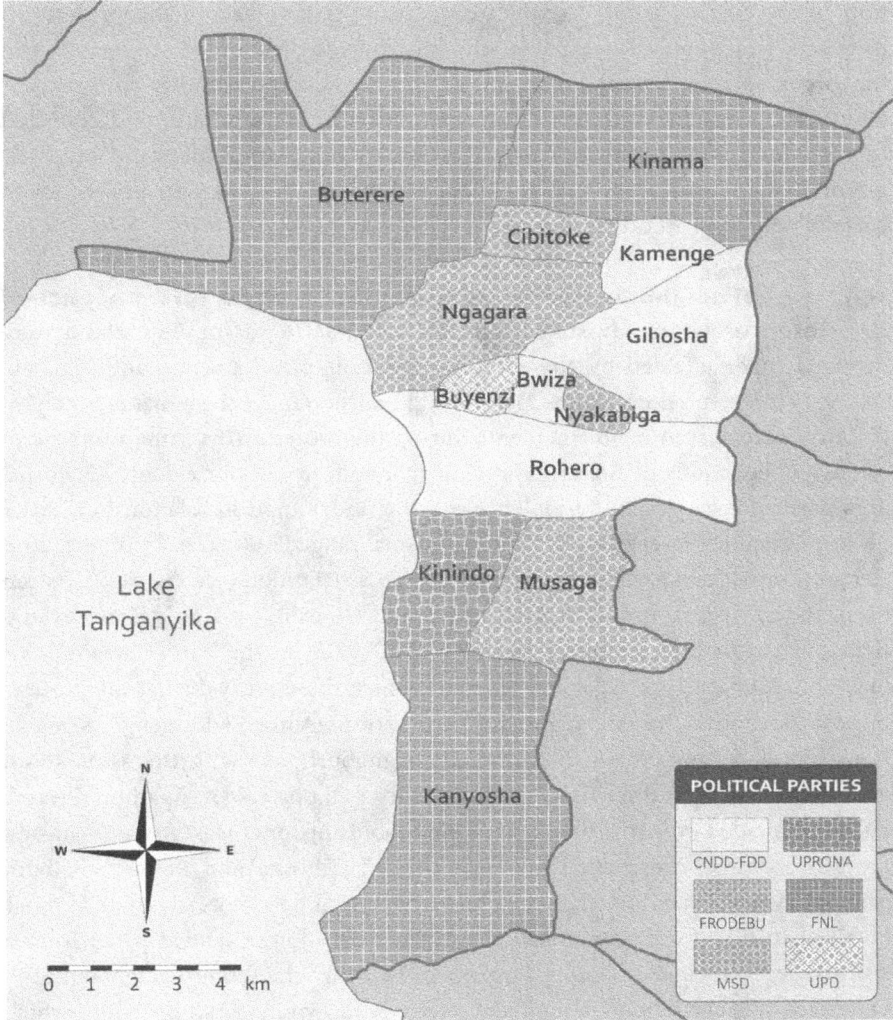

Figure 4: Distribution of votes in 2010 municipal elections, Bujumbura city. Map by Henrik Alfredsson, based on results announced by the National Independent Electoral Commission (CENI).

therefore, were decisive factors in the protests (see also Donovan-Smith and Ndayisaba 2015; Morice 2015).

To all the aforementioned motivating factors must be added the gains obtained or sought by a segment of the protestors. The mobilisation against Nkurunziza's third term was financially supported by many Burundians from the interior and the diaspora. Funds collected were allocated at the discretion of the donors to civil society organisations involved in the protests or to officials of opposition parties who themselves distributed these funds to the organisers of the demonstrations in the neighbourhoods concerned.[14] Obviously, these funds and the various items that were bought and collected (drinks, food, mobile charge cards, etc.) were a motivation for some, but their unfair distribution or mismanagement led to tensions among protestors in certain neighbourhoods.[15]

Why some neighbourhoods of Bujumbura were left untouched by violence As already stated, not all neighbourhoods of Bujumbura were involved in or affected by the protests. For example, Kamenge and Kinama, two very poor, predominantly Hutu, neighbourhoods in the northern part of the city, were spared major incidents during the protests. The same was true of the neighbourhoods of Rohero and Gihosha, and, to a lesser extent, Kanyosha. This particular geography of violence may be understood in relation to a series of demographic observations. Firstly, the mapping of the results of the 2010 elections provides a partial explanation for this distribution (see Figure 4). As can be seen, the neighbourhoods of Kamenge and Gihosha, and, to a lesser extent, Bwiza, voted in high numbers for the CNDD-FDD in the 2010 elections; this may be a primary reason for the relative calm in these areas during the protests in 2015. Secondly, the menacing Imbonerakure presence in Kamenge, Kinama, Kanyosha and Buterere – which are all neighbourhoods with the same social and ethnic configuration, and predominantly supporters of Agathon Rwasa's FNL – dissuaded potential dissidents from mobilising, or at least from organising protests within those particular areas. Thirdly, Gihosha and Rohero are both principally upper-middle-class neighbourhoods, and, as already stated, those involved in direct confrontations with the security forces tended to be from a less privileged socio-economic background. Fourthly, the Rohero neighbourhood has a generally ageing population, and relatively few young adult residents, which may account for the lack of mobilisation in that area. Finally, Kamenge is the neighbourhood where the armed conflict began in 1993–94 and is therefore considered to be the historical stronghold of the CNDD-FDD insurrection. Also, many members of the defence and police forces from the former insurrection live there. These historical ties may explain the reluctance of Kamenge residents to mobilise against the regime.

In addition to these dissuasive factors, the central location of the neighbourhood of Rohero, which includes most of the city centre, may have provided a major incentive for protests to be focused there. The protestors seem to have been acutely aware of the importance of achieving visibility, in part to emulate the successful mobilisations in Burkina Faso and Senegal in recent years. Furthermore, protestors were obviously not limited to mobilising in their own neighbourhoods. For example, it appears that Kinama residents were also active in Mutakura and Cibitoke, while people from Kanyosha went to support the neighbouring area of Musaga. Buterere joined the protest movement late or supported other protesting neighbourhoods such as Ngagara. This mobility of protestors across neighbourhoods essentially served to reinforce Bujumbura's geography of violence. Security forces focused their operations on neighbourhoods known to be critical of the regime, and, in response, protestors from other areas rallied to these zones of confrontation.

These micro-dynamics of popular mobilisation may account for a neighbourhood such as Buyenzi, which displayed voting patterns similar to those in the centres of confrontation in the city, being spared the large-scale violence of other areas. Its activist residents may have mobilised initially in other parts of the city, postponing the area's more direct involvement in the protests to a later stage when the conflict was already transitioning into a more militarised confrontation. In addition, Buyenzi's population is predominantly from the Muslim minority, which historically has taken a less confrontational role in relation to state authority. This is evident in the fact that Buyenzi was one of the few neighbourhoods spared interethnic violence in the 1990s.

Why violence in the provinces was limited to specific districts
From the beginning of the crisis, the situation in Burundi's interior regions was much more difficult to assess than in the capital. To observers in the capital as well as to those following the unfolding of events from outside the country, this was primarily due to the restricted media access outside Bujumbura, including the shutting down of the country's main radio stations, and the limited access to the interior for NGOs and international human rights organisations. These measures seem to have been reinforced deliberately by the authorities to hinder communications between actors in the capital and the interior, in order to limit the expansion of the protest movement to other parts of the country. In this regard, Human Rights Watch's press release of 27 July 2016 on the systematic sexual abuse of relatives of alleged opponents in the interior, committed by the Imbonerakure, revealed a reality that had previously been unknown to external observers (Human Rights Watch 2016).

Despite the official rhetoric insisting that protests and violence were confined to a few Tutsi neighbourhoods in Bujumbura, there were opposition mobilisations in most of the provinces, but these were quickly suppressed.

Ultimately, only a few rural municipalities, mainly located in the provinces of Bujumbura Rural, Bururi and Mwaro, could maintain the demonstrations and expose themselves to the violence of the police and the Imbonerakure. Apart from Bujumbura City, protests were observed in the following provinces: Bujumbura Rural, Bururi, Cankuzo, Cibitoke, Gitega, Kirundo, Makamba, Muramvya, Muyinga, Mwaro, Ngozi, Rumonge and Rutana. Only the provinces of Bubanza, Karuzi, Kayanza[16] and Ruyigi were left untouched. In the provinces listed, reports mainly located protests in the provincial centres, although rural municipalities were affected in several provinces (most notably Bujumbura Rural, Bururi, Gitega, Muramvya, Mwaro, Ngozi and Rumonge).

The protests in the provinces primarily occurred in rural municipalities where the opposition had achieved significant results in the 2010 municipal elections. In these districts, the MSD tended to be the largest party, with UPRONA and the FNL recording significant results as well. The CNDD-FDD generally performed poorly in these particular districts. Furthermore, the districts where protests were mobilised often had a relatively low presence of Imbonerakure militia. The violence outside the capital was therefore mainly limited to the provinces of Bururi, Bujumbura Rural and Mwaro, and political allegiance seems to have been one of the determining factors in this geography of violence.

In its attempts to deliberately ethnicise the crisis, the government has often argued that, even in rural areas, only the municipalities with a Tutsi majority were affected by the protests. This argument is partially true in that several of the protesting rural municipalities do have a large Tutsi population. The protesters in Bururi, Bujumbura Rural and Mwaro, often young people with a relatively high level of education, were undoubtedly sympathetic to the more targeted calls for action from civil society organisations: for instance, for the liberation of imprisoned human rights activists, against high prices, and against corruption. One would expect that this tendency may have been nourished by the fears aroused by the ethnic rhetoric of a government caught up in the same radical ethnic ideology that had characterised the CNDD-FDD as a military movement (Nindorera 2012). To this must be added the frustration felt in some provinces marginalised by the government because of their presumed association with the Tutsi elites of the past, among these primarily the province of Bururi, which had been the heart of power under the Tutsi military regimes. Moreover, several of the most active personalities in the 'Stop the Third Term' campaign came from some of these municipalities and wielded greater influence there because of their social networks (family, neighbourhood, etc.). Finally, it appears that one or more of the armed groups that mobilised when the opposition became more militarised retreated to these particular provinces, or at least used them as a support base. This was undoubtedly in line with the dual strategy of choosing a field of operation, primarily in certain rural municipalities of Bururi and Bujumbura Rural, that the police had difficulty accessing because of its steep terrain combined with the presence of a politically favourable environment.

The protests also extended to rural municipalities with a large Hutu majority loyal to the FNL, such as Kanyosha Rural and Nyabiraba, south of the capital where the presence of armed men had been reported for some time. Finally, the local branches of various civil society organisations involved in the campaign against the third term were active in mobilising protests in the provinces.[17]

A final factor related to the protests in the provinces was the closure of the University of Burundi. Most of the university's faculties and campuses are located near the Nyakabiga area in the capital. The university has more than 13,000 students,[18] although it can accommodate less than a third of this number on its campuses; the great majority of students have to find their own accommodation, and they often reside in modest neighbourhoods such as Nyakabiga, which has the advantage of being close by. During the first days of the demonstrations, many students went to show their support for the protestors in areas including Nyakabiga. To put an end to the student protests, the authorities immediately closed the university and expelled the students from the campus, thus forcing them to return to their homes in the provinces. In several localities in the interior of the country, demonstrations were subsequently fuelled in part by the students who had been expelled from their university and who, as a result, became idle and frustrated with the government.[19]

Conclusion

This chapter has analysed the historical and socio-political dynamics that informed the uneven distribution of violence in Burundi's 2015 elections. Through this prism, the chapter has explored the incentives of the main actors involved in the popular mobilisation against Pierre Nkurunziza's candidacy for a third term, as well as the motivations behind the brutal reprisals against these public protests. We have considered the links between the Imbonerakure youth movement, the national police forces, and the ruling CNDD-FDD, which were central to the state response to what were initially peaceful protests. The chapter thereby suggests that state violence was deployed by the Nkurunziza regime as part of a deliberate strategy to consolidate power and silence its opponents.

The violence linked to the elections in 2015 did not have a major impact on the living conditions of the people in the localities in the interior of the country who joined the wave of protest from time to time, as their repression was not as vigorous or as constant as in Bujumbura City. It was mainly the Musaga, Jabe, Nyakabiga, Cibitoke, Mutakura and Ngagara neighbourhoods that paid a price for the crisis and that recorded the greatest number of victims. The thousands of people who have been incarcerated in the prisons of Burundi since then are mostly young people from these locations. These areas saw the departure into exile of many young people and were virtually emptied of families, who preferred to settle in districts that were less exposed to police repression or to flee to the interior of the country, or to either Rwanda or Tanzania, which have received up to 85,000 and 250,000 Burundian refugees respectively (UNHCR 2017). The crisis also had an impact on the economic activity of these neighbourhoods, as many businesses had to close.

Residents of the protesting neighbourhoods first experienced police violence coupled with deprivation and harassment inflicted upon them by young demonstrators, as, for example, people were prohibited from going to work or pressured to take part in compulsory nocturnal security rounds. They subsequently experienced arbitrary arrests, kidnappings and ill-treatment by the police and the Imbonerakure before being subjected to killings and summary executions, which sometimes targeted entire families (Deutsche Welle 2015); the obvious aim of this was to create a climate of terror in these particular neighbourhoods. Beyond the visible effects of the crisis on these localities, other equally serious consequences have been less perceptible. These areas have lived – and, for some, continue to live – in a climate of fear and terror, with the police still making regular arrests. Therefore, it is difficult to assess the psychological consequences of the suffering endured by these populations.

The protests and the violent response from the Burundian security forces were mainly fuelled by a combination of political, identity, socio-economic and socio-demographic factors. Bujumbura is the main stronghold of the opposition because it concentrates the country's intellectual elite, reluctant to adapt to an authoritarian power characterised by poor governance and poor economic performance. It is also a locus for political opposition because of its large population of young people, most of whom are unemployed or underemployed and hence have uncertain prospects for the future. Living under precarious living conditions with many frustrations, these young people were more sympathetic to the mobilisation speeches of the campaign against the president's third term. To some extent, these urban youths were exploited by some of the political formations of the opposition and by part of civil society involved in the 'Stop the Third Term' campaign in their efforts to prevent President Nkurunziza's candidacy. These protests, perceived by the authorities as being essentially a Tutsi uprising with ulterior motives, resulted in the violent retaliation of the defence and police forces, which subsequently led to the emergence of an armed insurrection.

The causes of the election-related violence in Burundi in 2015 are charac-teristic of the crises affecting other African countries confronted with electoral processes and where the demands of a large part of the population contrast with the policies of governments obsessed with their own political survival and that resort to force and manipulation to maintain their positions (Höglund 2009). Unfortunately, the impotence and inability of African and international organisations to manage these conflicts tend to perpetuate and multiply these crises. The consolidation of democracy in Africa will be severely tested for a long time to come in the absence of a more sustained will and determination to prevent and/or stem crises and electoral violence, and without better coordination and coherence in the actions and initiatives of African regional organisations and the various international actors.

Inspired by the overall theme of this volume, it will be important to analyse further the micro-politics of electoral violence in Burundi; this could lead, for example, to better understandings of the impacts of local grievances (cf. Kalyvas 2003) on the geography of violence, and of the inner workings of the networks and hierarchies of power and patronage within the Nkurunziza regime. This call for further research seems particularly urgent as the prospects for sustainable peace and political stability in Burundi continue to deteriorate at the time of writing. In the transition from post-electoral violence to outright authoritarianism, the factors underlying Burundi's geography of violence considered here may prove to be a central component in the 'joint production' of continued political violence (Kalyvas 2003: 476; cf. Söderberg Kovacs, Introduction in this volume). Tragically, in the Burundian case, elections have indeed become the new battlegrounds, as Bøås and Utas (2014) have phrased it, and in a most acute sense.

Notes

1 *'Imbonerakure'* (literally 'those who see far' in Kirundi) is the official name of the ruling CNDD-FDD party's youth wing. Segments of this broad civilian organisation have been given military training and mobilised as militias. In this text, we primarily use the term 'Imbonerakure' to signify the youth militias active prior to and during the protests in April 2015 and during their aftermath.

2 The agreement is available at https://peaceaccords.nd.edu/accord/arusha-peace-and-reconciliation-agreement-burundi.

3 The 2005 constitution is available at www.assemblee.bi/Constitution-de-la-Republique-du.

4 They received 57 per cent of the votes in the municipal elections that determine the composition of the Senate and 58 per cent of the votes in the legislative elections.

5 'Militia units' is the categorisation accorded to the armed Imbonerakure groups by the United Nations (OHCHR 2015).

6 A majority of four-fifths of the votes is required to approve an amendment to the constitution.

7 Focus group with youths from neighbourhoods in the north of Bujumbura, June 2015.

8 Interview with the political scientist Jean-Salathiel Muntunutwiwe, professor at the University of Burundi, November 2015.

9 Focus group with youths from neighbourhoods in the north of Bujumbura, May 2015.

10 Focus group with youths from neighbourhoods in the north of Bujumbura, May 2015.

11 Ibid.

12 The 2014 Afrobarometer survey reveals that in the urban populations

surveyed, 76 per cent of respondents saw the economic situation of the country as 'bad' and 47 per cent as 'very bad'; 57 per cent of respondents described their living conditions as 'bad' compared with 11 per cent 'good', while 29 per cent did not want to express their opinion on this issue (Afrobarometer 2014).

13 Of the urban population questioned in the 2014 Afrobarometer survey, 72 per cent were of the opinion that their living conditions were worse than in the previous year (Afrobarometer 2014).

14 Interviews with civil society leaders in Bujumbura, May–November 2015.

15 Focus group with youths from neighbourhoods in the north of Bujumbura, May 2015.

16 At the beginning of July 2015, Kayanza experienced brief clashes between an armed group, which was quickly neutralised, and the police.

17 Interviews with civil society leaders in Bujumbura, May–November 2015.

18 The total of 13,000 students is stated on the University of Burundi website (www.ub.edu.bi/).

19 Focus group with youths from neighbourhoods in the north of Bujumbura, May 2015.

References

Afrobarometer (2012) 'Survey Overview: The Quality of Democracy and Governance in Burundi'. Round 5. Compiled by Groupe de recherche et d'appui au développement des initiatives démocratiques (GRADIS) and the Institute for Development Studies (IDS), University of Nairobi. Available at http://afrobarometer.org/sites/default/files/publications/Summary%20of%20results/bdi_r5_sor_en.pdf.

Afrobarometer (2014) 'Résumé des Résultats, 6ème Tour de l'Afrobaromètre Enquête au Burundi, 2014'. Compiled by Groupe de recherche et d'appui au développement des initiatives démocratiques (GRADIS).

Arnould, V., A. Tor and A. Vervaeke (2016) 'Africa Uprising? The Protests, the Drivers, and the Outcomes'. Brief 33. Paris: European Union Institute for Security Studies (EUISS). Available at www.iss.europa.eu/publications/detail/article/africa-uprising-theprotests-the-drivers-the-outcomes/.

Ba, M. and N. Muhorakeye (2015) 'Burundi: Appels à la haine et ultimatum à hauts risque', Jeune Afrique, 6 November. Available at www.jeuneafrique.com/277636/politique/burundi-appels-a-la-haine-et-ultimatum-a-hauts-risques/.

Ben Hammouda, H. (1995) Burundi: Histoire économique et politique d'un conflit. Paris: Éditions l'Harmattan.

Bensimon, C. (2015) 'Crainte de violences au Burundi après le discours du président', Le Monde Afrique, 6 November. Available at www.lemonde.fr/afrique/article/2015/11/06/crainte-de-violences-au-burundi-apres-le-discours-du-president_4804870_3212.html.

Bøås, M. and M. Utas (2014) 'The Political Landscape of Postwar Liberia: Reflections on National Reconciliation and Elections', Africa Today 60 (4): 47–65.

Branch, A. and Z. Mampilly (2015) Africa Uprising: Popular Protest and Political Change. London: Zed Books.

Burihabwa, N. Z. (2017) 'Continuity and Contingency: The CNDD-FDD and its Transformation from Rebel Movement to Governing Political Party in Burundi'. PhD thesis, University of Antwerp.

CENAP (2014) 'Study on Security Needs in Burundi. Study Commissioned by the Office of the Ombudsman of Burundi'. Bujumbura: Conflict Alert and Prevention Centre (CENAP).

Deutsche Welle (2015) 'Des civils exécutés par la police au Burundi', Deutsche Welle, 14 October. Available at www.dw.com/fr/des-civils-ex%C3%A9cut%C3%A9s-par-la-police-au-burundi/a-18780117.

Donovan-Smith, O. and O. Ndayisaba (2015) 'La pauvreté et le chômage nourrissent le mécontentement populaire', *Equal Times*, 7 May. Available at www.equaltimes.org/la-pauvrete-et-le-chomage?lang=en#.Wdd35EoUmUk.

Goldsmith, A. (2015) 'Elections and Civil Violence in New Multiparty Regimes: Evidence from Africa', *Journal of Peace Research* 52 (5): 607–21.

Höglund, K. (2009) 'Electoral Violence in Conflict-ridden Societies: Concepts, Causes, and Consequences', *Terrorism and Political Violence* 21 (3): 412–27.

Human Rights Watch (2010) '"We'll Tie You Up and Shoot You": Lack of Accountability for Political Violence in Burundi'. New York NY: Human Rights Watch. Available at www.hrw.org/report/2010/05/14/well-tie-you-and-shoot-you/lack-accountability-political-violence-burundi.

Human Rights Watch (2016) 'Burundi: Gang Rapes by Ruling Party Youth: Attacks by Members of Youth League, Police on Relatives of Perceived Opponents'. New York NY: Human Rights Watch. Available at www.hrw.org/news/2016/07/27/burundi-gang-rapes-ruling-party-youth.

ICG (2005) 'Elections in Burundi: A Radical Shake-up of the Political Landscape'. Briefing 31/Africa. Brussels: International Crisis Group (ICG).

ICG (2010) 'Burundi: Ensuring Credible Elections'. Report 155/Africa. Brussels: International Crisis Group (ICG).

ICG (2016) 'Burundi: A Dangerous Third Term'. Report 235/Africa. Brussels: International Crisis Group (ICG).

Impunity Watch (2015) 'Burundi: Citizenship in Crisis', *Great Lakes Dispatches* 1 (August).

ISTEEBU (2015) 'Burundi: Profil et déterminants de la pauvreté. Rapport de l'enquête modulaire sur les conditions de vie des ménages 2013/2014'. Bujumbura: National Institute of Statistics and Economic Research of Burundi (ISTEEBU), African Development Bank Group.

Kalyvas, S. N. (2003) 'The Ontology of "Political Violence": Action and Identity in Civil Wars', *Perspectives on Politics* 1 (3): 475–94.

Le Monde (2016) 'Risques de génocide au Burundi selon l'ONU', *Le Monde*, 20 January. Available at www.lemonde.fr/afrique/video/2016/01/20/risque-de-genocide-au-burundi-selon-l-onu_4850494_3212.html.

Le Visionnaire (2010) 'Proclamation des résultats provisoires des communales dans la Mairie de Bujumbura', *Le Visionnaire*, 27 May. Available at http://levisionnaire-infos.blogspot.se/2010/05/proclamation-des-resultats-provisoires.html.

Madirisha, E. (2015) 'Marche de la paix ou campagne du Cndd-Fdd?', *Iwacu*, 31 March. Available at www.iwacu-burundi.org/marche-de-la-paix-ou-campagne-du-cndd-fdd/.

Malagardis, M. (2015) 'Au Burundi, des massacres à huis clos', *Libération*, 13 December. Available at www.liberation.fr/planete/2015/12/13/au-burundi-des-massacres-a-huis-clos_1420446.

McAdam, D. and S. Tarrow (2010) 'Ballots and Barricades: On the Reciprocal Relationship Between Elections and Social Movements', *Perspectives on Politics* 8 (2): 529–42.

Ministry of Higher Education and Scientific Research (2015) *Directory of Higher Institutions of Public and Private Education*. Bujumbura: Ministry of Higher Education and Scientific Research.

Ministry of the Presidency (2008) 'Etude diagnostique sur la gouvernance et la corruption au Burundi; Rapport d'enquête Ministère à la Présidence chargé de la bonne gouvernance, de la privatisation, de l'inspection générale de l'état et de l'administration locale'. Bujumbura: Ministry of the Presidency.

Morice, F. (2015) 'La crise burundaise renvoie à des frustrations économiques, sociales et politiques', Radio France Internationale, 11 June. Available at www.rfi.fr/afrique/20150611-crise-burundi-frustrations-economiques-politiques-guichaoua-nkurunziza.

Ngayimpenda, E. (1998) *Histoire du conflit politico-ethnique: Les premières marches du calvaire (1960–1973)*. Bujumbura: Les Éditions de la Renaissance.

Nimubona, J. (2004) 'La perception de l'identité ethnique dans le processus électoral au Burundi'. Kigali: Ligue des droits de la personne dans la région des grands lacs (LDGL).

Nindorera, W. (2012) 'Le CNDD-FDD au Burundi: Le cheminement de la lutte armée au combat politique'. Berghof Transitions Series 10. Berlin: Berghof Foundation.

OHCHR (2015) 'Increased Militia Violence "Could Tip Burundi Over the Edge" – Zeid', United Nations High Commissioner for Human Rights, 9 June. Available at www.ohchr.org/EN/NewsEvents/Pages/DisplayNews.aspx?NewsID=16059&LangID=E.

OHCHR (2016) 'Alarming New Patterns of Violations Emerging in Burundi – Zeid', United Nations High Commissioner for Human Rights, 15 January. Available at www.ohchr.org/EN/NewsEvents/Pages/DisplayNews.aspx?NewsID=16953.

Raleigh, C. (2015) 'Urban Violence Patterns across African States', *International Studies Review* 17: 90–106.

Reilly, B. (2011) *Democracy in Divided Societies: Electoral Engineering for Conflict Management*. Cambridge: Cambridge University Press.

Reyntjens, F., S. Vandeginste and M. Verpoorten (eds) (2015) *Annuaire de l'Afrique des Grands Lacs (2013–14)*. Paris: Éditions l'Harmattan.

Reyntjens, F., S. Vandeginste and M. Verpoorten (eds) (2016) *Annuaire de l'Afrique des Grands Lacs (2014–15)*. Paris: Éditions l'Harmattan.

RFI (2015) 'Burundi: Une contestation qui se construit dans la rue', Radio France Internationale (RFI), 29 April. Available at www.rfi.fr/afrique/20150429-burundi-contestation-troisieme-mandat-pierre-nkurunziza-construit-rue-jeunesse-oppo.

Rufyikiri, G. (2016) 'Echec de la transformation du CNDD-FDD en parti politique au Burundi: une question d'équilibre entre le changement et la continuité'. Working Paper 2016.12. Antwerp: Institute of Development Policy and Management, University of Antwerp.

Schedler, A. (ed.) (2006) *Electoral Authoritarianism: The Dynamics of Unfree Competition*. Boulder CO: Lynne Rienner.

Schedler, A. (2013) *The Politics of Uncertainty: Sustaining and Subverting Electoral Authoritarianism*. Oxford: Oxford University Press.

Söderberg Kovacs, M. and S. Hatz (2016) 'Rebel-to-Party Transformations in Civil War Peace Processes 1975–2011', *Democratization* 23 (6): 990–1008.

Taylor, C., J. Pevehouse and S. Straus (2013) 'Perils of Pluralism: Electoral Violence and Competitive Authoritarianism in Sub-Saharan Africa'. Simon Papers in Security and Development 23/2013. Vancouver: School for International Studies.

Themnér, A. (2017) *Warlord Democrats in Africa: Ex-military Leaders and Electoral Politics*. London and New York NY: Zed Books.

UN Security Council (2011) 'Report of the Secretary-General on the United Nations Office in Burundi'. Secretary's General Report S/2011/751. New York NY: United Nations.

UNCAT (2016) 'Concluding Observations of the Committee on the Special Report of Burundi Requested under Article 19 (1) in Fine of the Convention'. CAT/C/BDI/CO/2/

Add.1. New York NY: United Nations Committee against Torture (UNCAT). Available at http://tbinternet.ohchr. org/_layouts/treatybodyexternal/ Download.aspx?symbolno=CAT/C/ BDI/CO/2/Add.1&Lang=Fr.

UNDP and MFPDE (2014) *Rapport sur le développement humain 2013 au Burundi: 'Croissance économique, promotion des innovations et emploi des jeunes'*. Bujumbura: United Nations Development Programme (UNDP) and Burundian Ministry of Finance and Planning of Economic Development (MFPDE). Available at www.bi.undp.org/content/dam/ burundi/docs/publications/Povred/ NHDR_2013_Burundi_Web.pdf.

UNHCR (2017) 'Burundi Situation 2017. Supplementary Appeal January–December 2017'. Geneva: United Nations High Commissioner for Refugees (UNHCR). Available at www. unhcr.org/59244aa77.pdf.

5|Competition, uncertainty and violence in Sierra Leone's swing district

Ibrahim Bangura and Mimmi Söderberg Kovacs

Introduction

At the end of December 2015, a parliamentary by-election was held in one of the eight constituencies in the eastern district of Kono in Sierra Leone. Two candidates from the dominant political parties in the country – the incumbent All People's Congress (APC) and the opposition Sierra Leone People's Party (SLPP) – campaigned for the seat. During the final campaign days, both parties sent well-known national political figures from the capital Freetown to the constituency to demonstrate support for their local party candidate. In both cases, their convoys were accompanied by a large number of supporters. The process soon turned violent, with clashes between stone-throwing youth. The ensuing riot – in which a vehicle belonging to a deputy minister was burnt out and several people sent to hospital – prompted President Ernest Bai Koroma to issue a decree for the deployment of the national army to assist the police in quelling the violence (*Sierra Leone Telegraph* 2015; *Patriotic Vanguard* 2015).

The incident is not unusual. Since the beginning of party politics in Sierra Leone in the early 1950s, elections in Kono have seen higher levels of electoral violence than most other districts in the country.[1] Such violence has ranged from attacks on both political candidates and voters to the destruction of property including houses, vehicles and offices of rival parties and their representatives, and the disruption of campaign rallies and meetings. Why is it that a local parliamentary by-election of seemingly limited political value far away from the capital would warrant the presence of national politicians and generate such tension, violence and destruction? The purpose of this chapter is to address this puzzle. More precisely, we ask the following research question: why are elections in Kono District more likely to be accompanied by election-related violence compared with other areas in the country?

We argue that the answer is to be found in the district's unique role as an electoral swing district. In a country strongly governed by an overlapping ethnic and regional divide that splits the country into two almost equally sized voting strongholds, Kono is both ethnically diversified and cosmopolitan in character. Its electorate may swing in either direction, thereby potentially determining the outcome of national elections. This raises the stakes of all elections in the area, including local by-elections in between the general elections, and renders Kono a highly courted district by all political parties. In their efforts to gain the upper hand in electoral contests, both national and local politicians resort to a wide range of violent or coercive strategies for the purpose of both mobilising voters and preventing potential supporters of other parties from casting their votes in favour of the competition. However, in order to carry out and implement such strategies on the ground, the political elite need to enter into precarious relationships with local actors – notably local chiefs and local youth gangs – who in turn are dependent on political connections to gain access to resources and maintain their own power platforms. In this way, national and local interests collide in the establishment of mutually dependent relationships that together contribute to the specific character of violence around elections in Kono.

This chapter primarily draws on findings from interviews and focus group discussions carried out in Kono and Freetown between December 2015 and November 2016. We begin with a short discussion of the theoretical literature pertaining to swing states and electoral violence, particularly in the African context. This is followed by an overview of political dynamics in Sierra Leone, with focus on trends of electoral violence at the national level. Against this background, Kono as a swing district is analysed from a historical perspective, and the various and plentiful manifestations of electoral violence at the local level are described in greater detail. We consider violent dynamics around the general elections, but also violence in between elections and intra-party electoral violence. In order to better understand the linkages between national-level competition and violent dynamics at the local level, we dicuss the mutually dependent relations between political elites, traditional chiefs and youth, particularly organised youth gangs. Lastly, some concluding remarks are presented.

Political competition, swing areas and electoral violence

We argue that the key explanation for why we see electoral violence in Kono District – particularly during close electoral races – is the perception that Kono stands out among the fourteen districts of Sierra Leone as one of the most important potential swing districts when it comes to election results. While the notion of 'swing areas' or 'swing voters' is relatively new to the literature on African politics, it is frequently referred to, albeit rarely defined, in media reporting from more established democratic settings. Due to the firmly entrenched two-party system, a winner-takes-all electoral system, and often highly competitive elections, swing voters and so-called battleground states are commonly perceived to play a key role in determining the outcome of national elections. In spite of this, the concept of 'swing voters' remains relatively undeveloped in the scholarly literature, with many different understandings and empirical operationalisations (Weghorst and Lindberg 2013).[2] According to Mayer (2007: 359), a swing voter is 'a voter who could go either way, a voter who is not solidly committed to one candidate or the other'. Their final allegiance is undecided right up until the day of the election. The concept of battleground states, while related, is conceptually different, in that it refers to states that 'cannot be firmly counted on to support one candidate or the other, those states that are potentially winnable by both major-party candidates' (ibid. 361). Individual voters in such states may not be potential or actual swing voters, but the outcome of the final vote in the state is contested and relatively few votes in one direction or the other could swing the entire state, following the logic of the majoritarian electoral system. But it could also be that the 'electoral volatility' (Lindberg and Morrison 2005) of such states are high, with significant changes in voting patterns across time.

In the scholarly debate on African elections, the notion of 'core' versus 'swing' voters has been largely missing. Instead, the debate has been dominated by two narratives: one that suggests that voting patterns are largely driven by identity markers, notably ethnicity (e.g. Bates 1983; Posner 2005); and one that highlights the importance of clientelism and the distribution of private goods in exchange for votes (e.g. Bratton and van de Walle 1997; Gyimah-Boadi 2007; Kitschelt and Wilkinson 2007). However, with the strengthening of competitive multiparty elections on the African continent, additional narratives are emerging that suggest a more complex picture of voting patterns that are not readily understood from the perspective of one prism alone. Lindberg and Morrison (2008) suggest that analytical concepts traditionally used to analyse politics in more established democracies may increasingly gain importance in explaining the nuances of politics in Africa's new democracies, alongside other, more well-established notions of ethnic policies and clientelism. For example, they argue that the two-party alignment in Ghana builds on the existence of a core voting population, defined as those who consistently vote for the same party in each election on the basis of party loyalty determined by regional or ethnic ties and swing voters whose allegiance switches between elections depending on government performance and political issues (Lindberg and Morrison 2005). This is echoed in the work of Whitfield (2009), who argues that in close electoral races in Ghana, the outcome of elections is likely to be determined by voting in critical swing regions. Importantly, however, increasingly competitive party politics does not appear to have undermined traditional patronage politics. In these hotly contested areas, the practices of clientelism become even more intensified and widespread. 'When a small number of swing voters can shift the plurality one way or the other, the value of each potential swing voter increases, thus creating incentives for candidates to use all available means in their campaigns,' Lindberg and Morrison argue

(2008: 120). Collier and Vicente (2011) likewise argue that in situations of close electoral competition, violence is a particularly effective strategy in intimidating swing voters and will be the preferred method for weak political parties, whether incumbent or challenger. Asunka et al. (2017) suggest that, all other things being equal, party incentives to manipulate the election, using either fraud or violence, are greater in competitive areas.

This reasoning is supported by previous works on electoral violence, where close races have been identified as an important explanatory factor (Norris, Frank and Martinez i Coma 2015). For example, Wilkinson's (2004) study of ethnic riots in India shows that in situations of close electoral competition at the community level, party elites have incentives to polarise the population along ethnic lines through the instigation of violent incidents for the purpose of securing electoral support from pivotal swing voters within their own ethnic community or to intimidate their ethnic opponents. Wilkinson's study is particularly important as it can help to explain not only why but also when and where we are likely to see incidents of electoral violence on the subnational level. Hence, the risk of electoral violence in perceived swing areas is likely to be higher precisely in situations where there is real political competition between parties and genuine possibilities to change existing power relations.

Based on these insights, we propose that in situations of close political competition, when much is at stake, politicians in new democracies are more likely to resort to the use of violent strategies for the purpose of both mobilising and intimidating a large number of potential swing voters. Perceived swing areas are much more likely than other areas to be the target of such strategies, as traditional means of mobilisation, notably appealing to ethnic loyalties, in combination with the distribution of largesse is unlikely to be regarded as sufficient. Engaging in violent strategies also requires national politicians to seek out local alliances with local actors who can act as proxy perpetrators, resulting in the 'joint production' of violence (Kalyvas 2003). Such local alliances – and the mixture of motives that this entails – help explain the specific patterns and trends of violence that emerge on the ground.

Elections and violence in Sierra Leone

Since the start of party politics, elections in Sierra Leone have been dominated by the competition between the SLPP and the APC, and the bulk of inter-party violence in the country since then can be traced back to the power struggle between them. In situations of parity in particular – that is, in close electoral races with significant prospects for a change in government – inter-party violence tends to increase, while at times of one-party dominance election-related violence subsides. Two of the most competitive general elections in the post-independence era, in 1967 and 2007, stand out in particular for also being the most violent elections recorded in the country. In both elections, the incumbent SLPP was challenged by the APC in opposition, and eventually had to concede power.

The SLPP was formed in 1951 when party politics was introduced in what was then still a British colony. At that time, the party had its primary electoral base outside the capital of Freetown. As such, the SLPP worked in close cooperation with traditional authorities and chiefs from the outset, and was dependent on their support and mobilisation of the electorate in rural areas (Harris 2011: 41–3). While the first elections in the 1950s and early 1960s were characterised by relative openness and fair electoral play, the first decade of independence saw increasing levels of violence around elections throughout the country as the APC gradually emerged as the key national competitor to the SLPP. The ethno-regional logic was evident from the start, with the SLPP drawing most of its core supporters from the Mende ethnic group in the south-east of the country and the APC being the party of choice among the Temnes and Limbas of the north and the north-west, as well as the Creoles in the western area including Freetown (ibid. 61–4). Following highly contested and violent elections in 1967, the APC won the national elections for the first time, with Siaka Probyn Stevens emerging as prime minister. In 1969, a de facto one-party state was declared.

State decay and widespread repression under Stevens, combined with a range of other factors, contributed to the onset of civil war in 1991, and a decade of violent destruction followed. In 1992, a group of lower-ranking front-line soldiers, fed up with the incapacity of the APC to manage the war, overthrew the government and established a military junta, the National Provisional Ruling Council (NPRC). After three years in power, the NPRC was forced by growing internal and international pressure to organise elections to re-establish civilian rule, and Ahmed Tejan Kabbah of the SLPP was elected president. The civil war continued, however, and the next few years would see both another violent coup and several attempts by the armed opposition to enter the capital with force (see, e.g., Abdullah 2004; Gberie 2005; Keen 2005). It was not until February 2002 that the war was officially declared ended, with the first post-war elections scheduled for May the same year. The SLPP and President Kabbah were able to benefit greatly from the perception of having brought peace to the country, and won with over 70 per cent of the votes cast. By then, the APC was still suffering from the negative perceptions of its days in power during the one-party regime, but still succeeded in securing 23 per cent of the votes, which was a major step forward compared with the elections of 1996, when the party had gained a mere 5 per cent of the national votes (Kandeh 2003). The stage was therefore set for a re-emergence of the pre-war SLPP–APC competition in the post-war period.

In the general elections in 2007, the APC was again able to challenge the SLPP in a closely contested race. The SLPP was perceived by many to have failed to deliver the peace dividends despite significant international support. The selected flag-bearer Solomon Ekuma Berewa held limited support among large parts of the SLPP electorate, who expressed concerns that the long-serving SLPP leadership was out of touch with realities on the ground.[3] Meanwhile, the APC had carried out a major reorganisation to distance itself from its past, and party leader Ernest Bai Koroma was able to convincingly promise an agenda for change. At the national level, the election campaign was highly contested, with widespread violence not only between supporters of the APC and the SLPP, but also between the SLPP and the People's Movement for Democratic Change (PMDC), a splinter party from the SLPP, led by Charles Margai, who had bitterly lost the SLPP primaries to Berewa. The split in the traditional SLPP support base in the south-east of the country was instrumental in the victory of the APC, as the PMDC threw its support behind the APC in a very violent run-off, in which Koroma eventually emerged as the winner (Kandeh 2008).

The APC spent the subsequent years attempting to take maximum advantage of its role as incumbent by attempting to consolidate its control over state institutions and making inroads into electorally contested areas, including Kono. The period leading up to the general elections in 2012 saw a number of violent by-elections in traditional SLPP areas. The third post-war general elections also saw a close race between the APC and a reinvigorated and more militant SLPP led by former NPRC junta leader Julius Maada Bio, with tensions running high in several parts of the country. However, the elections were generally less violent than in 2007. This was at least partly due to the increased security measures implemented throughout the country. Koroma eventually secured an APC victory and a second term in power. None of the other candidates, apart from Bio, were able to secure more than 1.5 per cent of the votes cast, confirming the polarisation of the political landscape in post-war Sierra Leone. Bio initially refused to concede electoral defeat, suggesting that the elections were rigged, and the immediate post-election period saw minor incidents of electoral violence, especially in SLPP strongholds (Söderberg Kovacs 2012). The SLPP contested the result officially, but the Supreme Court eventually dismissed the petition. After the 2012 elections, inter-party political competition temporarily subsided, but contentious internal power struggles ensued.

As this brief overview demonstrates, the general pattern of electoral violence in Sierra Leone can be explained by the electoral competition between the two major contenders for power at the national level. However, we are yet to understand the subnational patterns of the geography of violence, and why some areas of the country are more likely than others to see outbreaks of election-related violence.

The strategic logic of electoral violence in Kono

In a country otherwise strongly driven by a relatively predictable ethno-regional logic when it comes to voting patterns, Kono is an exception. Located in the east of the country, the district is situated between the northern APC/Temne voting block and the southern SLPP/Mende voting block. People belonging to the Kono ethnic group are considered the 'indigenes' of the area, but they are not in a majority, and the district is characterised by its cosmopolitan nature with many different ethnic groups. Neither of the two main contenders can safely consider the district to belong to their electoral stronghold. The outcome of the vote in the district is always uncertain, and, over time, it has shifted considerably. In the general elections in 2012, the APC claimed six out of the eight constituencies in Kono, while the SLPP won two. However, only ten years earlier, in the first post-war elections in 2002, the pattern was the direct opposite, with the SLPP winning six constituencies and the APC only two. In the 1996 elections, during the civil war, the SLPP won all eight constituencies. This has given Kono a reputation for being politically unstable and unpredictable.[4]

Due to the strategic importance of the outcome of the vote in Kono, the district usually attracts a disproportionate amount of attention from national politicians at the time of elections. This is especially the case in close races, when the chance of a change of government is high. In these instances, Kono's role as a swing district becomes more important, and both the major parties use violence to galvanise voters of their own party and to prevent the other party from campaigning and its supporters from accessing the polls. Both the 1967 and the 2007 general elections are cases in point, and the developments in Kono around these two elections will be discussed in greater detail below. However, a closer look at Kono also reveals a strategic pattern of violence between the general elections, as the political parties attempt to hold ground and make inroads in preparation for the next general elections. By-elections in particular have seen outbreaks of election-related violence. Findings from our case study also point to the strategic role of intra-party violence as various contenders struggle for power and positions.

Swinging the vote and tipping the balance In 1967, the general elections were closely contested on the national level between the ruling SLPP and the APC. One of the cornerstones of the APC's strategy was to attempt to tip the vote in Kono. Grievances against the ruling SLPP had been mounting among the population in the district since independence due to the party's involvement in the exploitation of the area's diamonds in collaborations with some of the local chiefs. The APC was able to capitalise on this local power divide, and built up a local network of its own in the district primarily consisting of wealthy but excluded Lebanese diamond dealers, disenfranchised miners, and the locally based opposition party Kono Progressive Movement (KPM). All the KPM leaders came from marginalised chieftaincy households in constituencies that lacked diamond resources. Importantly, the licensed dealers presided over youth gangs originally set up to defend and protect illicit mining operations. The liaison with these gangs became instrumental for the APC, which undertook a violent election campaign in the district (Reno 1995: 72–8). At the last minute, Chief Brewah, the paramount chief heading the district, also decided to support the APC. The Kono vote tipped the national balance in favour of the APC, which won the national elections and brought Siaka Stevens to power. In return for their electoral support, local Kono politicians were rewarded with cabinet positions and high-profile appointments throughout Stevens' one-party regime.

In 2007, the country again experienced a very close electoral race with significant prospects for regime change as the APC challenged the incumbent SLPP. Early on, it was clear to the APC that the deciding votes would come from Kono, something that directly affected their campaign strategy.[5] The APC leadership assessed – rightly, as it turned out – that they could capitalise on the widespread perception in the district that Kono had not benefited much from the post-war Kabbah regime. Some of the most vocal critics were found in the ex-combatant community, where many were unhappy with the disarmament, demobilisation and reintegration process they went through after the conflict. Together with the unpopularity of the SLPP presidential candidate Solomon Berewa and the formation of the PMDC, the APC leadership believed the conditions were ripe for a power shift.[6] Alliances with local power holders were struck and ex-combatants were recruited in order to gain an inroad into the communities and to mobilise potential voters. In the words of a high-ranking APC member:

At this point, the previously SLPP loyal chiefs began to waver in their support of the government. They turned a blind eye to APC activities on their land. There were also critical turncoats, important people who went from SLPP to APC. Sia Koroma, the wife of the APC presidential candidate Ernest Bai Koroma, also came from Kono. Kono was critical for us and we focused hard on winning there. We went there to say to everyone, 'Look, APC is the party of the people. We are your party. Have you benefited anything from the SLPP since the end of the war?' Ex-combatants were recruited. We called them 'Security Task Forces', and the leaders 'Marshalls'. We gave them black uniforms and bandanas to look more fearful. We attacked the SLPP, they attacked us back and a cycle of retaliation began.[7]

As the quote demonstrates, the APC leadership consciously used Kono indigenes to convince the local population to vote for their party.[8] The fact that the APC flag-bearer Koroma was married to a woman from Kono certainly helped. But perhaps even more importantly, Koroma strategically selected a running mate from the district, Chief Samuel Sam Sumana, a well-known local strongman. These local alliances also enabled the party to recruit youth as foot soldiers of violence through Sam Sumana's patronage network. Consequently, the entourage of Berewa was attacked when he went to campaign in Kono and many SLPP candidates in the district were assaulted and harassed by youth loyal to Sam Sumana. This caused several local SLPP candidates to drop out of the race and traditional SLPP voters were scared away from the polling stations.[9] But several sources also testify to violent acts carried out by SLPP supporters who were neither prepared nor willing to face the reality of defeat. For example, there were alleged assassination attempts on both Koroma and Margai as they campaigned in the district (Kandeh 2008: 618).

The patterns and trends of electoral violence in Kono clearly speak to the strategic logic at work. The key purpose of every election campaign is to ensure access to territory: to hold speeches, distribute resources and promises, and build new alliances and patronage relations. This is why local election rallies are seen as an instrumental component of the national election campaigns. In the words of a local businessman in Kono:

The common villager is easily persuaded, easily moved, as they have little other information at hand to compare with. Many are illiterate, and only a few have radios. The rallies and campaigns are therefore of critical importance to the politicians. This is when you have the chance to appeal to people's loyalties, to send messages and make promises.[10]

For the same reason, it is perceived as crucial to prevent the other party from gaining territorial access to your claimed areas. Most politicians believe that, if their opponents have access, there is a risk that they will be able to convince the people with their promises and the distribution of largesse. Party loyalty cannot be counted on, especially in Kono. In the words of a high-ranking APC member in Kono:

Money is very important here. You have to show strength. That is very important in delivering people. You can sway them if you are strong enough, if you have money. They will be on your side. The economy in the area is going down. The diamond mining is no longer as lucrative for the average person. Before you could just go out and take your sieve with you. Now the youth are much more dependent on politics. But you cannot trust these people. They are not stable. They will fool you.[11]

In order to prevent the other party from gaining access to potential swing voters, violence is often used to obstruct or interrupt the rival party's rallies. Youth gangs are used to make sure that roads become inaccessible and bridges cannot be crossed, or to directly attack campaign vehicles, in order to prevent the other party from gaining entry.[12] But electoral violence does not always target members and supporters of the other party and competing candidates. In contested areas or in areas that are the stronghold of the competitor, violence by the challenger is sometimes directly aimed at the electorate to scare away potential voters for the other side. By making sure that the rival party gets as few votes as possible, the challenger hopes to increase the parity of the election results. In such circumstances, youth supporters are deliberately imported from outside the local district to orchestrate the violence. Rumours of violence, especially by unknown perpetrators, tend to make people stay at home and avoid travelling long distances.

Holding ground and making inroads But a closer look at electoral dynamics in Kono reveals that the district's role as a swing district also helps explain occurrences of violence and coercive intimidation in less competitive national elections and in between general elections. Even in situations of relative power asymmetry, both political parties have used violence in the district as a long-term strategic tool to 'hold ground' and make strategic 'inroads'. The 2002 general elections in Kono are a case in point. After the end of the civil war, the SLPP emerged with the political upper hand and was strongly favoured to win the first post-war elections. In war-ravaged Kono in particular, the APC stood little chance of winning in any of the district's constituencies. In spite of this, the SLPP used all means possible to protect its influence in the district, including violence and widespread intimidation of APC candidates and potential supporters. For example, local SLPP members mobilised the Poro secret society to come into Koidu town the day before voting day, to make sure that 'outsiders' ran away. According to local traditions, non-initiates are not allowed to see the so-called 'devil' (the masked spirit of a secret society) and doing so is associated with punitive measures, or even death. APC politicians also testify to great difficulty campaigning in the area. At the time, the APC did not have a local party office in Kono and few people dared to host the APC in their houses, as they feared retaliation and attacks by local SLPP strongmen. Consequently, all APC party meetings in the district were held at night and in secrecy.[13] In addition, both parties recruited ex-combatants for protection and intimidation. According to a high-ranking national APC official:

> We called on the leaders of our ex-combatants. We told [them] we needed their help. Some were on contract and payroll. Others were paid in kind with alcohol and small money. It was all very organised. We were attacked. We attacked back. Fire for fire. The 'security task forces' went to several places. Killed and maimed. Ex-combatants were recruited both locally and from other areas of the country. The local combatants could not necessarily be trusted, so we needed spies as a security measure.[14]

In the eyes of the APC, their strategy paid off although they predictably lost the national elections. In Kono, the APC did not win a single constituency, but the voting patterns showed that they had been able to make significant inroads in the district, which they believed would be instrumental in future elections. According to a senior member of the APC, this was due to the fact that they 'put up a good show' in the district.[15] As the quote above shows, they were also able to build local alliances and patronage relationships that could be activated in the next general election.

In addition, because of Kono's role as a potential swing district, by-elections there are seen as important opportunities for strategic manoeuvring in between general elections, and have often been marred by violence. According to the APC district chairperson in Kono:

> By-elections are very critical as it is very important not to lose any seat. They will be important in determining the outcome of the next general election. In between elections, it is vital to have a strategy in place. The opponents are hoping to gain ground, and you have to hold the ground.[16]

As demonstrated by the quote, the parties generally believe that by increasing their political influence in a constituency, however small and remote, they will improve their chances of running a successful electoral campaign in the area in the next elections. But the purpose is also symbolic. The intention is to send a signal of strength, in order to convince potential turncoat politicians and swing voters who may be convinced to cross the floor in the run-up to the next elections. In the words of a high-ranking APC member:

> We spend about four times as much on some of these by-elections as we spend on the general elections. All resources are concentrated in one area, instead of being divided and spread across. Here all efforts are concentrated [in] one place. Either you coerce them or you convince them. In reality, the importance of by-elections is mostly symbolical. It does not guarantee you support in the general elections. So it makes no sense. But it is perceived as an important signal.[17]

The by-election in Constituency 25 in Kono in December 2015, described in the introduction to this chapter, illustrates this point. In the 2012 general elections, the APC was able to win six of the eight parliamentary seats in the district. Constituency 25, however, was relatively evenly split between the two parties, and the APC was able to secure only a very narrow victory. The unexpected death of the elected APC parliamentarian in 2015 was thus a major source of concern for the APC, which was keen to hold the seat. The SLPP, meanwhile, considered the by-election as an important opportunity to retake an area lost with a very small margin.[18]

According to a local councillor in Kono, it is sometimes worth spending resources in by-elections even in perceived strongholds of the other party. Even if you get a very small percentage, you are still seen as making important inroads in an area you may later claim. This phenomenon is referred to in Sierra Leone's politics as a 'top-up' strategy. For example, after the APC came to power in 2012, the party was able to win in several strategically important areas generally believed to be firm traditional SLPP strongholds, including Kailahun, Bo and Kenema.[19]

The intra-party struggle for power A different kind of electoral violence – and one that has significant importance for understanding political dynamics in Kono in the last few years – has been intra-party violence within the two main political contenders. Just as the political as well as the electoral system is shaped on a winner-takes-all logic, there is little room for losers within party hierarchies. Party members are involved in a constant struggle to create and maintain the right connections that will ensure they can remain on or move up the party ladder. This struggle normally intensifies during transition periods, which are often riddled with weak or non-existing succession plans and a large playing field of prospective candidates competing for power. At such times, 'camps are formed and alliances are shaped'.[20] In this process, violence is frequently employed as a strategy to intimidate or frighten competitors and display strength and power.

For example, in the period following the general elections in 2012, violent incidents relating to intra-party politics far overshadowed traditional APC–SLPP animosity in the country as a whole, but perhaps particularly in Kono.[21] Maada Bio lost the presidential race in 2012, and many in the party believed that it was time for him to step down. Other contenders – such as Alpha Timbo and Kandeh Kolleh Yumkella – emerged and agitated for change in the party's leadership. Maada Bio, however, strongly opposed this critique and did not hesitate to use his loyal network of youth, including ex-militias from the days of the NPRC regime, to forcefully resist any such attempts through violent intimidation.[22] The most contentious intra-party fighting in the post-2012 period, however, was associated with the ruling party. The re-election of President Koroma for a second and last term in office signalled the beginning of an intense struggle in the party, with a large number of contenders competing to succeed him. In this process, several individuals were forced to the sidelines. One of the most controversial cases was the dismissal from office of the vice president – Kono strongman Samuel Sam Sumana – by President Koroma in March 2015.[23] The event effectively split APC members and supporters into two camps, with fierce and far-reaching consequences, including several incidents of violence.

In Kono, the Sam Sumana controversy had particularly damaging effects. Because he was a local Big Man, his patronage networks ran deep through the district. Some APC party members and supporters decided to remain loyal after his dismissal, hoping that they would be rewarded on his return. This group of people found themselves barred from the local party office, and many had to leave the district altogether. Other perceived loyalists were reshuffled out of power. For example, the mayor of Koidu Town was suspended in July 2016, together with a group of other colleagues within the local district administration. The formal allegations concerned corruption, but many speculate that it was rather the mayor's close ties to the former vice president that was the reason behind his political downfall.[24] The suspension of the mayor brought the local district council to a virtual standstill for months, and the councillors were deeply divided over the issue. Other APC party members and supporters were quick to shift camp and throw their support behind other Big Men who remained in the good books of the president and his closest allies. Due to the almost complete politicisation of the socio-economic space in Sierra Leone, there is little room for impartiality. Consequently, all individuals in Sam Sumana's patronage networks were forced to take sides, including the paramount chiefs and the local youth gangs, which split into two camps.[25] These divisions were strongly played out in social media, houses were vandalised and there were several cases of violent interruptions of party meetings.[26] According to the Office of National Security (ONS) and the Political Party Registration Commission (PPRC), the Sam Sumana controversy was the number one cause of election-related violence in Kono in the 2015–16 time period.[27]

Forceful intermediaries: local chiefs and traditional authorities

In order to understand the specific character of electoral violence in Kono, we also need to better understand the precarious relationships that national politicians enter into with local actors in order to implement violent strategies for mobilisation and intimidation. Traditional authorities are one of the most important political intermediaries between the political elites and people at large in areas outside city centres in Sierra Leone. In Kono, in particular, many local chiefs are considered to hold great influence and legitimacy in their chiefdoms. As such, they play an instrumental role as both instigators and victims of electoral violence.

According to the Constitution of Sierra Leone, chiefs are the 'custodians of the land' in all the rural areas of Sierra Leone, where they are responsible for law and order and serve as agents of administration for the government, with the right to collect local tax. According to the Chieftaincy Act of 2009, they are also expected to contribute to development in their chiefdoms (Conteh 2016: 34–5). Although chiefs are not expected to 'take active part in partisan politics', they often end up being one of the most important political intermediaries for politicians seeking to influence elections at the grassroots level (ibid. 35). This is a practice with historical roots in Sierra Leone. The British were dependent on local chiefs to carry out tasks that the colonial state was unable to perform from the distant capital. The chiefs, in return, were rewarded with money and goods that gave them authority at the local level. This allowed them to grow rich and powerful locally, while serving the government of the day. This practice was later formalised through the establishment of geographical chiefdoms, each headed by an assigned paramount chief (Reno 1995: 32–3).

In Kono, the role of the chiefs as informal power brokers grew increasingly important after the discovery of diamond and gold in the 1930s, as both the local state administrators and the international mining companies found themselves dependent on the chiefs to control illegal diamond mining (Reno 1995: 45–6). With the introduction of party politics, the chiefs were immediately drawn into the competition between parties as 'vote-catching agents' (Conteh 2016: 12–13). For the incumbent party in particular, the chiefs became the most important local intermediaries. Financial rewards were distributed for chiefs to actively mobilise electoral support for the party in government and violently harass and intimidate the opposition. In exchange for their loyal support, local strongmen gained cabinet posts in the capital (Reno 1995).

After the end of the civil war in Sierra Leone, the chiefdom system was revitalised with only limited reform. This allowed the chiefs to retain much of their traditional influence at the local level (Harris 2011: 121; see also Jackson 2006). In Kono in particular, decision making over land leases and surface rent in diamond-rich chiefdoms has allowed some chiefs to grow both wealthy and influential (Acemoglu, Reed and Robinson 2014: 333; Murphy 1990: 30). As such, the political elite has a strategic interest in entering into alliances with chiefs at election time.[28] In the 2012 election campaign in Kono, for example, the incumbent APC was seen using both carrots and sticks to get the support of the local chiefs.[29] Most chiefs also have a vested interest in sustaining favourable connections with the government in power. In order to fulfil their duties and secure contracts for development projects in their chiefdoms, they are dependent on political connections.[30] Chiefs are therefore the ultimate swing actors, known as always 'favouring the government of the day'.[31] Their political leverage, however, is dependent on their ability to deliver voters; hence, they participate actively in election campaigns and put pressure on section chiefs to follow their lead. Sometimes they go around calling for people to vote or provide transport to the polling stations.[32] In traditional strongholds of the other party or in contested areas, this has often put the chiefs in direct opposition to the political preferences of people in their own chiefdoms, and their attempts to mobilise voters often involve the use of threats and intimidation, and occasionally violence.[33] They may also attempt to prevent supporters of the other party from participating in party rallies or voting, sometimes through threats of violence or force. According to a civil society activist in Kono:

Chiefs are controlled by politicians and they simply do what they want. If the interest of the politician is to see violence, the business of the chiefs will be to mobilise the youth and get them ready to act out the politician's wish.[34]

Occasionally chiefs also punish voters after the election results have been announced. For example, in one of the two chiefdoms in Constituency 25, after the by-elections in December 2015, the local chief put up the election results showing the APC victory on the office wall for everyone to see, with the idea of publicly shaming the minority who had voted for the SLPP. In addition, the chief used his local influence to make sure schools were closed and roads were blocked, and motorcyclists in Koidu Town, so-called 'okada riders', were prevented from picking up passengers in villages with suspected SLPP voters.[35]

Local gangs and foot soldiers of violence

Although mainly orchestrated from the top, electoral violence in Kono – like elsewhere in the country – is primarily carried out by people who are generally referred to as 'thugs' in Sierra Leone: youths who are recruited by politicians to orchestrate violence.[36] While the national and local elites are dependent on these individuals and groups to do their dirty work on the ground, the youth are equally dependent on their Big Men networks for survival and possibilities for social advancement. The character of this mutually destructive dependency explains the specific shape and form of electoral violence in Kono.

A number of context-specific factors make Kono stand out as a particularly fertile area for recruiting such youth as foot soldiers for violence. Since the discovery of gold and diamonds in the 1930s, Kono has generated significant wealth for the political elites yet remains one of the poorest districts in the country. This discrepancy is a common source of grievance among people in the district. In the post-war period, this frustration has increased due to the decline of alluvial diamond mining, which is no longer as productive as it used to be. Kono was also heavily affected by the civil war and was one of the last areas to be held by the rebel forces. After the war, many former fighters stayed in the area to work in artisanal mining and the district is commonly thought to hold the largest concentration of ex-combatants in the country.[37] Fifteen years after the end of the war, however, it is often hard to separate ex-combatants from urban youth in general, and the dividing lines are often blurred.

In Kono, many young people are pessimistic about their prospects and see compliance with the wishes of the elites as their only way out. A type of patronage system referred to locally as godfatherism has thus emerged, where youth turn to the elites and those with perceived economic resources and ask 'Bra u borbor dae?' ('Boss, is there anything for your boy?'). This dependence has played into the hands of the politicians, particularly around election time. In the words of Kallay, a diamond miner:

> There is nothing to fight against in the system. At the end you fail, you can never beat them. You can only survive with the help of a patron. When they say jump, you ask how high. When they say throw stones at the other party, you do so. Don't question them, just do it and when they trust you, they give you some money and even help you to get minor jobs. Our youth have learned this survival strategy and they are effectively using it.[38]

The dependency goes both ways, and engaging in electoral violence on behalf of a political party is often seen as an opportunity to access ready cash or a ticket to a more promising future. Most of the violence is organised by youth gangs – or 'cliques', as they are known in Kono. Much like the chiefs, gang leaders are dependent on and follow orders from the top, while they also have an interest in offering their services to the highest bidders on the market. In 2016, it was estimated that there were about twenty such gangs in Kono, although two major gangs dominated the district: one led by Adamou, a former Armed Forces Revolutionary Council (AFRC) mid-level commander and the chairperson of the APC 'security task force' in Kono, and one led by Ali, alias 'Gun Point', a former Revolutionary United Front (RUF) commander. Following the Sam Sumana controversy, Adamou's crew changed their name to 'Friends of Sam Sumana', while a breakaway faction declared its political allegiance to Diana Konomanyi.[39] When elections draw near, politicians approach the gangs to offer money, alcohol and cigarettes – so-called 'moral boosters' – in exchange for violent assignments. These rewards are deliberately short term, which serves as a guarantee of long-term dependence. As noted by Christensen and Utas (2016: 29), building on Sahlins (1963), this is a typical feature of these Big Man networks: the tendency to postpone (sometimes indefinitely) expected reciprocities and thereby create extended and far-reaching mechanisms of debt. At other times, the gangs engage in activities that demonstrate their loyalty and support, hoping that such acts will be recognised and rewarded.[40] Or, in the words of Christensen and Utas (2016), they invest in the future through the creation of perceived debt. When the stakes of elections are particularly high in a specific locality, however, national politicians usually bring in loyal instigators of violence from outside the local district. This serves to increase the level of violence, as the perpetrators are unlikely to be familiar with the victims and hence show less restraint, but it also increases fear, as local people are unable to recognise them.[41]

The incumbent always has an advantage in these situations, as they both have the capacity to mobilise greater resources and can make use of the institutions of the state, including the police, to protect their foot soldiers of violence. This contributes to establishing a culture of impunity for violence committed.

Although some individuals have been arrested and rearrested several times, they are often seen on the streets again the following day. At times, election officials have also been intimidated and sometimes attacked, with few repercussions.[42] Many therefore suspect that the local police protect these gangs, and that the police are under political influence from the capital.[43]

Concluding remarks

We began this chapter by asking why elections in the district of Kono have seen such high levels of electoral violence. We argued that the key explanation is the district's unique role as a national swing district. Since the outset of party politics, the voting pattern in Sierra Leone has been strongly driven by an ethno-regional logic, which at times of close electoral races divides the country in two almost equally sized strongholds, the north/north-west and the south/south-east. Kono is a key exception to this trend, with important implications for its potential to swing the national vote and determine the outcome of general elections, which has happened in a couple of critical instances. Consequently, the district is heavily courted both in the run-up to the general elections and in between elections, for example during by-elections, with the two major party contenders trying to hold ground in perceived strongholds and making strategic inroads into perceived opposition areas or in contested constituencies. The findings from Kono clearly speak to the instrumentality of electoral violence in this context. Geographical control is the key mechanism at work. In order to win elections, the political elite not only need to display strength in numbers in local rallies and distribute resources and political promises; they also need to make sure that competitors are kept from doing the same. To this end, roads and bridges are blocked, campaign vehicles attacked, and the rallies and campaign meetings of the opposition are disrupted and disturbed. On the day of the election, violence serves an additional purpose: to frighten opposition supporters and keep them away from the voting stations. By affecting the turnout in contested areas, parties can swing the outcome in a small single-member constituency. Even when a party stands little chance of winning a constituency, a local presence can ensure that they are able to 'top up' their numbers, and hence gain a foothold in the area – and this may pave the way for future electoral benefits. Another common source of electoral violence in Kono is intra-party violence relating to the struggle for control within political parties. In Kono, this type of violence has at times far exceeded inter-party violence in both frequency and intensity.

A number of additional factors tied to the socio-economic context of Kono and the Big Men networks between political elites, local chiefs and youth gangs serve to explain the more specific character and pattern of this violent dynamic. Traditional chiefs are known to largely favour the government of the day, as they are dependent on political connections and strategic alliances for maintaining their local authority, wealth and power. As such, they frequently engage in party politics and try to mobilise villagers in their constituencies to vote for their party or candidate of choice. In constituencies that are traditional strongholds of the opposition or in contested areas, such mobilisation often comes in the form of threats of violence and coercive harassment and intimidation, and the outcome of the ballot may be followed by collective punishments. The district's youth – consisting of large numbers of marginalised urban youth and ex-combatants organised in local gangs or cliques – are also central to the occurrence of violence in the district. Despite the wealth that the resources of the district has generated for the country and its elites for many decades, the great majority of the population in Kono have been left at the margins, struggling for their everyday survival. The alluvial diamond mining industry is less productive than before, the economy has stagnated and prices have gone up dramatically in the last few years. These developments have produced a readymade army dependent on and vulnerable to political godfathers. Such youth are used as instruments of coercion and intimidation of rivals in exchange for short-term benefits and long-term promises.

The findings from this case study point to the relevance of studying electoral violence as a strategic instrument used by the political elite in new and emerging democracies to influence the electoral contest and outcome. In this context, the notion of swing areas and swing voters proves a useful analytical tool. However, the case study also shows that more established theoretical views of the dynamic of elections in Africa – notably that of ethnic identity politics and clientelism – are equally relevant concepts in understanding the more intricate mechanisms at work. The strengthening of democracy in Sierra Leone in the post-war period and the (re-)establishment of elections as the most important mechanism for the distribution of political power have not led to the gradual undermining of either patronage politics or the traditional overlapping ethnic and regional divide in the country. In fact, our case study suggests the opposite: competitive multiparty politics in the post-war period has strengthened and reinforced the politicisation of ethnicity as an important tool for mobilising votes and has provided new resources, channels and rationales for Big Man politics.

Notes

1 Author interviews with intelligence officer at the Office of National Security (ONS), Freetown, January 2011; election officers at the National Electoral Commission (NEC) in Kono, Koidu Town, 22 November 2016.

2 Weghorst and Lindberg (2013) point to the existence of at least three different approaches to empirically measuring swing voters in previous literature, including self-reported ambivalence, lack of party affiliation and past voting behaviour.

3 Author interviews with SLPP members and supporters, Bo, Pujehun and Kenema, January 2011.

4 Author interviews with civil society activist, Koidu Town, 14 December 2015; staff of a local NGO, Koidu Town, 12 December 2015.

5 Author interview with high-ranking APC member, Freetown, 14 January 2016.

6 Ibid.

7 Ibid.

8 Ibid.

9 Author interview with high-ranking SLPP member, Freetown, 15 April 2016.

10 Author interview with businessman from Kono, Freetown, 15 January 2016.

11 Author interview with the APC District Chairperson in Kono, Koidu Town, 24 November 2016.

12 Ibid.

13 Author interview with high-ranking APC member, Freetown, January 2016.

14 Ibid.

15 Ibid.

16 Author interview with the APC District Chairperson in Kono, Koidu Town, 24 November 2016.

17 Ibid.

18 Author interview with election officers at the NEC office in Kono, Koidu Town, 22 November 2016.

19 Author interview with Kono District Council member, Koidu Town, 24 November 2016.

20 Author interview with high-ranking APC member, Freetown, 14 January 2016.

21 Based on author interviews with election officers at the NEC office in Kono, 22 November 2016; officers at the ONS office in Kono, 25 November 2016; representative of the West Africa Network for Peacebuilding (WANEP) in Kono, 22 November; Political Parties Registration Commission (PPRC) official in Kono, 22 November 2016, all Koidu Town.

22 Author interview with the SLPP District Secretary in Kono, Koidu Town, 24 November 2016.

23 Sam Sumana was first expelled from the APC and later removed as vice president. The decision was ruled as legal by the Supreme Court of Sierra Leone, but was later referred to the sub-regional court of the Economic Community of West African States (ECOWAS) in Abuja, Nigeria.

24 Author interview with representative of WANEP in Kono, Koidu Town, 22 November 2016.

25 Ibid.

26 Author interviews with officers at the ONS in Kono, Koidu Town, 25 November 2016; representative of WANEP in Kono, Koidu Town, 22 November 2016.

27 Author interviews with officers at the ONS in Kono, Koidu Town, 25 November 2016; PPRC official, Koidu Town, 22 November 2016.

28 Author interview with the APC District Chairperson in Kono, Koidu Town, 24 November 2016.

29 Author interview with civil society activist, Koidu Town, 15 April 2016.

30 Author interview with PPRC official, Koidu Town, 22 November 2016.

31 Author interview with Deputy Chief Administrator, Koidu New Sembehun City Council, Koidu Town, 24 November 2016.

32 Author interview with officers at the ONS in Kono, Koidu Town, 25 November 2016.

33 Author interview with Mandingo tribal head, Koidu Town, 25 November 2016.

34 Author interview with civil society activist, Koidu Town, 14 December 2015.

35 Author interview with PPRC official in Kono, Koidu Town, 22 November 2016.

36 As noted by Utas, 'youth' in the context of contemporary urban West Africa is not primarily a reference to an age group, but rather to a particular social status: 'a social category of people living in volatile and dire life conditions … who have yet to become *social* adults, people who have been marginalized

into what they see as a chronic state of youthhood (Utas 2012: 1, italics in original).

37 Author interview with representative of WANEP in Kono, Koidu Town, 22 November 2016.

38 Author interview with diamond miner, Koidu Town, 20 December 2015.

39 Author interviews with former member of the Gunpoint gang, Koidu Town, 23 November 2016; representative of WANEP in Kono, Koidu Town, 22 and 25 November 2016.

40 Author interview with former member of the Gunpoint gang, Koidu Town, 23 November 2016.

41 Author interview with officers at the ONS in Kono, Koidu Town, 25 November 2016.

42 Author interview with election officers at the NEC in Kono, Koidu Town, 22 November 2016.

43 Author interview with former member of the Gunpoint gang, Koidu Town, 23 November 2016.

References

Abdullah, I. (ed.) (2004) *Between Democracy and Terror: The Sierra Leone Civil War*. Dakar: CODESRIA.

Acemoglu, D., T. Reed and J. A. Robinson (2014) 'Chiefs: Economic Development and Elite Control of Civil Society in Sierra Leone', *Journal of Political Economy* 122 (2): 319–68.

Asunka, J., S. Brierley, M. Golden, E. Kramon and G. Ofosu (2017) 'Electoral Fraud or Violence: The Effect of Observers on Party Manipulation Strategies', *British Journal of Political Science*. Available at https://doi.org/10.1017/S0007123416000491.

Bates, R. H. (1983) 'Modernization, Ethnic Competition and the Rationality of Politics in Contemporary Africa' in D. Rothchild and V. Olorunsola (eds), *State Versus Ethnic Claims: African Policy Dilemmas*. Boulder CO: Westview Press.

Bratton, M. and N. van de Walle (1997) *Democratic Experiments in Africa: Regime Transitions in Comparative Perspective*. Cambridge: Cambridge University Press.

Christensen, M. M. and M. Utas (2016) 'Ex-militias and Ambiguous Debt Relations during Post-war Elections in Sierra Leone', *African Conflict and Peacebuilding Review* 6 (2): 23–47.

Collier, P. and P. Vicente (2011) 'Violence, Bribery and Fraud: The Political Economy of Election in Sub-Saharan Africa', *Public Choice* 153 (1–2): 117–47.

Conteh, M. N. (2016) *Paramount Chieftaincy in Sierra Leone: History and Electoral Process*. Saarbrücken: Lambert Academic Publishing.

Gberie, L. (2005) *A Dirty War in West Africa: The RUF and the Destruction of Sierra Leone*. Bloomington IN: Indiana University Press.

Gyimah-Boadi, E. (2007) 'Political Parties, Elections and Patronage: Random Thoughts on Neo-patrimonialism and African Democratization' in M. Basedau, G. Erdmann and A. Mehler (eds), *Votes, Money and Violence: Political Parties in Sub-Saharan Africa*. Uppsala: Nordic Africa Institute.

Harris, D. (2011) *Civil War and Democracy in West Africa: Conflict Resolution, Elections and Justice in Sierra Leone and Liberia*. London: I. B. Tauris.

Jackson, P. (2006) 'Reshuffling an Old Deck of Cards? The Politics of Local Government Reform in Sierra Leone', *African Affairs* 106 (422): 95–111.

Kalyvas, S. N. (2003) 'The Ontology of "Political Violence": Action and Identity in Civil Wars', *Perspectives on Politics* 1 (3): 475–94.

Kandeh, J. D. (2003) 'Sierra Leone's Post-conflict Elections of 2002', *Journal of Modern African Studies* 41 (2): 189–216.

Kandeh, J. D. (2008) 'Rogue Incumbents, Donor Assistance and Sierra Leone's Second Post-conflict Elections of

2007', *Journal of Modern African Studies* 46 (4): 603–35.

Keen, D. (2005) *Conflict and Collusion in Sierra Leone.* Oxford: James Currey.

Kitschelt, H. and S. I. Wilkinson (2007) *Patrons, Clients, and Policies: Patterns of Democratic Accountability and Political Competition.* Cambridge: Cambridge University Press.

Lindberg, S. I. and M. K. C. Morrison (2005) 'Exploring Voter Alignments in Africa: Core and Swing Voters in Ghana', Journal of Modern African Studies 43 (4): 1–22.

Lindberg, S. I. and M. K. C. Morrison (2008) 'Are African Voters Really Ethnic or Clientelistic? Survey Evidence from Ghana', *Political Science Quarterly* 123 (1): 95–122.

Mayer, W. G. (2007) 'The Swing Voter in American Presidential Elections', *American Political Research* 35 (3): 358–88.

Murphy, W. P. (1990) 'Creating the Appearance of Consensus in Political Discourse', *American Anthropologist* 92 (1): 24–41.

Norris, P., R. W. Frank and F. Martinez i Coma (2015) *Contentious Elections: From Ballots to Barricades.* New York NY: Routledge.

Patriotic Vanguard (2015) 'Kono: SLPP's Gbondo Was No Match for APCs Tucker', *Patriotic Vanguard,* 21 December. Available at www.thepatrioticvanguard.com/kono-slpp-s-gbondo-was-no-match-for-apc-s-tucker (accessed 15 April 2017).

Posner, D. N. (2005) *Institutions and Ethnic Politics in Africa.* Cambridge: Cambridge University Press.

Reno, W. (1995) *Corruption and State Politics in Sierra Leone.* Cambridge: Cambridge University Press.

Sahlins, M. D. (1963) 'Poor Man, Rich Man, Big-man, Chief: Political Types in Melanesia and Polynesia', *Comparative Studies in Society and History* 5: 285–303.

Sierra Leone Telegraph (2015) 'Did Sierra Leone Vice President Foh's Hate Speech Spark Violence in Kono?', *Sierra Leone Telegraph,* 18 December. Available at www.thesierraleonetelegraph.com/?p=11061 (accessed 15 April 2017).

Söderberg Kovacs, M. (2012) '"Ampa Ampoh!": Sierra Leone after the Announcement of the 2012 Election Results'. Mats Utas blog, 30 November. Available at https://matsutas.wordpress.com/2012/11/30/ampa-ampoh-sierra-leone-after-the-announcement-of-the-2012-election-results-guest-post-by-mimmi-soderberg-kovacs/ (accessed 15 April 2017).

Utas, M. (ed.) (2012) *African Conflicts and Informal Power: Big Men and Networks.* London and New York NY: Zed Books.

Weghorst, K. R. and S. I. Lindberg (2013) 'What Drives the Swing Voter in Africa?', *American Journal of Political Science* 57 (3): 717–34.

Whitfield, L. (2009) '"Change for a Better Ghana": Party Competition, Institutionalization and Alternation in Ghana's 2008 Elections', *African Affairs* 108 (433): 621–41.

Wilkinson, S. I. (2004) *Votes and Violence: Electoral Competition and Ethnic Riots in India.* Cambridge: Cambridge University Press.

6 | Ex-militants and electoral violence in Nigeria's Niger Delta

Tarila Marclint Ebiede

Introduction

Electoral violence has shaped the outcomes of elections since Nigeria returned to democratic rule in 1999. The overarching narrative that has emerged from research on this subject is that electoral violence in Nigeria is driven by unbridled neopatrimonialism (Omotola 2010; Albert 2005; Adetula 2014). As a theoretical lens, neopatrimonialism tends to view elections as a process dominated by elites competing for political power. Other actors in the field of play are often conceptualised as 'clients' of the dominant political actors. However, electoral competition is not limited to political elites alone. It involves a broad range of actors belonging to different socio-economic groups in society. In most cases, these actors are youths. There is a tendency to view these youths as 'clients' who express their agency in the interests of a political 'patron'. This view does not provide a complete picture of the agency of youths in the electoral process, especially as it relates to electoral violence. In this chapter, I argue that these youths, just like the elites, are similarly competing for power and influence as they engage in the electoral process. There is a need to explain the agency of these youths in the study of electoral violence in Nigeria's prevailing democratic order.

To explain the agency of youths in electoral violence in Nigeria, this chapter focuses on ex-militants in the Niger Delta region. Ex-militants are an important youth group in conflict-affected societies. Ex-militants are often categorised as marginalised youths (Maclay and Özerdem 2010), whose agency is predetermined by the actions and interests of their political patrons (Themnér 2015; Themnér and Utas 2016). However, Iwilade (2017) argues that ex-militants act in their own self-interest. According to him, ex-militants use their past history and profile as violent actors to negotiate for opportunities with political patrons. In this chapter, I argue that ex-militants engage in the political process as individuals in a struggle to maintain their place of power in their local communities and the political processes within the state. While not denying the important place of perverse competition for political power among elites in Nigeria's electoral process, the perspective that emphasises the agency of ex-militants provides a nuanced explanation of the factors that shape the political process in conflict-affected societies such as the Niger Delta. Although this is not a general rule, ex-militants are likely to engage in electoral violence in pursuit of their interests in the political process. Therefore, to explain the motivations of people who are not within the conceptual frameworks of 'elites' in the political process, this chapter seeks to examine when and why ex-militants engage in electoral violence.

The central argument in this chapter is that ex-militant leaders mobilise their ex-fighters to carry out electoral violence with the aim of influencing the outcome of elections in ways that maintain their position of power and influence in their communities. I argue that there is a greater level of violence where there is political factionalism among ex-militant leaders. This is especially the case in societies where more than one militant group exists. Leaders of these groups, who are often in competition with each other, align themselves with different political parties. As opposing political parties compete during elections, ex-militant leaders tend to mobilise their ex-fighters to carry out acts of violence that can determine the outcome of the electoral process. This action is motivated by the ambitions of ex-militant leaders to maintain or gain access to patronage networks or political power at the governmental level. Ex-militant leaders use the power they gain from political processes within the state to assert themselves in their local communities. Hence, electoral violence is as much an outcome of elite competition for power within the state as it is of competition for power by ex-militant leaders within their own communities.

Methodologically, this chapter draws on fieldwork conducted in Nigeria's Niger Delta region. Data from this fieldwork includes interviews conducted with ex-militants and members of communities, members of political parties and government officials in the Niger Delta. The chapter also relies on data on events documented by the Partners for Peace (P4P) project (Partners for Peace 2015), which is available online. The P4P project collects data on political violence in the Niger Delta, including incidences of electoral violence that involve ex-militants. In addition, the chapter relies on newspaper reports. These different sources are triangulated to produce a coherent empirical narrative of electoral violence during the 2015 general elections in three states in the Niger Delta region: Delta, Bayelsa and Rivers states. These states are often referred to as the 'geographic Niger Delta' (Tamuno 2008).[1] The focus on the three core Niger Delta states is deliberate; although all oil-producing states have a history of protest movements against the Nigerian government, these states are known to have been the stage for armed militancy in the region. Ex-militants, the focus of this chapter, have a greater presence in the political processes of these states.

The chapter is structured as follows: this introductory section is followed by an overview of the current literature on ex-combatants and electoral violence in post-conflict societies.[2] The subsequent section discusses the relationship

between electoral violence and armed militancy in Nigeria's Niger Delta region.
The main arguments are set out in the fourth section, in which I present and analyse the data that explains why ex-militants were involved in electoral violence during the 2015 general elections in the Niger Delta. The chapter ends with a conclusion that highlights theoretical insights gained from the empirical data presented. These insights seek to enhance current understandings of ex-militants' involvement in electoral violence in the Niger Delta, and in other societies that have experienced organised armed insurgencies.

Ex-combatants and electoral violence in post-conflict societies

Mainstream peace and conflict studies often maintain that there is a need to manage ex-combatants' transition from violence to civilian life in societies emerging from violent conflict (Berdal 1996). Disarmament, demobilisation and reintegration (DDR) programmes are usually initiated to manage this transition (Schulhofer-Wohl and Sambanis 2010; United Nations 2010). It is expected that the implementation of DDR programmes will ensure that fighting groups have no weapons after disarmament (Berdal 1996), and that networks and groups will be disbanded through demobilisation programmes. Finally, ex-combatants commonly receive support and training to ensure that they can earn sustainable incomes and participate in the socio-political life of their communities without resorting to violence (Spear 2006; Özerdem 2012).

The trajectory of ex-combatants in post-conflict societies is subject to political, economic and social realities they encounter after participating in DDR programmes. Research on ex-combatants has shown that their group structures continue to be relevant even when conflicts end (De Vries and Wiegink 2011). These networks could be significant for the economic survival of ex-combatants (Peters 2007; Reno 2010) and could also serve as political capital for ex-combatants and their leaders (Utas 2012). This chapter focuses on the ways in which ex-combatants use their networks in the political processes of their societies in ways that can lead to electoral violence.

Politics in post-conflict societies can be contentious. According to Lyons (2002: 6), political processes in such societies – and particularly elections – aim to 'settle the contentious issues of internal and external legitimacy and must be organized under the difficult circumstances of societal disorder, general insecurity, fear, distrust, and institutional breakdown'. This contentious politics is even more evident when democracy is introduced as a path out of conflict (Jarstad and Sisk 2008). Elections in post-conflict societies are an exercise that can reveal the existing rifts in such societies, expose historical animosities and generate politicised criminality as societies seek to produce a new political order (Kynoch 2005). Not all societies emerging from violent conflicts enter into democratisation processes or hold elections to create political consensus, and there is a high possibility that the very issues that shape violent conflicts are at the heart of electoral politics in post-conflict societies seeking to democratise.

As citizens, ex-combatants also participate in the post-conflict electoral process. This participation takes different forms, often depending on the way in which the conflict was terminated. Armed groups might emerge as political parties as part of the peace agreements that lead to the termination of conflict. In this case, ex-combatants often become members of the political party that evolves out of their former armed group. Political parties that emerge from armed groups in post-conflict societies are shaped by structures and networks that were created during the armed conflict (Söderström 2011a). In the absence of a transition from armed group to political party, ex-combatants still partici-pate in the political process, but as part of political structures that include other members of society who may not have been part of any armed group. Whether or not political parties emerge out of armed groups, ex-combatants who are interested in politics tend to seek membership of political groups to enable them to register their presence in the political process of their societies.

Ex-combatants' interest in asserting themselves in political processes could take different forms. In Liberia, it has been shown that the involvement of ex-combatants in politics can be driven by democratic ideals such as inclusion, as well as by non-democratic confrontational discourses (Söderström 2011a; 2011b). Maclay and Özerdem (2010) argue that involving ex-combatants in political processes in societies emerging from conflict enhances their civil participation in politics. However, the reality of ex-combatant involvement in politics does not necessarily reflect these ideals of democratic political partici-pation. Instead, existing evidence shows that the shape and form of political involvement reflect the nature of politics in societies emerging from conflict (Bøås 2011; McGregor 2002; Reno 2010; Utas 2012). In many of these societies, politics is characterised by patron–client relations, perpetuating relationships and norms that were forged during the time of conflict. In fact, some of these patron–client relationships and norms may have been responsible for the outbreak of violence in the first instance (Peters 2007).

A core feature of patronage politics is the relationship between those who seek to gain and maintain political power (patrons) and those who are used to achieve this goal (clients) (Alapiki and Ukiwo 2013). In societies charac-terised by such politics, patrons buy the support of clients through promises of rewards and access to political patronage when the patrons gain control of the state. Competition for control of the state emerges from the reality of state domination in state–society relations and economic activities in most African postcolonial countries (Ake 1996). The economic approaches adopted by most African states following independence ensured that policies such as the nationalisation of assets, increased state investment in service delivery and control of the sale of privately grown commodities such as cocoa, groundnuts, kola, cotton and oil palm were implemented through so-called government marketing boards. These policies ensured that resources that were available in post-independence countries were increasingly bestowed on the state, which increased the value of power at the centre. This, Ake (ibid. 6) notes, meant that state power remained 'immense, arbitrary, often violent, always threatening', and that the political class sought to obtain and maintain power 'by all means'. This description can be extended to post-conflict states in Africa. According to Arowosegbe (2011), such states fit Ake's conception of the postcolonial state; however, politics and governance are not only shaped by colonial history, but also by violent conflicts that have occurred in such societies (Vlassenroot and Raeymaekers 2004). Unbridled competition for power is a common practice in post-conflict societies, and, as in the postcolonial state, it creates a violent political culture that often manifests during elections.

Ex-combatants are drawn into the political culture of their societies when they seek to participate in post-conflict political processes such as elections. In many instances, it is argued that the agency of ex-combatants in post-conflict politics is influenced by political patrons (Themnér 2015; Themnér and Utas 2016). I argue that a nuanced perspective on the actions of ex-combatants would take into account how they are located within the politics of their local communities. While ex-combatants may seem to be acting in the interests of political elites whom they see as patrons, they could also be acting in their own interests within the politics of their immediate communities. Therefore, it is important also to examine how ex-combatants act in the electoral process to advance their own interests within their community. This theoretical perspective can provide new answers to the question of why ex-combatants engage in electoral violence in post-conflict societies.

Electoral violence and armed militancy in Nigeria's Niger Delta

Armed militant groups emerged in Nigeria's Niger Delta in the mid-2000s. The overarching narrative popularised by scholars, civil society activists and militant groups is that armed militancy is an expression of community grievances against the Nigerian state and international oil companies (IOCs) (Ibaba 2005; Obi 2009). Research has shown that armed militants emerged through different trajectories (Ebienfa 2011). Youths who joined militant groups are known to have participated in various forms of violence, including intra-communal, inter-communal, intra-ethnic, political and criminal violence. The foundations of what became known as armed militancy were laid by a complex network of political violence in the Niger Delta.

The relationship between electoral violence and armed militancy can be traced to the run-up to the 2003 general election in the core Niger Delta states. Members of the political class recruited and armed youths from street gangs and youth movements, which led to the proliferation of small arms and light weapons in local communities in the Niger Delta (Best and Von Kemedi 2005). As Asuni (2009) shows, politicians who provided arms to youths did not recover those weapons after the 2003 elections. Armed with different types of weapons, some of these youths began to engage in criminality in their local communities. However, in a remarkable turn of events, Ateke Tom and Asari Dokubo, two notable youth leaders who had been hired by Peter Odili, the governor of Rivers State at the time, transformed into armed militants. Ateke Tom established the Niger Delta Vigilante (NDV), while Asari Dokubo started the Niger Delta People's Volunteer Force (NDPVF). This marked the beginning of the transition of youths who had been involved in electoral violence into armed militants engaged in a violent campaign against the Nigerian state and IOCs in the oil fields of the Niger Delta.

This anti-state violence became formalised in 2005 following the emergence of the Movement for the Emancipation of the Niger Delta (MEND) (Bøås 2011), an umbrella organisation for armed militant groups in the area. The formation of MEND also led to a proliferation of armed groups in the Niger Delta, as youth engaged in anti-state violence began to find a voice and a network through MEND. As MEND gained traction, it also became a powerful actor in the politics of the region. Armed militants affiliated with MEND gained more power and influence in their communities, which in turn changed the position of the militants – and particularly of the leaders of armed groups – in their local communities. Militant leaders who started as clients recruited by political patrons to carry out violence became dominant in community politics. This change is not surprising, as armed militant leaders have been able to build their own power independent of their erstwhile patrons. This was done through their engagement in oil theft, hostage taking and patronage from IOCs and gave such leaders the leverage to negotiate their position in the political processes of their communities on their own terms. Hence, MEND was not simply a platform for the expression of anti-state violence; it was also a means for youths to gain a position of power and influence in communities where violence plays an important role in the political process.

The limits of Nigeria's DDR programme In June 2009, President Umaru Musa Yar'Adua announced an amnesty and DDR programme for armed groups in the Niger Delta. The DDR programme was designed to facilitate the termination of the insurgency in the region and was meant to disband militant groups and facilitate their reintegration into society. It started with the disarmament phase. Armed militant groups, led by their leaders, handed in their weapons and each fighter signed an oath of repentance. The militant leader was responsible for identifying members of his group, but each militant took the oath as an individual fighter. This was followed by the encampment of repentant militants. Technically, the armed groups were demobilised in the camps, where repentant militants were given non-violent advocacy training as part of a two-week demobilisation exercise. Ex-militants were asked to select individual educational or vocational training programmes that would enable them to gain the necessary skills and knowledge for employment. Ideally, implementation of the DDR programme would therefore prepare them for reintegration into society.

If successful, DDR is likely to reduce the power and influence of leaders of armed groups. This is because the network of armed combatants and their ability to perpetrate violence are the basis of the political power of militia leaders. A successfully implemented DDR programme means that leaders of armed groups are likely to lose their position of power in their communities as well as in broader political processes. This is especially the case when such leaders have no other source of power. If militant leaders lose their power, they are likely to return to their status as clients of political patrons. The implementation of an amnesty and DDR programme in the Niger Delta is therefore a test case for how militant leaders will seek to maintain their power and influence in communities and political processes in post-conflict societies. In this chapter, I argue that the involvement of ex-militants in electoral violence during the 2015 general elections in Nigeria's Niger Delta is an outcome of ex-militant leaders' struggle to maintain a position of power and influence in their communities and in political processes within the state.

The reality for most ex-combatants differs from what was envisioned by the DDR programme. First, the role of armed leaders in enrolling fighters into the DDR programme reinforced the existing relationship between fighters and their leaders (Ebiede 2016). Although all fighters were eligible to enter the DDR programme, they needed their leaders to submit their names. This is captured in an interview with an official of the Presidential Amnesty Programme (PAP):

> During the interview, he [the ex-militant leader] reports that he has 2,000 people and brings them. Who brought them? The leader. He brought them during disarming, they lined up and during disarming you registered them as individuals. If you are not careful, he can even decide not to bring forward some of his fighters at the point of demobilisation.[3]

As this quote illustrates, it was the leaders of the militant groups who guaranteed the participation of their fighters in the amnesty and DDR programme, and, in some cases, the 'fighters' included freeloading youths who were not part of an armed group (Nwajiaku-Dahou 2012). This process tended to sustain the loyalty of ex-militants towards their leaders. An example of this loyalty can be seen in a response from an ex-militant fighter during an interview:

> I would do what my leader tells me to do. Why not? He is my boss na …
> Yes. He is my boss; he is caring for me. He is caring for me more than the

government. How much are they paying us? Is it not 65,000 naira? He is doing more than that. He started our journey in life to be somebody. Every leader you see, if he says, 'My men, I want to see you today and this is what I want you to do' ... Why not?[4]

In this statement, the ex-militant fighter explained the logic behind his loyalty to a militant leader. He demonstrates that his loyalty towards his 'boss' supports his social status, which he conceptualises as his 'journey in life to be somebody'. He notes that this loyalty also guarantees his livelihood, as the limited payment from the DDR programme is not enough to sustain him. For this reason, he believes, he and other ex-militants will always remain loyal to their leaders and do their bidding if the need arises. This is also confirmed by ordinary civilians in communities who report that members of armed militant groups 'are still together' despite having participated in the DDR programme.[5]

The loyalty of ex-fighters to their ex-militant leaders has implications for the mobilisation for violence during the electoral process. As an ex-militant from Ologbobiri in Bayelsa State explained: 'I will do what master says I should do. Nobody can stand us in that river.'[6] This means that the ex-militant and his group will ensure that political rivals do not pilot their boats on the river leading to rural communities where voting is expected to take place. Most communities are accessible only via the waterways, and so armed groups can disrupt the political campaigns of opposition groups and capture electoral materials when they are being transported by water. This example shows that one way in which ex-militants demonstrate loyalty to their former leaders is by doing their bidding during elections – and this can include violence. Ex-militant fighters who continue to benefit from the support of their leaders are easily mobilised by these leaders for election purposes.

Those who do not rely on such support or patronage tend to be independent. For example, another ex-militant fighter associated with Africa Ukparasia explained that he no longer participates in the political activities of his ex-militant leader, even though he still remains friendly with him. The reason he gave for this was that he does not rely on him for financial support. According to him, 'I have my business and I can take care of myself. Africa remains my man, but I don't like politics.'[7] The different positions of ex-militants who remain loyal to and available for mobilisation by their ex-militant leaders and those who are not available for mobilisation demonstrate the importance of a patron–client relationship in the mobilisation of ex-militants during elections. This relationship is similar to that between the ex-militant leaders and their own political patrons – the ex-militant leader can be a client as well as a patron.

Nigeria's 2015 general election was an election with high stakes – and in the Niger Delta region, the stakes were particularly high for the regional political elites. The incumbent president, Goodluck Jonathan (People's Democratic Party or PDP), an ethnic Ijaw from Bayelsa State, was competing against Muhammadu Buhari (All Progressives Congress or APC), an ethnic Fulani from Katsina State in the country's North West region. Goodluck Jonathan's term in office had given political elites in the Niger Delta an opportunity to come closer to the presidency and gain from its benefits (Owen and Usman 2015). Apart from statutory appointments, political elites from the Niger Delta had secured opportunities within the national government, something they had historically been denied due to the ethnic nature of Nigerian politics. In the run-up to the elections, former President Obasanjo criticised President Goodluck Jonathan thus: 'For you to allow yourself to be "possessed", so to say, to the exclusion of most of the rest of Nigerians as an "Ijaw man" is a mistake that should never have been allowed to happen' (*Premium Times* 2013). In response, Edwin Clark, a notable member of the Ijaw ethnic group, noted Obasanjo's allusion to Goodluck Jonathan's Ijaw ethnicity in his governance style as 'contemptuous', 'myopic' and 'pejorative' (*The Will* 2014). As a result, the 2015 election was one of high stakes for the political elites in the Niger Delta.

Ex-militant leaders also emerged as prominent political actors in their communities as a result of armed militancy (Ukiwo and Ebiede 2012). The new power of ex-militant leaders is exemplified by their inclusion by government in oil industry patronage schemes, such as the pipeline protection contract, and their patronage in waterways security through the Nigerian Maritime Safety Agency (NIMASA) (*PM News* 2016). These perks and the ethnic-based political mobilisation made most ex-militant leaders support the PDP during the 2015 general elections. Thus, in the 2015 elections, most ex-militant leaders declared their support for President Jonathan (Eziukwu 2015).

Key ex-militant leaders campaigned for PDP candidates in their local communities. Using their influence and power gained over the years, some ex-militants went as far as nominating other ex-militants within their armed groups or other civilian loyalists to run for elected positions during the elections. Ex-militants received opportunities within political parties to nominate their preferred candidates for political appointments and elected positions at the regional level.[8] At the national level, ex-militants seem to represent the interests of the Niger Delta region; however, politics at the local level showed that ex-militants who were in support of the PDP sought to entrench their place as 'patrons', 'godfathers' and 'Big Men' in community politics. What was at stake for ex-militants was not simply the loss of power at the national level, but their position of influence within their own communities. Hence, ex-militant leaders used their networks of ex-fighters, financial resources and influence to support candidates during the elections with the aim of maintaining their position of power within local communities. The actions undertaken by ex-militant leaders in support of their preferred political parties, mostly the PDP, led to electoral violence during the 2015 general elections.

Regional dynamics The popularity of the PDP in the Niger Delta did not deter some regional political elites from joining the APC. The Rivers State governor at the time, Rotimi Amaechi, was among five PDP state governors who defected to the APC due to political differences within the PDP. The other four were Rabiu Musa Kwankwaso (Kano), Murtala Nyako (Adamawa), Abdulfatah Ahmed (Kwara) and Magatakarda Wamakko (Sokoto), all from states in Northern Nigeria. In Bayelsa State, Timipre Sylva, a former governor and prominent member of the PDP, also moved to the APC. The defection of Rotimi Amaechi and Timipre Sylva and their supporters to the APC was evidence of deep elite factionalism in the Niger Delta during the 2015 general elections.

Elite factionalism also extended to ex-militant leaders in the Niger Delta, something that was particularly evident in Bayelsa State during the 2015 electoral process. Generally, most ex-militant leaders in the state declared their support for President Goodluck Jonathan and the PDP (Eziukwu 2015). However, a faction of ex-militants led by ex-militant leader Africa Ukparasia defected to the APC. Ukparasia's personal declaration of cross-carpeting was significant because many ex-militant fighters remained loyal to him, their former leader.[9] Ukparasia's political move was the result of his post-militancy political experience, which had been informed by the alliance that had been established and formalised with Timipre Sylva when the latter was governor of Bayelsa State, from 2007 to 2012. During this period, Sylva established links with ex-militant leaders in Bayelsa State by managing the peace process that led to the end of militancy in the state. Within this process, he provided opportunities for militant leaders to nominate their allies for positions on the Bayelsa State Peace Committee. Ukparasia's ally and preferred candidate, Chief Tiwei Timipa Orunimighe, was also given the position of chairman of Southern Ijaw Local Government Council in 2009 (Ukiwo and Ebiede 2012). This appointment served to integrate Ukparasia into Chief Sylva's patronage network in Bayelsa State.

The PDP denied Sylva the opportunity to run for a second term in the state elections (Oyadongha 2012), which left him in a political wilderness immediately after the 2011 elections. Hence, he also quickly transferred his allegiance to the APC when it was established in 2013. Ukparasia's local political ally, Orunimighe, was also removed from his position as local government chairman by Henry Seriake Dickson, the new governor of Bayelsa State. As a result, Orunimighe also defected to the APC and became the party's chairman in Bayelsa State. Sylva continued to enjoy the loyalty of some local politicians who had served in his government and in his old political networks. Ukparasia, one of the most prominent ex-militant leaders in Bayelsa State, was among those who continued his political relationship with Sylva. But this support was also based on expectations of rewards if the APC emerged as victorious. An ex-militant fighter loyal to Ukparasia explained that the government of Goodluck Jonathan had not kept the promises offered to their leader and had denied him the patronage other ex-militant leaders were receiving.[10] This shows that the participation of ex-militant leaders in the electoral process in Bayelsa State is clearly driven by the patronage they can gain.

There was less factionalism in Delta State. Government Ekpomopolo (commonly known as Tompolo), the key ex-militant leader in the state, remained in the PDP. He is a beneficiary of security contracts from NIMASA for the waterways and from the Nigerian National Petroleum Company (NNPC) for oil pipelines (Edegbe, Midat and Okhomina 2015). The governor of Delta State at the time, Emmanuel Uduaghan, also remained in the PDP and supported the re-election of Goodluck Jonathan. Both ex-militants and the ruling political elite in the PDP shared a common agenda in the re-election of Jonathan. In addition, Ekpomopolo nominated the PDP's candidate for the deputy governorship, in addition to supporting several other aspiring political office holders in Delta State. Although there were active members of the political opposition within Delta State, there were no divisions between PDP members within the state; any divisions in Delta State were based on pre-existing political opposition lines. Both Bayelsa State and Rivers State were significantly different in this regard from Delta State. In the period leading up to the elections, the contest in Rivers State was between a faction led by Amaechi and another led by the PDP gubernatorial candidate, Nyesom Wike. All the ex-militant leaders within Rivers State were aligned with the PDP.

The examples described above illustrate the way in which ex-militant leaders are nested within the political competition for power in the Niger Delta. The situation explained here reinforces earlier theoretical discussions on the fragile nature of politics in societies emerging from violent conflicts and the unbridled competition for political power by actors in such societies. Ex-combatants are just one subset of those actors. But, as seen in the Niger Delta, a dominant factor in the involvement of ex-combatants in election processes is the involvement of the leaders of former armed groups in those processes.

Ex-militants and electoral violence during the 2015 elections

The Niger Delta was one of the regions in the country with the most reports of election-related incidents in connection to the 2015 electoral process (Partners for Peace 2015). Different forms of violence took place: for example, election materials were destroyed, there were clashes between supporters of political candidates, ex-militants were used as hired political 'thugs', political rallies were violently disrupted and shootings were reported. There were, however, important geographical variations between the different states of the region. In Delta State, there were disruptions of political rallies and attacks on political leaders, but little or no violence in areas dominated by ex-militants. This was due to the relative consensus among the leading political elites and ex-militant leaders. Government Ekpomopolo, the ex-militant leader of MEND in Delta State, supported the PDP. Ekpomopolo's charismatic leadership and large following meant that there was little or no dissent within the communities where he operated as a warlord. Bayelsa State had a different experience. The factionalism that occurred as a result of the defection of Africa Ukparasia meant that he was likely to lose his place of power in community politics and within the state if the APC did not emerge victorious in any of the state-level elections. Other ex-militant leaders in Southern Ijaw Local Government Area – the locality where Ukparasia had influence and power – maintained their support for the PDP, thereby intensifying the competition for power. In Rivers State, ex-militant leaders continued to support the PDP. However, the APC led by Governor Rotimi Amaechi made significant efforts to campaign in communities where ex-militant leaders wielded power and influence. This brought both parties into a space of confrontation, which often led to violence. The increased probability of violence in Rivers and Bayelsa states calls for a closer analysis of events there.

Bayelsa State The presidential election held in March 2015 did not result in widespread electoral violence in Bayelsa State. In sharp contrast, the December 2015 governorship election in Bayelsa State recorded incidences of violence.[11] This election was declared inconclusive following an outbreak of violence involving ex-militants in Southern Ijaw Local Government Area. Henry Seriake Dickson, the governor of Bayelsa State, described the elections as a 'war' due to the intensity of the violence. Reports of violence recorded during this period showed that it was related more to the legislative elections: for example, ex-militants destroyed campaign materials belong to a politician campaigning for legislative office in Brass on 25 January 2015 (Partners for Peace 2015). In Ekeremor, supporters of PDP and APC candidates clashed on 7 February 2015 and PDP party loyalists destroyed opposition campaign materials in Kolokuma Opokuma on 5 February (ibid.). Violent confrontation involving supporters of different political parties was also seen in Nembe on 31 January 2015 (ibid.). These examples show the specific pattern of election violence in Bayelsa State during the 2015 legislative elections; however, they also show that ex-militants were not involved in all cases of election violence. The only instance where ex-militants were involved occurred in Southern Ijaw Local Government Area during a local legislative election in Constituency 4 (ibid.). This constituency was home to ex-militant leaders Africa

Ukparasia and Joshuan Mackiver, who supported different candidates for the Constituency 4 legislative office: Ukparasia supported the APC candidate, while Mackiver supported the PDP candidate. Interviews conducted with community members confirmed that the confrontation between ex-militants during this election was the result of rivalry between the two ex-militant leaders in the area[12] – they struggled to ensure that politicians and community members who belonged to their network occupied positions of public authority within the state and the community.

Electoral violence occurred across Bayelsa State during the governorship elections held on 4 December 2015. The Southern Ijaw Local Government Area[13] in particular witnessed a violent confrontation between armed ex-militants that led to the cancellation of the election results for the entire local government area (Ukpong 2015). A witness to the event provided the following account:

> We were going to the local government secretariat. Africa and his boys were on one side of town and Joshua and his boys were on the other. Africa told Joshua and his boys to allow him to take the election materials. But they refused. It was not too long afterwards before Ogun Boss and other Africa boys started shooting at Joshua boys. Several persons were injured.[14]

The quote above illustrates the role the ex-militant leaders and ex-militant fighters had in the election violence and shows that the violence seemed to be a confrontation between two factions. However, it does not tell us why ex-militant leaders, who had previously collaborated in an insurgency against the Nigerian state, engaged in a violent confrontation against each other during the elections. In order to answer this question, we need to understand the political alliances of these ex-militant leaders at the end of the insurgency in which they participated. Africa Ukparasia had joined the APC, while Joshua Mackiver joined the PDP. Both men tried to use violence, a method they had both used during the insurgency, as a means to enhance the chances of their political parties.

The quote also contains information that reflects the dynamic nature of the ex-militant leaders' loyalty to their political parties and patrons. The respondent noted that it was Ogun Boss[15] who started shooting. This information is important for a number of reasons. Ogun Boss had supported the PDP during the presidential and legislative elections in Bayelsa State. During this period, he had opposed Africa Ukparasia, who supported the APC. However, Boss had disagreements with the PDP over the control of oil infrastructure security contracts in the state (*Premium Times* 2015). The state governor sought to control these contracts, but Ogun Boss wanted total control. Boss's failure to be awarded these contracts led him to oppose the PDP government that he had once supported. This clearly shows that, even though ex-militant leaders may be seen as clients in a patron–client relationship with political office holders, they also exercise their agency in negotiating their place in this relationship. To do this, they resort to violence or the threat of violence. Thus, ex-militant leaders should not be seen as clients without agency, but rather as actors who use their history and socio-political categorisation as entrepreneurs of violence to negotiate a place in the political system of the Niger Delta. In order to do this, the ex-militant leader mobilises his ex-fighters, especially those who continue to benefit from his continued dominance in the political system. This struggle is one factor that leads ex-militant fighters to participate in election violence even after participating in a DDR process.

The outcome of the Bayelsa State election shows the plausibility of this argument. Henry Seriake Dickson of the PDP was finally declared winner of the governorship election in Bayelsa State. In return, he appointed Joshua Mackiver, an ex-militant leader who had been engaged in the violent confrontations in support of his governorship candidacy, as chairman of Southern Ijaw Local Government Area (Oyadongha 2016). Africa Ukparasia lost his position of influence in the politics of the local government area and in Bayelsa State in general. This illustrates that the expectations of reward serve as a motivation for support, and that this leads ex-militants to engage in election violence.

Rivers State There were repeated incidences of violence in the period leading up to and during the elections in Rivers State. Data from the Partners for Peace project shows that violence occurred in several local government areas in Rivers State. For example, armed youths attacked and destroyed the campaign materials of the APC in Asari Toru Local Government Area on 18 January 2015. Also, armed youths bombed the site of a planned APC rally in Port Harcourt, the capital of Rivers State, on 24 January 2015. Reports also show that ex-militants, using violence against election officials and party agents, hijacked election materials in Degema Local Government Area on 23 January 2015. Attacks were also reported in Gokana and Obio Akpor Local Government Areas during the period of the elections (Partners for Peace 2015).

Reports of electoral violence in Rivers State show that not all acts of violence involved ex-militants. Some of these acts were carried out by youths who were not involved in armed militancy. This does not come as a surprise, as election violence was a common phenomenon in the region long before the involve-ment of ex-militants in politics (see Human Rights Watch 2007). However, cases of election violence reported in areas dominated by ex-militants tended to be more intense and destructive during the 2015 elections in Rivers State. For example, an APC campaign rally in Okrika, the home town and base of Ateke Tom, was violently disrupted by ex-militants (Ibanga 2015). After the elections, the Rivers State government set up a commission of inquiry on violence during elections, and witnesses testified that members of the APC were also violently attacked during the general elections in Akuku-Toru Local Government Area (Rivers State Government 2015).

The motives behind the involvement of ex-militant leaders in election violence in Rivers State during the 2015 elections could be compared with those in Bayelsa State. Such a comparison would highlight differences in the workings of the political networks in the two states. The election violence in Bayelsa State, as discussed earlier, shows that ex-militant groups confronted each other during the election process. However, in Rivers State, ex-militant leaders tended to remain in the then ruling PDP. Thus, the violence carried out by ex-militant fighters targeted those in the opposition parties, who were not necessarily ex-militant fighters and were not necessarily armed. With the exception of this difference, the role of ex-militant leaders in election violence was similar in the two states.

The violence that occurred in Okrika Local Government Area was credited mainly to ex-militant fighters under the control of Ateke Tom, the ex-militant leader of the NDV (Ibanga 2015). Ateke's interest in the 2015 elections was defined by his support for the PDP (Olapade 2013): like many Ijaw elites, he benefited from the patronage of the PDP-led government, and, like other ex-militant leaders, this patronage gave him a position of privilege and power within Okrika, where he had most influence. There were fears that a government led by the APC would terminate these patronage contracts, which would displace Ateke from his privileged position in the community. These fears became reality after the APC's Muhammadu Buhari was sworn in as president on 29 May 2016 and cancelled all contracts to ex-militant leaders. This highlights the anxieties of ex-militant leaders, such as Ateke, who mobilised their ex-fighters to ensure that the PDP won the elections in their local areas.

Ex-militant leaders also have an interest in ensuring that their preferred candidates emerge victorious at the state level. Thus, Ateke's interest did not end with trying to ensure the victory of the PDP in the presidential elections. Historically, Ateke's involvement in election violence goes back beyond the 2015 elections. In fact, his foray into armed militancy started when he was a so-called 'thug' hired for election violence by the PDP during the 2003 elections (Asuni 2009). Ateke's continuous membership in the PDP creates a relationship and a motivation for him to continue to ensure that the party emerges victorious within his domain. This is because the success of the PDP at the level of the subnational state creates possibilities for continued patronage. Ateke therefore engages in this process by mobilising his ex-militant fighters, who then become involved in the hijacking of election materials, intimidation of voters and harassment of members of the opposition.

The defection of Amaechi to the APC also played a significant role in the anxieties that fuelled election violence in Rivers State. As already noted, ex-militant leaders remained in the PDP despite the emergence of the APC as a governing party in the state. Thus, the continued governance of the APC in Rivers State would probably have meant the political alienation of ex-militant leaders who supported the PDP. This risk of political alienation increased the stakes of the elections for ex-militant leaders such as Ateke Tom, who were driven by these anxieties to mobilise ex-militant fighters who remained loyal to them during the elections in Rivers State.

Ex-militant leaders in Rivers State were reported as being involved in election violence even before the emergence of armed militancy in the Niger Delta (Human Rights Watch 2004). In fact, as argued by (Ukiwo 2011: 27), 'militancy has thrived in the region because guns rather than votes count during elections'. However, the analysis so far shows that the continuous involvement of ex-militant leaders and ex-militant fighters in election violence does not lie within the linear patron–client relationships that characterise mobilisations for political violence. Instead, ex-militant leaders have emerged as actors who continuously negotiate their place within the political context of their communities. They use resources available to them to negotiate this place, including their ex-fighters. In situations where the electoral process is susceptible to influence by violence, they deploy their ex-militant fighters to carry out violent actions that could influence the outcome of the elections. The PDP emerged victorious in the governorship elections and in a majority of state legislative elections in Rivers State. This victory was an outcome of a violent contest that led to the repeated cancellation of elections in certain areas. The violence could be interpreted as an unbridled contest for political power by the political elite, but one could also argue that it is also the result of the struggle of ex-militant leaders to remain powerful in their communities and to maintain informal positions of influence in state politics.

Conclusion

This chapter has examined when and why ex-militants engage in electoral violence in Nigeria's Niger Delta. The theoretical premise is that ex-militant leaders have gained power in their communities and in the wider political processes of the state. To maintain this power, ex-militant leaders have to ensure that the political party they support emerges victorious in elections, which is why they engage in the electoral process. This goes beyond the notion that ex-militants and their leaders are clients whose agency is mainly expressed in support of political elites. The evidence and analysis show that ex-militant leaders tend to act as patrons or 'Big Men' themselves in their communities and local governments, and that they maintain this status due to patronage contracts they have with Nigeria's oil industry. In addition, ex-militant leaders remain influential among their ex-fighters because of the nature of the Niger Delta DDR programme, which ensures that ex-militant leaders control the participation of their ex-fighters in the DDR process. To maintain their power and privilege locally and in the broader political processes of the state, ex-militants tend to mobilise their material resources and militia networks to carry out electoral violence with the aim of influencing the outcome of elections in the Niger Delta.

The findings in Rivers and Bayelsa states show that this theoretical claim manifests in different ways. Ex-militant leaders in Rivers State tend to focus on maintaining the power of the PDP in the state. Hence, their focus was on violently attacking members of the APC during the 2015 electoral process. This resulted in electoral violence that impacted on the outcome of the elections in areas where ex-militant leaders had influence and control. Unlike Bayelsa State, there was no internal factionalism among ex-militants in Rivers State during the elections. The major electoral violence that was recorded in Bayelsa State occurred among ex-militants who were in support of opposing political parties. This shows that electoral violence is likely to be more intense in states where militant groups are split along party lines.

The findings and analysis in this chapter show that ex-militant leaders tend to exercise their agency in their own interests: that is, to maintain their positions of power and privilege in their communities. Electoral violence is a way for ex-militant leaders to maintain the power they have gained as a result of the violent conflicts and militancy in the Niger Delta. It is a struggle for them not to revert to being disposable 'clients' of 'Big Men' in the political process. For ordinary ex-militant fighters, their continued relationship with ex-militant leaders is what leads them to engage in electoral violence. This chapter argues that the networks behind electoral violence are complex and multilayered. An important insight drawn from this complexity is that the conception in the literature of ex-militant leaders as 'middle-men', 'brokers' and 'clients' in the politics of societies emerging from conflict is incomplete. Instead, ex-militant leaders tend to act as Big Men and patrons in such societies. In this way, ex-militants see elections as a zero-sum game, since their positions of power and influence tend to depend on the outcomes of elections.

This chapter demonstrates the need for policy makers and electoral institutions to engage with ex-militant leaders when preparing for elections in societies emerging from armed conflict. Often, ex-militant leaders and ex-fighters are viewed as potentially dangerous actors in the political process. It is assumed that the concerns of ex-militants should have been addressed by DDR programmes. But this assumption falls short of the reality. Ex-militants focus on the broader political processes of their society after attending DDR programmes. In this chapter, I show that, while ordinary ex-fighters may focus on economic opportunities, ex-militant leaders are concerned about political power in their communities and within the state. Clearly, ex-combatants are not passive actors in post-conflict political processes. Hence, there is a need for policy makers and electoral institutions to develop specific policy instruments that seek to engage ex-combatants in post-conflict elections.

Notes

1 Other states included in the official definition of the Niger Delta are Abia, Imo, Ondo, Akwa Ibom, Cross River and Edo states. This definition emerged in 2000 following the creation of the Niger Delta Development Commission (NDDC).

2 Ex-militants as a social category are often referred to as ex-combatants in the literature of peace and conflict studies.

3 Author interview with DDR official, Abuja, January 2014.

4 Author interview with ex-militant in Ologbobiri, Bayelsa State, January 2014.

5 Author interview with community member, Ologbobiri, Bayelsa State, December 2013.

6 Author interview with ex-militant, Ologbobiri, Bayelsa State, 14 December 2014.

7 Author interview with ex-militant member, Ologbobiri, Bayelsa State, September 2015.

8 Author interview with Ibaba S. Ibaba, a Nigerian scholar, Yenagoa, Bayelsa State, February 2014.

9 Author interviews with ex-militants from Africa Ukparasia's faction in Ologbobiri, Southern Ijaw Local Government Area, Bayelsa State, November 2014.

10 Author interview with ex-militant in Yenagoa, Bayelsa State, 12 September 2015.

11 The election in Bayelsa State occurred later because of a judicial process that extended the tenure of a governor in 2011 owing to an election that was re-run in 2008. This meant that the governorship election calendar in Bayelsa State was disrupted and no longer followed the general election calendar that is common across Nigeria.

12 Author interviews with community members, Ologbobiri, Bayelsa State, September 2015.

13 All armed militant groups in Bayelsa State were based in this local government area during the period of the armed insurgency in the Niger Delta.

14 Telephone interview by the author with Coronation Topko, 10 December 2015.

15 This is an alias. The original name of the ex-militant is Paul Eris. He is an indigene of Peremabiri community in Southern Ijaw Local Government Area.

References

Adetula, V. (2014) 'Money Bags, Violence and Electoral Democracy in Nigeria'. Paper presented at the Nordic Africa Days (NAD), Nordic Africa Institute, Uppsala, Sweden, 26–27 September.

Ake, C. (1996) *Democracy and Development in Africa*. Washington DC: Brookings Institution.

Alapiki, H. and U. Ukiwo (2013) 'Anxious Godfathers, Errant Godsons: Neopatrimonialism and Democratisation in Nigeria', *Politeia* 32 (1): 40–58.

Albert, I. O. (2005) 'Explaining "Godfatherism" in Nigerian Politics', *African Sociological Review/Revue Africaine de Sociologie* 9 (2): 79–105.

Arowosegbe, J. (2011) *Reflections on the Challenge of Reconstructing Post-conflict States in West Africa: Insights from Claude Ake's Political Writings*. Uppsala: Nordic Africa Institute.

Asuni, J. B. (2009) *Understanding the Armed Groups of the Niger Delta*. Washington DC: Council on Foreign Relations.

Berdal, M. (1996) 'Disarmament and Demobilization after Civil Wars', *Adelphi Papers* 36 (303): 88.

Best, S. G. and D. Von Kemedi (2005) 'Armed Groups and Conflict in Rivers and Plateau States, Nigeria' in N. Florquin and E. Berman (eds), *Armed and Aimless: Armed Groups, Guns, and Human Security in the ECOWAS Region*. Geneva: Small Arms Survey.

Bøås, M. (2011) '"Mend Me": The Movement for the Emancipation of the Niger Delta and the Empowerment of Violence' in C. Obi and S. A. Rustad (eds), *Oil and Insurgency in the Niger Delta: Managing the Complex Politics of Petro-violence*. London and New York NY: Zed Books.

De Vries, H. and N. Wiegink (2011) 'Breaking Up and Going Home? Contesting Two Assumptions in the Demobilization and Reintegration of Former Combatants', *International Peacekeeping* 18 (1): 38–51.

Ebiede, T. M. (2016) *Beyond Rebellion: Alternative Narratives of Violent Conflicts and the Implications for Peacebuilding in the Niger Delta*. New York NY: African Peacebuilding Network, Social Science Research Council.

Ebienfa, K. I. (2011) 'Militancy in the Niger Delta and the Emergent Categories', *Review of African Political Economy* 38 (130): 637–43.

Edegbe, O., J. Midat and O. Okhomina (2015) 'Nigeria: NIMASA Pays Tompolo N1.5 Billion Monthly – Ex-Chairman', AllAfrica, 3 June. Available at http://allafrica.com/stories/201506030113.html (accessed 12 December 2017).

Eziukwu, A. (2015) 'Ex-militants Canvass Support for Jonathan's Re-election', *Premium Times*, 25 February. Available at www.premiumtimesng.com/news/top-news/177483-ex-militants-canvass-support-for-jonathans-re-election.html (accessed 1 June 2016).

Human Rights Watch (2004) *Nigeria's 2003 Elections: The Unacknowledged Violence*. New York NY: Human Rights Watch.

Human Rights Watch (2007) *Election or 'Selection'?: Human Rights Abuse and Threats to Free and Fair Elections in Nigeria*. New York NY: Human Rights Watch.

Ibaba, S. I. (2005) *Understanding the Niger Delta Crisis*. Port Harcourt: Amethyst and Colleagues Publishers.

Ibanga, I. (2015) 'Explosions, Gunshots Disrupt APC Rally in Patience Jonathan's Home Town', *Premium Times*, 17 February. Available at www.premiumtimesng.com/news/headlines/177011-breaking-explosion-gunshots-disrupt-apc-rally-in-patience-jonathans-home-town.html.

Iwilade, A. (2017) 'Slipping through the Net: Everyday Agency of Youth and Politics of Amnesty in Nigeria's Niger Delta (2009–2015)', *Journal of Contemporary African Studies* 35 (3): 266–83.

Jarstad, A. K. and T. D. Sisk (2008) *From War to Democracy: Dilemmas of Peacebuilding*. Cambridge: Cambridge University Press.

Kynoch, G. (2005) 'Crime, Conflict and Politics in Transition-era South Africa', *African Affairs* 104 (416): 493–514.

Lyons, T. (2002) 'Postconflict Elections: War Termination, Democratization, and Demilitarizing Politics. Working Paper 20. Arlington VA: School for Conflict Analysis and Resolution, George Mason University.

Maclay, C. and A. Özerdem (2010) '"Use" Them or "Lose'" Them: Engaging Liberia's Disconnected Youth through Socio-political Integration', *International Peacekeeping* 17 (3): 343–60.

McGregor, J. (2002) 'The Politics of Disruption: War Veterans and the Local State in Zimbabwe', *African Affairs* 101 (402): 9–37.

Nwajiaku-Dahou, K. (2012) 'The Political Economy of Oil and "Rebellion" in Nigeria's Niger Delta', *Review of African Political Economy* 39 (132): 295–313.

Obi, C. (2009) 'Nigeria's Niger Delta: Understanding the Complex Drivers of Violent Oil-related Conflict', *Africa Development* 34 (2).

Olapade, A. (2013) 'As Wike, Obuah and Ex-militant Ateke Tom Hold Rally, They Say "Returning Jonathan to Aso Rock is our Agenda"', *The Scoop*, 18 November. Available at www.thescoopng.com/as-wike-obuah-and-ex-militant-ateke-tom-hold-rally-they-say-returning-jonathan-to-aso-rock-is-our-agenda/ (accessed 12 June 2016).

Omotola, S. (2010) 'Explaining Electoral Violence in Africa's "New" Democracies', *African Journal on Conflict Resolution* 10 (3): 51–73.

Owen, O. and Z. Usman (2015) 'Why Goodluck Jonathan Lost the Nigerian Presidential Election of 2015', *African Affairs* 114 (456): 455–71.

Oyadongha, S. (2012) 'Sylva Has Not Dumped PDP – Aides', *Vanguard*, 9 January. Available at www.vanguardngr.com/2012/01/sylva-has-not-dumped-pdp-aides/ (accessed 2 April 2016).

Oyadongha, S. (2016) 'Ex-militant leader, 7 Others Make Local Government Caretaker List in Bayelsa', *Vanguard*, 2 April. Available at www.vanguardngr.com/2016/04/ex-militant-leader-7-others-make-local-govt-caretaker-list-bayelsa/ (accessed 2 June 2016).

Özerdem, A. (2012) 'A Re-conceptualisation of Ex-combatant Reintegration: "Social Reintegration" Approach', *Conflict, Security and Development* 12 (1): 51–73.

Partners for Peace (2015) 'Peace Building Map'. Available at www.p4p-nigerdelta.org/peace-building-map (accessed 12 June 2016).

Peters, K. (2007) 'From Weapons to Wheels: Young Sierra Leonean Ex-combatants Become Motorbike Taxi-riders', *Journal of Peace, Conflict and Development* 10 (10): 1–23.

PM News (2016) 'We Still Have Contract with Tompolo's Company', *PM News*, 30 October. Available at www.pmnewsnigeria.com/2016/10/30/we-still-have-contract-with-tompolos-company-nimasa/ (accessed 22 September 2017).

Premium Times (2013) 'Exclusive: Obasanjo Writes Jonathan, Accuses President of Lying, Trying to Destroy Nigeria, Promoting Corruption', *Premium Times*, 11 December. Available at www.premiumtimesng.com/news/151275-exclusive-obasanjo-writes-jonathan-accuses-president-lying-destroying-nigeria-promoting-corruption.html (accessed 22 September 2017).

Premium Times (2015) 'Bayelsa State Government and Ex-militants on War Path over Pipeline Surveillance Contract', *Premium Times*, 15 March. Available at www.premiumtimesng.com/regional/south-south-regional/178515-bayelsa-government-ex-militants-on-war-path-over-pipeline-surveillance-contracts.html (accessed 22 September 2017).

Reno, W. (2010) 'Transforming West African Militia Networks for Postwar Recovery' in K. B. Harpviken (ed.), *Troubled Regions and Failing States: The Clustering and Contagion of Armed Conflict*. Comparative Social Research 27. Bingley, UK: Emerald Group.

Rivers State Government (2015) *Report of the Commission of Inquiry to Investigate all the Politically Motivated Killings and Damage to Property in Rivers State Immediately Before, During and After the 2015 General Elections*. Available at www.icla.up.ac.za/images/un/commissionsofinquiries/files/Nigeria%20Rivers%202015%20final%20report.pdf (accessed 12 December 2017).

Schulhofer-Wohl, J. and N. Sambanis (2010) *Disarmament, Demobilization, and Reintegration Programs: An Assessment*. Research Report. Sandöverken, Sweden: Folke Bernadotte Academy.

Söderström, J. (2011a) 'Politics of Affection: Ex-combatants, Political Engagement and Reintegration Programs in Liberia'. PhD thesis, Department of Government, Uppsala University.

Söderström, J. (2011b) 'Dissent and Opposition among Ex-combatants in Liberia', *Democratization* 18 (5): 1146–67.

Spear, J. (2006) 'From Political Economies of War to Political Economies of Peace: The Contribution of DDR after Wars of Predation',

Contemporary Security Policy 27 (1): 168–89.

Tamuno, T. T. (2008) 'The Geographic Niger Delta'. Paper presented at the International Conference on the Nigerian State, Oil Industry and the Niger Delta, organised by the Department of Political Science, Niger Delta University, in collaboration with the Center for Applied Environmental Research, University of Missouri-Kansas City.

The Will (2014) 'Chief Edwin Clark's Letter to Obasanjo', *The Will*, 3 January. Available at http://thewillnigeria.com/Chief-Edwin-Clarks-letter-to-Obasanjocompressedpdf.pdf (accessed 13 December 2017).

Themnér, A. (2015) 'Former Military Networks and the Micro-politics of Violence and Statebuilding in Liberia', *Comparative Politics* 47 (3): 334–53.

Themnér, A. and M. Utas (2016) 'Governance through Brokerage: Informal Governance in Post-civil War Societies', *Civil Wars* 18 (3): 255–80.

Ukiwo, U. (2011) 'The Nigerian State, Oil and the Niger Delta Crisis' in C. I. Obi and S. A. Rustad (eds), *Oil and Insurgency in the Niger Delta: Managing the Complex Politics of Petro-violence*. London and New York NY: Zed Books.

Ukiwo, U. and T. M. Ebiede (2012) 'Beyond Amnesty: The Challenges of Democracy and Sustainable Peacebuilding in the Niger Delta', *Niger Delta Research Digest* 6 (2): 109–33.

Ukpong, C. (2015) 'Bayelsa: INEC Cancels Elections in Southern Ijaw Local Government, Declares Elections Inconclusive', *Premium Times*, 7 December. Available at www.premiumtimesng.com/news/headlines/194772-breaking-bayelsa-inec-cancels-election-in-southern-ijaw-declares-election-inconclusive.html (accessed 2 June 2016).

United Nations (2010) *Second Generation Disarmament, Demobilization and Reintegration (DDR) Practices in Peace Operations: A Contribution to the New Horizon Discussion on Challenges and Opportunities for UN Peacekeeping*. New York NY: United Nations Department of Peacekeeping Operations.

Utas, M. (ed.) (2012) *African Conflicts and Informal Power: Big Men and Networks*. London and New York NY: Zed Books.

Vlassenroot, K. and T. Raeymaekers (2004) *Conflict and Social Transformation in Eastern DR Congo*. Ghent: Academia Press.

7 | The winner takes it all: post-war rebel networks, Big Man politics, and the threat of violence in the 2011 Liberian elections

Mariam Bjarnesen

Introduction

In October 2011, Liberia faced one of its sternest post-war challenges – the second general elections following two brutal civil wars (1989–96 and 1999–2003). While the international peacekeeping mission, United Nations Mission in Liberia (UNMIL), had organised the first post-war elections held in 2005, this time the Liberian state resumed full responsibility. The elections were widely seen as a test of the country's security-political situation, and as an opportunity to consolidate Liberia's fragile peace. Yet there were also fears of renewed instability, or even violence. The elections would be telling, and not only in terms of the final electoral results. More importantly, the pre-election political mobilisation and the manner in which the elections were conducted would, it was thought, be a powerful gauge of Liberia's security system and how far the country had come since the 2003 peace agreement.

In most post-conflict countries, much is at stake and tensions are high during elections (e.g. Harris 2011; Lyons 2005; Obi 2007). The 2011 Liberian elections were no exception. Specifically, they illustrated how important it is for many ex-combatants to become what they regard as 'politically active', but, more than this, they highlighted the importance of supporting the 'right' political candidate. During elections, Liberians in general, and perhaps ex-combatants in particular, partly due to their violent potential, have access to opportunities that are usually out of their reach. These political events are the moments when the otherwise distant political elite has to listen to the Liberian people. But the difference between winning and losing in Liberia can be immense, something that can be demonstrated by following networks on both sides of the dividing line. For my informants, political involvement was very advantageous for one side; for the other, it was disastrous.

In this chapter I use the elections as a point of departure for analysing the role of Liberian ex-combatants, and how such a political event can highlight the relevance of talking about what I refer to as 'post-war rebel networks', eight years after the war came to an end. The empirical research that informs this chapter was gathered through in-depth interviews with a distinct category of Liberian ex-combatants: namely, ex-combatants for whom the networks established during the war remain important. The focus here, in other words, is on former rebel soldiers who have actively maintained their links to each other, or to other former combatants, in an organised, but not formalised, manner. I choose to use the term post-war *rebel* networks simply because the individuals I have followed within these structures mainly have a past as rebel soldiers. For this chapter, I specifically followed ex-combatants in support of the presidential candidates who, ultimately, were the most important candidates in the 2011 elections – the incumbent president Ellen Johnson Sirleaf from the Unity Party (UP) and Winston Tubman, the presidential candidate from the Congress of Democratic Change (CDC) – before, during and after the elections.

The chapter analyses whether a lingering temptation to mobilise such networks as potential perpetrators of electoral violence still existed during the time leading up to, and during, the 2011 Liberian elections. It takes its point of departure from the concept of Liberian 'Big Man politics' as a form of clientelism (see, e.g., Utas 2012a; Jörgel and Utas 2007). This conceptualisation embraces the idea that in Liberia, as elsewhere where there is an apparent lack of a well-functioning state, people depend on individual Big Men with important positions in business, politics, the military or perhaps illegal activities who use their resources to provide their followers with mutual benefits for them and their networks. Furthermore, a general perception of ex-combatants is that they are intimately linked with post-war violence and instability. Following this logic, the mobilisation of ex-combatants during post-war elections would run a great risk of ultimately resulting in violence. One of the central findings of this chapter suggests that, while there are examples of violent outcomes, the mobilisation of ex-combatants by political candidates during times of post-war elections is not necessarily done for the purpose of winning elections through the use of violence. This conclusion underscores the more general point that ex-combatant involvement in such political events does not automatically result in electoral violence.

Post-conflict elections – the final break with war?

Elections in post-conflict countries are often seen as important markers of a state's transition from war to peace. Elections are therefore prioritised within international efforts aimed at rebuilding states and promoting democracy after violent conflicts. In high-profile international interventions in particular, elections also have an important symbolic value, signalling in both the domestic and the international arena that a legitimate government authority has prevailed. This is seen as representing an essential step in the process of state reconstruction, and thus a central part of post-conflict state building (Reilly 2013). Yet, when electoral violence still occurs, it naturally makes us question the sustainability of the newly achieved peace and the state of the democratisation process in general. Electoral violence – together with its causes, perpetrators and consequences – has received increased attention for these reasons in recent years (e.g. Höglund 2009; Laakso 2007; Mehler 2007). Such research is of great value, not least because it can tell us something about the level of stability that a country has reached after a conflict. But should this lead to the conclusion that the absence of electoral violence is a sign of a state's final break with war? In this chapter, I suggest otherwise. Moran (2006), in her research on violence and democracy in Liberia, notes the Western tendency to view these two concepts as occupying opposite ends of an evolutionary scale whereby the successor to widespread violence is imagined to be democracy. Moran questions whether democracy and violence really are separate, or even separable, or whether there is violence in democracy and democracy in violence. Moran asks if a people really can be said to 'choose' democracy over war and vice versa. In answer to these questions, she argues that in Liberian political discourse violence and democracy are not conceptually opposed, but rather are aspects of the same understanding of legitimacy. She suggests that Liberian history can be understood as an ongoing interplay between themes of democracy and violence enacted at both local and national levels (ibid.). In this chapter, I approach the 2011 Liberian elections from a similar perspective. I suggest that the elections, despite the relatively low levels of violence, cannot be seen as a final break with war. On the contrary: the elections in this case make Liberia's wartime past more evident. War and peace are entangled, not opposed, and the elections illustrate this continuity. For instance, as pointed out by Harris and Lewis (2013) in their analysis of the Liberian elections, many of the political actors with high levels of popularity who had built on their war records returned in 2011, illustrating that the time that had passed since the war did not appear to have altered the political environment. The use of post-war rebel networks during post-conflict election processes, whether or not this leads to the use or threat of violence, is an illustrative example of these war–peace entanglements.

Liberia's recent history of electoral violence

The use of wartime structures and ex-combatants in order to win elections is not a new phenomenon in Liberia. As Lyons (1998), among others, observed during the 1997 elections after the first civil war, the former National Patriotic Front of Liberia (NPFL) rebel leader Charles Taylor converted his military organisation into an efficient mass-mobilising political party where patronage replaced guns and rallies roadblocks, in order to win the political competition. Taylor's political party – the National Patriotic Party (NPP) – provided a civilian platform from which he could compete for votes during the elections, but in reality the organisation remained fundamentally militarised (Lyons 2005). Taylor then convinced the UN monitors to accept the result of the elections in which his NPFL had intimidated voters, and he was elected president (Reno 2011). As noted by Reilly (2013), the easiest way to attract voters in post-conflict societies is often to appeal to the very same insecurities that generated the original conflict in the first place. In such cases, Reilly argues, instead of attempting to win support with policy appeals, post-conflict parties have a strong incentive to downplay policy choices and instead mobilise voters along identity lines. In the Liberian case this seems to be true, as wartime insecurities as well as aspects of identity appear to have played an important role in all post-conflict elections. It should be noted, however, that a remarkable aspect of the 2005 elections was the virtually complete disappearance of rebel groups in the political process, as neither the rebel group LURD (Liberians United for Reconciliation and Democracy) nor MODEL (Movement for Democracy in Liberia) transformed into political parties. Sekou Conneh, the former chairman of LURD, reappeared in the elections as a presidential candidate of his own political party, but the attempt was rather ineffectual as his estranged wife and former co-leader Aisha Conneh decided to support Johnson Sirleaf and the UP instead (Harris 2011).

According to Harris (2011), many rebel generals and leaders of insurgent forces seemed to have been satisfied with unseating Taylor and pursuing lucrative deals within the National Transitional Government of Liberia (NTGL) and in business. Still, the war and former rebel soldiers continued to have a significant impact on the elections even after the peace agreement had been signed in 2003. As demonstrated by Sawyer (2008), the ending of the war and the removal of the oligarchy and warlords did not make Liberia a political *tabula rasa*. During the 2005 elections, as noted by Sawyer, the candidates who could claim to have provided security for local communities during the wars were favoured by the voters. Candidates associated with armed groups with credible records among their people were elected. In Nimba County, both elected senators had a past as combatants. Prince Johnson, the former leader of the rebel group Independent National Patriotic Front of Liberia (INPFL), who constantly reminded voters of his protection of them during the conflict and his ability to defend them again should there be another war, won the senior senate seat by a landslide. The former NPFL commander Adolphus Dolo,[1] who won the second senator seat, campaigned on his record of defending Nimba County against LURD forces in 2001. Sawyer (ibid.) notes that a similar pattern could also be seen in other parts of the country during the elections, although to a lesser extent. Such dynamics of rebel transformation at election time in post-war democracies raise important questions. As noted by Anders Themnér (2017), the evolution of a wartime general such as Dolo into a post-war democrat highlights a central problem facing many war-torn countries: that electoral politics often becomes a game contested by Big Men with violent backgrounds in a context of façade institutions and weak authoritarian political parties. As Themnér observes, a central question is therefore what this recurring tendency implies. Will former warlords on the political scene continue to employ wartime tactics, such as inflicting fear, orchestrating violence, committing abuses and engaging in criminal activities? Or will they choose more democratic paths and seek to reconcile war-affected groups? In his research on warlords turned politicians, Themnér comes to the important conclusion that these actors are not a priori reckless and irrational, bent on spoiling peace processes and democratisation, and that there is little evidence that they would automatically engage in aggression. On the contrary, Themnér (ibid.) finds that most so-called 'warlord democrats' act in a warlike manner only under very specific conditions. In this chapter, following a similar logic, I examine the consequences of how, why and when post-war rebel networks, rather than individuals, become involved in electoral politics, particularly considering the risk of violence, instability and the continuation of wartime logics.

The 2011 Liberian elections and the involvement of ex-combatants

In August 2003, the government of Liberia, and the two rebel groups the LURD and the MODEL, signed the comprehensive peace agreement that came to mark the end of war in Liberia. Years of brutal fighting had left the war-torn republic with overwhelming challenges. The fragile state was to be rebuilt and security re-established. With major assistance and funding from the international community, Liberia underwent a disarmament, demobilisation, rehabilitation and reintegration (DDRR) process of ex-combatants, which disarmed over 100,000 combatants. With this process, which lasted until 2009, Liberia was to integrate former combatants into civil society and disrupt lingering post-war rebel networks (*UNMIL Today* 2009). Nevertheless, in 2011, at the time of the second post-war elections, these networks were mobilised in different capacities by the main political candidates, as we shall see in this chapter.

Winston Tubman and the vigilante leader In 2009, I met Alex for the first time. Alex had emerged as a leader of a vigilante group in Sinkor, Monrovia a few years earlier. The group saw themselves as local defenders: defenders of their community in an area that the Liberian National Police (LNP) did not dare enter at night. At dusk, the young men of the group gathered. Following Alex's instructions they were divided into smaller groups and took turns to patrol the neighbourhood until the early morning hours. Anyone not belonging to the community who was found wandering in their streets was stopped and questioned. Suspected criminals, or anyone caught committing a crime, were to be brought directly to Alex and then handed over to the police for further investigation. This did not always happen, however. From time to time, the vigilantes not only took it upon themselves to be the neighbourhood's watchmen; they also considered themselves fit to determine the captured individual's guilt or innocence after an on-the-spot interrogation, as well as to inflict the punishment (see also Kantor and Persson 2011).

Alex had not been a rebel soldier. Among the approximately fifty men who made up the vigilante group, that made him an exception. The group's members came from different backgrounds, ethnic groups, parts of Liberia and rebel factions. What they now shared was not only their community and their status as ex-combatants but also poverty and unemployment. The members of the community could not afford to pay the vigilantes, but most contributed a little money or food to keep the group going. In this way, for some of these young men, being a vigilante was a way to secure a daily meal, but it was also a way to make use of skills learned during the war. According to vigilante members and other members of the community, Alex had been chosen because he was well respected, well known, and a trusted man in the neighbourhood. He, in turn, made good use of the ex-combatants' skills as informal neighbourhood security providers. Their years of service in different rebel movements had taught them how to organise themselves, how to secure an area, and where to take positions in order to protect their neighbourhood and ambush suspected criminals. They knew how to fight, but, more importantly, as Alex and others in the community often pointed out, they were fearless and feared by others for their perceived violent nature. The knowledge that the vigilante group was primarily composed of ex-combatants, in other words, had a deterrent effect on outsiders.

But the advantages of having former rebels as vigilantes also came with its perils. The ex-combatants were more likely to take the law into their own hands when it came to punishment. The rule that the suspected criminal was to be brought to Alex first and then to the police was, as noted above, broken from time to time. The ex-combatants' past experiences from war and their fearless attitude to violence made them unpredictable and difficult to control. Catching a person in the act of committing a crime, the ex-combatatants were more likley to resort to spontaneous violence. The community's attitudes towards the vigilante group were thus ambivalent. As a community member who was not part of the vigilante group told me, the group enjoyed strong support in the community because the alternative was non-existent: the LNP were neither present nor trusted. The ex-combatants' skills in security and fearless attitude made them valuable security providers in the eyes of the community, while at the same time, at least to a certain extent, they could be controlled as they worked for the community instead of constituting a threat against it.

When I met Alex again in September 2011, life had taken a new turn for him and his group. Alex and the men around him had 'gone into politics', as they saw it themselves.[2] One might also say that Liberian politicians had reached out to the ex-combatants. Alex had been approached by Winston

Tubman – the man who, in May 2011, had been chosen as the presidential candidate for the CDC party. After being nominated, Tubman set out to arrange his personal protection, primarily by establishing his own informal security group. Tubman wanted men around him who could work as his personal bodyguards, and who could protect him when campaigning but possibly also show force, power and status. To find men suitable for the job, Tubman turned to Alex. This was not the first time Tubman had run for president and not the first time he had approached Alex. Like Ellen Johnson Sirleaf, Tubman, the nephew of Liberia's longest-serving president, William Tubman, was part of and brought up within the old Americo-Liberian elite.[3] He had degrees from the London School of Economics, Cambridge and Harvard University and had owned his own law firm. During Samuel Doe's years in power, Tubman served as Liberia's Minister of Justice. After the fall of Doe, Tubman had continued his career as a diplomat within the UN and had just left a position as the UN Special Representative of the Secretary-General on Somalia in time for the 2005 elections (BBC News 2005). Tubman then ran for Doe's old party, the National Democratic Party of Liberia (NDPL) (see also Harris 2011).

Tubman had got to know Alex and had called on him to establish an informal security force of ex-combatants to accompany him during his campaigning in the 2005 elections. Tubman had lost the race against Ellen Johnson Sirleaf back then, and Alex and his men had returned to their normal life and business. But for the 2011 elections, Tubman needed the vigilante leader and his network once again. The security force established around Tubman and the CDC party came to resemble a military unit in many ways. Alex and four other men, the others being former rebel generals, were chosen as the unit's main commanders. Some of these men had also worked for Tubman in 2005, while others were new recruits. Each commander had a specific task and main responsibility for areas such as Tubman's overall day and night-time security, campaigning and motorcade security, private residence and party headquarters security, and so on. Under each commander, Alex assigned ex-combatants from his vigilante group to work as security providers. The group closest to Tubman was composed of approximately twenty-five men. However, the overall informal security network around CDC was much larger. George Weah, the well-known footballer and former CDC presidential candidate from 2005, ran for the vice presidency under Tubman during the 2011 elections. He also had his own personal informal security force, resembling in structure the one organised for Tubman. Finally, there was an additional informal security group working for the CDC party, which some informants called the 'Battle Cry'. The Battle Cry was a much larger group, composed of approximately 1,000 men and a few women, most of whom were ex-combatants. The Battle Cry did not operate autonomously but was under the command of Tubman's security group. The group's members were located both in Monrovia and out in the counties and worked as reinforcements for Tubman's security group during his campaigning. For example, the group was to check and secure an area before Tubman and his closest security group arrived in towns and villages to campaign. The members of Battle Cry never received any regular payment from the CDC party but were often given food and drinks and, sometimes, small amounts of money. The members of Alex's security group closest to Tubman could count on somewhat more regular payments from the CDC party but, for them, as for the members of the wider security structures of the party, what mattered were the hopes and promise of an eventual electoral victory for Winston Tubman. When I talked about this with Alex and the other commanders of the security group, they were all very enthusiastic. If Tubman were to win the elections, they felt sure that the victory would imply permanent security jobs. At the very least, the commanders would be incorporated into the official security system, either as bodyguards or in other positions within the formal security institutions. They did not even want to think about where they would end up if Tubman lost, but they were sure that a defeat would leave them with their struggle with unemployment and poverty. A victory for the incumbent president Ellen Johnson Sirleaf, they argued, would not give them any benefits at all.[4]

Ellen Johnson Sirleaf and the former LURD general Michael had achieved what many only dream of and had secured employment in the formal sector: a senior position within one of the country's security institutions. If 'reintegration is the process by which ex-combatants acquire civilian status and gain sustainable employment and income' (as stated in UNDDRRC 2005), Michael had certainly been socially and economically integrated into civilian life. But Michael's success lay not in his abandonment of his wartime rebel networks, but rather the opposite.

At the end of the second Liberian civil war in 2003, a network of an estimated 5,000 ex-combatants (predominantly ex-LURD rebels) took control of one of the country's lucrative rubber plantations, then known as Guthrie and later renamed Sime Darby plantation (UNMIL 2006). Although the illegal occupation officially ended in 2006, networks of ex-combatants stayed on as informal security providers for the new management (Bjarnesen forthcoming). As the 2011 elections approached, it became more and more evident that this post-war rebel network had a new role to play in political developments in Liberia. Three former rebel generals had remained active at the plantation following the government takeover, and, through them, the ex-combatants within the plantation security force were connected to influential political actors. The mutual dependence between key political actors, on the one hand, and key former rebel commanders with the ability to influence post-war rebel networks, on the other, becomes particularly evident by following the trajectory of Michael as one of the three main commanders at the plantation. Through Michael, the ex-combatants at the plantation could be used for political purposes, and through him the ex-combatants could take advantage of this political event.

Michael had already successfully managed to secure and leverage political connections during his time in control of Guthrie. Authorities and politicians, even at the highest level of the transitional government (the NTGL), cooperated with the rebel leadership occupying the plantation after the war. In doing so, they managed to take advantage of the financial resources generated by the rubber industry. After the 2005 national elections, Johnson Sirleaf's government negotiated with the rebel commanders in order to regain control over Guthrie, and Michael was the main negotiator on the side of the occupiers. He thus became the gatekeeper between the political and economic elite and the ex-combatants at the plantation. The elite needed the ex-combatants and the ex-combatants needed the elite. Michael could operate as the link between these actors, making cooperation possible and a mutual dependence fruitful for both sides. Even after he and the other ex-combatants had officially handed over control of Guthrie in 2006, Michael remained an important actor for the politicians and the ex-combatants alike. He successfully negotiated reintegration benefits for his former combatants with the Sirleaf Johnson government, but he also stayed in close contact with the ex-combatants who remained at the plantation as informal security providers (Bjarnesen forthcoming). Michael also used the contacts he gained during his time managing the plantation for his own benefit in order to secure employment within Liberia's official security structures, namely the Intelligence Department of the LNP. Furthermore, Michael had done what few ex-combatants have had the ability to do: he had invested some of his resources in university studies and, in 2012, he obtained a degree in criminal justice.[5] While using his skills and contacts, Michael continued to progress within the official security structures, as he later attained a senior position in one of Liberia's formal security institutions.

For the 2011 elections, Michael once again became important for the political elite as well as for the ex-combatants in his network. In March 2011, during the voter registration process, he launched an ex-combatant organisation based around the Sime Darby plantation area. When Michael first had the idea, he presented it to a senior local politician in Sirleaf Johnson's government in Bomi County, where the rubber plantation is located, who decided to sponsor the project. Michael came up with the idea because he wanted an organised network for ex-combatants' rights. He wanted, he said, to keep them out of trouble, drugs and criminal activities, and he wanted to work for their employment opportunities by using his links to the political elite. Whatever motives Michael had for starting the organisation, it was evident that, for the politicians facing a forthcoming election, supporting Michael's organisation was a strategic way of gaining votes. Michael soon had over 1,000 ex-combatants enlisted in his organisation and politicians at the highest level approached the network.

Michael and two other former rebel generals, constituting the leadership of the organisation, even had a few meetings with the president herself. The outcome of these meetings was that Michael and the former commanders promised to promote Ellen Johnson Sirleaf and the UP in the elections and during the pre-election phase in exchange for financial support and promises of scholarships for higher education for some of the ex-combatants, should the Sirleaf Johnson government remain in power. As Michael explained, he first encouraged the ex-combatants to register for the elections, then, as he said, 'I told them why, when and how to vote.'[6] In this way, Michael's influence over the ex-combatants as voters became equally significant.

Winners and losers in the 2011 elections

The results of the first round of the presidential elections, held on 11 October 2011, were released on 25 October, giving incumbent president Ellen Johnson Sirleaf the lead with 43.9 per cent of the votes, followed by Winston Tubman with 32.7 per cent. The former rebel leader Prince Johnson, now a presidential candidate for the National Union for Democratic Progress (NUDP) party, came in third with 11.6 per cent of the votes (NEC 2011a). As none of the candidates managed to secure an absolute majority, Johnson Sirleaf and Tubman faced a run-off election to be held on 8 November 2011. However, Winston Tubman and the CDC claimed that the election had been rigged in Johnson Sirleaf's favour. Tubman and the CDC pulled out of the second round and urged their supporters to boycott the run-offs. For Alex and my other informants who supported Tubman and the CDC, this decision had immeasurable consequences. They felt cheated out of the election victory and were convinced that the elections had been fraudulent, regardless of the approval of international observers. Their frustration grew rapidly, and Liberians and election observers now started to fear renewed violence despite the relatively calm pre-election period. On 7 November, the day before the second round of the presidential elections, the protests eventually turned deadly, on a day that my informants refer to as 'Bloody Monday'. Thousands of CDC supporters had gathered outside the party headquarters to urge voters to boycott the run-off elections. Violence broke out as police backed by UN forces blocked a road to prevent the CDC activists from marching into the city. Tear gas was used but also live bullets, and at least one young man among the CDC activists died after being shot in the head.[7] These events marked the beginning of the end for the hopes and dreams of a better future that Alex and the men around him had held during the pre-election phase. President Johnson Sirleaf's victory was declared a few days later.

Alex was dejected when I met him after the elections. Tubman had left the country, leaving Alex and his men without work. Not only was Alex without a job, he seemed to be unable to find a new one because of his former commitment. Alex's main strength, which Tubman had clearly exploited – namely, that he had been a well-known and respected man in his community with the ability to mobilise whole networks of ex-combatants – had now become a weakness. The opposition knew him well and no one wanted to employ him. With the victory of President Johnson Sirleaf, security positions within the formal security institutions were now completely out of reach, Alex and all my pro-CDC informants argued. But these positions were not beyond reach for ex-combatants on the winning side, those who had supported the president before and during the election process. Now Johnson Sirleaf had to pay them back with whatever means she had, leaving nothing for the losing side. As Alex explained: 'CDC can do nothing for the ones they mobilised. They are left with nothing. And now things are even worse than before as the winning side don't want to have anything to do with them.'[8] Alex had not only looked for jobs within the formal security institutions, he had also visited almost all the private security companies, but no one, he said, was willing to offer a position to a man who so clearly was connected to the losing side. For Alex and the ex-combatants working for him this was a 'winner-takes-all' situation, and they had supported the 'wrong' candidate.

Furthermore, Alex was not only miserable due to his inability to find a job; he was also afraid. In December, only a few weeks after the Johnson Sirleaf victory, Alex's house was attacked. Masked men broke into the house in the middle of the night. They took everything of value and smashed the rest, leaving Alex's small home completely ravaged. Alex and others in the neighbourhood strongly believed that this was a retaliatory act, due to the fact that he was a CDC man, that he had not been loyal to the ruling elite of Liberia. The police, he said, had not investigated the incident and could even have been involved. He had no evidence of this suspicion, but this was what he and others believed. From then onwards, Alex did not dare spend another night in his old house. He feared another attack, he feared revenge and retaliation, and he even feared for his life. For six months, he had been moving around all over Monrovia, spending the nights at different friends' houses. He never wanted to stay in the same place for long, and he was careful not to let too many people know his whereabouts. In all the years I had known him, Alex had been proud to be a well-known man in his neighbourhood. Now he saw this distinction as his biggest disadvantage. He and many ex-combatants around him had staked everything when they took sides in the elections. This political event had been their most promising option, and a risk they considered worth taking. But they had lost everything.

For Michael, the outcome of the elections meant something entirely different. As I could see when we met again in April after the elections, Michael and his network of ex-combatants had clearly benefited from Ellen Johnson Sirleaf's victory. The victory meant that Michael could feel more secure in his position at the security institution, a position he most likely would have lost if there had been a new political leadership. For his ex-combatants, Michael had used his personal contacts with senior politicians to get funding for over twenty scholarships for university studies. He had been the one who appointed the candidates for the scholarships, choosing among those ex-combatants in his network who already had a high school diploma and whom he saw as promising. He had managed to recommend several others for different informal security positions through his contacts at various institutions and private organisations.[9] This was the government's way of paying him back for the support he had mobilised during the electoral campaign. The official election results from the first round of voting in Bomi County, where Michael's ex-combatant organisation was based and where he had the main part of his network, gave Ellen Johnson Sirleaf 65.3 per cent of the votes, compared with Winston Tubman's 28.7 per cent. In the second round, as Tubman had boycotted the elections, Johnson Sirleaf won a clear victory with 92.4 per cent (NEC 2011b). Michael often laughed and told me that *he* had 'won Bomi for Ellen'. He said this jokingly, but it was not hard to tell that he saw some truth behind his statement. It is, of course, impossible to say precisely how much influence Michael and his network of ex-combatants actually had on the Liberian elections, but what is evident, judging from how much the politicians invested in their contacts with him and his former fighters, is that the impact was significant.

Michael has remained important for a large network of ex-combatants, despite the war being over for many years. They come to him for favours and small handouts, but, most importantly, because through him, if they are lucky, they have the possibility of finding employment. For the Liberian elite, on the other hand, Michael is just as valuable. His network of ex-combatants is large and loyal, and through him politicians and others can access these post-war rebel structures whether for personal gain, mobilising votes, unofficially employing security providers, or other social, financial or political purposes.

The potential of post-war rebel networks for electoral violence

During the Sierra Leonean general elections in 2007, Christensen and Utas (2008) followed what turned out to be a remobilisation of ex-combatants into 'security squads' for the major political parties. The exact motives for mobilising ex-combatants were never officially specified, but as Christensen and Utas found, the former fighters themselves argued that, alongside a lack of trust in the formal security institutions, political leaders chose to employ them as they were afraid of the consequences of *not* mobilising them. The politicians, in their eyes, feared another uprising and were therefore forced to work with them. Other statements indicated that the task forces, in addition to providing security for the politicians, were also used by the political elite to intimidate voters and to 'create a general state of panic' (ibid.). Furthermore, Christensen and Utas's informants also regarded the elections as an opportunity to benefit in ways the end of the war had never offered them. But the most important motivating factor for the ex-combatants was their expectations for the future. Their participation in the security squads, they believed, could bring future benefits such as jobs and education.

Many of these incentives were also relevant for my informants in the 2011 Liberian elections. However, during the elections, Liberia witnessed far fewer violent incidents than Sierra Leone did. Although it is beyond the scope of this chapter to explore why the use of post-war rebel networks led to more violence in Sierra Leone, the issue of time passed since the war might be a factor worth mentioning in brief. In the Sierra Leonean 2012 elections, the levels of violence decreased compared with those in 2007, and were only a matter of small-scale and localised incidents, which did not suggest a high level of central planning, as noted by Conteh and Harris (2014). As the same authors have pointed out, it may be that violence in the Sierra Leonean case was no longer an efficient vote-collecting strategy for the main parties. More importantly for this study is the fact that the Liberian case questions the assumption that post-war rebel networks are used simply with the motive of mobilising electoral violence, a conclusion one might otherwise be tempted to draw if one analysed the 2007 Sierra Leonean case in isolation. In the Liberian case, the use of networks of ex-combatants does not seem to have been intended to create an overall state of panic in any sense, even though the politicians surrounded by ex-combatants while campaigning could have had an intimidating effect on the public. For Winston Tubman, for example, campaigning in the company of the network of ex-combatants Alex could provide could also have been a way to show force, power and status, thereby attracting votes. Hoffman (2011) found examples of a similar logic during the 2005 Liberian elections, when a businessman from Grand Cape Mount County decided to run for the House of Representatives. The businessman found a former rebel commander an indispensable ally, as he had the capacity to mobilise 'supporters' in Monrovia. Due to his connections higher up in the Liberian hierarchy, the commander, who kept a network of ex-combatants close to him, learned that the businessman needed young men who could rally for him on appointed days, taking to the streets wearing his party colours on T-shirts. The businessman needed, as Hoffman argues, a display of force and support. With ex-combatants dancing, shouting and marching in his name he manifested power. With his army of 'violent labour' he could make it clear to the Liberian people that he had the strength to govern (ibid.).

Tubman's mobilisation of the ex-combatants in 2011 could be seen from a similar perspective, as a public display of force and power, partly through demonstrating his ability to control ex-combatants. But perhaps even more importantly in the case of the 2011 elections, having access to these networks could be an effective way to mobilise votes in exchange for promised benefits, given that the networks of ex-combatants and their dependants were still well connected, operational, large and loyal. This, I would argue, shows how the violent potential of post-war rebel networks is only one – and not necessarily the most important – aspect of why the political elite finds these actors valuable during political events such as elections even long after war has ended.

At the same time, the strategic use of post-war rebel networks by the political elite should not overshadow the equally strategic use of the political elite by post-war rebel networks. As noted by Laakso (2007), groups mobilised as potential perpetrators of violence should not be disregarded as merely a passive reserve manipulated by political leaders. Violent campaigning for the winning party can be a strategy for marginalised groups to gain political power after elections. This argument fits well with the case of the Liberian ex-combatants during the 2011 elections, although their networks were not being used for the specific purpose of violent campaigning as such. The fact that the political elite wanted to make use of and manipulate post-war rebel networks for their own benefit does not take away from the ex-combatants' own agency and ability to make strategic choices in their support of political candidates. This observation does not imply that all of the ex-combatants within the post-war rebel networks had the same freedom of action when it came to taking sides in the political game. An actor such as Michael, who ultimately had become a gatekeeper between the two sides, obviously had more room for manoeuvre than most low-ranking ex-combatants. Still, post-war rebel networks were far from passive tools in the hands of the political elite in this regard. The elections were rather an opportunity, albeit a risky one, to take advantage of their wartime pasts as rebel soldiers – both for ex-combatants who had secured more influential positions in post-war Liberia and among the majority who had not.

Post-war rebel networks as a resource for stability and livelihood

Lyons (2005) emphasises selective incentives – such as patronage – as one of the major ways in which political parties mobilise support during post-conflict elections in militarised societies. Selective incentives may take the form of material benefits, such as salary or employment, or non-material benefits such as prestige or a feeling of efficacy. Individuals might be willing to join a political party, social movement or insurgency because the selective incentives are available only to those who participate. In order to maintain the benefits of selective incentives, a difference in the treatment of one's in-group and out-groups is required. Patronage distributed only to supporters of political parties is an example of this (ibid.). In the case of the 2011 Liberian elections, it is clear that the political elite used this strategy to mobilise support among ex-combatants and that both the material and non-material benefits of the selective incentives were significant for the mobilised ex-combatants. For my informants, the elections were above all else an opportunity to find employment. As pointed out by Jennings (2008), among others, in Liberia, the language and expectations of what the reintegration process was to bring about were clearly incompatible with the implementation and resources assigned for this task. As Jennings notes, the reintegration concept in itself is vague, and could refer to either a minimalistic or a more ambitious reintegration agenda. In the Liberian case, this led to heightened expectations, followed by frustration and dissatisfaction among the ex-combatants. Many were unable to find paid employment after completing the DDRR training courses, accusing the DDRR process of failing to improve their situations and leaving them with unfulfilled promises. As early as December 2003, disappointment in the process had led to riots that caused the deaths of nine people and a temporary suspension of the DDRR (ibid.).

One of the fundamental issues was that ex-combatants were under the impression that completion of the DDRR would automatically lead to employment. This, in fact, was impossible for the weak Liberian state and economy to accomplish. Ex-combatants, like most Liberians, had to find their own way to rebuild their lives and secure their livelihood. For some of the ex-combatants who had spent years in the war with their fellow fighters, leaving their closest network, their wartime rebel structure, was not a realistic alternative. Munive (2010) has analysed the concept of unemployment in Liberia in relation to youth and ex-combatants. With an estimated 85 per cent unemployment rate, finding work for Liberia's youth is, of course, an enormous challenge. However, as Munive concludes, since most of the economy is informal in Liberia, the term 'unemployed' is of questionable utility. The international community, Munive argues, has viewed ex-combatants and young people in general from a bureaucratic perspective, casting those without formal employment as unproductive, making it imperative to transform 'unruly' ex-combatants into productive citizens. But in reality, Munive shows, contrary to these representations, young people are actively engaged in economic activities for survival, activities that constitute the backbone of the Liberian post-war economy. As formal employment is not an option for Munive's informants, informality becomes the sole means of survival (ibid.).

For the Liberian ex-combatants I have followed before, during and after the elections, the use of their wartime rebel structures became a way to access the informal labour market in post-war Liberia. And as the case studies have shown, their particular labour was in high demand during this time. Ex-combatants draw on their skills in security learned during the war; they are potentially violent and they can be influential and efficient in mobilising support for their candidate, as their networks are often large and loyal to former commanders. I would argue that, for many ex-combatants, it therefore becomes strategically important to *preserve*, rather than abandon, wartime rebel structures in order to find employment. The 2011 elections undeniably illustrate that the reintegration of ex-combatants and the dissolution of post-war rebel structures would be counterproductive to the interests of the Liberian political elite, contrary to the messages of official policy. In this way, a mutual dependence between the ex-combatants and the elite still existed eight years after the war was declared over. And during events such as national elections, this mutual dependence becomes even more visible. Nonetheless, the stakes are incredibly high for the ex-combatants when they take sides in political events. While this can sometimes provide an opportunity even to gain formal employment, it may also end disastrously, as survival in Liberia is connected in many ways to having the right connections to the political elite.

The disbanding of rebel structures is commonly considered vital due to the general view that ex-combatants in lingering rebel structures constitute an imminent security risk and have the potential to drive a post-conflict country back into warfare. I would argue that the image of a rebel – and consequently that of an ex-combatant – is not only a consequence of violent acts committed during the war, but also a product of the stereotypical, superficial and often misleading ways in which the war and its combatants have been described and represented in the media and elsewhere. As McMullin (2013) points out in his assessment of the discourse and practice of DDRR in Liberia, a threat narrative that portrays ex-combatants as inherently and naturally threatening to post-conflict peace dominates the debate on ex-combatants. According to McMullin, ex-combatants tend to be monitored and discussed in terms of how their disappointment could lead to renewed warfare, independent of other variables that could result in war and independent of the ways in which this dissatisfaction might be linked to these other variables. All ex-combatant activity is thus monitored in terms of the risk it poses to the recurrence of war. As McMullin argues, this view of ex-combatants as threats is anchored in the assumptions that ex-combatants are antisocial, lack education, ideology and political beliefs, are irrational, barbarically violent, apolitical, greedy and nihilistic, and that, after the end of war, they naturally gravitate towards criminal lives.

Following this critical reading of preconceptions about ex-combatants, we cannot assume unconditionally that the use of post-war rebel networks in the 2011 Liberian elections necessarily contributed to a risk of renewed war. Such an assumption would rely on the notion that organised networks of ex-combatants would automatically perpetrate violence. In fact, I would suggest that the involvement of post-war rebel networks during the election process could possibly have had conflict-*mitigating* effects, as the elections gave many ex-combatants some form of employment opportunity, albeit informally. Furthermore, there were no signs of any remobilisation to new rebel factions during the elections. Clearly, as Mitton (2009) points out, success in politically reintegrating ex-combatants should not be judged solely by the absence of renewed violence or the conduct of free and fair elections. The extent to which ex-combatants have faith in the political system and peace to deliver solutions to their problems of social and economic disparity is more relevant (ibid.). Applying this understanding to the 2011 Liberian elections, we must conclude that the relatively peaceful completion of the elections is not sufficient to say that a successful demobilisation of ex-combatant networks has been achieved, nor that these first post-war elections organised by the Liberian authorities signalled a final break with the country's wartime past. Former fighters were instead politically useful in their capacity as *ex*-combatants, highlighting how war and peace continue to be intimately linked in Liberia. Bøås and Utas (2014) come to a similar conclusion. With a point of departure in the historical background of the country's conflict, they conclude that Johnson Sirleaf's electoral victory should be interpreted neither as an indication that the country has entered into a new stage of peace and reconciliation, nor as evidence of a strengthening of the country's democratisation. Instead, the authors suggest, the electoral results could even be seen as cementing the old cleavages that led to civil war in the first place (ibid.). The 'winner-takes-all' effects of the Liberian 2011 elections for the ex-combatants considered in this chapter support this analysis.

Conclusions

This chapter has reached two overarching conclusions. Firstly, the 2011 elections in Liberia did not bring about the envisioned final break with past wars. The lingering presence of post-war rebel networks and their continued usefulness to political Big Men are clear indicators of this continuity. Rebel networks can remain relevant long after war has come to an end despite years of demobilisation and reintegration efforts. In times of elections, they can become important pawns in the political game. The elections proved to be an opportunity for Liberian ex-combatants that could lead to post-election advantages, though only on the winning side. In this sense, a genuine democracy was far from strengthened, as, in the eyes of the losers, the winning side was not considered more legitimate than it had been before the elections.

Yet, these continuities with Liberia's wartime past might not be the real problem, which leads us to the second overarching conclusion of this chapter:

that the presence and use of post-war rebel networks in times of elections may not necessarily, or automatically, result in violence. The past wars are part of Liberia's social and political reality and the country must continue to deal with – and sometimes incorporate – both the actors and the structures responsible for past atrocities, as they do not simply vanish at the end of the war. From the perspective of ex-combatants themselves, their mobilisation for the 2011 elections was primarily part of an entrepreneurial strategy to secure employment, rather than being motivated by a desire to take part in potential electoral violence or renewed warfare. The Liberian case shows that the involvement of organised ex-combatants in political events such as elections, or for other tasks and in other contexts, is not an inevitable precursor to violence, as is often assumed. This is a central finding as the general perception of post-war rebel networks is that their mere continued existence may automatically lead to renewed violence – in connection with important political events such as elections, or, in the worst case, in a return to war. This chapter has shown that the use of post-war rebel networks can have positive outcomes for the ex-combatants themselves but also for post-war stability, as these actors are given opportunities otherwise closed to them.

We might therefore be forced to view post-war rebel networks in a rather different light than traditionally has been the case. Their continued presence, in times of post-war elections and post-war societies in general, is a far more complex issue than often assumed. During elections, and in post-war contexts in general, post-war rebel networks can be used to perpetrate violence – or merely to intimidate, due to their violent potential – but they may also be used for entirely non-violent purposes. The spectrum of post-war activities in which these networks can engage is broad and needs to be analysed from such a perspective in order to be fully understood. If we assume that all actors with a history of active engagement in war, including post-war rebel networks, are predetermined to resort to violent methods after the war, we fail to appreciate how such constellations could be used in positive ways. We will also fail to understand the circumstances that may lead to these networks being used for violent ends: we should not forget that they are accustomed to and capable of violence and warfare. Used in the wrong way by the political elite or by other financially powerful and influential actors, they are potentially dangerous to the future stability and peace of Liberia. There is no doubt that the Liberian political elite was playing a dangerous game with its strategic use of post-war rebel structures during the 2011 elections. And, as can be seen from their experiences on the losing side of the elections, so too were the ex-combatants.

Notes

1 Adolphus Dolo was also known as General Peanut Butter during the war.

2 This was a common expression among my informants in order to explain their participation primarily as informal security providers during the 2011 elections.

3 The Americo-Liberians are descendants of freed American slaves of African background who were sent to Liberia between 1817 and 1867. The group ruled the country in an apartheid state manner and declared Liberia independent in 1987.

4 Personal communication with Alex and two of the other main commanders of the informal security group at various occasions in Monrovia during September and October 2011.

5 While few ex-combatants have had the ability to study at university, some of the more influential former commanders appear to have earned degrees in criminal justice sponsored by politicians or other influential actors.

6 This section is mainly based on personal communication with Michael in September and October 2011 and April 2012. However, much of the information in the chapter is also based on several interviews and meetings with ex-combatants and workers at Guthrie, Bomi County, Liberia, from 2010 to 2012.

7 See, for example, BBC News (2011) and Utas (2012b).

8 Conversation with Alex, Monrovia, 12 April 2012.

9 Personal communication with Michael on several occasions in Monrovia in April 2012.

References

BBC News (2005) 'Liberian Poll: The Main Contenders', BBC News, 5 October. Available at http://news.bbc.co.uk/2/hi/africa/4309302.stm.

BBC News (2011) 'Liberia Election: CDC Monrovia Protest Turns Deadly', BBC News, 7 November. Available at www.bbc.co.uk/news/world-africa-15624471.

Bjarnesen, M. (forthcoming) 'From Perpetrator to Protector?: Post-war Rebel Networks as Informal Security Providers in Liberia'. Athens GA: University of Georgia Press.

Bøås, M. and M. Utas (2014) 'The Political Landscape of Postwar Liberia: Reflections on National Reconciliation and Elections', Africa Today 60 (4): 47–65.

Christensen, M. M. and M. Utas (2008) 'Mercenaries of Democracy: The "Politricks" of Remobilized Combatants in the 2007 General Elections, Sierra Leone', African Affairs 107 (429): 515–39.

Conteh, F. M. and D. Harris (2014) 'Swings and Roundabouts: The Vagaries of Democratic Consolidation and "Electoral Rituals" in Sierra Leone', Critical African Studies 6 (1): 57–70.

Harris, D. (2011) Civil War and Democracy in West Africa: Conflict Resolution, Elections and Justice in Sierra Leone and Liberia. London: I. B. Tauris.

Harris, D. and T. Lewis (2013) 'Liberia in 2011: Still Ploughing its own Democratic Furrow?', Commonwealth and Comparative Politics 51 (1): 76–96.

Hoffman, D. (2011) The War Machines: Young Men and Violence in Sierra Leone and Liberia. Durham NC: Duke University Press.

Höglund, K. (2009) 'Electoral Violence in Conflict-ridden Societies: Concepts, Causes, and Consequences', Terrorism and Political Violence 21 (3): 412–27.

Jennings, K. M. (2008) 'Seeing DDR from Below: Challenges and dilemmas Raised by the Experience of Ex-combatants in Liberia'. Fafo Report 2008:03. Oslo: Fafo.

Jörgel, M. and M. Utas (2007) The Mano River Basin Area: Formal and Informal Security Providers in Liberia, Guinea and Sierra Leone. Stockholm: Swedish Defence Research Agency.

Kantor, A. and M. Persson (2011) 'Liberian Vigilantes: Informal Security Provision on the Margins of Security Sector Reform' in M. Ekengren and G. Simons (eds), *The Politics of Security Sector Reform: Challenges and Opportunities for the European Union's Global Role*. Farnham: Ashgate.

Laakso, L. (2007) 'Insights into Electoral Violence in Africa' in M. Basedau, G. Erdmann and A. Mehler (eds), *Votes, Money and Violence: Political Parties in Sub-Saharan Africa*. Uppsala: Nordic Africa Institute.

Lyons, T. (1998) 'Liberia's Path from Anarchy to Elections', *Current History* 97 (619): 229–233.

Lyons, T. (2005) *Demilitarizing Politics: Elections and the Uncertain Road to Peace*. Boulder CO: Lynne Rienner.

McMullin, J. (2013) 'Integration or Separation? The Stigmatisation of Ex-combatants after War', *Review of International Studies* 39: 385–414.

Mehler, A. (2007) 'Political Parties and Violence in Africa: Systematic Reflections against Empirical Background' in M. Basedau, G. Erdmann and A. Mehler (eds), *Votes, Money and Violence: Political Parties in Sub-Saharan Africa*. Uppsala: Nordic Africa Institute.

Mitton, K. (2009) 'Engaging with Disengagement: The Political Reintegration of Sierra Leone's Revolutionary United Front' in M. Berdal and D. Ucko (eds), *Reintegrating Armed Groups after Conflict: Politics, Violence and Transition*. London and New York NY: Routledge.

Moran, M. H. (2006) *Liberia: The Violence of Democracy*. Philadelphia PA: University of Pennsylvania Press.

Munive, J. (2010) 'The Army of "Unemployed" Young People', *Nordic Journal of Youth Research* 18 (3): 321–38.

NEC (2011a) '2011 Presidential and Legislative Elections: National Tally'. Monrovia: National Elections Commission (NEC). Available at www.necliberia.org/results2011/.

NEC (2011b) '2011 Presidential and Legislative Elections: Bomi County'.

Monrovia: National Elections Commission (NEC). Available at www.necliberia.org/results2011/county_3_1.html.

Obi, C. (2007) 'Introduction: Elections and the Challenge of Post-conflict Democratisation in West Africa', *African Journal of International Affairs* 10 (1–2): 1–12.

Reilly, B. (2013) 'Elections and Post-conflict Political Development' in M. Berdal and D. Zaum (eds), *Political Economy of Statebuilding: Power after Peace*. London and New York NY: Routledge.

Reno, W. (2011) *Warfare in Independent Africa: New Approaches to African History*. Cambridge: Cambridge University Press.

Sawyer, A. (2008) 'Emerging Patterns in Liberia's Post-conflict Politics: Observations from the 2005 Elections', *African Affairs* 107 (427): 177–99.

Themnér, A. (2017) *Warlord Democrats in Africa: Ex-military Leaders and Electoral Politics*. London and New York NY: Zed Books.

UNDDRRC (2005) 'What Is DDR?', United Nations Disarmament, Demobilization and Reintegration Resource Centre (UNDDRRC), May. Available at www.unddr.org/what-is-ddr/introduction_1.aspx.

UNMIL (2006) *Human Rights in Liberia's Rubber Plantations: Tapping into the Future*. Monrovia: United Nations Mission in Liberia (UNMIL).

UNMIL Today (2009) 'DDR Wraps Up', *UNMIL Today* 6 (2): 1.

Utas, M. (ed) (2012a) *African Conflicts and Informal Power: Big Men and Networks*. London and New York NY: Zed Books.

Utas, M. (2012b) 'Liberia Post-election: On CDC Popularity and Odd Election Results', Mats Utas blog, 5 April. Available at http://matsutas.wordpress.com/2012/04/05/liberia-post-election-on-cdc-popularity-and-odd-election-results/.

8 | Parasitic politics: violence, deception and change in Kenya's electoral politics

Jacob Rasmussen

Introduction

> We are not a violent organisation. But I can't say that some of our members weren't violent [during the 2008 post-electoral violence]. It is young men; of course they are angry. The government can't tell them not to be angry.[1]

Since the introduction of multiparty elections in Kenya in 1992, the electoral process has been characterised by violence in one way or another (Fjelde and Höglund, Chapter 1 in this volume). In 1992 and 1997, interethnic violence and militia-driven persecution of opposition supporters in the run-up to the elections killed several hundreds of people (Kagwanja 2001). The 2007 December elections erupted into interethnic and militant violence that killed 1,500 people and displaced more than half a million (Kagwanja and Southall 2010). Even the supposedly peaceful elections of 2002 and 2013, where a lot of resources were put into preventing and containing violence, saw hundreds of people killed in the months leading up to the elections (Merino 2014; Mutahi 2005). The dynamics and expressions of violence might have differed from one election to the next, and some of the violent actors have also changed over time, but the politicisation of ethnic identities, the instrumentalisation of youth militias, and the excessive use of force by the state security services have been central components of the violence that has surrounded and affected democratic elections in Kenya (Mueller 2008; Thibon 2014). As shown in the introduction to this volume, these elements are far from unique to Kenya; on the contrary, they are driving factors in much electoral violence across the world.

This chapter approaches electoral participation as anything from voting to violent action (Laakso 2007). The chapter investigates the Mungiki movement, one of the most dominant violent non-state actors in Kenyan electoral politics since the late 1990s. Looking at Mungiki's shifting roles as youth grassroots organisation, violent ethnic militia, political party and religious organisation across the last three elections (2002, 2007 and 2013), the chapter approaches electoral violence – in line with the ambitions of this volume – as violent acts or threats of violence affecting the electoral results or the electoral process prior to or after the actual vote. As such, the analysis of Mungiki's role in electoral violence is not necessarily limited to periods of close proximity to the elections; rather, electoral violence in an emerging and transformative democracy such as Kenya can occur in temporal isolation from the elections yet have a huge impact or be informed by the electoral process (cf. Bekoe 2012; Burchard 2015). To add perspective to the analysis of Mungiki's peculiar practices, the chapter draws parallels with the wider characteristics of Kenyan politics. Hence, the analysis of Mungiki as a central actor in Kenya's recent history of electoral violence also provides a contextual analysis of the movement's relation to the Kenyan state and Kenyan politics, which has strong elements of ethnic politicisation and patronage politics (cf. Bratton and van de Walle 1997; Utas 2012).

Politics in Kenya is often described as a politics of deception or a politics of intrigue, known in the lingua franca Kiswahili as 'Siasa za kumalizana'. Politics in this perception is a game concerned with outsmarting the opponent by all means, often for personal gain or the gains of the ethnic community.[2] This aspect of Kenyan politics and political practice is often emphasised during national elections and it relates to another recurrent phrase characterising the ethnic dimension of electoral politics and the hopes of winning: 'It is our turn to eat.' This expression refers to the politicisation of ethnic identities and the expectation of politicians with a particular ethnic association to take care of their ethnic constituencies after electoral victory (Branch and Cheeseman 2010: 1). This effectively captures politics as a zero-sum game with a winner and a loser, where the gains of the winner equal the losses of the loser. As emphasised in the introduction to this volume and repeated in the literature on electoral conflicts, the higher the stakes in the elections, the more likely the risk of violence (Collier 2010).

Through the notion of 'parasitic politics', the chapter explores how the Mungiki movement buys into the noted characterisations of Kenyan politics as deceptive and driven by an appetite for power and the hope for ethnic redistribution. Parasitic politics is used to diagnose and explain a particular kind of political practice in which democratic participation and violent practices merge through the ability to transform, deceive and live of one's 'other' (in the case of Mungiki, the 'other' is either the Kenyan state, the Kikuyu political and economic elite, or the population as a whole). The merger of democratic politics and the potential for violence in the same concept does not mean that Kenyan politics is violent by default, but the concept can help us unpack the situated behaviour and rationale of some of the central actors.

The chapter is based on long-term ethnographic fieldwork in Kenya on the Mungiki movement in the aftermath of the post-electoral violence in 2008, during the extra-judicial persecution by the police of Mungiki in 2009, during the constitutional referendum of 2010, and during the 2013 elections.[3] The ethnographic material on Mungiki's practices and political engagements is set in relation to existing literature on the movement and to the bulk of literature on Kenyan elections and the country's continued struggle for democracy.

The chapter continues by setting out the analytical foundation before going into three empirically founded sections: the first focuses on Mungiki's mass actions and mobilisation, the second on the movement's ideological baggage from the Mau Mau and its ability to transform, and thirdly on the parasitic nature of politics and violent action. Each section is organised in subsections providing analyses of Mungiki's involvement across the three general elections from 2002 until 2013 and the role of violence or the struggle to contain it in these elections. In the conclusion, the chapter argues that electoral violence, as we can understand it through the notion of parasitic politics, reveals itself as relational, fuelled by competing claims and counter-claims, and groomed by the actualisation of historical misrecognitions and the instrumentalisation of collective identities, rather than being driven by a lack of civility and a lack of trust in the democratic aspect of elections.

Deception and violence as political participation

Cheeseman (2015) and Collier (2010) have investigated the political economy of the dynamics of democracy and violence in Africa from a cross-country comparative perspective. They both depart from the positive potential for legitimacy and accountability inherent in democratisation, and the possibility for changing the course of events through the electoral process. Both authors point out that political participation – and maybe even the idea of democracy itself – is often boiled down to the electoral process of casting the vote, and the dynamics of contestation and violent conflict are often linked to the possibility for change.

The fact that all Kenyan elections since the introduction of multiparty democracy have been violent in one form or another testifies to the increased stakes for politicians in maintaining power; violence thus becomes a means to that end, even if the stakes and therefore the level of violence seem to drop at elections where the incumbent's term comes to an end, like the 2002 and 2013 elections in Kenya (Cheeseman 2015). Kenya's history of ethnic voter mobilisation, which has created identity-based loyalties between politicians and their support bases, has also limited voters' mobility to other political camps and has increased the risk of ethnic violence (cf. Collier 2010; Fjelde and Höglund, Chapter 1 in this volume).

In addition, sub-Saharan Africa is facing a demographic challenge due to the enormous increase in the youth population, which casts poor and young first-time voters as the central actors of electoral democracy. On the one hand, the youth have the numbers to gain influence through the vote; on the other, they often constitute a marginalised group due to their lack of jobs and education and their limited possibilities for political participation.

This is problematic in countries such as Kenya where voter registration and actual voting are time consuming and costly for the poor. Often, poor youths are considered a threat to democracy, and in many instances on the continent they constitute the main perpetrators of electoral violence (Anderson 2002; Christensen and Utas 2008; Strauss 2011). Paradoxically, the threat of violence or the violent act itself can be seen as a particular form of electoral participation in which the youths voice their dissatisfaction with the existing order and their chances for political participation and societal inclusion (Laakso 2007: 227). This is no different in Kenya, where the Mungiki movement claims to represent the masses of poor youth, and where its political mobilisation has come to evoke immediate public fears of violence.

The Mungiki movement embodies what I call 'parasitic politics' through its ability to transform and deceive, and to combine democratic participation and violent practices. Empirically, parasitic politics is derived from Mungiki's use of two metaphors from Kikuyu mythology: the chameleon and the Mugumo tree (a parasitic fig tree). Mythologically, the latter is considered the tree of life and the former as the harbinger of death. Both metaphors inhibit the ability to transform: the chameleon through its ability to continuously change colour and blend in with its immediate surroundings, and the parasitic Mugumo tree through its ability to consume the host tree and take on a new form. The two metaphors point to Mungiki's transformative and violent potential and also allude to ideas of a hidden core and a potentially deceptive surface. As such, Mungiki's metaphors embrace notions of secrecy, deception and violence in relation to societal transformations, as well as reintroducing mythology and ancestral traditions as integral parts of Kenyan politics.

In his work on the parasite as a grand metaphor for human relations, French philosopher Michel Serres (1982) merges notions of politics and mythology to describe how existing orders are challenged and re-worked (Brown 2002: 1). At the core of Serres' characteristic of the parasite is the asymmetrical relation. Even if the preying parasite and the host might depend on each other, their relationship is always asymmetrical: one is feeding on the other (Serres 1982: 55). Yet, together, the parasite and the host merge into a new and different whole. Through this parasitic process the normal flow of things – the existing order – is interrupted in order for something new to appear (ibid.). It is the characteristics of interruption, the inherently violent takeover, and the relational asymmetry and interdependence that make the parasite an intriguing metaphor for describing Mungiki's mythologically infused political practice and its role in electoral violence in Kenya. While unpacking the chameleon and Mugumo tree metaphors, the chapter investigates the productive potential of deception for understanding Mungiki's role in the dynamics of electoral violence in Kenya.

'The born-again Mau Mau': Mungiki's economic and cultural background

Mungiki is a movement dominated by youth from the Kikuyu tribe. Mungiki was founded in the rural parts of central Kenya in the late 1980s based on a revival of Kikuyu traditional religious beliefs (Wamue 2001). While formed in opposition to President Moi's oppressive regime, Mungiki also had grudges against the Kikuyu political elite (Gecaga 2007). The movement claimed to be the biological and ideological grandchild of the Mau Mau movement that had fought for land and freedom during the struggle for independence in the 1950s.

Ideologically, Mungiki is fighting against poverty, political and social exclusion, and for a correction of what their members perceive as historical injustices committed against the poor Kikuyu population. Mungiki adopted a range of secret rituals and operational structures from the Mau Mau. As such, Mungiki is founded on and guarded by a combination of revolutionary ideals and ritually sanctioned secrecy (Rasmussen forthcoming). In Kenya, any reference to Mau Mau oathing raises concern, as the oaths are widely associated with violent religiosity and obscenity (Blunt 2013: 168). Furthermore, Jomo Kenyatta used mass oathing in a deliberate attempt at secretly mobilising the Kikuyu population behind his presidency in 1968 (Knighton 2010), which also associates oathing with the politicisation of ethnic identities and patronage politics.

Over the years, Mungiki has increased in numbers and gained strongholds in the Kikuyu-dominated areas of the poor neighbourhoods in Kenya's major cities, where it has become involved in economic activities in the flourishing informal economy (Rasmussen 2012; Servant 2007). Through the involvement in the security sector and the public transport industry, Mungiki became involved in criminal and violent activities. It also became increasingly politicised (Anderson 2002; Kagwanja 2005a). Due to the movement's involvement in crime and violence, as well as its problematic relationship to some Kikuyu politicians, Mungiki was subjected to systematic police persecution in 2002 and 2003 and most severely between 2007 and 2009 (Alston 2009; KNCHR 2008; Oscar Foundation 2007; 2008). These events cast Mungiki members as not only perpetrators of violence but also victims of political violence, thus entering into a larger cycle of Kenyan electoral violence which is about settling old scores.

Since Mungiki's foundation, the members' public appearance has changed from dreadlocked young men flagging the movement's colours of green, white, black and red, through snuff-taking lumpen youth in the *matatu* industry (Kenya's informal means of public transportation), to Sunday church-goers wearing shirts and jackets. In terms of their public declaration of faith, members have moved from being Kikuyu traditionalists, through a brief flirtation with Islam in 2002 that saw them move back to the Kikuyu base, before converting to Pentecostalism in 2009. Mungiki simultaneously presents itself as a religious movement, a political party with widespread economic activities and with a militant wing, and a movement engaged in social development activities and farming on a local level. All these aspects testify to Mungiki's potential to appear transformative and multiple at one and the same time. However, the leadership claims to remain true to the ideological core of fighting poverty, inequality and historical injustices.

While the ability to change while staying true to the core ideals of the movement is important, especially in relation to the chameleon and Mugumo tree metaphors, the changes have often coincided with the violent persecution of the Mungiki leadership. The brief conversion to Islam in 2002 has largely been considered a diversion when the movement was seeking shelter from police persecution under the banner of a minority religion. Years later, local Mungiki members in Kayole playfully showed off Islamic registration cards, claiming that they could appear in a range of different identities.[4] Similarly, when in October 2009 Maina Njenga and his followers publicly dissolved Mungiki and converted to Pentecostalism after Njenga's release from prison, it was widely perceived as yet another sham intended to free Mungiki of its reputation as the perpetrator of the 2008 electoral violence.

This doubt was only fuelled by the organisation's initial choice of joining the controversial and opportunistic Bishop Margaret Wanjiru's church, 'Jesus Is Alive Ministries' (JIAM). Wanjiru had pursued her political ambitions via the church and mobilised the support of her congregation to become a member of parliament (Kavulla 2008). She was hoping to benefit from the electoral support of the Mungiki members. However, these electoral ambitions never materialised for Wanjiru as Mungiki had its own agenda. For Mungiki's members, the explicit combination of religion and politics resonated well with their former traditionalist beliefs, where religion and politics were not considered separate domains. Thus, the conversion paved the way for Maina Njenga's 'rebirth' as a bishop and a politician and for the Mungiki members to present themselves as the 'born again Mau Mau'.[5] On the one hand, the dual meaning captured in this sentence describes a resurrection of the Mau Mau movement; on the other, it captures the former Mau Mau sympathisers who have converted to Pentecostalism through a ritual rebirth and conversion. The rebirth of the Mau Mau, even at the symbolic level, is associated with violence and political struggle for change.

Mobilising the masses *Mungiki* means multitude in the Kikuyu language, and there is an inherent claim and ambition of both being and representing the masses. Mungiki's core recruitment base has been among the poor urban youth and the landless and disenfranchised young Kikuyu population. The power of Mungiki's multitude ultimately has two potential expressions: that of a democratic threat to the established political elite through the vote; and as a threat to democracy through violent outbursts and rioting by the dissatisfied and unruly youth population.

The latest census on the demographic development in Kenya reveals that 50 per cent of the population is below twenty-five years of age (KNBS 2009). Mungiki's main recruitment base among the rapidly increasing youth population – many of them first-time voters – has only added to the uncertainty about the movement's potential impact, as this group is perceived to be easily influenced by their patrons. The potency of this indeterminable base of young Kikuyu voters is evident in the recurrent attempts by established politicians to mobilise Mungiki's youth support. Being the largest ethnic group in Kenya, the Kikuyu make up an attractive constituency and the Kikuyu heartlands are traditionally among the most contested electoral constituencies as politicians strategise on how to either unify or divide the Kikuyu votes (Cheeseman 2008: 168; Fjelde and Höglund, Chapter 1 in this volume; Mulli 1999).

Over the years, Mungiki spokespersons and commentators on the movement have differed over the size of the movement and the level of commitment of the members; the estimated numbers have ranged from several million supporters down to 30,000 core members (Rasmussen 2013; Ruteere 2008). The uncertainty about Mungiki's size has itself been part of the movement's political leverage, and the leadership has deliberately used this uncertainty to argue for their potential in influencing electoral results. By mobilising several thousand rowdy young men and creating visibility around their political gatherings, the movement has continuously managed to present the uncertainty of numbers as a potential voter base that should be taken seriously. The threat of violence through mass action prior to elections has been a central element of Mungiki's force. We can situate this practice somewhere between voting and actual violence, as it is an act that potentially influences the turnout of opposition voters at the polling stations, yet it may not involve casting a vote nor the shedding of blood.

In 2002, departing president Daniel arap Moi (from the Kalenjin tribe) and his chosen successor Uhuru Kenyatta (Kikuyu) – posing as the youthful candidate to bring about the long-sought-for generational change of power – reached out to Mungiki. The relationship between the politicians and Mungiki was then described as a patron–client relation (Kagwanja 2005a: 64). A similar characterisation would suffice for Uhuru Kenyatta's alleged use of Mungiki as a youth militia in the 2008 post-election violence. In 2003, President Mwai Kibaki (Kikuyu) – after winning a landslide victory against Uhuru Kenyatta in the 2002 elections – tried to counter Mungiki's opposition and reach out to their members by commemorating and restoring their idol – the Mau Mau leader Dedan Kimathi (Kikuyu) – to national hero (Branch 2010: 316). And in 2013, Raila Odinga (from the Luo tribe) posed alongside Mungiki's leader

Maina Njenga at the family home of Dedan Kimathi in a similar attempt to tap into Njenga's support base of young Kikuyu voters in Central Province, an area where Raila Odinga and Luo politicians traditionally have little support (*Daily Nation* 2012b). These attempts by successive politicians to reach out to Mungiki for electoral support testify to the importance of the Kikuyu youth as an electoral force that is recognised, but it also reveals the somewhat instrumental approach politicians often have towards the youth constituency. While hardly any politicians want to be directly associated with violent youths, the potential of numbers seems to outweigh the fear of association with electoral violence or the threat of it.

Mobilising the youth for change Over the years, Mungiki has proven its ability to mobilise in large numbers, thus putting action behind its claims of being indeterminate and representing the masses. But underlying the ability for mass mobilisation is also a strong ambition of mobilising for social change. In the campaigns prior to the 2002 elections, Mungiki displayed its strength in mobilising its members for direct political action by gathering several thousand people in Nairobi in support of Uhuru Kenyatta (Kagwanja 2005a: 63). Mungiki's leadership argued that their support for Uhuru Kenyatta was an ideological support for generational change and for a youth revolution, not an issue of ethnic politics (Kagwanja 2005b). During the demonstrations, Mungiki members waved machetes and so-called '*rungus*' (the Swahili word for a blunt wooden club used for fighting), alarming the press with their potential for violence (ibid.; Maupeu 2003). The police apparently turned a blind eye to the Mungiki members' unruly behaviour and their display of weapons, which led to heavy criticism when the police shut down and dispersed a political rally by the opposition the following week (Kagwanja 2005a: 63). The police was criticised for using double standards, raising questions concerning the relation between the Moi–Uhuru alliance and the security forces. Moi was known for keeping close relations with the security forces and special units within the police (Katumanga 2013), a central element in maintaining political power, not only in Kenya (cf. Collier 2010). Mungiki's display of its violent potential in 2002 occurred mainly prior to the elections.

In April 2008, thousands of Mungiki members rioted in Nairobi, bringing traffic and businesses to a standstill; this followed months of violent ethnic and politically motivated clashes as a reaction to the disputed 2007 elections, which saw Mwai Kibaki claim the presidency from Raila Odinga. The rioters protested against the extra-judicial killing of two of their leading figures and the wife of their chairman, Maina Njenga, allegedly carried out by secret police death squads (KNCHR 2009). Despite Mungiki members' role as perpetrators in the preceding post-election violence, the movement's sudden mass appearance in the centre of the capital was a shock to many Kenyans. The fact that Mungiki members were able to enter the city in large numbers and cause havoc despite police awareness of the movement and in spite of the re-emerging violent persecution of Mungiki members was a boost for the movement's recruitment.[6] In important ways, the riots also marked a shift in Mungiki's violent mass appearance, as they were driven by the movement's grievances against the current political regime (led by the Kikuyu Mwai Kibaki), whereas previous mass appearances had been mobilised by changing political patrons for voter support or violent intimidation, or had been centred around religious initiation rituals, or were turf wars with other youth groupings. The April 2008 Nairobi riots showed Mungiki members taking charge of their own agenda and directing their violent potential against the state that had allegedly mobilised them and called for their persecution.

In March 2010, hundreds of Mungiki members participated in a peace rally in Eldoret in the heartlands of the Kalenjin parts of Rift Valley. The rally saw Mungiki's leadership appear on stage alongside former President Moi, both preaching peace and unity between the Kalenjin and Kikuyu ethnic groups and bringing together the most violent sections of their respective communities in the post-electoral violence of 2008. Interestingly, while Maina Njenga appeared on stage, Mungiki members dressed in suits and sunglasses were lined up in front of the crowd to provide security, whereas armed officers from the Administration Police stepped up when Moi entered the stage.[7] Mungiki's appearance at the Eldoret peace rally reveals its ability to strike deals with politicians controlling local segments of the security forces. Suddenly, Mungiki appeared as an advocate of peace. Simultaneously, the police persecution of Mungiki members saw them rebrand themselves as nationalist, in support of the progressive and rights-based constitution. In the period between the 2008 post-electoral violence and the 2010 constitutional referendum, secret police units had systematically persecuted Mungiki and the International Criminal Court (ICC) had opened cases against Uhuru Kenyatta for mobilising Mungiki for retaliatory attacks during the 2008 elections. Central Mungiki members were among the proposed ICC witnesses and Mungiki saw the violent persecution as a politically led attempt at silencing witnesses. In these circumstances, Mungiki could pursue its ambitions for societal change and the correction of historical injustices through a change to a pro-constitutional rights-based agenda. Mungiki's violent post-electoral engagements now saw the movement drawn into a cycle of state persecution, where the police were killing its members in order to cover up previous violent deeds in the fear of legal persecution from the ICC. Söderberg Kovacs' example from Burundi in the introduction to this volume accounts for similar dynamics of cyclical electoral violence instated to secure impunity.

The 2013 elections took place in the dark and gloomy shadows of the post-electoral violence of 2008, and enormous resources were invested in preaching peace and preventing a recurrence of electoral violence (Long et al. 2013). The ICC case against the Kikuyu Uhuru Kenyatta and the Kalenjin William Ruto brought the two candidates together in a political alliance where they respectively ran for president and vice president in the 2013 general election, an alliance that quickly became known as the 'alliance of the accused' (Lynch 2014). Kenyatta and Ruto succeeded in capitalising on this political climate and managed to turn the ICC case against them into a question of national sovereignty and of international attempts at scapegoating the entire Kikuyu and Kalenjin societies for the violent deeds of a few (Mueller 2014).

In the early stages of the 2013 electoral campaigns, Mungiki participated in a series of religious and political mass rallies using its usual tactics of displaying its ability to mobilise hordes of young men, only this time it made an effort to communicate its ability to contain their unruliness. However, its violent potential was constantly shimmering under the surface. In line with its stance in the constitutional referendum, Mungiki deliberately took up a position against ethnically infused politics. For instance, the Limuru rally in April 2012 was a peace meeting arranged as a direct critique of the ethno-cultural associations GEMA (Gikuyu, Embu, Meru Association) in Central Province and KAMATUSA (Kalenjin, Maasai, Turkana, Samburu) in Rift Valley for advocating tribalism and ethnic division.[8] When the police interrupted and cancelled the political meeting in Limuru, the Mungiki crowd behaved relatively peacefully compared with previous years, when meetings often ended in running battles with the police (*The Star* 2012). Similarly, at a political gathering at Kamukunji Grounds in Nairobi in June 2012, where Mungiki's leadership announced their effective takeover of the political party Mkenya Solidarity and launched their ambitions of running for seats at various electoral levels, Mungiki's security team seemed to cooperate with the police in controlling the masses.[9]

The 2013 elections were largely non-violent. A lot of resources had been put into advocating peace and preventing hate speech. The political leaders of the two warring factions of 2008 had teamed up in a political alliance. Mungiki's leadership ended up withdrawing their political candidatures and encouraged their members to support the Luo candidate Raila Odinga. Mungiki's role during the actual vote, however, seemed to have a limited impact on Raila Odinga's result in the constituencies covering Mungiki's strongholds, as Uhuru won landslide victories in the Kikuyu-dominated areas (IEBC 2013). Maina Njenga's public support for a non-Kikuyu candidate did not go uncontested in the ranks of Mungiki, and some members decided to go against the public recommendations of their chairman and voted for Uhuru Kenyatta.[10] In Nakuru, members posed as bodyguards for opposing political candidates, testifying both to the internal split in Mungiki and to the pragmatic logic of lending one's muscle to the best-paying patron.

The highest stake in the 2013 elections was legal persecution for instigating human rights abuses carried out by Mungiki. The dominant narrative of peace in the 2013 elections was a constant reminder of the violence of 2008, and the campaigns effectively turned the elections into a fight against foreign legal intervention (meaning the ICC). The elections might have been peaceful, but the violence was omnipresent. Mungiki's members again proved their ability to mobilise and contain huge crowds in the run-up to the elections, but they did not influence the vote. Their ability to initiate change seemed to be reduced to their violent capacity or the threat of violence.

Harbingers of death: religious appearances, mythological references and violent potential

When members of Mungiki refer to their transformations they often use metaphors, especially the chameleon and the Mugumo tree. As noted earlier, metaphorically the chameleon refers to the ability to adapt to changing situations, and to appear as something different from and other than what it seems to be. Analytically, it concerns the ability to transform, and opens up for discussion the question of whether the chameleon's true character is its ability to change colour and surface appearance or whether its true character is to be found in its shape or behaviour. The Mungiki members' use of the chameleon metaphor accentuates this problem, as the metaphor constantly teases out questions of whether their façade shrouds a concealed truth or whether it is solely a surface appearance or a diversion. In this sense, the chameleon metaphor diverts attention from the movement's religious and political project. This is also where the power of the chameleon lies, as it assumes that there is a depth or a truth that is hidden; that underneath the façade there is something politically important and potent yet hidden from public view and knowledge.

However, the chameleon can refer to more than unpredictability and the ability to transform itself and appear in multiple forms. In Kikuyu mythology, the chameleon is presented as the harbinger of death. To summarise briefly, the chameleon was sent by God to tell the Kikuyu people that they should never die, but he failed to deliver the message properly and ended up being humiliated by the Kikuyu people who chased him away. Soon afterwards, the Kikuyu started dying.

Mungiki was made illegal prior to the 2002 general elections following a turf war with a rival Luo gang in the Nairobi estate of Kariobangi, where the intergroup fighting resulted in running battles in the streets and targeted killings with machetes (Maupeu 2002). The fighting became known as the Kariobangi massacre. The rival gangs competed over the right to provide informal security in the neighbourhoods of Nairobi's Eastlands and over control of lucrative *matatu* routes. Politicians saw the potential in linking up with the disaffected youth in charge of the provision of everyday services such as security, transport and rubbish collection, as they could serve the purposes of anything from voting fodder to violent intimidation. Mungiki proved especially skilled in capitalising on the political interest of violent youth militias, and, instead of facing persecution, Mungiki stuck a deal whereby the police turned a blind eye to Mungiki's forceful takeover of the most lucrative *matatu* routes in Eastlands in return for political support. Mungiki leaders even made public declarations about being protected by the government (Anderson 2002: 538–40; Kagwanja 2005a: 64). The Kariobangi massacre not only instilled a fear of Mungiki among the public, it also affected the 2002 elections in direct ways, as it helped Mungiki carve out an economic platform for political and violent engagements. However, due to the level of violence, Uhuru Kenyatta and Moi also had to publicly disassociate themselves from the unruly youth they had reached out to. The ban of Mungiki was a central element in this process, and so was the barring of Maina Njenga's parliamentary candidature later in the year.

Despite the ban, which was still in force, and the erratic persecution of Mungiki, the movement managed to make a new deal of non-persecution prior to the 2007 elections, as their numerical and violent potential was called on once again by the Kikuyu political elite (ICC 2015; TJRC 2013; Waki Commission 2008). The late December announcement of the electoral result granting the incumbent Mwai Kibaki victory over Raila Odinga was immediately disputed and sparked countrywide protests and riots. In Rift Valley in particular, many ordinary Kikuyus suffered politically and ethnically motivated attacks, once again bringing old grievances over land to the fore (see Fjelde and Höglund, Chapter 1 in this volume). According to the ICC prosecutor's pre-trial briefs, Uhuru Kenyatta and other politicians held meetings with Mungiki, paying its members to conduct retaliatory attacks, helping them get hold of weapons, and granting them passage through police roadblocks (ICC 2015: 18–21).[11] Mungiki's violence killed several hundred people and displaced thousands. All human rights briefs and commission reports looking into the post-election violence present Mungiki and the police as the main perpetrators. In addition to these gruesome effects of the post-electoral violence, a further consequence was the ICC charge of human rights violations against Uhuru Kenyatta. As already mentioned, the ICC case greatly affected the 2013 elections and resulted in the extra-judicial persecution of Mungiki members, and it continues to cast shadows on Kenyan politics despite the ICC dropping the charges against Uhuru Kenyatta in 2014, due to a lack of evidence and what the court claimed was witness intimidation (ibid.).

Mungiki's involvement in the post-electoral violence and the brutality of the Kariobangi massacre earned the movement an image of youth militants for hire and a threat to democracy. The media similarly presented them as a menace to society, associated with crime, ritualised obscenity, and brutal violence. If we think of the mythological meaning of the chameleon, the members' use of the chameleon metaphor takes on an ironic (and perhaps unintended) twist, because Mungiki literally is perceived as the harbinger of death.

But the metaphor allows for additional interpretative twists. Recall Mungiki's experience as being marginalised and excluded, then think of it as analogous to the fate of the vanishing and humiliated chameleon being chased away by the (now deadly) Kikuyu people who hoped to grow fat from the land. In this rendition, the chameleon metaphor captures the continuous tension between Mungiki and the Kikuyu political elite, a tension that unfolds around perceptions of betrayal, failure and exclusion – which, as we have seen, is particularly prominent around elections. The persecution and the extra-judicial killings of Mungiki by the police and the trade-offs guaranteeing safety in exchange for violence and votes can be understood as outcomes of interrupted and failed communication, resulting in a troubled and conflictual relationship causing death and grievance.

And there is yet another twist to the mythological prophecy of the chameleon bringing death to the fat Kikuyu people. Uhuru Kenyatta, son of Kenya's first independent president, Jomo Kenyatta, and heir to the Kenyatta family's wealth, was accused by the ICC of planning and instigating part of the post-election violence of 2008. Key witnesses against Uhuru Kenyatta at the ICC were former Mungiki members. Prior to the 2013 elections, there was still a possibility of Mungiki witnesses exposing Uhuru Kenyatta and bringing political death to Kenya's most celebrated political family. At that time, and before the ICC dropped the charges, the chameleon was still shimmering in its skin.

The numerous possibilities of interpretation and for merging mythological meaning with politically and violently infused action provide the chameleon metaphor with its explanatory strength. One can choose to focus either on the chameleon's changing colour or on its interior character, but, either way, the metaphor will always reveal the possibility of the other – and thus it is strategically incomplete. This is an important element in understanding Mungiki's shifting political alliances and its constant potential.

Parasitic politics: forceful takeovers from the inside

In Kenyan politics there is a long tradition of using violent youth militias for support and to intimidate opponents (Kagwanja 2001; 2009; Mueller 2008: 189), and Mungiki members have acted in this capacity in the past. Even if the Mungiki members have reformed and abandoned their criminal and violent ways, their violent activities of the past still maintain political power. On several occasions, the movement has hinted at the possibility of using inside knowledge of past alliances to discredit former political patrons. In May 2012, Maina Njenga claimed that almost all politicians from the Kikuyu heartlands in Central Kenya have used Mungiki for their political survival at some point (*Daily Nation* 2012a), indicating that no one has clean hands and that no one should feel safe from exposure.

The idea of gaining political leverage from secret knowledge of others recalls Mungiki's other metaphor, the Mugumo tree – the parasite that grows on other trees. The tree has aerial roots that stretch to the ground and entangle and subsume the host tree. Metaphorically it evokes images of strength and power inherent in its parasitic nature, but it also points to relational aspects between host and parasite, a violent and antagonistic yet symbiotic process through which a new tree emerges. The Mugumo tree and the parasitic process direct our attention to Mungiki's ever-changing relationship with its political patrons and to the police who violently persecute the movement.

For Mungiki members, the Mugumo tree is a powerful and ambiguous metaphor. It allows Mungiki members to think of themselves as part of a potent collective with the capacity to act as parasites on the *matatu* industry, on Margaret Wanjiru's JIAM church, on the Mkenya Solidarity party and on the Kikuyu political elite. As has been shown, Mungiki managed to gain economically and politically from the Kariobangi massacre, and its violent takeover of lucrative *matatu* routes and its continuous forceful control have allowed the movement to raise money and create jobs for its members. In that sense, they are living off – or acting as parasites on – the *matatu* industry (Katumanga 2005; Rasmussen 2012).

In a blunt statement, Maina Njenga admitted a similar parasitic approach to the movement's Pentecostal conversion, as a newspaper quoted him telling Bishop Margaret Wanjiru in front of her congregation: 'This church is no longer yours. Now it is ours!' (*Daily Nation* 2009). By bringing in numerous Mungiki members to the congregation, he implied that they would take over her church. A similar process took place when Mungiki effectively took over the political party Mkenya Solidarity in 2012. As early as 2008, individual Mungiki members began registering as ordinary members of the Mkenya Solidarity party immediately after the government had turned down Mungiki's registration of its own political wing, the Kenya National Youth Alliance.[12] These registrations to Mkenya Solidarity continued until June 2012, when Maina Njenga publicly declared his leadership of the party at a rally on Kamukunji Grounds in Nairobi, much to the surprise of the original founder, G. G. Kariuki. Both examples reveal a swallowing of the host from within.

The symbiotic relationship between the parasite and the host as described by Serres (1982) reveals that the transformative aspect of parasitism does not free the parasite of the host when it has entangled it. Rather, the host is subsumed and becomes part of the new collective body. Understanding Mungiki through the Mugumo tree metaphor thus allows for an inside perspective that is still contextually open.

Through Mungiki's violent activities in relation to electoral and political events, we can see how the movement acted as a parasite on its political patrons by accepting money or negotiating a truce with the police. At the same time, it acted as a parasite on the local Kikuyu communities by extorting money from the *matatu* industry or by inserting its members as dreaded security providers. Through some of its actions, Mungiki effectively acted in a state-like manner or claimed a state-like authority; by doing so, Mungiki acted as a parasite on the state while embodying its character.

The Mugumo tree The explanatory qualities of the Mugumo tree metaphor go beyond its parasitic capacity revealed through the ambiguous and transformative aspects that characterise the relationship between host and parasite. Like the chameleon, the Mugumo tree also features in Kikuyu mythology. It is perceived as sacred and as the tree of life under which the Kikuyu tribe came into being. Furthermore, it serves a range of ritual purposes, and a legend reveals how the Mugumo tree is a medium through which the Kikuyu people communicate with their god through sacrifice and daily prayers (Beech 1913: 4; Karangi 2008: 122). Traditionally, some of the initiation rituals for the transition to adulthood were performed under the Mugumo tree, and the Kikuyu council of elders would hold its meetings there (Kenyatta 1938). In reference to these rituals and meetings, the Mau Mau took some of their oaths under the Mugumo tree.

Karangi (2008) has argued that the Mugumo tree has been neglected in attempts at understanding the cosmology of the Kikuyu. He sees the Mugumo tree as a reference point for the continuity of the social, religious and political world of the Kikuyu, with the tree symbolising fertility, survival, protection, belonging, religious access and political power (ibid. 117, 127–8). Therefore, when Mungiki members describe their movement as being like the Mugumo tree they not only refer to the immediate parasitic qualities of the tree; they also symbolically refer to themselves as having access to a vast register of past cultural, social, religious and political knowledge in the present and for the future. Mungiki's metaphorical references to the mythology invest the movement with the power of the Mugumo tree and fill it with parasitic agency, and its members become agents of change. Their parasitic behaviour is legitimised not only through notions of fairness and due to experiences of historical and structural injustice. More importantly, it is legitimised by reference to the mythology. As such, Mungiki advocates and practises a different form of politics, even if it sometimes mirrors the wider perception of Kenyan politics as deceptive.

However, former Mungiki members do not have exclusive ownership of the symbolic power of the Mugumo tree, nor of Kikuyu rituals such as oathing. In the spring of 2012, there were widespread rumours of secret oathing ceremonies in support of Uhuru Kenyatta taking place at night, allegedly initiated by Kikuyu elders in order to unite the Kikuyu voters behind a Kikuyu presidential candidate and to oppose the ICC intervention. In February 2013, a Mugumo tree fell in Nyeri; this, according to legend, signals a generational change of guard within the Kikuyu community. In other words, the departing President Kibaki would be succeeded by a younger Kikuyu, which in this case could only mean Uhuru Kenyatta.[13] These examples show that other parts of the Kikuyu community are also influenced by secret ritualistic, prophetic and mythical knowledge in their political practices.

If we return to the idea of parasitic practices and the question of who is acting as a parasite on whom, it can also be argued that the Kenyan state and the Kikuyu political elite have been parasites on the Mungiki movement and its militant services. They have used the movement's violent and numerical services whenever they needed them, but Mungiki has been violently discarded through extra-judicial persecution whenever it posed a threat. Mungiki, for its part, has used its bad reputation as a weapon to disentangle itself from its previous patronage networks. Through its ability to continuously transform and appear politically relevant, Mungiki has managed to take a position in Kenyan politics where its patronage cannot be taken for granted. Mungiki members posing as key witnesses at the ICC is the best illustration of this. Mungiki uses its reputation as a dreaded militant sect to remain important, yet the ability of the movement to transform from anti-Christian ethnic traditionalists to a nationalist rights-based pro-constitution movement reveals that nothing is static. Parasitic politics is inherently violent, whether conducted by Mungiki or used as a characteristic of Kenyan politics in general.

Conclusion

This chapter has shown how narratives (traditional and ritually infused) as a source for violent political mobilisation draw on a vast register of perceived injustices; this is similar to Fjelde and Höglund's (Chapter 1) convincing argument that a historical analysis of conflict patterns reveals how contemporary electoral violence is often informed by the past politics of differentiation and the politicisation of past identity conflicts. The chapter has shown how Mungiki, through its violent and parasitic practices, has played a central role in electoral violence over the last couple of decades. In the 2007 elections, Mungiki's violent potential – first displayed in 2002 – grabbed the headlines and defined the post-electoral chaos. Even in the supposedly peaceful 2013 elections, when the central concern was maintaining peace and containing violence, the process was tainted by past violence; this is best exemplified by the influence of the ICC case as a decisive theme. The chapter has shown how the potential for violence becomes a powerful resource for influencing the political agenda, even if the potential is not actualised. Through the skilful play of the threat of violence, secret knowledge and mythological power, the Mungiki movement practises politics in a different way from that of the established political elite – though it is far from unfamiliar. By focusing on the role of deception and on parasitic feeding on one another, the chapter has revealed how we can understand the former Mungiki movement's quest for political inclusion, influence and power.

Furthermore, informal institutions such as youth militias that were established for political ends during authoritarian rule in Kenya have lived on after the turn to multiparty democracy; these informal political actors, like Mungiki, are used by the formal state as well as acting on their own. The chapter has shown how the continued existence and influence of informal political and violent organisations in the democratic era threatens the establishment of formal institutions and easily informs electoral conflicts (cf. Söderberg Kovacs, Introduction in this volume). The chapter has revealed that similar methods of secrecy and deception are at play at the centre of Kenyan politics. The aim here is not to argue that Kenyan politics is inherently immoral or by default corrupt. Rather, the aim has been to investigate the workings of violence and deception in relation to the electoral process. The tension between politicians and Mungiki in the ICC case presents itself as an extreme case for unfolding the deceptive work going on in the quest for power because it plays out across several electoral periods, drawing from the first engagements between Mungiki and the Kikuyu political elite, covering the 2007 post-electoral violence, and continuing until the abandoned ICC court case. Youth militias such as Mungiki and their influence on elections have historical roots, and they are intimately linked to politicians and remain influential in formal politics and on the ability of formal and legal institutions to function.

Mungiki's ability to change and constantly transform has been an essential part of the movement's power, as it is constantly transgressing the boundaries between the formal and the informal, the legal and the illegal. This is captured in the chameleon metaphor, where the true appearance of the movement – whether there is a true appearance at all – is constantly questioned. As such, Mungiki has not been stabilised and it presents a constant potential for violence to outsiders. This has provided the movement with influence on politics, and not only at election time.

Mungiki's role in Kenyan politics as an institutionalised political, religious and violent movement is best explored by looking at the relation between violence and elections, as elections have become critical encounters for Mungiki's parasitic practices. Through its metaphorical reference to Kikuyu mythology, Mungiki merges not only politics and violence but also politics and mythology, which allows for an analytical understanding of electoral violence in Kenya as more than merely anti-democratic and uncivil. Electoral violence must be understood as a form of participation that draws on other registers of knowledge that we usually associate with democratic practice and politics.

In doing so, the relational aspect of electoral violence as it has taken place in Kenya in recent years reveals itself, and it resonates with broader notions of deception and patronage that characterise Kenyan politics.

The existence of informal institutions with the potential for violence close to the core of formal political decision making and electoral politics has enormous implications for policy, as different logics are at play simultaneously. When such logics are present, yet hidden or denied, planning for peaceful electoral processes risks overlooking not only the vested interests at various levels, but also – and just as importantly – how these interests are interlinked and connected in intricate ways.

Notes

1 Author interview with Mungiki leader from Nakuru commenting on the movement's role in the 2008 post-electoral violence, March 2009.

2 The 1992 general elections in Kenya are a good example of how ethnic interests were strategically protected through the orchestration of violence (see Fjelde and Höglund, Chapter 1 in this volume).

3 I appreciate the financial support for fieldwork from the Danish Research Council for Culture and Communication between 2008 and 2010, and from the UK's Foreign and Commonwealth Office for funding fieldwork during the 2013 elections.

4 Author's fieldnotes, December 2008.

5 This was a recurrent phrase used by Mungiki members in the months after the Pentecostal conversion.

6 In interviews with Mungiki members carried out between August 2008 and May 2009, the Nairobi riots were mentioned more than twenty times by different members, referring to the movement's ability for mass mobilisation, but especially to its ability to disrupt and bring the capital city to a halt.

7 Author observations from the Eldoret peace rally, March 2010.

8 GEMA and KAMATUSA respectively supported the Kikuyu candidate Uhuru Kenyatta and the Kalenjin candidate William Ruto. Promoted as a peace meeting, the Limuru meeting presented the former Mungiki movement with the chance of distancing itself from the old ethnic organisations and instead allowed it to claim a pro-peace nationalist agenda.

9 Kamukunji observations conducted for the author by Armstrong Obissa, a Kenyan sociologist, 9 June 2012.

10 Interviews and observations with Mungiki members in Kayole and Nakuru, December 2012 and February 2013.

11 The former spokesperson of Mungiki, Nguguna Githau, accounted for the same process in a conversation with this author in February 2009. He was shot dead in April 2009.

12 Author's fieldnotes and interviews, November 2008.

13 According to an old prophecy by the Kikuyu prophet Mugo wa Kibero, a fallen Mugumo tree in Thika would symbolise the end of colonial rule, which actually happened in 1963, and the fallen Mugumo tree in Nyeri was interpreted along similar lines (*The Standard* 2013).

References

Alston, P. (2009) *UN Special Rapporteur on Extra-judicial, Arbitrary or Summary Executions: Mission to Kenya 16–25 February 2009*. Geneva: United Nations.

Anderson, D. M. (2002) 'Vigilantes, Violence and the Politics of Public Order in Kenya', *African Affairs* 101: 531–55.

Beech, M. W. H. (1913) 'The Sacred Fig-tree of the A-kikuyu of East Africa', *Man* 13: 4–6.

Bekoe, D. A. (ed.) (2012) *Voting in Fear: Electoral Violence in Sub-Saharan Africa*. Washington DC: United States Institute for Peace Press.

Blunt, R. (2013) 'Kenyatta's Lament: Oaths and the Transformation of Ritual Ideologies in Colonial Kenya', *HAU Journal of Ethnographic Theory* 3 (3): 167–93.

Branch, D. (2010) 'The Search for the Remains of Dedan Kimathi: The Politics of Death and Memorialization in Post-colonial Kenya', *Past and Present* 206 (5): 301–20.

Branch, D. and N. Cheeseman (2010) 'Introduction: Our Turn to Eat' in D. Branch, N. Cheeseman and L. Gardner (eds), *Our Turn to Eat: Politics in Kenya since 1950*. Münster: Lit Verlag.

Bratton, M. and N. van de Walle (1997) *Democratic Experiments in Africa: Regime Transitions in Comparative Perspective*. Cambridge: Cambridge University Press.

Brown, S. (2002) 'Michel Serres: Science, Translation and the Logic of the Parasite', *Theory, Culture and Society* 19 (1): 1–27.

Burchard, S. M. (2015) *Electoral Violence in Sub-Saharan Africa: Causes and Consequences*. Boulder CO and London: First Forum Press.

Cheeseman, N. (2008) 'The Kenyan Elections 2007: An Introduction', *Journal of Eastern African Studies* 2 (2): 166–84.

Cheeseman, N. (2015) *Democracy in Africa: Successes, Failures, and the Struggle for Political Reform*. Cambridge: Cambridge University Press.

Christensen, M. M. and M. Utas (2008) 'Mercenaries of Democracy: The "Politricks" of Remobilized Combatants in the 2007 General Elections, Sierra Leone', *African Affairs* 107 (429): 515–39.

Collier, P. (2010) *Wars, Guns and Votes: Democracy in Dangerous Places*. London: Vintage Books.

Daily Nation (2009) 'Is This the End of Mungiki?', *Daily Nation*, 25 October.

Daily Nation (2012a) 'MPs Used Mungiki, Says Njenga', *Daily Nation*, 27 May.

Daily Nation (2012b) 'Plan to Honour J. M. Kariuki', *Daily Nation*, 2 August.

Gecaga, M. G. (2007) 'Religious Movements and Democratisation in Kenya: Between the Sacred and the Profane' in G. Murunga and S. Nasong'o (eds), *Kenya: The Struggle for Democracy*. London: Zed Books.

ICC (2015) 'The Situation in the Republic of Kenya: In the Case of the Prosecutor vs. Uhuru Muigai Kenyatta'. The Hague: Office of the Prosecutor, International Criminal Court (ICC).

IEBC (2013) *Election Data. 4th March 2013 General Election*. Nairobi: Independent Electoral and Boundaries Commission (IEBC). Available at www.iebc.or.ke/uploads/resources/EIqEo3LuiB.pdf.

Kagwanja, P. M. (2001) 'Politics of Marionettes: Extra-legal Violence and the 1997 Elections in Kenya' in M. Rutten, A. Mazrui and F. Grignon (eds), *Out for the Count: Democracy in Kenya*. Kampala: Fountain Publishers.

Kagwanja, P. M. (2005a) 'Power to Uhuru: Youth Identity and Generational Politics in Kenya's 2002 Elections', *African Affairs* 105 (418): 51–75.

Kagwanja, P. M. (2005b) 'Clash of Generations? Youth Identity, Violence and the Politics of Transition in Kenya, 1997–2002' in J. Abbink and I. van Kessel (eds), *Vanguards and Vandals: Youth, Politics and Conflict in Africa*. Leiden and Boston MA: Brill Publishing.

Kagwanja, P. M. (2009) 'Courting Genocide: Populism, Ethno-nationalism and the Informalisation of Violence in Kenya's 2008 Post-election Crisis', *Journal of Contemporary African Studies* 27 (3): 365–87.

Kagwanja, P. M. and R. Southall (2010) 'Kenya's Uncertain Democracy: The Electoral Crisis of 2008', *Journal of Contemporary African Studies* 27 (3): 259–77.

Karangi, M. M. (2008) 'Revisiting the Roots of Gikuyu Culture through the Sacred Mugumo Tree', *Journal of African Cultural Studies* 20 (1): 117–32.

Katumanga, M. (2005) 'A City under Siege: Banditry and Modes of Accumulation in Nairobi, 1991–2004', *Review of African Political Economy* 106: 505–20.

Katumanga, M. (2013) 'Morphing Mirror Images of Military Culture and the Emerging Nation State Insecurities' in F. Vrey, A. Esterhuyse and T. Mandrup (eds), *On Military Culture: Theory, Practice and African Armed Forces.* Cape Town: UCT Press.

Kavulla, T. (2008) 'Our Enemies are God's Enemies: The Religion and Politics of Bishop Margaret Wanjiru, MP', *Journal of Eastern African Studies* 2 (2): 254–63.

Kenyatta, J. (1938) *Facing Mt. Kenya: The Tribal Life of the Gikuyu.* New York NY: Vintage Books.

KNBS (2009) 'Single and Grouped Ages in Years by County and District' in *Kenya Population and Housing Census 2009.* Nairobi: Kenya National Bureau of Statistics (KNBS).

KNCHR (2008) *The Cry of Blood: Report on Extrajudicial Execution and Disappearances.* Nairobi: Kenya National Commission for Human Rights (KNCHR).

KNCHR (2009) 'Extra-judicial Executions: The Testimony and Subsequent Execution of the Late Bernard Kiriinya Ikunyua'. Press release, 24 February. Nairobi: Kenya National Commission for Human Rights (KNCHR).

Knighton, B. (2010) 'Going for Cai at Gatundu: Reversion to a Kikuyu Ethnic Past or Building a Kenyan National Future' In D. Branch, N. Cheeseman and L. Gardner (eds), *Our Turn to Eat: Politics in Kenya since 1950.* Münster: Lit Verlag.

Laakso, L. (2007) 'Insights into Electoral Violence in Africa' in M. Basedau, G. Erdmann and A. Mehler (eds), *Votes, Money and Violence: Political Parties in Sub-Saharan Africa.* Uppsala: Nordic Africa Institute.

Long, J. D., K. Kanyinga, K. E. Ferree and C. Gibson (2013) 'Kenya's 2013 Election: Choosing Peace over Democracy', *Journal of Democracy* 24 (3): 140–55.

Lynch, G. (2014) 'Electing the "Alliance of the Accused": The Success of the Jubilee Alliance in Kenya's Rift Valley', *Journal of Eastern African Studies* 8 (1): 93–114.

Maupeu, H. (2002) 'Physiologie d'un massacre: la tuerie du 3 mars 2002, Kariobangi North (Nairobi, Kenya)' in *Annuaire de l'Afrique Orientale.* Paris: Éditions l'Harmattan.

Maupeu, H. (2003) 'Les elections comme moment prophétique. Narrations Kikuyu des Élections Générales de 2002', *Politique Africaine* 90: 57–77.

Merino, M. (2014) 'The March 4 2013 General Elections in Kenya: From Latent Tensions to Contained Violence' in C. Thibon, M. Fouere, S. Mwangi and M. Ndead (eds), *Kenya's Past as Prologue: Voters, Violence and the 2013 Elections.* Nairobi: IFRA/ Twaweza Publications.

Mueller, S. D. (2008) 'The Political Economy of Kenya's Crisis', *Journal of Eastern African Studies* 2 (2): 185–210.

Mueller, S. D. (2014) 'Kenya and the International Criminal Court (ICC): Politics, the Election and the Law', *Journal of Eastern African Studies* 8 (1): 25–42.

Mulli, L. (1999) 'Understanding Election Clashes in Kenya, 1992 and 1997', *African Security Studies* 8 (4): 75–80.

Mutahi, P. (2005) 'Political Violence in the Elections' in H. Maupeu, M. Katumanga and W. Mitullah (eds), *The Moi Succession: Elections 2002.* Nairobi: IFRA/Transafrica Press.

Oscar Foundation (2007) *The Killing Fields*. Nairobi: Oscar Foundation.

Oscar Foundation (2008) *Veil of Impunity*. Nairobi: Oscar Foundation.

Rasmussen, J. (2012) 'Inside the System, Outside the Law: Operating the Matatu Sector in Nairobi', *Urban Forum* 23 (4): 415–32.

Rasmussen, J. (2013) 'Kenya: Mungiki Regroup Pre-election in Search of Political Influence', *African Arguments*, 1 February. Available at http://africanarguments.org/2013/02/01/kenya-mungiki-regroup-pre-election-in-search-of-political-influence-by-jacob-rasmussen/ (accessed 2 September 2017).

Rasmussen, J. (forthcoming) 'Sacrificial Temporality: Mungiki's Ritualised Mobilization' in H. Vigh and S. Jensen (eds), *Sporadically Radical. Ethnographies of Organised Violence and Militant Mobilization*. Copenhagen: Museum Tusculanum Press/University of Chicago Press.

Ruteere, M. (2008) 'Dilemmas of Crime, Human Rights and the Politics of Mungiki Violence in Kenya'. Occasional Paper 01/08. Nairobi: Kenya Human Rights Institute.

Serres, M. (1982) *The Parasite*. Baltimore MD: Johns Hopkins University Press.

Servant, J. (2007) 'Kikuyus Muscle in on Security and Politics: Kenya's Righteous Youth Militia', *Review of African Political Economy* 34 (113): 521–26.

Straus, S. (2011) '"It's Sheer Horror Here": Patterns of Violence during the First Four Months of Côte d'Ivoire's Post-electoral Crisis', *African Affairs* 110 (440): 481–9.

The Standard (2013) 'Mystic Mugumo Tree's Fall Sparks Succession Debate', *The Standard*, 6 February.

The Star (2012) 'Police Stop Limuru 2B', *The Star*, 18 April.

Thibon, C. (2014) 'Kenyan Elections: When Does History Repeat Itself and Does Not Repeat Itself?' in C. Thibon, M. Fouere, S. Mwangi and M. Ndead (eds), *Kenya's Past as Prologue: Voters, Violence and the 2013 Elections*. Nairobi: IFRA/Twaweza Publications.

TJRC (2013) *Final Report Vol. II*. Nairobi: Truth Justice and Reconciliation commission (TJRC).

Utas, M. (ed.) (2012) *African Conflicts and Informal Power: Big Men and Networks*. London and New York NY: Zed Books.

Waki Commission (2008) *Report of the Commission of Inquiry into the Post-election Violence*. Nairobi: Waki Commission.

Wamue, G. N. (2001) 'Revisiting our Indigenous Shrines through Mungiki', *African Affairs* 100 (400): 453–67.

9 | Eclectic ties and election touts: Chipangano's cyclic governance agenda in Mbare, Zimbabwe

Tariro Mutongwizo

Introduction

Elections in Zimbabwe since independence in 1980[1] have been accompanied or controlled by coercion (Hove 2013). These have been events where violence has come to be expected; it is only the form of such violence that has shifted over time, and the means through which violence and intimation are dispensed. It has been suggested that places where state institutions are controlled by patronage networks present the most complex conflicts (de Waal 2009). This is because the eradication of such conflicts requires the intervention of the state, and the state is incapable of intervening when it too is embroiled in the conflict. The prevalence of informal networks of patron–client relations is a constant and prominent feature of politics in Africa (Bratton and van de Walle 1997). These relations may take varied forms and violence can be deployed or occur as a consequence of these ties. Elections in Zimbabwe are no exception.

In the 2008 and 2013 general elections in Zimbabwe, electoral violence was meted out by a group known as 'Chipangano', which despite garnering various definitions,[2] will be referred to in this chapter as a criminal network. Chipangano mainly operates within the low-income township of Mbare and the surrounding areas in Harare, the capital of Zimbabwe. It is a site where, for many years, patronage networks have caused havoc in people's day-to-day lives – and even more so before, during and even shortly after elections (LeBas 2014; Moore 2014; Mutongwizo 2014). The activities of Chipangano reflect the fact that the city and the state can be used for different purposes than those intended, by 'keeping the official structure operative' while 'using official space for private entrepreneuring' (Simone 2004a: 409).

This chapter intends to explore these patronage networks between Chipangano and the Zimbabwe African National Union – Patriotic Front (ZANU-PF) government and how they appear and diminish during and outside election periods. The chapter analyses how the ties between Big Men in the ZANU-PF party and unemployed youth and touts (individuals who are part of Chipangano's day-to-day activities) are strengthened closer to elections, leading to different types of profiteering in which Big Men and Chipangano indulge by meting out violence in order to control Mbare. This chapter examines the alternating activities of Chipangano in Mbare, with a particular focus on its activities during election periods. The chapter responds to questions relating to the micro-level processes in Mbare that prompt Chipangano, its identity and its activities around election time. An investigation of Chipangano's leadership is essential to respond to these questions, as is an analysis of the mechanisms the group exploits and what it stands to lose from a loss of control of the Mbare area in an election. Of similar importance is an analysis of how, in this instance, Big Men enlist criminal networks and vice versa; this is particularly relevant when considering the nature of the relationship between ZANU-PF and Chipangano, as well as the allegiance that Chipangano shows to ZANU-PF. The key argument made is that Chipangano's ties to specific ZANU-PF individuals in power bolster the network and allow it to exert violent control over Mbare's businesses. In exchange, the network is used to mobilise voters at the time of elections. Such links, supported by outright violence, may in fact be the predominant manner in which electioneering is conducted in Zimbabwe.

Through an examination of Chipangano, this chapter contributes to this volume and more broadly to the literature on electoral violence by pointing to evidence that Big Men enlist groups to dispense violence in order to secure support garnered through coercion. The shifts in the strength of ties between Big Men and violent groups over time illustrate how both parties exploit these ties at varying points to each party's benefit. Médard's (1992) use of Sahlins' (1963) 'Big Man' model in exploring African politics points out how African Big Men alter economic resources and turn them into political authority. This chapter also demonstrates the converse relationship: how political authority is converted into economic profits.

In order to gain insight into the issue, data has been triangulated from three sources. The primary source is data from a household survey conducted in 2010 among 200 residents of Mbare, Harare.[3] In addition, interviews with representatives from local governance organisations, the Combined Harare Residents' Association (CHRA) and the Harare Residents' Trust (HRT) were conducted in 2011 and 2012. These organisations are non-state entities that aim to ensure reliable and equitable service delivery to Harare's residents and represent residents in matters pertaining to local governance. When reporting the statements from participants, pseudonyms are used in order to honour anonymity and protect the identity of these individuals. Finally, and of great value, media accounts were followed in order to establish a clearer picture of the nature and activities of Chipangano. Each of these three methods comple-mented each other in broadening an understanding of a topic that has long remained underexplored.

The chapter begins by briefly discussing the history of electoral violence in Zimbabwe. The background of Chipangano is then outlined: how it came into being, its activities and ties, and how it has operated since it first appeared in 2001. The chapter illustrates that Chipangano is a localised, specific and recent example of a phenomenon that is by no means novel in Zimbabwean politics. In the past, war veterans, youth militia and even ethnic tensions have been relied on by the ZANU-PF to intimidate voters and push them to vote in the party's favour (Hove 2013). This background is followed by an assessment of Chipangano's lifespan and endurance. The relationship between Chipangano's activities and its aim to maintain a ZANU-PF stronghold in urban areas is then unpacked. One key element of this criminal network is its *supposed* links with ZANU-PF office holders. The chapter argues that the alleged ambiguity of these ties is the main reason why Chipangano thrives and manages to maintain hegemony for ZANU-PF in Mbare through the use of force, particularly around election times. The chapter ends with some concluding remarks.

The background to violent electioneering in Zimbabwe

Chabal and Daloz (1999: 80) point out that:

> There is an overlap between the world of politics and business and this is salient in Africa. Politicians are 'licensees' of violence; they can access or restrain official force. Politicians are the key players in the informal sector where success depends on the ease with which economic transactions can evade official control or hindrance.

Such politicians act as Big Men when licensing violence that may benefit them, or those who conduct violent acts on their behalf. Simone (2004b: 145) observes that local order can be 'disrupted in order to intensify authoritarian control, with the effect of loosening the population from its former social and political ties'. Thus, violence is used to control individuals and their voting behaviour, 'giving rise to "big man" systems operating more as commercial firms than as states' (ibid. 145).

The links between states and criminal networks where state officials with Big Man status co-opt individuals to mete out terror have been documented globally. Carey, Colaresi and Mitchell's (2015) valuable analysis of over 200 informal state militia and violent criminal networks worldwide (including Chipangano) is useful for uncovering the ways in which the informal delegation of violence to these groups can assist some states in avoiding taking responsibility for the violence perpetrated by these militia. Carey, Mitchell and Lowe (2013) refer to these groups as pro-government militias. The responsibility for violence is shifted through state officials relying on militia and criminal networks to gain control through violence. Fiorina (1985) refers to this as a 'disguise' the state uses to accomplish aims that otherwise would not have been possible using the state's official identity. The local or national government sponsors such pro-government militias, but they are not part of the official security forces such as the police or army. In most cases, the militias are armed and have some level of organisation and links to the government, but those links are clandestine or not officially recognised. While Chipangano has not been documented as being armed, in some respects the description proffered by Carey, Mitchell and Lowe (2013) describes Chipangano, particularly its covert links with the state.

Relying on criminal networks and militias to enforce control ensures that the state can deny involvement in these activities. Staniland (2012) observes that governments avoid accountability in this way. In Zimbabwe, politicians have long relied on violence to achieve their ends. Tracing the history of maintaining hegemony and order in Zimbabwe, Sachikonye (2011) notes that the colonial and postcolonial state used violence as a tool to control citizens, and that this has also protected perpetrators of violence. This can be noted in inter- and intraparty violence between liberation movements, violence by state institutions in the independent state, ethnic violence, electoral violence, violence in the land reform process and the violence used in Operation Murambatsvina.[4] Mungure (2014) points out that violent groups have often been sanctioned by the Zimbabwean state as a means of preserving power. Unlike the pro-government militias discussed earlier, Operation Murambatsvina and the land reform process actually involved the state's security apparatus. Further, these instances also coincided with elections. This evidence illustrates that accumulation through violence and the control of voters is not a new phenomenon in Zimbabwe. Such methods arise from a long history of conquest. Violence is the means through which power is sought and maintained (Moore 2012).

In some instances, the state's use and condoning of violence in Zimbabwe was legislated. Sachikonye (2011) uncovers some of the laws passed to license the use of violence by the state: these included the Amnesty Ordinance 3 of 1979, the General Pardon Ordinance 12 of 1980 and the Clemency Order of 2000. The legitimising of violence by the state has led to the development of an 'informal economy of violence' (Ibeanu and Luckham 2007) in Zimbabwe, where force and intimidation are tools used in day-to-day governance and political processes.

The violence dispensed by Chipangano differs slightly from previous instances in that its existence and scope were more localised to Mbare and the surrounding high-density areas. Additionally, this criminal network's relationship with Big Men who mobilise violence is more loosely characterised; here, ties are resorted to and disregarded at specific times. Chipangano is enlisted by Big Men when necessary, and, in this case, when votes are being violently canvassed. It is important to note that Chipangano's loose and changeable relationship with Big Men is characteristic of these patron–client relationships. Utas (2012: 8) points out that 'bigmanity' involves 'fluid and ever-changeable webs of relations'. This flexibility will be illustrated in this chapter when considering the alleged leadership of Chipangano and how it has shifted over time, consequently affecting Chipangano's existence.

The continuation of instances when violence is used as a tool for governance with the state's overt or tacit endorsement has therefore plagued Zimbabwe for a long time. This chapter focuses on how Big Men have used violence in the Mbare area to garner support and control businesses by partnering with Chipangano at specific times.

Introducing Chipangano's informal economy of violence

Chipangano means pact in Shona, the most widely spoken language in Zimbabwe. Nyasha from the HRT described Chipangano as a pact among criminals to plunder public resources for the benefit of the criminal network.[5] Whether or not this pact extends to government officials is unclear. Chipangano was led and managed at the outset by the former ZANU-PF Harare Province Youth leader Jim Kunaka. Kunaka, however, lost his position in 2013, and was later ousted from ZANU-PF in 2014 after the party alleged that he was showing support for former vice president Joice Mujuru's Zimbabwe People First (ZimPF) party. Allegedly, Tendai Savanhu, ZANU-PF shadow MP for Mbare and a member of the politburo, initially supported Chipangano financially. Following its establishment, members were paid from the criminal network's spoils after it was granted immunity to plunder resources (Shumba 2011; *The Zimbabwean* 2012).[6] While the association between Chipangano and these individuals has been established, and it is widely believed that Chipangano has assisted with the mobilisation for support of these individuals and other ZANU-PF youth members, particularly during election time, there have also been various instances where the links between Chipangano and these individuals have been denied (*The Daily News* 2012).[7]

Isolating all Chipangano allegiances to ZANU-PF to these two individuals would be inaccurate, however, although it has been established that they have the strongest ties to Chipangano (Crisis in Zimbabwe Coalition 2012). Despite strong links with ZANU-PF being discernible, this criminal network has evaded prosecution by remaining conveniently ignored by the state as far as pertinent aspects of its existence are concerned, such as the individuals behind its sponsorship. Chipangano therefore operates with outright impunity through its association with Big Men who hold political office.

The emergence of Chipangano and its subsequent fading and re-emergence since 2001 is a topic that has garnered much attention in the media. Chipangano has caused immense strife in many of Harare's merchandising hubs. It is notably present in various forms across Harare's informal business areas, and towns such as Norton (Kibble 2013) and the high-density areas of Highfield and Mufakose have experienced Chipangano's dominance in one form or another.

However, this criminal network primarily operates in Mbare, a site close to the city centre and a place where informal businesses thrive. Chipangano's main activities include, but are not limited to, seeking to mobilise support for ZANU-PF candidates in the area, preventing the penetration of the political opposition, and aiming to maintain control of Harare municipality properties (see Shumba 2011; *The Zimbabwean* 2012; Chirau and Chamuka 2013; McGregor 2013; LeBas 2014; Moore 2014; Mutongwizo 2014).[8]

There is very little known about the members of Chipangano – who they are and how many there are – but the HRT has generally characterised them as 'youth'. In 2011, the HRT asserted that, in many cases, people travel to Mbare and work with ZANU-PF members in order to exploit the available opportunities to make money by terrorising informal business people.[9] The HRT notes that many individuals are only loosely and occasionally connected to Chipangano in Mbare; when they return to their communities – which tend to be other high-density areas such as Epworth, Chitungwiza, Mabvuku, Highfield and Budiriro – they are apolitical and in some cases may even be supporters of Movement for Democratic Change (MDC), the opposition party. In their communities, the fact that they are Chipangano members remains unknown. Patrick, a member of the CHRA, argued in 2011 that anyone who is unemployed might be tempted to join Chipangano as it provides a sure way to make a living.[10] Those without access to alternative modes of survival may in fact be easily drafted into Chipangano (Moore 2012). As such, the activities of Chipangano are not limited to election-related violence.

Chipangano's governance agenda: controlling elections and earnings

Chipangano's pursuits range from relying on violence to control economic activity in Mbare and the surrounding areas to mobilising support for the ZANU-PF ruling party before and during elections. The shifts in Chipangano's undertakings are discussed below.

Violent electioneering While the existence of Chipangano was not formally documented until 2001, it was the establishment of the opposition in the form of the MDC in 2000 that prompted its emergence. According to LeBas (2014), voters in Harare, particularly those supporting the MDC, began to experience fear and intimidation in 2000. Until then, such terrorisation of voters had occurred only in Zimbabwe's rural areas.

Various scholars describe the manner in which Chipangano mobilised urban residents to support ZANU-PF as violent and coercive. Chipangano also held campaigns for ZANU-PF in Mbare, where they coerced residents into attending during the 2008 and 2013 elections (Mutongwizo 2014). Chirau and Chamuka (2013) note that vendors in the Magaba area held deep concerns and fears about elections, as they led to violence and an interruption of their livelihoods in Mbare.

Moore (2014) observes that Chipangano coerced urbanites to cast votes in favour of ZANU-PF. McGregor (2013) points out that, aside from engaging in pervasive physical violence, Chipangano used the surveillance of voters to ensure compliance with directives to vote for ZANU-PF. Some of the surveillance tactics involved following the movements of MDC activists, keeping registers to note attendees at ZANU-PF meetings and rallies, and checking members of the public for ZANU-PF cards. McGregor (ibid.) adds that some prominent MDC councillors and activists were expelled from Mbare. This benefited ZANU-PF greatly, as it resulted in other MDC activity losing momentum and operating more discreetly, thereby leading to the weakening of the opposition party.

In a 2011 interview, participants from the CHRA raised the issue that Chipangano had disrupted meetings and activities aimed at providing equitable services for urban residents on many occasions. CHRA participants added that any activity that was designed to enlighten citizens on their rights in any way was targeted in one way or another by Chipangano. As stated by Rufaro of the CHRA:

Our satellite office in Mbare was very popular, it became a hub for many activities and before we set it up, penetrating Mbare had been very difficult. But then, the office was closed down by Chipangano earlier in 2010. By force. They felt that we were threatening their existence and taking over Mbare since they somehow began to perceive us to be an affiliate of the MDC.[11]

Victor, also from the CHRA, said:

We had a monthly newsletter known as *The Mbare Resident*. It was just a little paper that would talk about events in the community and also give people information on where to go if they needed help with community problems. We had harmless information in there like where to access water and other community facilities, but that was a threat to them [Chipangano] and they abolished it.[12]

Mbare residents highlight that Chipangano's terror was not unique to election periods. For example, people were also coerced into attending the funerals of declared national heroes. On one occasion, Chipangano forced residents to travel as far as the National Heroes Acre to show support for a departed ZANU-PF member (Dube and Chirisa 2012; Chirau and Chamuka 2013: 22).

Terror has been noted as continuing even after elections, with violence such as Operation *Makavhotera Papi* ('Who did you vote for?') being introduced to intimidate citizens and dispense violence (Mungure 2014). These actions are legitimised by the state since the entire election process is appropriated by

ZANU-PF; even after the election, violence is used to punish those known to have voted against the party or suspected of having done so. In such instances, Big Men who are office holders abuse their public positions and also legitimise practices in which 'the appropriation of such offices is not just an act of individual greed or ambition but concurrently the satisfaction of the short-term objectives of a subset of the general population' (Joseph 1987: 67).

Downsizing and sizing up Big Men: Chipangano's leadership The exploitation of public resources and offices by Big Men in association with criminal networks such as Chipangano in order to meet specific goals at clearly defined times is evident in Chipangano's former leader Jim Kunaka's changeable status within ZANU-PF. Much like Chipangano's foot soldiers, his status as a Big Man is also flexible and dependent on the time period. This can be observed in Kunaka's actions of October 2015, when, in an interview with South African News Channel ANN7, he referred to ZANU-PF as a 'cult' and apologised for his role in Chipangano (Ndlovu 2015).

However, months later, Kunaka re-joined ZANU-PF after being forced to leave the party in 2014 and later joining ZimPF. In an interview (Dlamini 2016), when asked about whether he would revive Chipangano, Kunaka responded by laughing at first and then vehemently saying:

> I can't continue using old systems, something that is no longer in fashion.
> We are coming on board with new strategies on how to win an election.
> I have said it before that, that was a time of madness and I was doing it
> because I was still young and now I am a matured politician. I know what
> is needed by the people of this country, it's not violence, it's not taking them
> to meetings by force and so forth. What they want to see is food on the
> table, so I will try by all means to encourage other young people to desist
> from violence. So I don't think that Chipangano would be revived. No, no,
> no we have got new systems of mobilising people, engaging people, one-on-
> one, in a peaceful manner.

While these are the most recent utterances from Kunaka, his return to ZANU-PF has nonetheless raised fears among people. Mbare residents in particular are gravely worried about the possible return of Chipangano to mobilise for ZANU-PF support in future elections (Dewa 2016). Kunaka's return to ZANU-PF prompted the MDC's Secretary for Information, Obert Gutu, to express the fears associated with such a move. Nehanda Radio (ibid.) quotes Gutu as saying:

> We are naturally disappointed that Kunaka is going to ZANU-PF after
> claiming to have repented. Our members in Mbare and its immediate
> environs have suffered at the hands of that group [Chipangano] and the

fact that its lynchpin, Kunaka, has re-joined the violent party is a cause for great concern.

The pattern represented here by Kunaka's return illustrates the cycle through which violence is meted out in Zimbabwe's elections, where Chipangano has been the vehicle through which violence has been dispensed in the 2008 and 2013 elections in order to ensure a victory. The departure and return of Kunaka reflects that the endurance of 'bigmanity' is not definitive. While some Big Men 'spend a lifetime at the centre of things', others – like Kunaka – 'come and go' (Utas 2012: 8). Examining the pattern displayed by Chipangano in the elections of 2008 and 2013, there is a detectable way in which it operates. This involves a focus on profiteering from Mbare's businesses on a day-to-day basis through being protected by Big Men who in turn have their positions of power preserved by Chipangano during election time, when citizens are violently mobilised for support for these Big Men. In this way, a reciprocal support system between Chipangano and Big Men is maintained. While there are breaks in the cycle – as seen in Kunaka's departure from ZANU-PF – it remains to be seen whether this is the very end of Chipangano and this form of violent electioneering in Mbare, seeing as such arrangements have been part of each of Zimbabwe's elections.

The decline and revival of Chipangano, and the criminal network's different focal points depending on the proximity of elections, demonstrate a cycle in its governance pattern within Mbare. The strength of the ties between Chipangano and Big Men also tends to be greater as elections approach, during the build-up to elections and throughout general and by-elections, but these ties are loosened during non-election periods.

It is clear that the activities of Chipangano have not been limited to election-related violence or only to activities seeking to promote ZANU-PF. This criminal network manages to constantly have an item on its governance agenda that creates a reason for its existence. Employing Chipangano to canvass votes through violence also benefits the ZANU-PF government because these actions can be denied and are challenging to verify (Kibble 2013). The Crisis in Zimbabwe Coalition characterises Chipangano not simply as a localised militia but as 'a parallel rogue security force' that receives logistical support from the state. Chipangano thus has dual roles: the criminal network has been employed as a tool for the repression of non-ZANU-PF supporters and as a force to generate revenue (Crisis in Zimbabwe Coalition 2012). This second role will be discussed in the next section.

Controlling informal sector earnings Outside election periods, the ZANU-PF youth identity is retained by members of Chipangano for their benefit in order to plunder public resources. Through their dual and fluid identities as

Chipangano and members of ZANU-PF's youth wing, they have been involved in the widespread terrorisation of urban dwellers, particularly those making a living in the informal sector. Chipangano uses violence to intimidate informal business owners, and to loot and control livelihoods by demanding a share of these business people's earnings as a form of tax (Chirau and Chamuka 2013: 21).

Chipangano is aware of the lucrative opportunities that exist in Mbare. There are wholesale markets known as Mupedzanhamo and Mbare Musika as well as retail and manufacturing industries in the Siya-so and Magaba areas. There is a strong presence of small businesses, and hence the opportunity to exploit individual business owners who need stalls and daily transportation. Chipangano's ability to plunder in such an environment is increased by the fact that there is little law enforcement and regulation in Mbare, thereby creating the opportunity for Chipangano to operate with impunity.

Further, ZANU-PF's denial of the existence of Chipangano has led to the police being unable to intervene in any way (Moyo 2011). In an interview with the HRT in 2011, participants argued that the police in Mbare are fearful of being victimised. This leads to Chipangano operating with impunity since there is no opposition from the police. If challenged by the police, members of Chipangano rely on their ZANU-PF allegiance to escape prosecution. The police remain partisan in terms of who is arrested, with perpetrators who support the government enjoying almost total immunity and individuals, especially opposition supporters and civil society figures, being subject to arbitrary arrest (Kibble 2013). The Harare City Council also lacks the capacity to confront Chipangano because members of the network use their ZANU-PF identity to hide behind political victimisation (Mutongwizo 2014).

Scholars who have had the opportunity to interview those affected by Chipangano's existence in Mbare have pointed out that the Chipangano network wholly controls business in the area. For instance, the majority of vendors operating in the Magaba area claimed that Chipangano has taken the law into its own hands. There is a constant atmosphere of fear, particularly during and after elections (Dube and Chirisa 2012). 'Bigmanity' is a response to a lack of formal structures (Utas 2012: 8), and, in this case, a lack of strong official control of public space and resources. Chipangano benefits from the Harare municipality's lack of influence in controlling public space and informally employs the known autocracy of the ZANU-PF government to achieve its ends – and, in the process, it garners support for ZANU-PF in Mbare and the surrounding areas by intimidating the public.

The media has noted that Chipangano halted the US$5 million Bill and Melinda Gates Foundation construction project of residential flats in Mbare in 2011. Chipangano threatened construction workers with violence, and demanded 51 per cent ownership of the project. The housing project was moved to Dzivarasekwa, another high-density area, south-west of the city of Harare. Chipangano is less active in Dzivarasekwa as this area does not have as many informal business opportunities as Mbare. Despite the project's formal approval by the City of Harare, the site of a proposed US$1.2 million service station and food court near Matapi police station was harassed in a similar way. Finally, as a third example of their control over public space in Mbare, Chipangano members destroyed the foreign-funded boreholes in Mbare, calling them 'enemy funded' (Shumba 2011; *The Zimbabwean* 2012; *The Daily News* 2012).

The control of market stalls and space allocated for trading in Mbare, as well as the charging of a toll to all transport operating in and around Mbare, creates a platform that bolsters Chipangano's dominance when elections approach. These activities ensures the day-to-day sustainability of Chipangano and are used to generate income for the network under the protection of Big Men such as Kunaka and Savanhu, who hold political power (McGregor 2013), since these Big Men have the capacity to command and prompt mass action (Sahlins 1963). The 2013 elections are a clear example where Chipangano controlled the unregulated informal vendors and voters in Mbare (Moore 2012).

During field research conducted between 2010 and 2012, participants in the household survey in Mbare and informants from the HRT and the CHRA pointed out that Chipangano relies on violence, torture and rape to intimidate people, civil society and the opposition. The HRT provided information on how Chipangano controlled public space, stating that it determined the allocation of market stalls in Mbare according to one's allegiance. Those paying a fee to Chipangano for market stalls or holding ZANU-PF cards or credentials received preferential treatment. Market stalls were further subdivided by Chipangano to allow members to charge more for the limited space by allocating more traders per stall. Market traders were supposed to have a licence from the City of Harare municipality, but Mbare councillor Paul Muleya points out that 'now you need a ZANU card' (McGregor 2013). Additionally, Chipangano charged all traders within the termini and minibus taxis a fee for operating in Mbare, usurping the control of the transport sector. Chipangano had therefore successfully taken control of the livelihoods of informal business people using the city council's infrastructure.

Nyasha from the HRT stressed that the government has 'allowed political thugs to masquerade as businessmen'.[13] Chipangano managed to take advantage of the state by usurping public resources and benefiting financially while posing as an entity working on behalf of ZANU-PF. By doing do, Chipangano members escape conviction. Due to the state's denial of Chipangano's existence, it has endorsed the group and has given it tacit permission to operate. In this way, the criminal creativity in which Chipangano engages is a form of security and adaptation in order to survive, and even to accumulate wealth.

The view that the state is preying on individuals (Buchanan 1999; Chabal 2007; Englebert 1997; Frimpong-Ansah 1991; Harsch 1997; Lund 2007; Shleifer and Vishny 1998) is demonstrated through Chipangano's existence in Mbare. Big Men such as Kunaka have outsourced criminality to Chipangano, which works to sustain both Chipangano and ZANU-PF.

Chipangano within the Big Man agenda: spillages for pillaging

Chipangano survived and perhaps proliferated between 2001 and 2014 because of its adaptation to the various economic environments in Zimbabwe. Chipangano altered its activities with each season that presented an opportunity for resources to be usurped or dominance to be used for securing resources and space. Success mainly rests on Chipangano's association with Big Men, who, in the form of Kunaka and Savanhu, provided a reprieve from the law, and in return worked as a network outsourced by ZANU-PF when necessary. The re-emergence of Chipangano before and during election periods and its re-focusing of energies towards controlling public space and resources during breaks from elections display the manner in which Chipangano undergoes various spillages from one identity and activity to another at different times. Chipangano possesses a fluid nature and undergoes numerous transformations in its bid to secure hegemony. In this way, Chipangano may be seen primarily as a business entity, driven mainly by greed and not necessarily by an allegiance to ZANU-PF.

In condoning Chipangano's activities, the state can, in Cohen's (2001) terms, be identified as a bystander to atrocities. In many respects, the state acts as an enabler of Chipangano's activity. Alluding to Chabal and Daloz (1999: 80), politicians are often the facilitators and licensees of the business of violence. It is clear that the success of networks such as Chipangano is not determined by their autonomy from the state, but is shaped more by their relationship with the state (Meagher 2010). In such instances, Big Men such as Kunaka emerge and use their positions to mobilise criminal networks for a mutually beneficial relationship based on plundering public resources. This case demonstrates that there are various sizes of Big Men in a hierarchy of control, assigning positions to each other in their plundering. It will be worth noting how Chipangano evolves, if at all, in future elections.

Elections and control in Mbare: elevating and relegating Big Men

Individuals are made into Big Men by small men. If anything, Chipangano's inestimable members benefited more from their activities in Mbare, since these individuals remain nameless and ousted Kunaka, whom they had made a Big Man within their sphere. Diamond (2008) notes that as more democratic processes and election observations are being encouraged and put in place, it has become more common for a ruling party or Big Man to lose an election. This may be one of the key reasons why criminal networks such as Chipangano exist, and Chipangano's aims tend to be dual for this reason. The first may be, as seen in the discussions above, to create a support base and build up or create Big Men; the second, as seen in Kunaka's case, may be to relegate these Big Men when the situation demands it. Hence, the label 'touts' describes both these individuals who are part of Chipangano's day-to-day activities in the various business opportunities in Mbare, and also their activities in terms of building up positions of power, and taking that power away from potential Big Men.

Therefore, it is debatable who is the patron and who is the client in the relationship, since the roles are somewhat reversed. Sahlins observes the fragility and the transient nature of Big Man power, 'as loyalty must continuously be reinforced and dissatisfaction among followers may have grave consequences for his authority' (Sahlins 1963: 292). The chapter therefore raises the point that criminal networks such as Chipangano are aware of and exercise their agency in their activities and are as much in control of the relationship as the Big Men who subcontract them to dispense violence in times when authority appears unachievable through legal means. Chipangano's withdrawal of support for Kunaka ended both his and Chipangano's terror in Mbare. This case also displays that both Big Men and Chipangano wielded power at different times, depending on what ends were being sought, and violence was the tool used to achieve their agendas.

It seems that criminal networks such as Chipangano emerge when a threat to hegemony exists, such as was the case between 2001 and 2014, when the MDC threatened ZANU-PF. Chipangano's most prominent years were between 2008 and 2013, which was the period when a global political agreement (GPA) existed in Zimbabwe and power was shared between ZANU-PF and the MDC. ZANU-PF's alleged reaction to the burgeoning of the opposition took the form of appropriating control through the use of Chipangano in places such as Mbare where the opposition was gaining widespread favour.

Electoral violence within the Mbare locality has been a consequence of the lack of regulation. The control of space in Mbare could be guaranteed by being associated with office holders representing the locality. Therefore, the violence in this instance can be understood as a direct struggle for power and control over the area, which is why individuals ranging from touts to stallholders to business people operating in Mbare sought involvement in Chipangano. This is spurred by lawlessness and the neglect of public space, where a blind eye can be turned to these battles for power. Thus, controlling the urban vote means controlling high-density suburbs such as Mbare. Kibble (2013) notes that the threat that Mbare poses to ZANU-PF is immense since it is a stronghold of the opposition. To ZANU-PF, control over Mbare is essential both because it is a stronghold of the opposition, and because a loss of control over Mbare would mean losing control over profitable business opportunities within the area's economic space.

Conclusion: the timely emergence of Big Men with specific agendas

This chapter has provided the basis for understanding the links that have been exploited by Chipangano and government officials acting as Big Men and how this association has benefited each party in different time periods. The government has condoned Chipangano because its existence is mutually beneficial for each actor. By observing Kunaka's rise in Chipangano, his exit from ZANU-PF and his subsequent return, it can be detected that individuals are elevated at distinct times and under specific circumstances, elections being the most crucial times. Chipangano was free to control and plunder public resources and space on a day-to-day basis, and the state relied on this criminal network's power in intimidating the public during election time in order to guarantee votes.

Therefore, Chipangano did not necessarily exploit the state by claiming allegiance to Big Men who hold political office; rather, it was a reciprocal relationship that was nurtured and flourished because of mutual benefits for Big Men and criminals, each supporting its proliferation at specific times. This indicates a 'pact' between prospective Big Men and the unemployed, youth and touts taking advantage of Mbare's opportunities, which thereby gave birth to Chipangano.

This chapter contributes to an understanding of the interplay between the links of this criminal network and ZANU-PF. The chapter has been useful for investigating how these networks are used, in this case through outright violence to support both the political interests of ZANU-PF and Chipangano's business agenda. Through examining Chipangano in Mbare, the chapter has shed some light on election-related violence and how it manifests within this locality. Furthermore, the chapter is useful as a lens through which to view the manner in which Big Men outsource services from criminal networks and how such links further guarantee the achievement of both parties' agendas and their impunity because of existing yet opaque ties.

What remains to be seen is whether Chipangano will yet again be revived in future elections, and if Chipangano – or similar criminal networks – will (re-)emerge in the same or a different form, supported by prospective Big Men who desire political power. The possibility of resurgence exists since Mbare remains an economic hub and a fertile breeding ground for various opportunities and opportunists. If Jim Kunaka does not take the position of the Big Man behind Chipangano in future elections, it will be worth noting whether another individual will be elevated to fill that void and mobilise citizens, as well as to control space and earnings in Mbare and the surrounding areas. The use of violence to maintain power when threatened by opposition may indeed be one of the ways in which ruling parties react to the risk of losing their dominance, thereby exerting more intense levels of control and violence during election periods.

Notes

1 Elections have been held in 1985, 1990, 1995, 2000, 2005, 2008 and 2013. For example, in 1985, the ruling party's Zimbabwe African National Unity – Patriotic Front (ZANU-PF) youths confronted the opposition Zimbabwe African People's Union (ZAPU) at a rally in Kwekwe, leading to violence and to the consequent result where ZANU-PF won seats in a ZAPU stronghold (Arnold, Garber and Wrobel 1986; Garber 1985). Furthermore, in the period leading up to the 2000 elections, the 'war veterans' militias' dispensed violence in support of ZAU-PF candidates. Kriger (2005) notes that over 200,000 incidents of violence against the opposition were reported in the first half of 2000.

2 Chipangano has also been described in the literature as an 'informal state-militia' (Carey, Colaresi and Mitchell 2015), as a 'stand-by militia' (Kibble 2013) and as a 'gang' (cf. *The Zimbabwean* 2012).

3 It was anticipated that the household survey would be sufficient to shed light on the nuances of the various governance mechanisms in Mbare. However, residents were extremely reserved when it came to discussing Chipangano. Only very few participants (3 per cent) openly discussed the existence of Chipangano; interestingly, they referred to them as ZANU-PF youth reservists. They said that this group was particularly involved in crime and violence during election time.

4 Operation Murambatsvina can best be described as a project of urban cleansing by the Zimbabwe government, targeting the poor. It began in May 2005 and for several months thereafter it razed informal sector activities (Coltart 2008). Murambatsvina is estimated by the United Nations (UN) to have directly affected at least 700,000 people who lost their homes or sources of livelihood (Tibaijuka 2005). It has been asserted that Murambatsvina aimed to chastise the urban poor for supporting the MDC (Bratton and Masunungure 2006).

5 Author interview with Nyasha, HRT, Harare, 10 February 2012.

6 Author interview with Brenda, HRT, Harare, 10 February 2012.

7 Ibid.

8 Author interview with Nyasha, HRT, Harare, 10 February 2012.

9 Author interview with Rufaro, CHRA, Harare, 18 March 2011.

10 Author interview with Patrick, CHRA, Harare, 18 March 2011.

11 Author interview with Rufaro, CHRA, Harare, 18 March 2011.

12 Author interview with Victor, CHRA, Harare, 17 March 2011.

13 Author interview with Nyasha, HRT, Harare, 10 February 2012.

References

Arnold, M. W., L. Garber and B. Wrobel (1986) *Zimbabwe: Report on the 1985 General Elections. Based on a Mission of the Election Observer Project of the International Human Rights Law Group*. Washington DC: International Human Rights Law Group. Cited in N. Kriger (2005) 'ZANU (PF) Strategies in General Elections, 1980–2000: Discourse and Coercion', *African Affairs* 104 (414): 1–34.

Bratton, M. and E. Masunungure (2006) 'Popular Reactions to State Repression: Operation Murambatsvina in Zimbabwe', *African Affairs* 106 (422): 21–45.

Bratton, M. and N. van de Walle (1997) *Democratic Experiments in Africa: Regime Transitions in Comparative Perspective*. Cambridge: Cambridge University Press.

Buchanan, A. (1999) 'Recognitional Legitimacy and the State System', *Philosophy and Public Affairs* 28 (1): 46–78.

Carey, S. C., M. P. Colaresi and N. J. Mitchell (2015) 'Governments, Informal Links to Militias, and Accountability', Journal of Conflict Resolution 59 (5): 850–76.

Carey, S. C., N. J. Mitchell and W. Lowe (2013) 'States, the Security Sector, and the Monopoly of Violence: A New Database on Pro-government Militias', *Journal of Peace Research* 50 (2): 249–58.

Chabal, P. (2007) 'State and Governance: The Limits of Decentralisation'. SNV Publication H0702-01. The Hague: SNV Netherlands Development Organisation.

Chabal, P. and J.-P. Daloz (1999) *Africa Works: Disorder as Political Instrument*. Oxford and Bloomington IN: James Currey and Indiana University Press.

Chirau, T. J. and P. Chamuka (2013) 'Politicisation of Urban Space: Evidence from Women Informal Traders at Magaba, Harare in Zimbabwe', *Global Advanced Research Journal of History, Political Science and International Relations* 2 (2):14–26.

Cohen, S. (2001) *States of Denial: Knowing about Atrocities and Suffering*. Cambridge: Polity Press.

Coltart, D. (2008) 'A Decade of Suffering in Zimbabwe: Economic Collapse and Political Repression under Robert Mugabe'. Development Policy Analysis 5. Washington DC: Center for Global Liberty and Prosperity, CATO Institute.

Crisis in Zimbabwe Coalition (2012) 'Zimbabwe Briefing Regional Office Weekly Report'. 28 March–3 April.

Dewa, T. (2016) 'Jim Kunaka Revives Violent Chipangano Scare', Nehanda Radio, 13 June. Available at http://nehandaradio.com/2016/06/13/jim-kunaka-revives-violent-chipangano-scare/ (accessed 17 June 2016).

de Waal, A. (2009) 'Mission Without End? Peacekeeping in the African Marketplace', *International Affairs* 85: 99–113.

Diamond, L. (2008) 'Progress and Retreat in Africa: The Rule of Law versus the Big Man', *Journal of Democracy* 19: 138–49.

Dlamini, N. (2016) 'No Plans to Revive Chipangano, Says ZANU PF Prodigal Son Jim Kunaka', *New Zimbabwe*, 11 June. Available at www.newzimbabwe.com/news-29666-Interview+Chipangano+terror+commander/news.aspx (accessed 17 June 2016).

Dube, D. and I. Chirisa (2012) 'The Informal City: Assessing its Scope, Variants and Direction in Harare, Zimbabwe', *Global Advanced Research Journal of Geography and Regional Planning* 1 (1): 16–25.

Englebert, P. (1997) 'The Contemporary African State: Neither African nor State', *Third World Quarterly* 18 (4): 767–75.

Fiorina, M. P. (1985) 'Group Concentration and Delegation of Legislative Authority' in R. G. Noll (ed.), *Regulatory Policy and the Social Sciences*. Berkeley CA: University of California Press.

Frimpong-Ansah, J. H. (1991) *The Vampire State in Africa: The Political Economy of Decline in Ghana*. Trenton NJ: Africa World Press.

Garber, L. (1985) 'Zimbabwe's 1985 Elections' in *Zimbabwe: Report on the 1985 General Elections*. Cited in N. Kriger (2005) 'ZANU (PF) Strategies in General Elections, 1980–2000: Discourse and Coercion', *African Affairs* 104 (414): 1–34.

Harsch, E. (1997) 'African States in Social and Historical Context', *Sociological Forum* 12 (4): 671–9.

Hove, S. (2013) 'Preventing Violence in Future Elections: Moving Towards an Early Warning System for Zimbabwe', *Journal of Peacebuilding and Development* 8 (1): 79–83.

Ibeanu, O. and R. Luckham (2007) 'Nigeria: Political Violence, Governance and Corporate Responsibility in a Petro-state' in M. Kaldor, T. L. Karl and Y. Said (eds), *Oil Wars*. London: Pluto Press.

Joseph, R. A. (1987) *Democracy and Prebendal Politics in Nigeria: The Rise and Fall of the Second Republic.* Cambridge: Cambridge University Press.

Kibble, S. (2013) 'Zimbabwe between the Referendum and the Elections', *Strategic Review for Southern Africa* 35 (1): 93–117.

Kriger, N. (2005) 'ZANU (PF) Strategies in General Elections, 1980–2000: Discourse and Coercion', *African Affairs* 104 (414): 1–34.

LeBas, A. (2014) 'The Perils of Power Sharing', *Journal of Democracy* 25 (2): 52–66.

Lund, C. (ed.) (2007) *Twilight Institutions: Public Authority and Local Politics in Africa.* Oxford: Blackwell.

McGregor, J. (2013) 'Surveillance and the City: Patronage, Power-sharing and the Politics of Urban Control in Zimbabwe', *Journal of Southern African Studies* 39 (4): 783–805.

Meagher, K. (2010) *Identity Economics: Social Networks and the Informal Economy in Nigeria.* Oxford and Ibadan: James Currey and HEBN Publishers.

Médard, J.-F. (1992) 'Le "big man" en Afrique: esquisse d'analyse du politician entrepreneur', *L'Année Sociologique* 42: 167–92.

Moore, D. (2012) 'Progress, Power, and Violent Accumulation in Zimbabwe', *Journal of Contemporary African Studies* 30 (1): 1–9.

Moore, D. (2014) 'Zimbabwe's Democracy in the Wake of the 2013 Election: Contemporary and Historical Perspectives', *Strategic Review for Southern Africa* 36 (1): 47–71.

Moyo, J. (2011) 'Zanu-PF's Militia Feeds on Extortion', *Mail and Guardian*, 18 November. Available at https://mg.co.za/article/2011-11-18-zanupfs-militia-feeds-on-extortion (accessed 23 February 2013).

Mungure. S. (2014) 'Informal Armed Formations and the State: The Case of Zimbabwe', *Journal of Peacebuilding and Development* 9 (2): 71–6.

Mutongwizo, T. (2014) 'Chipangano Governance: Enablers and Effects of Violent Extraction in Zimbabwe', *Africa Peace and Conflict Journal* 7 (1): 29–40.

Ndlovu, N. (2015) 'Ex-Chipangano Leader Jim Kunaka Apologises', NewsDay, 16 October. Available at www.newsday.co.zw/2015/10/16/ex-chipangano-leader-jim-kunaka-apologises/ (accessed 18 May 2016).

Sachikonye, L. M. (2011) *When a State Turns on its Citizens: 60 Years of Institutionalised Violence in Zimbabwe.* Johannesburg: Jacana Media.

Sahlins, M. D. (1963) 'Poor Man, Rich Man, Big-man, Chief: Political Types in Melanesia and Polynesia', *Comparative Studies in Society and History* 5: 285–303.

Shleifer, A. and R. W. Vishny (1998) *The Grabbing Hand: Government Pathologies and their Cures.* Cambridge MA: Harvard University Press.

Shumba, P. (2011) 'Chipangano: A Business Outfit Hiding Behind ZANU-PF', *The Zimbabwean*, 3 November. Available at www.thezimbabwean.co/2011/11/chipangano-a-business-outfit-hiding/ (accessed 18 March 2013).

Simone, A. (2004a) 'People as Infrastructure: Intersecting Fragments in Johannesburg', *Public Culture* 16: 407–29.

Simone, A. (2004b) *For the City Yet to Come: Changing African Life in Four Cities.* Durham NC: Duke University Press.

Staniland, P. (2012) 'Between a Rock and a Hard Place: Insurgent Fratricide, Ethnic Defection, and the Rise of Pro-state Paramilitaries', *Journal of Conflict Resolution* 56 (1): 16–40.

The Daily News (2012) 'How Chipangano Stalled Fuel Project', *The Daily News*, 26 February. Available at www.dailynews.co.zw/index.php/news/34-news/7563-how-chipangano-stalled-fuel-project.html (accessed 18 March 2012).

The Zimbabwean (2012) 'Violent Chipangano Gang Campaigning for ZANU PF', *The Zimbabwean*, 14 April. Available at www.thezimbabwean.co/2012/04/violent-chipangano-gang-campaigning-for/ (accessed 13 December 2017).

Tibaijuka, A. J. (2005) *Report of the Fact-finding Mission to Zimbabwe to Assess the Scope and Impact of Operation Murambatsvina*. Nairobi: UN Special Envoy on Human Settlements Issues in Zimbabwe. Available at www.un.org/News/dh/infocus/zimbabwe/zimbabwe_rpt.pdf (accessed 10 October 2010).

Utas, M. (2012) 'Introduction: Bigmanity and Network Governance in African Conflicts' in M. Utas (ed.), *African Conflicts and Informal Power: Big Men and Networks*. London and New York NY: Zed Books.

10 | Patronage politics and electoral violence in Lagos, Nigeria: understanding the micro-level dynamics

Daniel E. Agbiboa

Introduction

The patron–client framework in Africa is usually cast in absolute binaries that pay attention to the patron while relegating the client to residual status. A large corpus of work has shown that it is in the interest of ordinary citizens to seek attachment to so-called 'Big Men' for economic possibilities, social security and upward mobility (Utas 2012). What is regularly overlooked, however, are the tactical ways in which such attachment is sought, and the fact that it is also in the interests of Big Men to maintain political loyalists who will win them elections. The implication is that both the Big Man and his loyal supporters find themselves in a precarious position where they both need each other to survive and fulfil their aspirations. Faced with this manifest 'incompleteness' (Nyamnjoh 2015), conviviality is negotiated on the edge of conflict, imposed by necessity. This resonates with Francis Nyamnjoh's (ibid. 9) point that 'achievement is devoid of meaning if not pursued within, as part of, and on behalf of a group of people who recognize and endorse that achievement'. Thus, Big Men consolidate their interests best when these are pursued in acknowledgement of and respect for incomplete others.

Elections anywhere are times of radical uncertainties that lay bare the precarious positionality and incompleteness of a multiplicity of local actors who struggle to remain relevant and influential. Loyalties shift and mutate and insecurity increases. How does this particular uncertainty affect the behaviour of the actors involved? How do they cope with this specific insecurity around elections? What are the consequences in terms of violence? Drawing on primary data obtained from ethnographic fieldwork in Lagos, this chapter interrogates the micro-politics of election-related violence in Lagos, Nigeria, with a focus on the post-1999 electoral context and the urban transport sector. The chapter provides micro-level insights into why we see instances of election-related violence in transit spaces (i.e. motor parks), where practices of governance are exercised and contested daily. Along the way, the chapter foregrounds the interdependence between Big Men and their loyal foot soldiers, and provides some explanation for the rationale behind the latter's engagement in violent extortion with impunity. By focusing analytic attention on the ways in which the deeply local exigencies of insecurity and patrimonialism intersect with the manifestations of election-related violence in urban transport in Lagos, this chapter contributes to this volume's overriding focus on explaining the intricate causal mechanisms at work that link macro-level factors at the national level with the occurrence of election-related violence at the everyday level. In other words, the chapter demonstrates how insecurity surrounding elections leads to 'prebendal logics' (Pratten 2013) that underscore the precarious agency of both patrons and clients.

In terms of structure, the chapter begins with an analysis of the politics of transportation in Lagos, especially its structures and dynamics. This then forms a background for understanding electoral politics and related violence.

The politics of transportation

Various concepts have been used to capture the inherent contradictions and contingencies of everyday life, including Taussig's (1992) 'nervous system' or 'siege', Giddens' (1991) 'ontological uncertainty', Lubkemann's (2008) 'social condition of war', and Mbembe's (2003) 'state of war'. What these frameworks all have in common is the sense of uncertainty, mistrust and insecurity that speckles everyday life and ordinary forms of sociality. According to Mbembe and Roitman (2005: 324), insecurity in urban Africa may be framed in terms of 'the crisis' (*la crise*), or, in other words, the incoherence, uncertainty, instability and discontinuity caused by the mix of economic depression, instabilities, fluctuations and ruptures. For many transport operators whom I spoke to during fieldwork in Lagos, the struggle for survival and socio-physical security remains the overriding worry. As one *danfo* (minibus taxi) driver said to me, 'Man must *chop* [eat] because stomach does not take holiday.'[1] Given the relatively few full-time jobs that are available in the growing megacity, it is hardly surprising that public transport tends to attract plenty of labour in the form of unwaged youth, predominantly male. In fact, some *danfo* drivers and conductors in Lagos seem to constitute a reserve army of workers who are capable of relapsing into full-time touting should the need arise (Okpara 1988: 331). To my casual question 'How is life?', many transport operators in Lagos often responded: '*Aiye e le*' (this life is hard). The hard life of many operators is further complicated by the ubiquitous presence of *agberos* (motor park touts) on the road, acting as foot soldiers and tax collectors for the National Union of Road Transport Workers (NURTW), the most politicised and violent trade union in Nigeria (Albert 2007).

The term *agbero* itself is a euphemism for an army of antisocial and hard-boiled street youth who earn a living through their parasitic dependence on the control of passenger transport in Lagos. Largely a male youth affair, *agberos* use power and appropriate authority by redefining and inserting themselves into the interstices of state–society relations in the definition and maintenance of everyday order. They do this by usurping the public spaces of motor parks, bus stops and roads across Lagos, which they use as an operational base to collect illegal taxes and extort money from hapless *danfo* operators. Yet the appropriation of these transit spaces for private gain constitutes a usurpation of the constitutional function of local governments as specified in the Nigerian Constitution of 1999. My interview with Akeem Olawale, a *danfo* conductor in Oshodi local government area, revealed two types of *agberos* in Lagos:

> The *agberos* at the top they are somehow closer to the government. And the ones below they are the *eruku* – they are the ones dying for the ones up. The ones up they can travel abroad, have investment, but the one dying for them they don't have much.[2]

During fieldwork, I observed that every bus stop between Oshodi and Alimosho local government areas, where I conducted my fieldwork, has its own unit of *agberos*, who are armed with wooden clubs, sticks, whips and/ or iron rods so that they can brutally attack drivers and conductors who do not stop to pay financial tributes; at the time, these ranged from 50 naira (US$0.25) to 500 naira (US$2.50). These *agberos* usually conspire with traffic police officers to extort money from *danfo* operators. When a *danfo* driver hesitates in responding to their raucous demands of '*Owo da? Owo da?*' (Where is the money? Where is the money?), windscreens are smashed, side mirrors broken or forcibly pulled out, wipers and fuel tanks removed, seats broken off. A delay or refusal to pay the toll can also lead to a severe beating of the *danfo* drivers and conductors by a group of *agberos* who lurk around motor parks and bus stops to keep a close eye on tax collection. From my interviews with *danfo* operators, I learned that the intensity of violence increases during election seasons, when *agberos* are usually under immense pressure from the union to raise enough money to fund the expensive electoral campaigns of the ruling political party.

Among many Lagosians I spoke to, *agberos* are held in great contempt and represent objects of avoidance. This is largely because they reap where they have not sown, growing rich on the backs of the weak. As one *danfo* conductor in Oshodi said to me: 'Our case is like that of monkey dey work, baboon dey chop.'[3] A recurrent view among my interviewees was that senior officials in the union and local governments in Lagos share in the 'transport cake' collected daily by *agberos*. For many, this explains why *agberos* conduct their affairs with impunity, with *danfo* drivers referring to them as *omo ijoba* (a child of the government) or *apata* (rock). Other operators believe that local government politicians use these unlawful taxes collected by *agberos* to cover the huge expenses of their electoral campaigns. According to the popular view, *agberos* have their Big Men who position them at various bus stops and junctions across the state and expect returns later in the day. They are given high targets to meet and any failure to deliver the set amount spells trouble that could lead to the loss of their jobs. This view emerged in my interviews with *agberos* in Oshodi and Alimosho local government areas, at a time when Nigeria was preparing for its general elections in 2015 and when stakes and tensions ran very high. One *agbero* in a motor park in Oshodi told me that Oshodi has sixteen units that remit roughly 700,000 naira daily to the *oga agbero* (the head *agbero*) in charge of that area.[4] In Iyana Ipaja, another area, there are seven units that deliver around 200,000 naira daily to the *oga agbero*. In Alimosho area, the largest local government area in Lagos, *agberos* remit a daily sum of around 1 million naira to the *oga agbero*. Champion, a *danfo* driver in Oshodi, hinted at the strong connection between *agberos* and local politicians in Lagos when he said:

> If *ogas* [patrons] at the top were not supporting *agberos*, then they would be long gone from the motor parks because they are nothing but nuisance, making our jobs hell for us. They reap where they have not sown and scatter where they have not gathered. Let me tell you, in our business *agberos* are kings; they are untouchables. And many of these are just young men. They enjoy plenty support from top politicians up to the state governor and local government chairman. Now they even have uniform because *oga* Tinubu [the former governor of Lagos state] and *oga* Fashola [Tinubu's successor] installed them there to extort money for him and to harass people during elections. That is why they can do and undo. They are like gods here. Some of them now call themselves members of the NURTW. But these are all thieves and rogues. This is daylight robbery. But what can we do?[5]

Champion's statement calls for a rethink of the tendency to put urban or street youth on the Procrustean bed of the vulnerable and marginalised. The majority of *agberos* whom I encountered in Lagos were not marginalised, vulnerable or excluded in the strict sense of the words. If anything, these *agberos* were the dreaded and influential youth who have perfected the art of getting by or making do. Addressing the economic lack that underpins the political instrumentality of the *agberos*, an established editorial in Lagos writes:

> Our youths, for a good part of the life of a government, are starved of genuine opportunities; no employment, no education or training. And then come campaign time; the politicians sprinkle slush money and they unleash the beasts; rent a thug. These people are given money and small weapons to intimidate the opposition and ordinary citizens. They create fear and fan terror so that people are prevented from performing their constitutional obligations. (*Vanguard* 2015b)

There is a sense in which *agberos* mirror the behaviour of political leaders in Nigeria who often resort to devious ways to translate declining law and social order into patronage resources that oil the loyalty of their client networks. In early 2015, for example, former president Goodluck Jonathan criticised Nigerian politicians parading themselves as elder statesmen, whereas, by their actions and utterances, they are nothing but 'ordinary motor-park touts' who are 'planning to set the country ablaze because [they] did not get that particular thing [they] want' (*The Nation* 2015). With this statement, Jonathan implies two things: first, some Nigerian politicians are no different from *agberos* who use the instrument of violence to realise their selfish goals. And second, those politicians are likely to achieve their selfish interests when the country is in disarray. This point feeds the argument that social disorder works as a political instrument for Africa's elites (Chabal and Daloz 1999).

The continual re-enactment by the Nigerian ruling elites of practices in which the privileges of power are used for accumulation and to protect vested interests has permeated the social fabric down to the level of the police officer who demands bribes from taxi operators. As Marshall (1991: 26) notes, 'people must wield the little power and influence they have as a matter of survival'. This power dynamics is thrown into stark relief by the politics of patronage, and the violence that follows from it.

Transportation and the dynamics of patronage

The entangled layers of relations between *agberos* and the NURTW illuminate a model of urban youth clientelism. By this I mean 'the social production of dependency on patronage when local and national structures fail to provide for the social and economic needs of youth' (Murphy 2003: 62). Many *agberos* to whom I spoke in Oshodi and Alimosho areas told me that they became dependent on the generous patronage of NURTW elites as a way of rising above their own physical vulnerability and economic despair to 'become somebody in life', as one *agbero* in Oshodi told me.[6] By this, they mean gaining a source of income and respectability in the society in which they live. This view supports Patrick Murphy's (ibid.) youth clientelism model, which sees patronage as providing youth with a response to the political marginalisation and economic destitution enforced by the corrupt regimes of the nation state. In Lagos, the menace of *agberos* has been explained as symptomatic of a larger national unemployment crisis, where youth with few opportunities view politicians as a 'meal ticket'. As Adewale Maja-Pearce argues: 'there [are] too many young men hanging around, waiting for some action. All you have to do is go and meet them and pay them and they will do what you want … you can't blame the youths … they want to eat' (AFP 2015). Yet, Maja-Pearce omits the fact that urban youth (at least the *agberos* I encountered in Lagos) are not merely passive pawns in a political game of chess, but tactical agents capable of manipulating just as they are able to be manipulated. In other words, *agberos* can see opportunities and seize them (de Certeau 1984: xix). For example, during fieldwork I interviewed a group of *agberos* who bragged about how they would organise themselves and meet with local politicians on their own turf to broker a deal, which involved eliminating or threatening a political rival running for a position in the NURTW. As one *agbero* in Oshodi told me:

> When election is approaching, sometimes if we suspect that the politician
> is worried about someone taking over, we go to meet him and ask him if he
> wants us to 'sort that person out' [this can mean killing the person, beating
> him up, or threatening him]. Then we negotiate pay and job done! If he is
> reluctant or slow, we go to his rival and present him with the same offer. If
> he accepts or if his 'settlement' [payment] is better, the first one is in trouble.[7]

In this respect, the relationship of interdependence between *agberos* and the NURTW is best understood according to Anthony Giddens' (1979: 76, 93) association of autonomy and dependence in his 'dialectic of control', or Bayart's (1989: xiii) view that 'subjection can constitute a form of action'. A further interrogation of the micro-politics of relations between the *agberos* and the NURTW is thus expedient.

The NURTW was founded in 1978 with the goal of promoting the economic welfare of its members, who were professional taxi drivers in intra-city and inter-city transport. Since its establishment, the NURTW has grown rapidly to more than 1.5 million members throughout Nigeria. The NURTW controls 1,240 motor parks and 225 town service parking spaces, covering over 95 per cent of all motor parks in the 774 local government areas of Nigeria. This is in addition to private, federal and state government transport companies and other designated loading points (Agbiboa 2016). The union generates its funds through the dues it collects each day from transport operators through the *agberos*. The law establishing the NURTW assigned it the role of collecting check-off dues, such as deductions at source from the pay of each employee, with the employer's accounting office serving as collecting agent. However, these dues have now been multiplied by the NURTW in such a way that 'they are now used to oppress us', as one *danfo* driver told me.[8] The lucrative economy of motor park rackets is responsible for the explosion of motor parks across Lagos. While it is difficult to estimate the number of *danfos* plying Lagos roads, one *danfo* driver in Oshodi claims that: 'The NURTW chairman for Lagos pockets up to 5 million naira [about US$31,250] daily from the different units under him.'[9] However, the chairman does not pocket all the funds but distributes them among other union executives, police inspectors (for protection), local council chairmen and party officials. I learned that this system of distribution is in tune with the NURTW's guiding slogan 'Eat Alone, Die Alone'. In distributing the funds – or 'declaring surplus', as they say in

Lagos – the union chairman secures his Big Man status within the NURTW structure and the state political network.

Among Lagosians, there is a popular perception that the NURTW is home to an army of battle-ready *agberos* who not only collect illegal tolls from transport operators but also serve as political thugs for political parties across the country, especially during election times. Most of these *agberos* have been recruited from among a large, ready pool of jobless so-called 'area boys' (Momoh 1999) who roam the streets of Lagos. But to become an *agbero*, it is not enough to be jobless; you must also be feared. As one *danfo* driver told me: 'If you're in your street and you can create a scene, cut somebody's head, do whatever, they [the NURTW] will find a garage for you as an *agbero*. You're born to kill.'[10]

During fieldwork, I gathered that *agberos* are responsible for collecting and making returns to their respective unit chairman in their local government. This unit chairman reports to the zonal chairman, who reports to the local chairman, who in turn reports to the state chairman, who is the direct link to the national chairman. Along this chain, financial returns must be remitted on a daily basis. In Alimosho, I learned from a resident that, after the union chieftains receive their daily returns from their *agberos*, the ritual is for them to throw a huge roadside party (*faji*) where no cost is spared and people in the neighbourhood *chop awoof* (eat for free). The wife of one of the NURTW unit chairmen owns the shop that supplies alcohol and meat. Unit chairmen who fail to throw *faji* regularly are perceived as corrupt and self-centred, reinforcing Smith's (2007) point that ordinary citizens in Nigeria see their leaders as having forsaken the obligations of sharing associated with clientelism in favour of personal enrichment and unabashed venality. *Agberos* in Lagos are backed by their powerful union superiors and engage in extortion rackets as a way of partaking of the 'transport cake' in circulation. These *agberos* are encouraged by the fact that most unit chairmen started out as *agberos* in one of the many motor parks in Lagos. In fact, there were many 'grass to grace' stories in circulation in motor parks during the course of my fieldwork. To my question of why most *agberos* are so feared, Boniface, a *danfo* driver in Ikotun, replied:

> It is not about them, it is the chairman that protects them, so they must
> show loyalty to him at all cost. Even if you arrest the *agbero*, before you
> treat the wound they inflicted on you, they are back to their duty post,
> the NURTW unit chairman ensures they are freed. That is how the system
> works. They're all like mafias.[11]

In return for their services, *agberos* are offered cash rewards, which they often lavish on hard drugs (*igbo*), alcohol (*paraga*) and casual sex with prostitutes (*ashewo*). Fourchard (2010: 51) argues that the 'NURTW chairmen [in Lagos] act as providers of thugs recruited among the union to assist the state governor during his electoral campaigns' in exchange for 'large autonomy for levying taxes in the motor parks of the state'. Lagos is not unique in this regard. In Gombe State, for example, a group of touts known as Kalare boys have proven 'easy prey for politicians who offer them small amounts of money, drugs, alcohol and weapons in exchange for engaging in acts of intimidation and assaults or simply to accompany their campaigns in a demonstration of muscle' (Aniekwe and Agbiboa 2014: 12). The activities of the Kalare boys have included assault, rape, harassment, and extortion of ordinary civilians. Many of the Kalare boys worked for the People's Democratic Party (PDP) as political loyalists during the 2003 and 2007 elections. As Ma'azu, the PDP youth leader in Gombe State put it, 'thank God we have more boys than the opposition' (Human Rights Watch 2007: 94). Gombe aside, in the 2003 elections in the Niger Delta, Gaskia noted that:

> Politicians from the major political parties mobilized and surreptitiously
> armed groups of unemployed and disenchanted youths, and deployed
> them to cause mayhem and manipulate the electoral process. In this
> contestation and competitive arming of young groups, the party, which
> controlled the state government, got the upper hand. These political elite
> rivalries, coupled with a struggle for turf, contributed immensely to the
> rise of armed militancy and inter-militant armed violence, which preceded
> the 2003 elections and became consolidated in the period between the
> 2003 and 2007 general elections in the Niger Delta. (Cited in Ayoade and
> Akinsanya 2011: 295)

The above supports Pratten's (2013) argument that the need for 'hard men' who can deliver votes during elections fosters the patron–client relationship between political godfathers, office holders and candidates in Nigeria.

Politicised spaces

No study of the patronage dynamics of the NURTW in Lagos would be complete without a look at the violent battles for control of motor parks in the city, as well as the factionalism that undermines the NURTW from within. Motor parks are politically contested spaces. Since the 1950s, local government councils have been statutorily charged with responsibility for maintaining and collecting rates at motor parks. During the Nigerian Second Republic (1979–83), which ushered in the first elected civilian government under the 1979 constitution, however, motor parks, especially in Lagos, became a primary space of political antagonism when transport unions usurped their management and control. As Fourchard (2010: 50) recounts:

> The politicization of the management of motor parks started in Lagos as
> the capital was the site of two concurrent powers: the Federal government,

President Shehu Shagari and his party, the National Party of Nigeria (NPN) on the one hand, and the governor of Lagos State, Lateef Jakande and the UPN [Unity Party of Nigeria] on the other hand. NPN decided to enlist the support of members of a new union, the Nigerian Union [of] Road Transport Workers (NURTW), created a year before in 1978 under the leadership of Adebayo Ogundare, known as Bayo Success, who was given the assignment of winning all the motor parks in Lagos over to the UPN ... He did so by mobilizing his large clientele of drivers during the 1979 electoral campaign and by resorting to violence and killing his potential opponents in most of motor parks in Lagos.

Many transport operators believe that the impunity enjoyed by *agberos* in spaces such as motor parks is related to the close rapport between the NURTW, Lagos state elites and the ruling All Progressives Congress (APC) party. As one *okada* (commercial motorcycle taxi) rider in Alimosho told me: 'The leaders of NURTW wine and dine with the Governor of Lagos. *Egbe ko no ni wan* [they all belong to same party].'[12] Some operators were even more emphatic in their view that successive state governors have backed the NURTW leadership, which has supported their candidature, giving them the free hand 'to do and undo' within motor parks.[13] Given the lucrative nature of motor parks, they have become unsafe, factional and politicised spaces, and their control has become a do-or-die matter. As Albert (2007: 134) argues:

> The huge revenue collected by NURTW leaders, and the high social mobility this facilitates, explains why every member of the union aspires to become a chairman – whether at branch, city, state, zonal or national level. This partly explains why the members regularly engage one another in bloody skirmishes. It explains why NURTW members and members of other transport unions kill each other in defense of their position in most Nigerian cities.

A discussion of the NURTW chairmanship elections and related violence briefly illustrates the internal factionalisation of the union, and the means by which power struggles are contended. In 2008, Alhaji Saka Saula, chair of the NURTW (Lagos Chapter), was shot dead by masked gunmen outside his house in Iyana Ipaja. Alhaji Saula had taken over from Alhaji Baruwa, who held two positions: the Ogun State Chairman and the South West Zonal Chairman. There were palpable divisions and dissensions on all fronts. The redeployment of Alhaji Baruwa from Lagos to Ekiti State seemed not to have gone down well with him and his loyalists. Notably, three of the people who opposed Alhaji Baruwa's candidature for national president of the NURTW at the 2007 quadrennial conference in Jos died mysteriously. All suspects accused in relation to Alhaji Saula's death were eventually released on the grounds of insufficient evidence. In 2012, members of the NURTW (Lagos Chapter) clashed over the chairmanship of the union. The clash culminated in the killing of popular businessman Alhaji Ola Shehu Ekeniojuoti by gunmen suspected to be loyal to one of the chairmanship candidates. The deceased's brother, Abu Ekeniojuoti (aka Abu Stainless), was the former chairman of the NURTW on Lagos Island and a public supporter of the NURTW treasurer in Oshodi, Alhaji Musiliu Akinsanya, best known as MC Oluomo. Violence broke out after the NURTW national president, Alhaji Nasiru Yasiu, had a meeting behind closed doors with the five contestants at the union's office, with the outcome that an election would be held since the contestants could not present a consensus candidate. The followers of the former chairman, Alhaji Rafiu Olohunwa, were incensed by the outcome, as their expectation going into the meeting was that the union president would endorse their candidate for the position (*Vanguard* 2012).

On 30 September 2015, gunmen suspected to be members of a rival NURTW faction killed Olayinka Mamowora (aka Mamok), a close ally of MC Oluomo. Mamok was MC Oluomo's point man and allegedly led the unnamed gang that killed Baba Esi, a popular *agbero* in Oshodi, in April 2015 (*Vanguard* 2015a). In March 2015, Babajide Dosunmu (aka Mandos), NURTW chairman for Yaba Unit and vice chairman for the Lagos Mainland NURTW branch, was shot dead outside his house by gunmen. I had returned from fieldwork when the news of Mandos' violent death reached me. To glean more information surrounding the killing, I called Egungun (Masquerade) over the phone, an *agbero* in Oshodi whom I had interviewed and who had described how he benefited from the patronage of Mandos while he was still an *eruku*. Egungun told me that Mandos was killed by a rival NURTW gang in a bid to seize control of motor parks in the Tarmac area in Oyingbo, which was controlled by Mandos. Although he declined to name the rival group, he insisted that Mandos' death would be avenged. When the constant presence of lethal rival groups combines with the loss of murdered patrons, existence conforms with what Zygmunt Bauman describes as the postmodern tactic for warding off death: 'daily life becomes a perpetual dress rehearsal of death. What is being rehearsed ... is ephemerality and evanescence of things that humans may acquire and bonds that humans may weave' (Bauman 1992: 186). Within this context, *agberos* and their political patrons in Lagos are left not with death, but with 'the end of living' (ibid. 321): that is, death lived over and over again. No wonder, then, that 'anxieties about betrayal, loyalty, and envy should be high and that trust becomes something to be carefully constructed and difficult to obtain' (Caldeira 2006: 135–6).

My interactions with *danfo* drivers and conductors in Oshodi showed that one of the primary causes of factionalism in the NURTW relates to leadership tussles because of the 'winner-takes-all' syndrome, which seems to contradict the NURTW's constitutional provisions. I found that election, as a democratic tool of regime change, was hardly used by the NURTW chapter. Frequently, it was the more militant group that seized control. In early 2015, while I was finalising my fieldwork, a renewed clash between factions of the union in Oshodi left several dead or critically injured. The fight was reported as a 'spillover' from a previous 'supremacy fight over control of parks in Oshodi by NURTW members' (*Vanguard* 2015b). Since the majority of motor parks in Lagos do not have defined boundaries (for instance, it is difficult to know where a motor park in Lagos ends and a market begins), the presence of touts and *paraga* sellers in and around motor parks often accentuates violence and other antisocial practices. Indeed, many motor parks are hiding places for drug dealers and hardened criminals. It is no surprise, then, that many detained criminals interviewed on Lagos TV claim to have begun their 'careers' in motor parks (Albert 2007).

Tactical agency from below

Faced with such everyday violence and radical uncertainty, how do operators carve out meaningful temporalities? During fieldwork, I observed that *danfo* operators constantly devised tactics to avoid the violent extortion that they faced routinely. One tactic was to carry uniformed officers of authority – i.e. soldiers or members of the air force or mobile police – in the front seat in order to shield them from rampaging *agberos*. While this may lessen the usual level of assault, it does not completely prevent extortion, which has taken on a kind of de facto legitimacy. Also, operators are wont to align themselves with a Big Man (*oga nla*) who provides them with material security and shields them from the extortion and violence of *agberos*, in exchange for political loyalty transferred into votes at the time of elections. While some Big Men may assist poor operators in times of trouble (*wahala*), others may not.

Big Men who have the resources to help and actually do provide help are affectionately celebrated in vehicle slogans such as 'Givers never lack', '*Ola oga mi l'eko*' ('The benevolence of my Big Man in Lagos'), '*Oga nla* fans' ('Big Man fans'), '*Oga oga*' ('Big Man, Big Man'), '*Oga mi*' ('My Big Man'), '*Oga tie da?*' ('Where is your Big Man?'), '*Ere oga mi*' ('The benefits of my Big Man') and '*Oluwa ma pa alanu mi*' ('God do not kill my helper'). Big Men who have the means to help but fail to do so are labelled *awon aiye* (wicked world). The meaning of *awon aiye* is conveyed in an interview with a *danfo* driver in Oshodi:

The world [*awon aiye*] is an enemy of progress, the world is jealous of success. They want you to remain on one spot and not move upwards. They don't want you to be as successful as they are. Instead, they want to keep you at a point where they always give to you and you can't really become independent enough to take care of yourself and your family but continue to depend on them. This world is wicked and don't wish for good of others![14]

When Big Men disappoint, it is time for operators to console themselves, and to ponder on human frailty. This mood is best rendered in slogans such as 'Such is life', 'No condition is permanent', 'If men were God', 'Delay is not denial', 'No more person' and 'Who knows tomorrow'. However, the Yoruba believe that *ti ona kan ko ba di, ona mi ko le la* (if one door is not closed, another one will not be opened). To reduce the chances of disappointment in the hands of *awon aiye*, many operators tend to keep many Big Men simultaneously. The logic is simple: the more Big Men you have, the lesser your chances of disappointment (Utas 2012). However, the ultimate lesson of disappointment for *danfo* operators is that *igbekale omo araye, asan ni* (reliance on people in this world amounts to disappointment), because *olowo kin se olorun* (the Big Man is not God). The turn to God or the supernatural reinforces Gavin Williams' (1980: 114) point that in a context of everyday precarity, where fortunes are seen to be made and lost and one's own fortune frequently appears to be beyond one's control, 'God, fate and luck are common (and not unwarranted) categories for the explanation of success or lack of it'.

Having discussed the politics of transportation in Lagos, with particular focus on the notions of interdependency and precarity between patrons and clients, the next section engages with how this context influences the politics of electoral processes.

Elections and 'stomach infrastructure'

In 2012, the Lagos state government enacted a new road traffic law that restricted the activities of *okada* riders on 475 major routes across the city. Avowedly, the law was created to safeguard the lives and properties of Lagosians and to 'restore sanity' back to extremely congested Lagos roads. The state government went a step further and produced a documentary film titled *Aye Olokada* (*Life of an Okadaman*), aimed at educating Lagosians about the menace of *okadas*. To all intents and purposes, *Aye Olokada* was part of state propaganda to demonise *okada* riding and to discourage millions of Lagosians from using *okadas* as a means of transport. However, despite their legal restriction, *okada* riders have remained adamant by carrying out their activities on the prohibited routes. They argue that the government has not provided them with any alternative employment and that their restricted movement would 'further pauperise us and send members of our families to untimely graves'.[15] Such resistance has intensified a heavy clampdown by officers of authority (such as the police force and members of Kick Against Indiscipline (KAI)), including the confiscation of *okadas* and indiscriminate arrest of riders found on prohibited routes. Irked by the escalating situation, the All Nigerians Autobike Commercial Owners and Workers Association (ANACOWA) dragged the state government to court over the perceived violation of their right to move freely and not to be expressly discriminated against.[16]

Many *okada* riders whom I spoke to during fieldwork felt betrayed by the government led by Governor Babatunde Fashola (2007–15) and his ruling APC party. During the mass protest against the law, for example, one *okada* rider held a banner with the bold inscription: 'Fashola distributed helmets in 2011. NOW destroying OUR bikes.' Another *okada* rider held a banner that read: 'Used and Dumped.'[17] The import of both banners emerged in an interview with Fredrick Fasheun, chairman of the UPN:

> Lagos citizens must remember that this [APC] party used and dumped okada riders after harnessing their support and services in the elections of 1999, 2003, 2007 and 2011. During campaigns for those polls, APC politicians even donated to okada riders, branded helmets, motorcycles and reflective jackets. But no sooner did the Action Congress of Nigeria [now a part of the APC] come into power than they turned around to bite the finger that fed them, by banning okada all over Lagos. (Comment on *Premium Times* 2014)

Many *okada* riders whom I interviewed in Lagos claimed that they received their *okadas* from Governor Fashola's aides in the run-up to the 2011 elections, in exchange for their votes and loyalty to the APC.[18] Such a political stratagem, of course, is not a new development in Nigerian pre-electoral politics. We would recall that Orji Uzo Kalo, former governor of Abia (1999–2007), won great support in his state by pledging and then creating a programme to provide *okada* riders in his state with new motorbike taxis on credit (Smith 2007: 198). In the run-up to the 2015 elections in Nigeria, the enforcement of the law was appreciably relaxed across Lagos in what was a deliberate strategy aimed at securing the votes of *okada* riders (*Vanguard* 2014). In offering *okada* riders an instant reprieve, Lagos political elites have perfected the art of tactically 'manipulat[ing] the mechanisms of discipline and conform[ing] to them only in order to evade them' (de Certeau 1984: xiv). De Certeau's *The Practice of Everyday Life* is usually used to illustrate how actors in structurally weak positions deploy tactics in the absence of the possibility for more enduring strategising. Here, however, I ascribe these tactics to political elites, not to the *okada* riders.

Another point relates to the tactical ways in which political leaders from neighbouring states cashed in on the opportunity offered by the sour relations between transport (*okada*) unions and the government to shore up their patronage in the build-up to the 2015 elections, a period in which I conducted my fieldwork. Notably, in neighbouring Ekiti State, Governor Ayodele Fayose pledged not to ban *okada* activities as they had done in Lagos. Instead, Fayose required *okada* unions to partner with the government of Ekiti in registering all their members in view of the incessant robbery operations in the state through the efficient means of *okadas*. Addressing *okada* riders and owners in Ado Ekiti, Governor Fayose, the number one patron of Ekiti, said:

> If they cancel *okada* in every other state, that won't happen in Ekiti. But what I want is disciplined and responsible motorcyclists' association that can partner with government for meaningful development. Government alone cannot maintain security; I have to partner with an organisation like you. But I won't tolerate unruly behaviour. (*The Sun* 2014)

Certainly, since the Second Republic, political actors in Nigeria have intensified the patterns of prebendalism, which rests on the justifying principle that state power should be treated as 'congeries of offices which can be competed for, appropriated and then administered for the benefit of individual occupants and their supporters' (Joseph 1987: 8). The huge monetary premiums that can be gained by playing politics in Nigeria often give elections the stamp of a do-or-die affair. This is complicated by the fact that, in Nigeria, the winners in the competition for power win everything, and the losers lose everything. As a result, nearly everyone seeks power by every means, legal or otherwise, and those who already control state power try to keep it by every means. What emerges from this is a 'politics that does not know legitimacy, only expediency. This politics is not conducive to political stability, the rule of law or to democracy because it is constituted as warfare' (Ake 1976: 7, cited in Akinsanya and Ayoade 2013: 176). Today, Nigerian politicians attain a constituency by promising a piece of the national cake to their loyal supporters, in the process boosting their chances of regime survival. In the run-up to 2015 elections in Nigeria, seen by many as particularly competitive (both substantially and symbolically), I was struck by the number of political parties that placed huge emphasis on distributing 'stomach' items such as rice, milk, kerosene, chicken and staple foods to their supporters. The governor of Ekiti State, Ayo Fayose, notably distributed 80,000 chickens, 100,000 bags of rice and cash gifts to the people of Ekiti under the so-called 'stomach infrastructure' programme of his administration. Other states, such as Osun, Cross River and Lagos, followed suit (*Vanguard* 2014). In Oyo State, it is well documented that the political influence of the chief patron Lamidi Adedibu, aka the 'Godfather of Ibadan',[19] flowed primarily from his ability to mobilise money and violence in support of the politicians he sponsored (Agbiboa 2016; Albert 2007). Adedibu distributed cash and food to numerous supplicants on a daily basis from his Ibadan home, a brand of patronage known as *amala* politics, after a traditional dish common in Nigeria's south-western region.

In the face of severe hardship, it is not difficult to see why many lowly Nigerians seek instant gratification in exchange for their votes. In this respect, the practice of stomach infrastructure reclaims the 'wealth-in-people' that characterises the politics of 'bigmanity' in many African societies (Utas 2012). The idea of bigmanity has become linked in the literature to 'being for' someone (Bledsoe 1990; Utas 2012). As one vehicle slogan in Lagos puts it: 'A Stingy Rich Man is Still a Poor Man.' This slogan echoes Adrian Peace's (1979: 30) contention that if a Big Man is to enjoy prestige, he must combine the pursuit of his own gains with 'recognition of the interests and sentiments of others'. In other words, 'self-interest and the interests of others must wherever possible be made complementary' (ibid.). Furthermore, Peace (ibid. 30) argues that among the poor (*mekunu*) in Lagos, 'to acquire wealth, to dispose of it, and to exercise power in these ideal ways is considered right and proper because it is tradition and custom to do so'. This point resonates with Gavin Williams' (1980: 112) point that the values and goals in terms of which the success of the rich is defined are to a large extent shared by the poor. In short, the poor legitimise the rewards of the rich. In this respect, corruption is approached in this chapter as a perceived breakdown of a 'traditional' moral economy in which the haves were obliged to support the have-nots. Thus, many ordinary Lagosians (i.e. the *okada* riders) see their leaders as having forsaken the obligations of sharing associated with clientelism in favour of personal enrichment and unabashed venality (Smith 2007: 86). The outcome is the radical uncertainty and bankruptcy of everyday life.

Conclusion

This chapter has engaged with the dynamics of patronage politics in Lagos' transportation sector and how they intersect with electoral processes and election-related violence. Such violence has become a fundamental aspect of political competition in Lagos (and much of Nigeria), often occurring between gangs whose services are employed and rewarded by rival politicians. Street gangs are typically recruited from among the NURTW's *agberos* to attack their sponsors' opponents, coerce members of the public, rig elections, and protect their patrons from similar attacks. In this uncertain context, the interdependence between patrons and clients – and the precariousness of the Big Man position – is laid bare. During fieldwork, I spoke to a group of *agberos* in motor parks in Oshodi who admitted that they had been hired by members of the ruling party to disrupt the 2015 elections by intimidating opposition voters.[20] The masterminds of such violence – the union heads, politicians and party officials – often enjoy impunity due to the tacit acceptance of their conduct by police and state officials. Although the NURTW was founded to represent the collective interests of transport workers, the union has been converted into 'reservoirs of thugs for local politicians' (Human Rights Watch 2007). During fieldwork, public perception was that the government lacked the gravitas to call the union (and its *agberos*) to order because of the latter's strategic power structure in the electoral process in Lagos politics.

While the *pas de deux* between union and state undermines formal state capacity, it emboldens the union to gain a stronger foothold and legitimacy over the control of lucrative motor parks across Lagos, which, constitutionally, should be the domain of local government. This, in turn, leads to more predatory patterns of interaction between transport unions and the local community, destroying the moral certainties of ordinary citizens who are no longer sure who stands for what. Indeed, there is a sense in which both violence and order result from the shifting relations between the union and the state. For example, efforts by local governments in Lagos to reclaim their authority over the control of motor parks have often led to violent resistance from *agberos*. In a recent case, Oshodi witnessed a violent outburst when the local council's secretary ordered the immediate cessation of 'illegal' tax collection in motor parks in the area. Predictably, the decision did not go down well with *agberos* and their unit chairman. In a matter of days, *agberos* brutally attacked motor parks en masse, burning any *danfo* in sight. Worried about the growing threat to lives and properties, the secretary was forced to revoke his order within the same week of its announcement.[21] Normality in this context resembles what Paul Brass (1997) describes as a pre-Leviathan Hobbesian state of war in which there is a set of formal rules obeyed by a few people, a set of informal rules followed by most people, and a lack of legitimacy attached to both.

Notes

1 Author interview with *danfo* driver, Ikotun Egbe, November 2014.

2 Author interview, 22 October 2014.

3 Author interview with *danfo* conductor, Oshodi, October 2014.

4 Author interview with *agbero*, Oshodi, October 2014.

5 Author interview with *danfo* driver, Oshodi, December 2014.

6 Author interview, 13 November 2014.

7 Author interview with *agberos*, Oshodi, December 2014.

8 Author interview with *danfo* driver, Alimosho, November 2014.

9 Author interview with *danfo* driver, Oshodi, January 2015.

10 Author interview, Oshodi, December 2014.

11 Author fieldwork, Oshodi, October 2014.

12 Author interview, December 2015.

13 Author interview with *danfo* drivers, Oshodi, December 2014.

14 Author interview, December 2014.

15 Mr Aliyu Wamba, Chairman of the All Nigerians Autobike Commercial Owners and Workers Association (ANACOWA). Court affidavit deposed in Ikeja, 2012.

16 For a detailed study of this case, see Agbiboa (2016).

17 Author fieldwork observation, Alimosho, August 2014.

18 Interview with *okada* riders, Oshodi and Alimosho, December 2015.

19 'Godfatherism' refers to the process by which an individual establishes links with a senior within a given institutional hierarchy in the expectation of favoured treatment (Joseph 1987: 207).

20 Author interview with *agberos*, Oshodi, December 2014.

References

AFP (2015) 'Gangs Threaten Election Peace in Nigeria's Key City', Agence France Presse (AFP), 19 March.

Agbiboa, D. E. (2016) 'Frontiers of Urban Survival: Everyday Corruption and Precarious Existence in Lagos'. DPhil thesis, University of Oxford.

Akinsanya, A. A. and J. A. Ayoade (eds) (2013) *An Introduction to Political Science in Nigeria*. New York NY: University Press of America.

Albert, I. O. (2007) 'NURTW and the Politics of Motor Parks in Lagos and Ibadan' in L. Fourchard (ed.), *Gouverner les villes d'Afrique. Etat, gouvernement local et acteurs privés*. Paris: Karthala.

Aniekwe, C. C. and D. E. Agbiboa (2014) 'Civic Engagement and its Role in Mitigating Electoral Violence in Nigeria: Implications for the 2015 General Elections'. Working Paper, 21 December. Social Science Research Network. Available at https://papers.ssrn.com/sol3/papers.cfm?abstract_id=2541330.

Ayoade, J. A. and A. A. Akinsanya (eds) (2011) *Nigeria's Critical Election: 2011*. New York NY: Lexington Books.

Bauman, Z. (1992) *Morality, Immorality and Other Life Strategies*. Cambridge: Polity Press.

Bayart, J.-F. (1989) *The State in Africa: The Politics of the Belly*. London: Longman.

Bledsoe, C. (1990) '"No Success Without Struggle": Social Mobility and Hardship Foster Children in Sierra Leone', *Man* 25 (1): 70–88.

Brass, P. (1997) *Theft of an Idol: Text and Context in the Representation of Collective Violence*. Princeton NJ: Princeton University Press.

Caldeira, T. P. R. (2006) '"I Come to Sabotage your Reasoning!": Violence and Resignifications of Justice in Brazil' in J. Comaroff and J. L. Comaroff (eds), *Law and Disorder in the Postcolony*. Chicago IL: University of Chicago Press.

Chabal, P. and J.-P. Daloz (1999) *Africa Works: Disorder as Political Instrument*. Oxford and Bloomington IN: James Currey and Indiana University Press.

de Certeau, M. (1984) *The Practice of Everyday Life*. Berkeley CA: University of California Press.

Fourchard, L. (2010) 'Lagos, Koolhaas and Partisan Politics in Nigeria', *International Journal of Urban and Regional Research* 35 (1): 40–56.

Giddens, A. (1979) *Central Problems in Social Theory: Action, Structure, and Contradiction in Social Analysis*. Los Angeles CA: University of California Press.

Giddens, A. (1991) *Modernity and Self-Identity: Self and Society in the Late Modern Age*. Oxford: Polity Press.

Human Rights Watch (2007) 'Criminal Politics: Violence, "Godfathers" and Corruption in Nigeria'. New York NY: Human Rights Watch. Available at www.hrw.org/reports/2007/nigeria1007/4.htm (accessed 20 January 2017).

Joseph, R. A. (1987) *Democracy and Prebendal Politics in Nigeria: The Rise and Fall of the Second Republic*. Cambridge: Cambridge University Press.

Lubkemann, S. C. (2008) 'An Anthropology of the Social Condition in War', *Journal of Refugee Studies* 21 (3): 407–8.

Marshall, R. (1991) 'Power in the Name of Jesus', *Review of African Political Economy* 52: 21–37.

Mbembe, A. (2003) 'Necropolitics', *Public Culture* 15 (1): 11–40.

Mbembe, A. and J. Roitman (2005) *Figures of the Subject in Times of Crisis*. Chicago IL: Chicago University Press.

Momoh, A. (1999) 'The Youth Crisis in Nigeria: Understanding the Phenomena of the Area Boys and Girls'. Paper presented to the

Conference on Children and Youth as Emerging Categories in Africa, Leuven, Belgium.

Murphy, W. (2003) 'Military Patrimonialism and Child Soldier Clientalism in the Liberian and Sierra Leonean Civil Wars', *African Studies Review* 46 (2): 61–87.

Nyamnjoh, F. (2015) 'Incompleteness: Frontier Africa and the Currency of Conviviality', *Journal of Asian and African Studies* 52 (3): 253–70.

Okpara, E. E. (1988) 'The Role of Touts in Passenger Transport in Nigeria', *Journal of Modern African Studies* 26 (2): 327–35.

Peace, A. (1979) *Choice, Class and Conflict: A Study of Southern Nigeria Factory Workers*. Hassocks: Harvester Press.

Pratten, D. (2013) 'The Precariousness of Prebendalism' in W. Adebanwi and E. Obadare (eds), *Democracy and Prebendalism in Nigeria: Critical Interpretations*. New York NY: Palgrave Macmillan.

Premium Times (2014) 'Akinwunmi Ambode Wins Lagos APC Governorship Primaries', *Premium Times*, 5 December. Available at www.premiumtimesng.com/news/172484-breaking-akinwunmi-ambode-wins-lagos-apc-governorship-primaries.html.

Smith, D. J. (2007) *A Culture of Corruption: Everyday Deception and Popular Discontent in Nigeria*. Princeton NJ: Princeton University Press.

Taussig, M. (1992) *The Nervous System*. New York NY and London: Routledge.

The Nation (2015) 'When Jonathan Gets Angry', *The Nation*, 13 January.

The Sun (2014) 'I Won't Ban Okada – Fayose', *The Sun*, 27 November. Available at http://jesconaija.blogspot.com/2014/11/i-wont-ban-okada-in-ekiti-fayose.html (accessed 15 January 2017).

Utas, M. (ed.) (2012) *African Conflicts and Informal Power: Big Men and Networks*. London and New York NY: Zed Books.

Vanguard (2012) 'Lagos Wades into Bloody NURTW Fracas', *Vanguard*, 1 February. Available at www.vanguardngr.com/2012/02/lagos-wades-into-bloody-nurtw-fracas/ (accessed 6 March 2015).

Vanguard (2014) 'Fayose and Stomach Infrastructure', *Vanguard*, 8 July. Available at www.vanguardngr.com/2014/07/fayose-stomach-infrastructure/ (accessed 12 August 2014).

Vanguard (2015a) 'Police Yet to Arrest Killers of MC Oluomo's Aide', *Vanguard*, 2 October. Available at www.vanguardngr.com/2015/10/police-yet-to-arrest-killers-of-mc-oluomos-aide/ (accessed 18 August 2015).

Vanguard (2015b) 'Nigeria: Time we Moved the Dogma', *Vanguard*, 22 March. Available at http://allafrica.com/stories/201503232026.html (accessed 18 November 2015).

Williams, G. (1980) 'Political Consciousness among the Ibadan Poor' in G. Williams (ed.), *State and Society in Nigeria*. Idanre: Afrografika Publishers.

11 | 'Once they all pick their guns you can have your way': campaigning and talking about violence in northern Ghana

Afra Schmitz

Introduction

During a campaign trail in the Upper West Region shortly before Ghana's 2012 elections, the general secretary of the ruling National Democratic Congress (NDC) mockingly revealed the opposition's campaign strategy for the north: according to Johnson Asiedu Nketia, the New Patriotic Party (NPP) planned to instigate violence between various ethnic groups so that 'once they all pick their guns you can have your way'.[1] By drawing on past interethnic violent encounters (e.g. between the Dagaba and the Wala), the opposition party allegedly believed that it would cause tensions, insecurity and confusion in order to destabilise the region as an NDC support base and manoeuvre its way into taking over their stronghold.

Usually, violent encounters are associated with the northern part of the country. Over time, chieftaincy disputes, ethnic clashes and disagreements over land gave rise to a stereotype depicting 'northerners' as a primitive and violent people. Only at a second glance does it become apparent that these local conflict dynamics are closely intertwined with local and national politics and thus become efficacious during election times. In Ghana, outbreaks of electoral violence are comparatively rare and can be categorised as small-scale or low-intensity violence (Bob-Milliar 2014). Consequently, in an African context, Ghana serves as a role model for successful democratisation, based on peaceful, free and fair elections (Whitfield 2009). Since the country's return to multiparty democracy in 1992, however, no election has been entirely free from political turmoil and outbreaks of micro-level violence. Taking a closer look, the escalation of these conflicts can often be traced back to political key actors who use their local position as Big Men to politicise social tensions in their favour. As their clients, the youth become yet another target of prejudice: entangled in patronage relations, deeply entrenched in Ghanaian politics, they are identified as the driving force of electoral violence (Bob-Milliar 2014; Lamptey and Salihu 2012). Allegedly, they are ever ready to cause mayhem on command for their personal benefit while neglecting their own agency. However, in the Upper West Region, one of Ghana's poorest areas with a high unemployment rate, physical violence during elections is remarkably rare (NPC n.d.).

Drawing on various campaign strategies deployed by national and local political actors, this chapter addresses the ways in which talking about violence is strategically used in election campaigning in Ghana's Upper West Region, an environment shaped by powerful stereotypes, structural challenges, and local conflict dynamics. Thus, it makes the multi-layered reality of violence (Söderberg Kovacs, Introduction in this volume) tangible and at the same time carves out expressions of local democratic culture. The campaign speech of a high-profile politician during the 2012 presidential elections addresses strategies of integration and exclusion linked to identity politics, whereas the political mobilisation tactics of a youth group during the run-up to the local-level district elections in 2014 address patronage networks, political protest and agency. By analysing stereotypes of violence that evolve around ethno-regional diversity and clientelism, the interlinkages of elections, violence and campaign communication, as well as their consequences, become the subject of this chapter. The case studies show that countries praised for their peaceful use of democratic structures such as elections are still influenced by underlying patterns of structural violence. An analysis of talking about violence as a strategy, therefore, makes the links between verbal and physical violence approachable, while the choice of discourse connects national party politics with the local level.

The chapter is based on long-term ethnographic fieldwork in the Upper West Region, which I have conducted biannually since Ghana's 2008 legislative and presidential elections.[2] Thus, it covers the 2008 and 2012 general elections as well as the 2014 run-up to the elections of the district's administrative body, the District Assembly. The events and examples referred to are situations I experienced as a participant observer, supplemented by semi-structured in-depth interviews with politicians, party activists, the media and the electorate. The most important sources, however, are informal, cordial conversations with members of these groups.

The chapter discusses talking about violence as a political strategy and addresses the nexus between electoral violence and campaign communication. Subsequently, it provides an overview of Ghanaian elections by challenging the country's image as a role model for successful democratisation. Two case studies highlight the role that verbal violence plays in electoral campaigning locally and analyse common stereotypes of violence, their implications and their effects on the electorate, thereby covering questions of ethno-regional diversity, patronage and agency. The conclusion emphasises the entanglements of verbal violence and electoral campaigning in both national and local politics and ends with policy implications for Ghana and the region.

Talking about violence in electoral campaigns

In Ghana, violence as a socially and culturally constructed phenomenon constitutes an intrinsic part of social relations. Therefore, it needs to be incorporated in the examination of campaign strategies, whether it occurs in verbal or physical form. Performed comparatively easily, the effects of electoral violence are highly visible and concrete, opening a 'very efficient way of transforming the social environment and staging an ideological message before a public audience' (Schmidt and Schröder 2001: 3–4). Violence is not simply an arbitrary outburst of emotions; instead, hatred, fear and anger are used as strategic elements to further individual aims (Elwert 1995; Riches in Gabbert 2004: 98). In the emotionally charged atmosphere of election times when the end justifies the means, violence is a political resource, accompanied by the evocation of fear and strong feelings of loyalty. Yet, in the Ghanaian social setting, where physical violence is deemed illegitimate, conflicts are ignited and at the same time defused by means of communication.

The following analysis goes a little further when examining the political strategy of talking about stereotypes of violence in a micro-level setting. Notions about 'the other' essentially shape individual and collective identities. In this context, negative stereotypes, prejudices and images of the other are exploited to gain support. Consequently, '[s]uch negative attitudes and perceptions, which some may consider as simply ethnocentric, are in fact psychological weapons in conflict relations' (Amentewee 2007: 25). Considering these consequences, I define talking about stereotypes of violence as an element of a nuanced understanding of verbal violence that exceeds harassment, hate speech, intimidation or threat (Fischer 2002: 8). I argue that, even though political actors – be they high-profile politicians or local youth groups – apply verbal violence as a political resource to mobilise support, violence itself is hardly enacted but rather talked about. Communicated violence is closely entangled with physical violence as it evokes images and memories of past violent encounters and a fear of possible future events. To be effective, violence does not need to be physical: references to violence in campaign speeches alone can change realities.[3] Politicians use interpretations of reality that the electorate can easily relate to, and in doing so they shape political discourses on violence, peace and politics in their favour. The case studies discussed below examine dominant public discourses that become tangible during election campaigning.

In this context, anthropological research offers a meaningful perspective on micro-level election communication and enables us to gain insights into the topics addressed and manipulated during election campaigns that potentially lead to violence. To understand election-related violence on the African continent, Adolfo et al. (2012) approach electoral violence as a multifaceted phenomenon in comparative studies. This can be enhanced by including an anthropological view of the interconnectedness of campaigns, communication and violence. Political communication studies offer interesting perspectives on violent forms of electoral communication from a different angle. Notably, however, the scientific discussion on political communication is dominated by scholars from the United States and Europe (Klingemann and Voltmer 2002). This trend leads to a neglect of interpersonal communication processes that largely form election communication outside the North Atlantic realm. Case studies of countries in this wider area are rare, as is a focus on local-level democracy implemented through or based on direct communication (Lang 2003). A nuanced understanding of verbal violence in a micro-level setting of an African country such as Ghana, therefore, expands contemporary concepts of political communication by providing access to local political culture. This is of particular relevance in the Ghanaian electoral context, as the use of unrestrained language and verbal abuse in election campaigns can be observed as increasing over past elections (Danso and Afful 2012).

Challenging the model: elections and verbal violence in Ghana

Both scholars and the international community hail Ghana as an 'encouraging success story' and a 'beacon of hope' for democracy in Africa (Sithole 2012; Whitfield 2009). Elections since the re-establishment of multiparty democracy in 1992 have been declared peaceful, free and fair overall. Occasional outbreaks of electoral violence, such as the 2008 Gushiegu conflict in the Northern Region, in which clashes between NDC and NPP supporters prior to elections resulted in the destruction of forty-one houses by fire and the death of three people, are considered to be of low intensity (NPC n.d.: 63–4). In this regard, this case study differs from contemporary electoral violence studies: studies on countries perceived as peaceful and democratic are as rare as the research on electoral violence in war-torn or post-conflict African countries is elaborate (de Smedt 2009; Höglund, Jarstad and Söderberg Kovacs 2009; Laakso 2007; Nordstrom 1997). Laakso (2007: 225) states that 'elections in essence should be part of the democratic rules to solve political conflicts without force and violence'. Accordingly, violence is often seen as a hindrance to a successful democratic transition. Once overcome, as seems to be the case in Ghana, the scholarly focus remains on the macro-level but turns to the performance of (state) institutions, voting behaviour, or the role of political parties.

Like its neighbouring countries, Ghana as a nation evolved from a volatile history of military regimes that forcefully interchanged with civilian governments (Amankwaah 2013: 5). Still today, parallel structures such as patronage networks and neopatrimonialism remain firmly rooted and influential in Ghanaian politics (Gyimah-Boadi 2007: 28). After emerging from an authoritarian regime under Flight Lieutenant Jerry John Rawlings through multiparty elections in 1992, Ghana successfully transformed into a democracy.

Unsurprisingly, Rawlings and his NDC won the 1992 general elections with a landslide.[4] Over the following years, the NDC and the NPP (the strongest opposition party) evolved as the main political forces. In the process, the NPP was perceived as an exclusive Akan party, mainly dominated by Ashanti, southerners and elites. The NDC, on the other hand, established itself as the party of the 'small man', ethnically and socially inclusive (Nugent 1999: 296). The three northern regions emerged as a stronghold of the NDC due to the economic and administrative policies Rawlings initiated during the 1980s to strengthen the position of the north in the nation state (Bob-Milliar 2011).

Since 1992, the two parties have alternated power every eight years through general elections; the NPP was in government from 2000 to 2008, when the NDC recaptured power. The 2008 elections were fiercely contested and led to a run-off in Ghana's 'winner-takes-all' electoral system, followed by a peaceful transfer of power back to the NDC. Tensions during these elections were higher than in the preceding years and the presidential campaigns of the two main candidates were characterised by negative campaigning, inflammatory language and hate speech to a similar extent. The NDC presented the NPP's candidate, Nana Addo Dankwa Akufo-Addo, as a drug dealer and cocaine addict. Akufo-Addo and his NPP fought back by stigmatising the NDC's candidate, John Evans Atta Mills, as a walking corpse, weak and politically powerless (Danso and Lartey 2012: 45–6). Despite outbreaks of low-intensity violence, Ghanaians were awarded the status of 'mature democratic citizens' (Lindberg and Morrison 2008: 96). At the same time, they remained consciously aware of the possibilities of electoral violence. Localised acts of small-scale violence maintain an immense psychological effect by charging the political atmosphere and 'creat[ing] an urgent sense of insecurity in the minds of many Ghanaians' (Aning and Danso 2012: 26).

The run-up to the 2012 general elections was overshadowed by the sudden death of President Mills (NDC) in July 2012 after a long but well-hidden illness, which left his vice president, John Dramani Mahama, a Gonja from the Northern Region, in charge of the country. Continuing as a presidential candidate, Mahama opposed the NPP's candidate, Akufo-Addo, an Akan from the Eastern Region, in an intensely contested campaign. On the day of the election, the Coalition of Domestic Election Observers (CODEO) reported the highest critical incidents from Ashanti, Greater Accra and Northern Region in the areas of suspension of voting, harassment and intimidation as well as the violation of voting procedures (CODEO 2012: 108). Throughout the campaigns, verbal violence played a decisive role, as was shown by the infamous example of the NPP presidential candidate's call for 'all die be die' (all death is death no matter what happens). While his supporters interpreted this as a wake-up call to be vigilant, his opponents saw it as an instigation of violence (Danso and Afful 2012: 110–12).

When looking into verbal violence on a local stage, Ghana's Upper West Region serves as a meaningful unit of analysis. Even though the region is part of 'the north',[5] which is considered the most primitive and volatile area of the country, actual outbreaks of electoral violence have been rare. The National Peace Council (NPC) identifies the Upper West Region as the most peaceful region in the country (NPC n.d.). Politicians in north-western Ghana act within a framework where claims of land ownership and questions of autochthony, belonging and ethnic diversity play an important role in the web of social relations. As the following case studies show, these local conflict lines are intertwined with patronage networks that engage the youth and are easily exploited during election times to further individuals' political ambitions.

Presidential campaigning and the 'violent north'

> Oh, as for the north, all that you need to do is go and incite the Dagabas
> against the Walas. Go and incite the Konkombas against the Nanumbas.
> Go and incite the Dagombas against the Gonjas and once they all pick
> their guns you can have your way. They will feel that they shouldn't allow
> anybody from one tribe to be an overlord over all of them.[6]

Quoting insider information given to him by NPP acquaintances, the general secretary of the NDC, Johnson Asiedu Nketia, campaigned vigorously for his presidential candidate on the campaign trail in the Upper West Region in 2012. When speaking of the north, Ghanaian politicians and scholars all draw on its image as the remotest part of Ghana, underprivileged and marginalised in terms of infrastructure, education, employment and political relevance (Lund 2003; Tonah 2007). This impression is shared nationwide. Its origins date back to the neglecting politics of the British as the former colonial power (Bob-Milliar 2011; Ladouceur 1979). On the route to independence and beyond, the northern political elite felt the urge to further a distinct political representation of their interests within the national arena. Their common aim was to prevent a regime dominated by 'southerners' (Lentz 2006: 176–80). These dynamics led to a perception of the north as one single administrative unit[7] instead of the three regions it consists of in present-day Ghana – and this perception still persists today (Nugent 2001). Over time, supra-ethnic cleavages developed around the binary opposition of 'northerners' and 'southerners'. Nugent (ibid.) correctly argues that, in order to be effective, the category of 'the north' needs to distinguish itself from a category of 'the south'. The latter, however, does not constitute the focal point of identification for people living in the southern parts of the country (ibid. 7). People from the north, however, are constantly confronted with a stereotype degrading them as a remote and primitive people with a violent nature. 'Northernness' therefore constitutes a key element of their self-perception and forms the basis of a supra-ethnic identity.

That an overall northern political consciousness exists is challenged by
Bening and Kelly (2007); however, they do agree that a common identity
as 'northerners' has considerable influence within the political elite party
alignments, such as supporting the NDC rather than the NPP, a southern
Ashanti party.[8] But especially during elections, when one would expect a
natural solidarity of the northern electorate towards candidates of northern
origin, clientelism prevails because 'individual and self-interests are of growing
importance as social and economic changes impact on the area' (ibid. 181).
Thus, voting patterns expected to be based on belonging do not materialise.

Contrary to this assumption, the candidature of John Dramani Mahama, a
Gonja from the Northern Region, as the 2012 presidential candidate for the
NDC resulted in the successful mobilisation of votes along ethno-regional lines.
Left with only a few months to the elections, the NDC decided in favour of
Mahama as its presidential candidate despite his northern origin.[9] Subsequently,
the NDC's general secretary, Asiedu Nketia, campaigned vigorously in the
constituencies in north-western Ghana, drawing on Mahama's northern descent
to evoke solidarity and loyalty among the people. He constructed his speeches
around the pillar of 'equity' and pointed to the marginalised role northerners
had been assigned since independence in every relevant aspect of participation
in the Ghanaian state.[10] Marking northerners as marginalised, Asiedu Nketia
drew a clear territorial boundary and set the stage for his speech on differences. The passage quoted above reveals a skilful combination of stereotypes
and local interethnic conflict lines.

By drawing on a stereotype circulating in the southern part of the country
that claimed that northerners are a primitive and backward people and therefore, in their various ethnic compositions, prone to violence, Asiedu Nketia
made the connection between ethnic diversity and violence approachable. At
the same time, he enhanced the image of his own party by referring to the
cheap politics played by the opposition. After having argued in a way that was
unpleasantly familiar to people from the north, Asiedu Nketia claimed to have
an NPP document on the history of the Dagomba and their war against the
Gonja to hand, which came to the conclusion that President Mahama, being
a Gonja, was inadequate and dangerous as a political leader. The history of
conflict between the Gonja and other ethnic groups dates back to precolonial
times: Brukum (2007: 100–3) identifies the groups migrating into the area of
the Black Volta (such as the Gonja) as usurpers who forcefully introduced their
chiefdoms to people who had been organised mainly in acephalous groups.
According to one of the various settlement histories of the Dagara – whom
Asiedu Nketia addressed in his speech – they once formed part of the Dagomba
people. According to these stories, they 'felt that there was too much "dictator-
ship" and too little "autonomy" and "dignity", and therefore decided to break
away from the Dagomba kingdom' (Lentz 1994: 458). This narrative frames

the migration process as a 'Dagara rebellion against Dagomba rule' (ibid.) and reflects the complex interethnic tensions in the area. Listening to the general secretary, many people were confirmed in their perception of the NPP as an Akan party. As a consequence, the audience felt more connected to Mahama as 'one of them', adopting the stereotype as a basis for a defensive stance.[11]

It is noteworthy that, within Asiedu Nketia's deployment of the stereotype of 'the violent north', a phenomenon characteristic of the Ghanaian way of handling ethnic diversity becomes apparent. In the heterogeneous Ghanaian society, there is a strong feeling of illegitimacy with regard to the evocation of ethnic differences, because, if exploited, the potential for conflict would be explosive. This can be seen in the highly contentious statements made by various politicians from both the NDC and NPP that led to an outcry from wide sections of the population. Mahama allegedly campaigned on ethnic lines in 2012, an accusation that is supported by his speech in Nandom, Upper West Region. Being of northern origin, he presented himself as a 'son of the soil', thus aiming to mobilise an essential form of belonging to automatically generate support: 'And with your son leading the NDC, I am sure that my vote in this constituency ... is going to be massive!'[12] Within the opposition, a high-profile NPP politician linked the possession of the largest amount of resources to claims of political power; according to his line of argument, resources/power would without doubt belong to the Akan, represented by the NPP (*The Republic* 2015).

Even though it is 'un-Ghanaian' to openly attribute negative characteristics to any ethnic group or to condemn people on the basis of their ethnic background (Lentz and Nugent 2000: 24), ethnicity plays an important role in election campaigning as 'ethnic discourse in Ghana is deeply encoded rather than explicit: Often a choice proverb thrown into a speech is more effective than a lengthy diatribe' (Nugent 2001: 4). Asiedu Nketia takes a different turn to circumvent the 'diversity taboo': during his speech, different layers of ethnicity and regionalism are intertwined and the distinctions between territorial units and ethnic belonging dissolve completely. He draws on the 'northern stereotype' and, to underline his argument, he lists different interethnic conflicts. In my understanding, the term 'ethno-regionalism' captures the mobilisation of various elements constituting ethnicity that are included and adapted by a regionalist discourse. Articulated as a stereotype that is ascribed to a group of people and that draws distinct boundaries by marking them as different (backward, primitive, violent), the people concerned tend to build up a collective defence. By defining themselves intentionally as members of this group, they deprive others of the opportunity to use their place of origin as an insult. They reinterpret the stereotype and form an 'identity of defence' that binds them closely together in distinction to others. Through this process, just as the NDC general secretary intended, Mahama as the presidential candidate from the north was no longer a threat but became the inclusive candidate for all northerners.

It thus becomes apparent that, in the absence of actual outbreaks of violence that unify people against a common enemy, talking about violence has the same effect and generates a solid support base for Mahama as 'one of them'.[13] However, during election times, stereotypes that become potent are not only those that focus on ethno-regional discourses, as is shown by the case of a party youth group that is confronted with the cliché that denounces them as troublemakers.

Big Men politics, rumours and the youth

In 2014, some months ahead of the local elections for a new district assembly, young men and women took to the streets in a peaceful demonstration against the current NDC District Chief Executive (DCE). The DCE's reputation was dented by rumours of her selling contracts for a 10 per cent share and in the process neglecting the youth of the district, who constitute a strong political force. The leaders of the uprising, a local NDC youth group, saw her as being appointed by President Mahama not on merit but due to her close relationship with the First Lady. Worst of all, they felt, was her traditionally 'abominable' relationship with a married man who got her pregnant, a behaviour contradictory to everything she was supposed to embody as a role model. The demonstration did not, however, lead to the desired outcome: her removal from office by President Mahama. The youth group subsequently resorted to drastic measures, defacing her office with red paint reading 'Remove this whore Mr. President. Enough is enough' to make their voice heard. Additionally, they threatened to take up arms if that were the only way to get the president's attention. All actions by the youth group were supported by the NDC party executives of the district, as well as by the former MP. Local radio and news media covered the story and people aligned themselves quickly. The announcement of violence as the final step was publicly discussed and gained the group the intended attention, which conclusively led to the removal of the DCE in December 2014.[14] In informal conversations with the district's former MP, who lost the 2012 elections and planned his return in 2016, connections between him and the youth group became apparent, which supported rumours of his influential role in the removal of the DCE. Subsequently, he won the NDC primaries against the former DCE, making him the parliamentary candidate for 2016.

When analysing outbreaks of violence during elections, a high potential for conflict is attributed to the youth in their relations to Big Men. The youth offer their (sometimes violent) support in exchange for personal benefits: 'Those inclined to violence are encouraged, used and to some extent funded by politicians' (MacGaffey 2011: 66). Politicians act as Big Men and use their patronage networks to engage young party faithful for their political aims, or, as Bob-Milliar (2012: 195) puts it, foot-soldiers' activism 'is tied to the apron string of a "Big Man"'. The fairly recent term 'foot soldiers', established during the 1996 elections, refers to young Ghanaians, mostly men, with a poor educational background, who claim to act in the name of their parties or party patrons and often trigger violence. Their interactions with the party are mostly informal and personalised. Socially unacceptable behaviour and actions can thus be legitimised in the name of party interests (Bob-Milliar 2014). Critics often reduce the task of the foot soldiers to a simplified role: all they do is 'put their lives on a line, compromise the truth, and perpetuate lies' (Issakah 2010). Bob-Milliar (2012: 12) less judgementally notes that the youth form the pillar of the party and use their 'resources (time, money and civic skills)' to promote their party's policy goals, thus being central in mobilising support. In return, they expect to be rewarded with jobs, contracts or material gains to enable a better standard of living. Violent behaviour and illegal actions often derive from foot soldiers' frustration over risking their lives and reputation without receiving appropriate rewards as the system of reciprocity would suggest (Bob-Milliar 2014: 133). Besides their own individual motivation, physical assaults on the supporters of other parties are allegedly carried out on the orders of politicians.

In public discourse in Ghana, as well as in the scholarly literature (for an overview see Resnick and Casale 2011), youth who engage in politics are often reduced to the position of hired troublemakers. For instance, Bangura and Söderberg Kovacs (Chapter 5 in this volume) address a characteristic example of youth groups being engaged in electoral violence on command or autonomously, with a view to obtain personal benefits to counter hardship. In the last decades, northern Ghana has become infamous for an increasing number of interethnic as well as intra-ethnic clashes evolving around chieftaincy conflicts. Due to their links to national party politics, they have frequently erupted during general elections.[15] Youth were identified as the key actors involved in these clashes, as they have also been in the chieftaincy conflicts in Bawku in the Upper East Region and Yendi in the Northern Region (Amankwaah 2013; Lund 2003; MacGaffey 2011).[16]

During the 2008 elections, unemployed youth and so-called 'macho men' were identified as the main driving forces behind violent encounters between political parties (Lamptey and Salihu 2012: 196–7). The macho men play a prominent role in the Ghanaian public discourse on electoral violence. These young men capitalise on their well-built bodies for a living, often as security personnel or hired by politicians for 'dirty jobs'. Macho men are often used to cause chaos on the day of elections and to frighten the voters, stealing ballot boxes or rigging the polls. They are often said to be of northern origin (Amankwaah 2013: 13, 21). In the Upper East Region, for example, the Talensi by-election in 2015 was overshadowed by violent clashes between groups of macho men aligned to political parties fighting for the parliamentary seat.[17] The constituency witnessed clashes between groups of macho men (Azorka Boys versus Bolga Bull Dogs) that were instigated by the two main political parties, the NDC and NPP respectively, who interpreted the by-elections as a litmus test for the upcoming 2016 elections (Tornyi 2015). The strategic importance of influencing in-between elections to make a head start in the upcoming general elections, as pointed out by Bangura and Söderberg Kovacs (Chapter 5), gives the district assembly election a particular importance, as shown below.

Equating politically active youth with electoral violence is a gross oversimplification; however, it is a powerful prejudice that young people constantly have to deal with in their involvement with politicians at election times. As the example of the NDC youth group in a town in the Upper West Region shows, young men are often confronted by the allegation that they would sell themselves and their morals to the highest bidder and cause violence in return for personal gains. The group is led by well-educated peers who explicitly distance themselves from those who are 'being bought by politicians … who engage in violence because they are told to do so'.[18] Nevertheless, the group leaders would not decline money offered to them by their parliamentary candidate if they felt it was a reward for duties performed in campaigning. Prior to the election campaign in 2016, money was offered and discussed as a bribe for their support but collectively rejected on moral grounds.[19] However, they admit to strategically using their image as troublemakers to further their own political aims, as the incident of the DCE's removal shows.

The example of the involvement of young party supporters and their (suspected) links to party patrons shows that their awareness of the prejudices dominating the Ghanaian discourse on youth, violence and elections supports the argument of this chapter. They skilfully use their agency to further their own political aims, and, instead of resorting to physical violence, talking about the option of doing so gives them a powerful standing in political discussions, backed by the party executives of the district. Their acts of vandalism, supported by abusive language, complete the performance and underline the severity of their claims. Rumours surrounding their intended actions – and, in this case, the involvement of the former MP – play a decisive role in making their demands more relevant to the public, for whom it becomes difficult to distinguish facts from fiction. The groups' grievances are purposely encoded in a language of morality and tradition and thus are easily relatable for the public. In an atmosphere of uncertainty and political tension prior to elections, rumours provide information that is often perceived as knowledge in the absence of more credible sources. They are manufactured to shape a certain reality or 'truth' which itself is subject to interpretation, so that one might be led by their persuasiveness to act in a way that violates common rules of society, for example by engaging in violent encounters (Simons 1995: 43). The case study shows that rumours hovering around the connection of party politics and violence become increasingly powerful in the run-up to elections. Suddenly, the risk of a simmering social conflict erupting becomes real (Stewart and Strathern 2004: 184–5). Yet, as the example shows, for the threat of violence to be effective, no physical violence was necessary.

Conclusion

Electoral violence in Ghana is often traced back to ethnic diversity and regionalism, chieftaincy disputes, patronage networks and social and economic marginalisation. These factors are politicised and strategically manipulated by political elites to gain loyalty and support. In the last decades, the northern part of the country has become infamous for its outbreaks of violence during election periods in relation to interethnic conflicts, chieftaincy succession disputes and Big Man politics. At second glance, the interlinkages between long-standing local conflicts and national politics become apparent. The close links between party politics and local conflicts are strengthened by the main actors' involvement in patronage networks with the youth, who allegedly exchange services (at times of a violent nature) for personal gains.

These conflicts and the marginalised role the north has played in the nation state since colonial times serve as the basis for the stereotype of 'the primitive and violent northerner', supplemented by the cliché of politically active, violent youth, framed in militant terms as 'foot soldiers' or 'macho men'. By nominating a presidential candidate of northern origin in the 2012 elections, the NDC strategically used the stereotype of the 'violent northerner' and capitalised on the diversity factor that materialised and became tangible through talks about violence. The stereotype served as an enforcing, politically effective mechanism of integration and exclusion that resulted in a group identity of defence that subsequently manifested in loyalty to President Mahama as the overall candidate for the north. Thus, talking about the stereotype of violence contributed to a clear victory of the NDC in the three northern regions.

Being engaged in party politics, youth are similarly confronted with prejudices denouncing them as troublemakers who sell themselves to the highest political bidder for personal gain. The stereotype portrays them as closely tied to Big Men at the cost of their own agency. However, as the case study of a political youth group in the Upper West Region shows, the young party faithful actively engage with the allegation and skilfully use the stereotype to their advantage. Thus, talking about violence as the ultimate means to achieve their political aims gained them public attention and, backed by the party executives of the district, the necessary pressure to enforce their demands. As with the 'northerner' stereotype, physical violence during election times was not enacted but rather talked about, and yet it still took its full effect. In a social setting where violence itself is deemed illegitimate, the implications of the communicated allegations and possibilities of violence were consciously discussed in public. Conflicts were defused by containing and channelling tensions and emotions in a public discourse on violence, peace and politics. Talking about various notions of violence therefore works as a powerful strategy in election communication as it affects and changes realities without the outbreak of physical violence.

The findings of this case study emphasise the need for scholars and policy advisers alike to look beyond the macro-level links between elections and violence. The analysis of campaign communication on a micro-level enables us to identify and understand localised low-intensity electoral violence in seemingly peaceful democratic countries in the region. Structural violence might not necessarily express itself physically but nevertheless it has a high conflict potential, which finds its expression in verbal violence. To prevent the enactment of communicated violence and to defuse tensions in Ghana and in the region, talking about violence as a campaign strategy and its implications for the electorate should be taken into account.

Notes

1 Author's recording of a campaign speech by Johnson Asiedu Nketia in Nadowli, Upper West Region, 13 October 2012.

2 The findings of this chapter form part of my PhD project on electoral campaigning and political communication in north-western Ghana. I would like to thank the German Academic Exchange Service for funding my research in 2008 and 2014–15, as well as the Sulzmann Foundation for the generous support in 2010 and 2012. My special thanks go to Professor Carola Lentz for her advice and support throughout the years. Many thanks go to my Ghanaian counterparts who helped me gain a grounding in understanding the depths of local politics and to Cornelia Günauer for turning this chapter upside down. I am grateful to the editors for a fruitful workshop organised in 2015.

3 Danso and Adu Afful adduce securitisation theory to analyse hate speech and the abusive language that mark Ghanaian elections, in which 'language is inadvertently used to stimulate action' (2012: 102–4). An issue is labelled as a security threat and in the process becomes one, as Akufo-Addo's statement 'all die be die' shows.

4 The overwhelming victory was partly the result of the opposition's boycott of the parliamentary elections scheduled for December 1992 after Rawlings emerged from the presidential elections in November as the clear winner, allegedly by rigging the polls (Nugent 2004: 419). The NDC was formed without major changes of personnel out of the military Provisional National Defence Council (PNDC), which ruled Ghana from 1981 until it handed over to its successor party in 1993. When Ghanaians went to the polls again in 1996, general elections were to be held on 7 December every four years to avoid future boycotts. For a critical analysis of the manipulation charges summarised by the NPP in their official publication 'The Stolen Verdict', see Jeffries and Thomas (1993).

5 In the following, the concept of 'the north' is understood as an imagined and thus constructed entity covering the three northern regions. This category reflects a perception widely held by Ghanaians.

6 Author recording of a campaign speech by Johnson Asiedu Nketia in Nadowli, Upper West Region, 13 October 2012. In mentioning the conflict between the Nanumba and Konkomba, Asiedu Nketia refers to a long-standing dispute that originated in the establishment of power relations and the Nanumba's control over the Konkomba in colonial times. The most prominent outbreak of violence between the two ethnic groups, which had a spillover effect in surrounding ethnic groups, was the so-called Guinea Fowl War in 1994. This conflict had major implications in the area as about 2,000 people lost their lives and many more were displaced (Pul 2003).

7 Bening and Kelly (2007: 182–3) describe in detail the 'boundary changes' northern Ghana has undergone since colonial times and that have led to today's division into Northern Region, Upper East Region and Upper West Region.

8 See Lentz (2002) for a detailed analysis of local elites' party affiliations in the Upper West Region, which mainly reflect competition and rivalry among themselves.

9 Both major parties tend to field candidates from northern Ghana as running mates to their presidential candidates (Amoah 2003). In doing so, they believe that they cover the key parts of the electorate by promoting a presidential candidate from the south while having a representative from one of the minority groups (for example, a Muslim from the north) as the running mate in order to capture votes from the periphery.

10 Since independence, Ghanaian citizens have seen only one president from the north: Dr Hilla Limann was elected to power following Rawlings' first coup d'état in 1979 and subsequently was overthrown by him in 1981.

11 Field notes and author recordings, 13 October 2012.

12 Author recording of a campaign speech by John Dramani Mahama in Nandom, Upper West Region, 5 November 2012.

13 Danso and Lartey (2012: 43) highlight the same behaviour by former president John Evans Atta Mills during his 2008 election campaign and thus confirm that strategically playing the ethnic card during elections is deeply rooted in Ghanaian politics.

14 Group discussion with the youth group and NDC party executives, 21 November 2014; author field notes, September to December 2014.

15 Brukum (2007) gives detailed insights into various chieftaincy disputes in the northern regions since the 1980s.

16 For a detailed view of electoral violence within the Northern Region evolving around the Yendi chieftaincy dispute in connection with the 2008 elections, see NPC (n.d.: 46).

17 That some 'macho men' attempt to change their image by actively promoting peace during elections is easily forgotten (*Daily Guide* 2012).

18 Author field notes and informal conversations, February and August 2015.

19 Ibid.

References

Adolfo, E. V., M. Söderberg Kovacs, D. Nyström and M. Utas (2012) 'Electoral Violence in Africa'. Policy Notes 2012/3. Uppsala: Nordic Africa Institute.

Amankwaah, C. (2013) *Election-related Violence: The Case of Ghana*. Current African Issues 56. Uppsala: Nordic Africa Institute.

Amentewee, V. K. (2007) 'Ethnicity and Ethnic Relations in Ghana' in S. Tonah (ed.), *Ethnicity, Conflicts and Consensus in Ghana*. Accra: Woeli Publishing Services.

Amoah, M. (2003) 'Nationalism in Africa: Ghana's Presidential Elections', *Review* of *African Political Economy* 30 (95): 149–56.

Aning, K. and K. Danso (eds) (2012) *Managing Election-related Violence for Democratic Stability in Ghana*. Accra: Friedrich Ebert Foundation.

Bening, R. B. and B. Kelly (2007) 'Ideology, Regionalism, Self-interest and Tradition: An Investigation into Contemporary Politics in Northern Ghana', *Africa* 77 (2): 180–206.

Bob-Milliar, G. M. (2011) '"TE NYƆGEYƆNG GBENGBENG!" ("We Are Holding the Umbrella Very Tight!"): Explaining the Popularity of the NDC in the Upper West Region of Ghana', *Africa* 81 (3): 455–73.

Bob-Milliar, G. M. (2012) 'The Dynamics of Political Party Activism in Ghana: A Comparative Study of the Activists of the NDC and NPP in Wa Central and Lawra-Nandom Constituencies (1992–2008)'. PhD thesis, University of Ghana, Legon.

Bob-Milliar, G. M. (2014) 'Party Youth Activists and Low-intensity Electoral Violence in Ghana: A Qualitative Study of Party Foot Soldiers' Activism', *African Studies Quarterly* 15 (1): 125–52.

Brukum, N. J. K. (2007) 'Chieftaincy and Ethnic Conflict in the Northern Region of Ghana, 1980–2002' in S. Tonah (ed.), *Ethnicity, Conflicts and Consensus in Ghana*. Accra: Woeli Publishing Services.

CODEO (2012) *Final Report on Ghana's 2012 Presidential and Parliamentary Elections*. Accra: Coalition of Domestic Election Observers (CODEO). Available at http://codeoghana.org/assets/downloadables/Final%20Report%20on%20Ghana's%202012%20Presidential%20and%20Parliamentary%20Elections.pdf (accessed 15 September 2017).

Daily Guide (2012) 'Machomen Ready for Elections', *Daily Guide*, 26 November. Available at www.modernghana.com/news/432655/1/machomen-ready-for-elections.html (accessed 15 September 2017).

Danso, S. O. and F. A. Afful (2012) '"Fruitcake", "Madmen", "All-die-be-die": Deconstructing Political Discourse and Rhetoric in Ghana' in K. Aning and K. Danso (eds), *Managing Election-related Violence for Democratic Stability in Ghana*. Accra: Friedrich Ebert Foundation.

Danso, K. and E. Lartey (2012) 'Democracy on a Knife's Edge: Ghana's Democratization Processes, Institutional Malaise and the Challenge of Electoral Violence' in K. Aning and K. Danso (eds), *Managing Election-related Violence for Democratic Stability in Ghana*. Accra: Friedrich Ebert Foundation.

de Smedt, J. (2009) '"No Raila, No Peace!" Big Man Politics and Election Violence at the Kibera Grassroots', *African Affairs* 108 (433): 581–98.

Elwert, G. (1995) 'Gewalt und Märkte' in W. Dombrowski and U. Pasero (eds), *Wissenschaft, Literatur, Katastrophe. Festschrift für Lars Clausen*. Opladen: Westdeutscher Verlag.

Fischer, J. (2002) 'Electoral Studies and Violence: A Strategy for Study and Prevention'. IFES White Paper 2002-01. Arlington VA: International Foundation for Electoral Systems (IFES). Available at www.ciaonet.org/attachments/10188/uploads (accessed 15 September 2017).

Gabbert, W. (2004) 'Was ist Gewalt? Anmerkungen zur Bestimmung eines umstrittenen Begriffs' in J. Eckert (ed.), *Anthropologie der Konflikte. Georg Elwerts konflikttheoretische Thesen in der Diskussion*. Bielefeld: Transcript.

Gyimah-Boadi, E. (2007) 'Political Parties, Elections and Patronage: Random Thoughts on Neo-patrimonialism and African Democratization' in M. Basedau, G. Erdmann and A. Mehler (eds), *Votes, Money and Violence: Political Parties and Elections in Sub-Saharan Africa*. Uppsala: Nordic Africa Institute.

Höglund, K., A. K. Jarstad and M. Söderberg Kovacs (2009) 'The Predicament of Elections in War-torn Societies', *Democratization* 16 (3): 530–57.

Issakah, S. M. (2010) 'The Foot-soldier and Politics in Ghana', *Modern Ghana News*, 19 April. Available at www.modernghana.com/news/272172/1/the-foot-soldier-and-politics-in-ghana.html (accessed 15 September 2017).

Jeffries, R. and C. Thomas. (1993) 'The Ghanaian Election of 1992', *African Affairs* 92: 331–66.

Klingemann, H.-D. and K. Voltmer (2002) 'Politische Kommunikation als Wahlkampfkommunikation' in O. Jarren, U. Sarcinelli and U. Saxer (eds), *Politische Kommunikation in der demokratischen Gesellschaft*. Opladen: Westdeutscher Verlag.

Laakso, L. (2007) 'Insights into Electoral Violence in Africa' in M. Basedau, G. Erdmann and A. Mehler (eds), *Votes, Money and Violence: Political Parties and Elections in Sub-Saharan Africa*. Uppsala: Nordic Africa Institute.

Ladouceur, P. (1979) *Chiefs and Politicians: The Politics of Regionalism in Northern Ghana*. London and New York NY: Longman.

Lamptey, A. and N. Salihu (2012) 'Interrogating the Relationship between the Politics of Patronage and Electoral Violence in Ghana' in K. Aning and K. Danso (eds), *Managing Election-related Violence for Democratic Stability in Ghana*. Accra: Friedrich Ebert Foundation.

Lang, S. (2003) 'Local Political Communication and Citizen Participation' in G. Wolfsfeld and P. J. Maarek (eds), *Political Communication in a New Era: A Cross-national Perspective*. Routledge Research in Cultural and Media Studies 10. London: Routledge.

Lentz, C. (1994) 'A Dagara Rebellion against Dagomba Rule? Contested Stories of Origin in North-Western Ghana', *Journal of African History* 35 (3): 457–92.

Lentz, C. (2002) '"The Time when Politics Came": Ghana's Decolonisation from the Perspective of a Rural Periphery', *Journal of Contemporary African Studies* 20 (2): 245–74.

Lentz, C. (2006) *Ethnicity and the Making of History in Northern Ghana*. Edinburgh: Edinburgh University Press.

Lentz, C. and P. Nugent (2000) 'Ethnicity in Ghana: A Comparative Perspective' in C. Lentz and P. Nugent (eds), *Ethnicity in Ghana: The Limits of Invention*. London: Palgrave Macmillan.

Lindberg, S. and M. Morrison (2008) 'Are African Voters Really Ethnic or Clientelistic? Survey Evidence from Ghana', *Political Science Quarterly* 123 (1): 95–122.

Lund, C. (2003) '"Bawku is Still Volatile": Ethno-political Conflict and State Recognition in Northern Ghana', *Journal of Modern African Studies* 41 (4): 587–610.

MacGaffey, W. (2011) 'Tamale: Election 2008, Violence and "Unemployment"', *Ghana Studies* 14: 53–80.

Nordstrom, C. (1997) *A Different Kind of War Story*. Philadelphia PA: Philadelphia University Press.

NPC (n.d.) *Mapping Conflicts in Ghana*. Cape Coast: University of Cape Coast for the National Peace Council (NPC).

Nugent, P. (1999) 'Living in the Past: Urban, Rural and Ethnic Themes in the 1992 and 1996 Elections in Ghana', *Journal of African Studies* 37 (2): 287–319.

Nugent, P. (2001) 'Ethnicity as an Explanatory Factor in the Ghana 2000 Elections', *African Issues* 29 (1/2): 2–7.

Nugent, P. (2004) *Africa since Independence: A Comparative History*. Basingstoke: Palgrave Macmillan.

Pul, H. (2003) 'Exclusion, Association, and Violence: Trends and Triggers in Northern Ghana's Konkomba–Dagomba Wars'. Paper presented at the Annual Conference of the Midwest Political Science Association, Chicago.

Resnick, D. and D. Casale (2011) 'The Political Participation of Africa's Youth: Turnout, Partisanship and Protest'. Afrobarometer Working Papers 136. Available at http://afrobarometer.org/sites/default/files/publications/Working%20paper/AfropaperNo136.pdf.

Schmidt, B. and I. Schröder (2001) *Anthropology of Violence and Conflict.* London: Routledge.

Simons, A. (1995) 'The Beginning of the End' in C. Nordstrom and A. Robben (eds), *Fieldwork under Fire: Contemporary Studies of Violence and Survival.* Berkeley and Los Angeles CA: University of California Press.

Sithole, A. (2012) 'Ghana: A Beacon of Hope in Africa'. Policy and Practice Brief 18. Mount Edgecombe, South Africa: African Centre for the Constructive Resolution of Disputes. Available at www.accord.org.za/publication/ghana-a-beacon-of-hope-in-africa/ (accessed 15 September 2017).

Stewart, P. and A. Strathern (2004) *Witchcraft, Sorcery, Rumors, and Gossip.* Cambridge: Cambridge University Press.

The Republic (2015) 'Osafo Maafo's Tape: Kennedy Agyapong Takes NPP On', *The Republic*, 26 February. Available at www.ghanaweb.com/GhanaHomePage/economy/artikel.php?ID=348220 (accessed 15 September 2017).

Tonah, S. (2007) 'Theoretical and Comparative Perspectives on Ethnicity, Conflicts and Consensus in Ghana' in S. Tonah (ed.), *Ethnicity, Conflicts and Consensus in Ghana.* Accra: Woeli Publishing Services.

Tornyi, E. (2015) 'NPP "Bolga Bull Dogs" Clash with NDC "Azorka Boys". Eight Political Parties Have Been Cleared to Contest in the Talensi Constituency By-election', Pulse GH, 7 July. Available at http://pulse.com.gh/news/talensi-by-election-npp-bolga-bull-dogs-clash-with-ndc-azorka-boys-id3948513.html (accessed 15 September 2017).

Whitfield, L. (2009) '"Change for a Better Ghana": Party Competition, Institutionalization and Alternation in Ghana's 2008 Elections', *African Affairs* 108 (433): 621–41.

Conclusion: Beyond democracy and Big Man politics

Jesper Bjarnesen and Mimmi Söderberg Kovacs

Introduction

The holding of democratic elections has established itself as the most legitimate route to political office on the African continent. Yet, recent years have witnessed an increase in violence in African elections. How can this seeming paradox be explained? The scholarly debate in recent years has illuminated several critical findings that come a long way in shaping our understanding of electoral violence, but it has also generated new research questions beyond existing macro-level explanations. Primarily, we have yet to understand important variations across space and time within countries, and the relationship between national dynamics and incidents of electoral violence at the local level. Beyond the national political dynamics and the contentious politics at the elite level, we also need to better understand why and how other actors and groups are drawn into these processes and the effect this involvement has on the dynamics of violence. With this purpose in mind, we urged the contributors to this book to open up the many small black boxes we saw in current explanations of electoral violence in Africa's emerging democracies, and empirically study these processes from either a local perspective or with a focus on the causal mechanisms at work across space and time.

In this concluding chapter, we offer our reflections on some of the most significant themes that run across the empirical case studies, thereby outlining a set of theoretical avenues for understanding the micro-politics of electoral violence in the context of sub-Saharan Africa. We first consider the volume's insights for refining the conceptualisation of electoral violence, raising issues of the different and multiple expressions of such violent acts. Second, we discuss the roles that such acts play within the broader political structure, questioning the overall rationale of interpreting all acts of electoral violence as always inherently anti-democratic. We then highlight the volume's contribution to the turn beyond macro-level analyses and the theorisation of the variations and continuities in the spatial and temporal distribution of electoral violence on national and subnational scales. Subsequently, we discuss one of the lead themes of the anthology: the relationship between formal democratic structures and the politics of patronage, particularly the complex relationships and power dynamics between Big Men and foot soldiers of violence. Spurred by implicit and explicit analytical insights across several chapters, we also suggest that a more careful consideration of temporality and historicity might inform future theory building around the concept of electoral violence. In the last section of the chapter, we consider some implications for policy and practice in the broader field of electoral assistance and democracy support in Africa's new and emerging democracies.

Between and below: other expressions of electoral violence

This volume took as its point of departure a definition of electoral violence as *violent or coercive acts carried out for the purpose of affecting the process or results of an election*, building on the growing literature on electoral violence as a separate and specific phenomenon. A qualitative research approach must necessarily elaborate on such an overarching conceptualisation, and the case studies have added important nuance and variation regarding the scale, character and form of violent and coercive acts that relate to the holding of elections.

One of the contributions made by this volume has been to highlight the often subtle and elusive expressions of electoral violence. Several chapters explore threats and narratives of violence as practices that play an important part in shaping electoral outcomes in their own right. Ghana's remarkable political stability since the reintroduction of multiparty politics in the early 1990s may seem at first to be a counterintuitive case study to include in a book about electoral violence. However, Schmitz's discussion of the ways in which narratives of the so-called 'violent north', including hate speech and threats of violence, influence electoral campaigning in Ghana's Upper West Region suggests that the dividing lines between the use of force and subtler forms of aggression are more blurred than current conceptualisations of electoral violence allow. One implication of this observation is that there is room for conceptual expansion in many of the dominant theories on electoral violence, which tend to either take the forms of violence for granted or limit the analysis to instances of physical aggression, voter intimidation and the destruction of election material.

Electoral violence may take such subtle forms as words or gestures evoking past violence. In April 2015, the editors of this volume were conducting field-work in the Burundian capital of Bujumbura in the days leading up to the public protests, which marked a dramatic regression in the country's post-conflict democratic consolidation. We were told stories of the Imbonerakure youth militia marching past the RPA (Radio Publique Africaine) radio station, popping balloons to mimic the sound of gunshots, so frequently heard during the country's civil war. Here, the threat of future aggression was articulated with reference to a troubled past in eerily subtle ways, which would hardly register in a more restrictive analytical delimitation of violence. Rasmussen's chapter on the Mungiki movement in Kenya also shows how this movement's violent past (and potential) persists as a central factor in its claim to power and influence in Kenyan politics, despite its transformation in recent years into a less confrontational movement, redefined as vested in the ideology of Pentecostalism. Both Rasmussen and Fjelde and Höglund demonstrate that Kenya's relatively peaceful elections of 2002 and 2013 were still undercut by the ethno-political cleavages and accompanying patronage dynamics that incited the alarming levels of violence during the 1992 and 2007 elections. These ominous continuities are also present in Sjögren's analysis of the systemic oppression underlying Uganda's ebbs and flows in electoral violence across successive presidential elections during the past three decades. Further, the chapters by Ebiede and Bjarnesen also illustrate how the instrumental remobilisation of and association with ex-militants by the political elite are not only a matter of sheer use of force, but also a compelling demonstration of latent power that may be sufficient to shape electoral processes and voting behaviour without actually engaging in physical violence. As Schmitz suggests, subtle communications of the threat of violence may thus provide an analytical entry point to studying the underlying forms of structural violence that may otherwise be overlooked or underestimated in the face of more visible and overt forms of aggression.

Another finding that relates to the conceptualisation of electoral violence and is noted in several chapters has been the benefit of removing the existing, often relatively arbitrary, temporal delimitations when studying electoral violence. Precisely because of the importance of electoral politics and its all-encompassing nature in many of Africa's electoral democracies, many important alliances and strategic moves occur outside the formal election period, including different forms of electoral violence. Bangura and Söderberg Kovacs highlight the many violent by-elections that have taken place in Sierra Leone in between general elections. They also illustrate how intra-party violence within the major political parties has far exceeded inter-party violence at times, as different political contenders are positioning themselves for the next elections. These are significant expressions of electoral violence that have previously gone largely unnoticed in the literature. In this book, we view these acts as indicators of everyday electoral violence. This by no means diminishes the relevance of a continued focus on the high-intensity violence often connected to the holding of general elections. In fact, the findings in this book point to the unequivocal connections between such large-scale events and the myriad of smaller stories that take place behind the scenes and beyond the limelight of international attention.

Electoral violence as contentious politics?

While the chapters of this volume thereby point to new and promising avenues in research regarding both subtler and additional expressions of electoral violence, the contributions also offer nuanced understandings of the multiple and ambivalent roles that such violence may play in a broader political structure. As a catch-all term for a multitude of acts and practices, perpetrated by actors on all sides and by all levels of the political spectrum, the concept of electoral violence runs the risk of conflating acts and incentives of significantly different scopes and scales. What are the differences and parallels between, say, assassinations of opposition politicians in Burundi and the day-to-day intimidation of *agbero* traffic tax collectors in the streets of Lagos? What, indeed, are the differences and parallels between violent acts committed by actors empowered by the incumbent regime and similar acts committed by actors loyal to, or sustained by, the political opposition or actors who may not be defined clearly, or strictly, as belonging to the political class? Should the actions of movements such as Mungiki in Kenya or Chipangano in Zimbabwe, with their ties to organised crime, be seen as part of civil society or as a shadow political class outside formal politics? All of these questions are tinged with a normative urge to see formal politics as more proper and productive than subversive forms of social and political action and activism. But understanding the negotiability of the definitions and exercise of state-sanctioned violence, or of the incentives of violent actors outside formal party politics, does not imply a value judgement of their legitimacy. The perspectives taken in the chapters of this volume are grounded in qualitative contextual analysis that foregrounds the incentives and manoeuvring spaces of specific actors at specific moments and in specific socio-political locations within a political landscape. These constitute the spectrum of micro-level dynamics that lend depth and complexity to this volume's approach to the study of electoral violence.

On this basis, while state-sanctioned violence may be seen to revolve around regime survival in a classical Weberian sense, the generally lenient attitude taken by the international community towards African rulers implies that the incumbent political class should be seen as lacking incentives to *refrain* from violence, as much as being driven by reasons for *engaging* in such practices of excessive use of force. Sjögren's analysis suggests that Yoweri Museveni's dominance in Ugandan politics over the course of three decades may be ascribed to a combination of the lenience of regional and international actors towards his autocratic governance and the lack of a space in which the political opposition can mobilise effective resistance. In quantitative terms, electoral violence in sub-Saharan Africa is predominantly state-sanctioned by a considerable margin, but actors in the political opposition should also be considered, along with actors outside the political class whose loyalties may be far from obvious. From a qualitative perspective, the frequency or scale of electoral violence provides an entry point, or context, for an in-depth analysis of the incentives and effects of these violent acts. One does not have to condone violent acts to appreciate that aggressive mass mobilisation or small-scale acts of coercion and intimidation by actors outside the formal political spectrum may be understood as a form of political participation in their own right, as Rasmussen suggests in the case of the Mungiki movement.

The violent demonstrations that broke out in Bujumbura in the run-up to the 2015 elections and following President Pierre Nkurunziza's announcement of his candidacy for a third term, as discussed by Nindorera and Bjarnesen, provide an interesting case study in that they challenge much of our conventional understandings of electoral violence as inherently anti-democratic. In so many ways, it could be argued that the strong reactions among parts of the population in the capital were indicators of democratic progress and a widespread acceptance that the holding of democratic elections is the key mechanism for the distribution of power. People took to the streets in organised, and originally largely peaceful, protests precisely because Nkurunziza's move was considered a violation of the democratic advances made since the Arusha peace accords. Large-scale and organised violence broke out only when these protests were met with repression and force by the government in power, at which point the resistance went underground and became increasingly militarised. The Burundi example thus illustrates the potential usefulness of studying electoral violence as one expression among many in a larger dynamics of contentious politics.[1]

The micro-level turn in studies of electoral violence

The micro-level variations within and across cases are perhaps the most valuable contribution of the volume to the study of electoral violence. Despite the significant contextual variations, the case studies included in this volume are all examples of how going beyond the macro-level has enabled the authors to tease out significant variations on different subnational levels. Rather than suggesting a clear divide between national and subnational political arenas, several chapters demonstrate the intricate interlinkages across these levels of governance. In doing so, they illustrate how local actors interact with national-level political dynamics to produce violence in the context of electoral processes. The overarching narratives that dominate political rhetoric at the national level are shaped from below by a multitude of local conflicts, grievances and alliances. These multi-layered competitions and collaborations combine to produce the particular trends and patterns of electoral violence that emerge across time and space.

In Nindorera and Bjarnesen's contribution, Burundi's recent political conflict is shown to have displayed a specific geography of violence in which the capital, Bujumbura, became the central battleground in the clashes between protestors and security forces. But their analysis also shows that the demographic variation within the capital city posited some neighbourhoods as central to the confrontations because of their status as historical strongholds of the main opponents to the incumbent government. In this account, the political legacies from Burundi's civil war can be traced through a cartography of the distribution of voting within the city, exposing a geography of violence based on the combination of ethno-political loyalties and socio-economic inequalities. Fjelde and Höglund also evoke the notion of a specific geography of violence to explain the centrality of Kenya's Rift Valley in electoral politics, due to the region's history as a locus of the unequal distribution of land.

Bangura and Söderberg Kovacs explain why the Kono District of Sierra Leone has been the scene for such high rates of electoral violence over the last few decades by pointing to the district's role as a critical swing area in a country otherwise driven by a relatively sharp and predictable regional and ethnic logic in terms of voting patterns. In situations of intense political competition and close races in particular, the political elite have incentives to use violence – as one strategy among many others – to influence the outcome of the vote. Similarly, evoking Kalyvas's (2003) influential conceptualisation, Mitchell's analysis of land conflict dynamics in south-western Côte d'Ivoire shows how central political actors on the national scene tap into local land conflicts to generate a 'joint production of action' that provides local actors with elite patronage in exchange for the electoral support needed to swing the national elections. In both these cases, national-level politics are intimately linked to specific subnational actors in particular regions or districts, whose leverage is based on their power to mobilise supporters for either peaceful or violent participation in the electoral process.

But to reduce the mutual benefits of central and local elite collusion in relation to electoral politics to a question of patronage clearly simplifies our understanding and obfuscates the complex interplay of political and financial interests at stake, which are obviously not specific to the countries under consideration, nor to African politics writ large. As we discuss in the following section, the volume's findings thus contribute to a refinement of our understanding of patronage politics in Africa's electoral democracies and beyond.

Reciprocal relations and mutually reinforced dependencies

The complex and ambivalent roles that electoral violence plays in different political contexts cut to the core of the relationship between formal democratic politics and institutions, including elections, and the underlying political logic of patronage. In the title of this volume and in the introduction to this book, this is expressed as the inherent tension between formal democracy and Big Man politics. Although this juxtaposition has served as a useful conceptual entry point, the contributions show that it really does not make much sense to think of these two notions as diametrically opposed.

This analytical sensibility becomes particularly valuable in relation to cases that are often classified according to well-established dogmas about neopatrimonialism and African politics, for example when ex-combatants are involved in electoral politics. Here, conventional views would most likely posit the influence of post-conflict networks of former fighters as a symptom of a failed demobilisation and reintegration process, and perceive ex-combatants unequivocally as a threat to the post-conflict consolidation of political stability and democratic integrity. In Bjarnesen's analysis of Liberian post-war rebel networks, however, the multiple roles played by ex-combatants in electoral politics demonstrate that these actors are adept at adjusting their skills to a non-violent political context. The real source of potential electoral violence is the 'winner-takes-all' nature of Liberia's political system, where the losing candidate and his or her supporters are left with nothing while the winning side virtually takes over the entire state bureaucracy. In this political structure, the privilege of engaging in patronage relations is almost exclusively reserved for the ruling party or coalition, a combination that greatly raises the stakes of elections.

Elaborating on the more nuanced view of the politics of patronage considered above, several chapters explore the reciprocal relations between so-called Big Men and their dependants in the context of electoral politics. Ebiede argues that former combatants in Nigeria's Niger Delta are more than mere clients in an asymmetrical relationship with the region's political elite. He demonstrates how former commanders within non-state armed groups have risen to claim a place in the political elite, thereby renegotiating their place in the patronage hierarchy. He further suggests that even the less influential actors in these post-war networks are able to enact considerable agency over their own position in the local political context. Agbiboa, through his case study of urban transportation workers in Lagos, affirms the observation that the dynamics between Big Men and their dependants are less straightforward than commonly assumed. He emphasises that dependency in these relationships runs both ways, with Big Men equally dependent on the support of their so-called clients as vice versa. The Lagos *agberos* thereby claim a central place in the region's electoral politics, as their drivers' unions become attractive for political actors intent on harnessing their support during election season.

Similar reciprocal relationships underscore both Rasmussen's chapter on the Mungiki movement and Mutongwizo's analysis of Zimbabwe's Chipangano network. Both cases portray a political elite acutely aware of the potential benefits of involving violent actors in their electoral campaigns, but also the debts they owe their dependants if they are to sustain their support. One factor favouring the elite, of course, is the large number of young people without employment, who provide a replaceable workforce with limited bargaining power. But through their subnational anchorage and diversified resource base, these non-state actors provide links between central political actors and their electorates, thereby merging a grassroots anchoring of electoral politics with coercive practices. Inspired by the Mungiki movement's symbolic evocation of the fig tree, which enters into a symbiotic relationship with a host tree from which it extracts nourishment, Rasmussen conceptualises the mutual interdependence of the political elite and its dependants as a 'parasitic politics'. Similar to the parasite–host relationship in plant ecology, neither the patron nor the client in a patronage relationship is able to retain their autonomy; rather, they enter into a symbiosis that produces a different entity from its constituent parts. These micro-political dynamics place limits on elite actors as well, as their symbiosis with dependants alters their outlook and their possibilities for substituting one set of clients for another, should the relationship prove to be less advantageous.

This parasitic dynamic is also evident in the two chapters on ex-combatant involvement in electoral politics. The 'winner-takes-all' nature of Liberian politics structures loyalties that endure long after the votes are cast, and both ex-combatants and their patrons are locked in a symbiosis that forms the basis of either their access to or their abjection from state power. By blurring the lines between state and non-state actors, the ex-militants in Nigeria's Niger Delta further underscore this symbiosis as the former secessionist movement has become integrated into the regional political competition, and the political competition in turn has become increasingly militarised. But foot soldiering is not limited to ex-combatants, as the chapters on Ghana and Sierra Leone illustrate. In both countries unemployed youths, mostly men and often from underprivileged backgrounds, have been identified as key culprits in acts of electoral violence. While associated with labels such as 'gangs' or 'cliques' in Kono and 'macho men' in Ghana, they claim to act on behalf of their patrons or local political leaders who hire their muscle to achieve their political aims. But just as often, the youth engage willingly in violent activities that they hope will be recognised and eventually rewarded. Schmitz convincingly demonstrates how the phenomenon of foot soldiering has gained a prominent role in the Ghanaian public discourse on electoral violence, where stereotypes about young troublemakers for hire are widespread. But these simplistic narratives and derogatory discourses are also double-edged, and many youths skilfully use their agency to reinforce this picture in order to negotiate private benefits without resorting to actual violence. The Kenyan case also demonstrates that the tendency for ethnic block voting can be understood on the basis of patronage dynamics, whereby ethnic favouritism may be tolerated on the anticipation of a future redistribution of the implied advantages in subsequent elections. By locking political candidates and their ethnically homogeneous electorates in an interdependent relationship, the incentive to break these loyalties is difficult to overcome, as it would imply a fundamental rupture in the politics of redistribution.

Towards a 'historical turn' in the study of electoral violence

Running counter to an analytical strategy that approaches instances of electoral violence in relative isolation, several chapters in this volume emphasise a deeper temporal dimension of electoral politics. Fjelde and Höglund propose a 'historical turn' in the literature on electoral violence on the basis of their analysis of Kenya's transition into multiparty democracy in the early 1990s, and the enduring structures of ethno-political redistribution underlying the varying levels of electoral violence in subsequent decades. Rasmussen's discussion of the Mungiki movement's violent legacy, which lends its bargaining power to contemporary politics, adds a micro-level perspective to these complex dynamics. Fjelde and Höglund suggest that, in addition to the changing national and international standards of electoral governance, the elite's capacity to learn from and adapt to the effects of violent electoral strategies in the past plays a crucial role in either retaining or discouraging electoral violence. These insights are theorised in Sjögren's contribution, which emphasises the sequential aspects of elections as a backdrop for understanding contemporary and future configurations of elite strategies and opposition responses. All three chapters thereby argue against the tendency to view particular instances of violence, or a specific electoral cycle, in isolation. Sjögren's case study, however, is more oriented towards explaining the significant *variations* in the forms and scale of electoral violence in Uganda during the long reign of Yoweri Museveni, while both Kenyan case studies illustrate the underlying *continuities* in political institutions – state as well as non-state – that sustain electoral violence as a viable strategy. Seen in conjunction, these theoretical insights articulate the volume's overall contribution to a heightened conceptual sensibility to the historical legacies that lie behind contemporary instances of violent electoral strategies.

This longitudinal view of factors that contribute to electoral violence also sheds light on another shortcoming in framing the analytical core of electoral violence as the tension between democracy and Big Man politics. Although elections as an institutional mechanism are intimately linked to the idea of democracy as a political system, elections are regularly held in many countries that score low in almost all democracy indexes, display very few features normally associated with liberal and consolidated democracies, and, perhaps most importantly, show no signs of moving towards increased democratisation.[2] Previous research has suggested that these illiberal democracies are more likely than others to see election-related violence (Salehyan and Linebarger 2015). This suggests that the core of the problem may not be so much the clash between democracy and Big Men politics as the illiberal nature of current electoral processes.

Policy implications

How are these findings relevant for policy and practice when it comes to supporting electoral processes in new and emerging democracies on the African continent? In this final section, we offer five broad statements that we believe are relevant for translating the research findings presented in this volume into more tangible advice for practitioners in the fields of election assistance and support, election observation, and democracy promotion in Africa's new and emerging democracies.

Encourage processes and reforms that lower the stakes of elections One of the key messages reinforced in this volume is that we cannot understand election-induced violence in these contexts, whether at macro- or micro-level, without taking into consideration the incentive structures of the political elite. Governments as well as opposition parties deliberately plan, support and engage in violent and coercive activities to affect the process or result of an election because the stakes of electoral outcomes are so high. As long as most political and economic resources remain concentred at the centre, this is unlikely to change. There are two separate, yet related, sets of remedies to this problem. First, the benefits of winning must be reduced. Political and economic power must be fundamentally decentralised and redistributed in a meaningful way. Institutions that serve as checks and balances on the executive power need to be strengthened. Holding political office should not be a guaranteed route to impunity for life for violence and human rights abuses. The choice of electoral systems is also important in this respect, and electoral reform can play a key role in circumventing winner-takes-all logics and encourage more broad-based political solutions. Second, there must be a role for political losers in the system. The role of parliaments must be strengthened; political opposition must have access to expression, influence and resources; and local governance structures must become more independent and self-sufficient. The problem is not patronage politics per se. It is that all networks are organised in such a manner that they are ultimately tied to the top office.

Support the broader process of democratisation beyond election support The findings from this book support the claim that it may be precisely because multiparty elections are gaining ground that we see a rise in election-related violence. As genuine political competition emerges and becomes an integral part of the political system – as it has done in countries such as Kenya, Ghana, Nigeria and Sierra Leone – the outcome of elections matters more than ever. Traditional means of controlling and manipulating electoral processes and outcomes through fraud and ballot stuffing have faced increasing challenges as election technology has improved and election observation techniques are becoming more sophisticated and advanced. Yet, while elections may have emerged as the only game in town, democracy has not (Linz and Stephan 1996). Most of the states discussed in this book display few of the signs normally associated with consolidated democracies (e.g. Diamond 1999; Linz and Stephan 1996; Przeworski 1991). Political tolerance for divergence of opinion is generally low; institutions are often weak or manipulated; the rule of law is largely absent; and large parts of civil society are politicised. Importantly, impunity for political violence is widespread. Hence, one of the most important and fundamental remedies for addressing electoral violence may not be to strengthen the credibility of electoral processes, institutions and systems, but to support the continued democratisation of the political landscape beyond elections.

Expand the concept and practice of election observation and monitoring Several chapters also enhance our understanding of the character, form and timing of electoral violence. Previous research has primarily focused on general elections, the time period immediately before and after the elections, and high-intensity outbreaks of violence, riots and large-scale killings. This narrow focus is reflected in most policy documents and has dominated international practice on election monitoring. While we believe that the growing attention to electoral violence has contributed to improving the work of many international organisations that engage with these issues at headquarters level and in the field, not least in terms of conflict prevention and management, it has also led to a concentration of resources and activities that do not necessarily reflect realities on the ground. This book has highlighted the many instances of everyday electoral violence that take place long before election day, in between general elections, and within political parties. It has also suggested that we should pay more attention to subtler forms of election-related aggression. Verbal threat constructions and belligerent narratives may play an instrumental role in de-securitising social processes, especially in the context of elections in new and fragile democracies and post-conflict societies (e.g. Sjöstedt, Söderberg Kovacs and Themnér 2017). Previous research in the field of social psychology has established the critical role played by processes of de-humanisation and de-individuation in the escalation of violent conflict (e.g. Pruitt and Kim 2003).

This suggests that more time and resources should be devoted to the period between general elections, not least the holding of strategic and contentious by-elections, and to domestic election observation that has the capacity to remain in place for much longer and ensure a presence in remote locations. It also suggests that more support should be given to programmes and processes that aim to strengthen intra-party democracy, such as codes of conduct for political parties and intra-party mediation, not only at the time of general elections but as permanent institutions. Considering the large number of armed groups that converge on political parties and the multitude of individuals in many African post-war settings who lay down their arms to pursue electoral politics, more effort should probably also go into supporting such transformative processes in a peaceful and democratic direction.

Rethink electoral security Related to the point made above, we believe that more effort should be put into ensuring that international actors do not collude with incumbents clinging to power by too swiftly and non-critically securitising electoral processes. As noted in the Introduction, previous research has established that governments in power are often the key perpetrators of election-related violent incidents on the African continent (Straus and Taylor 2012). Several of the contributions in this volume confirm this picture and point to the many intricate processes of violent intimidation and mobilisation that occur, both around and between general elections. One of the cards incumbents often play in order to manipulate the electoral process to their advantage is to deliberately securitise the electoral process in order to justify the need for increased security measures (Jenkins 2017). For example, in the run-up to the 2012 general elections in Sierra Leone discussed in the Introduction to this book, the All People's Congress (APC) government equipped police officers with advanced weaponry normally only carried by military personnel. Furthermore, the legal regulation known at the time as Military Aid to Civil Power (MAC-P) was revoked, allowing the president as Head of the National Security Council to order the military to assist the police in mitigating and managing security situations. While law and order is the duty of the government in power, such measures also carry critical risks in countries where the government is often accused of conflating the party with the state. International actors involved in electoral assistance and support need to be aware of this dynamic at work and ensure that civil liberties and rights are not circumvented too easily under the guise of security measures.

Address unresolved conflicts at the local level Another important finding emerging from this book with direct implications for policy is the critical link between national electoral dynamics and unresolved conflicts and grievances at the local level. Several chapters have illustrated how such lingering issues may feed into and reinforce processes of electoral violence at the local level. Although not the main focus in Schmitz's chapter on Ghana, recurring chieftaincy disputes have played a major role in the production of electoral violence in the northern parts of the country. Bangura and Söderberg Kovacs also point to the many underlying and lingering post-war grievances in the district of Kono in Sierra Leone, which amplify the possibilities for the elites to recruit and mobilise people for electoral violence. Mitchell's discussion of electoral violence in Côte d'Ivoire is perhaps the most apparent example. Because local land disputes are so widespread and frequent throughout the African continent, his findings are of great concern. One of the most important elements in the prevention of electoral violence may therefore be to support and strengthen land reforms. This finding is in line with recent research that suggests that questions concerning origin are among the most crucial and contested issues in political life on the African continent (Bøås and Dunn 2013). However, as noted by Fjelde and Höglund in their study of elite incentives for instigating or mitigating ethnic distinctions in Kenya during election time, such unresolved land disputes are often an integral component of a greater pattern of political, social and economic inequalities, and may be difficult to address in isolation.

Notes

1 We owe this point to one of the anonymous reviewers of this book.

2 We owe this point to one of the anonymous reviewers of this book.

References

Bøås, M. and K. Dunn (2013) *Politics of Origin in Africa: Autochthony, Citizenship and Conflict*. London: Zed Books.

Diamond, L. (1999) *Developing Democracy: Toward Consolidation*. Baltimore MD: Johns Hopkins University Press.

Jenkins, S. (2017) 'The Politics of Fear and the Securitisation of African Elections: Evidence from Tanzania 2015'. Paper presented at the 7th European Conference on African Studies (ECAS), Basel, 29 June–1 July.

Kalyvas, S. N. (2003) *The Logic of Violence in Civil Wars*. Cambridge: Cambridge University Press.

Linz, J. J. and A. Stephan (1996) *Problems of Democratic Transition and Consolidation: Southern Europe, South America, and Post-Communist Europe*. Baltimore MD and London: Johns Hopkins University Press.

Pruitt, D. G. and S. H. Kim (2003) *Social Conflict: Escalation, Stalemate, and Settlement*. New York NY: McGraw Hill.

Przeworski, A. (1991) *Democracy and the Market: Political and Economic Reforms in Eastern Europe and Latin America*. New York NY: Cambridge University Press.

Salehyan, I. and C. Linebarger (2015) 'Elections and Social Conflict in Africa, 1990–2009', *Studies in Comparative International Development* 50 (1): 23–49.

Sjöstedt, R., M. Söderberg Kovacs and A. Themnér (2017) 'Demagogues of Hate or Shepherds of Peace? Examining the Threat Construction Processes of Warlord Democrats in Sierra Leone and Liberia', *Journal of International Relations and Development*. Available at https://doi.org/10.1057/s41268-017-0111-3.

Straus, S. and C. Taylor (2012) 'Democratization and Electoral Violence in Sub-Saharan Africa 1990–2008' in D. A. Bekoe (ed.), *Voting in Fear: Electoral Violence in Sub-Saharan Africa*. Washington DC: United States Institute for Peace Press.

About the contributors

Daniel E. Agbiboa is Assistant Professor at the School for Conflict Analysis and Resolution at George Mason University, Arlington, Virginia.

Ibrahim Bangura holds a PhD in Economics from the Leipzig Graduate School of Management in Germany. He works as a consultant and as a lecturer at the Peace and Conflict Studies Programme at the University of Sierra Leone.

Mariam Bjarnesen is Assistant Professor at the Department of Security, Strategy and Leadership at the Swedish Defence University.

Tarila Marclint Ebiede is a Research Fellow at the Centre for Research on Peace and Development, University of Leuven, Belgium.

Hanne Fjelde is Associate Professor at the Department of Peace and Conflict Research at Uppsala University.

Kristine Höglund is Professor at the Department of Peace and Conflict Research at Uppsala University.

Matthew I. Mitchell is Assistant Professor at the Department of Political Studies at University of Saskatchewan.

Tariro Mutongwizo is a postdoctoral researcher at the University of New South Wales Law School.

Willy Nindorera works as a consultant and independent political analyst in Bujumbura, Burundi.

Jacob Rasmussen is Associate Professor at the Department of Social Sciences and Business at Roskilde University.

Afra Schmitz is a PhD candidate in the Department of Anthropology and African Studies at Johannes Gutenberg University Mainz.

Anders Sjögren is Associate Professor in Political Science and Senior Researcher at the Nordic Africa Institute.

Index

land law 1998, 75, 81; regions nativist discourse, 71, 73; 2010-11 electoral crisis, 56, 61, 67-8; 2015 election, 80
Crook, R.C., 76

Dagomba, -Gonja conflict, 239
Dahl, Titus, 50
Daloz, J-P., 11, 199, 208
danfo drivers, 220-1; defence tactics, 225-6; operators money extortion, 217
Daxecker, U.E., 16
DDR (disarmament, demobilisation and reintegration) programmes, 137, 148, 150-1, 160; employment expectation, 170; Liberia, 171; Niger Delta, 140-2;
De Certeau, M., 227
de-humanisation, processes of, 260
Democratic Alliance, Uganda, 59
Democratic Party (DP), Kenya, 32
Democratic Party, Uganda, 53
Democratic Republic of Congo, electoral violence, 2, 67
democratic transition, heightened violence, 29
Diamond, L., 208
diamonds, 120-1, 127-8, 131
'diversity taboo', Ghana, 240
Doe, Samuel, 162
Dokubo, Asari, 140
Dolo, Adolphus, 159
Dosunmu, Babajide (Mandos), killing of, 224
Dunn, K., 5

Ebiede, Tarila Marclint, 19, 252
economic resources, political authority creating, 198
Egypt, military takeover, 60
Ekeniojuoti, Abu ('Abu Stainless'), 224
Ekiti State, Nigeria elecions, 13, 227
Ekiti, Ado, 228
Ekpompolo (Tompolo), 145-6
Eldoret peace rally 2010, 184
elections: Burundi 2010, 106; coercive intimidation, 8; -democracy distinction, 260; do-or-die, 228; electoral commissions, 16; fraud accusations, 1; international prioritised, 157; loss costs, 15; majoritarian systems, 116; 'our turn to eat', 177; party rally interruptions, 15; resources imbalance, 12; sequential aspect, 48; stakes-violence relations, 28, 259; strategic violence, 5; sub-national level analysis, 4, 245; uncertainty moments, 215; winner-takes all dynamic, 10, 38, 166, 172, 224, 237, 256-7
elections monitoring, 38; limited parameters of, 260-1; violence contribution, 16
electoral violence, Africa: absence significance, 158; act of participation, 192; Burundi history and geography, 87-90, 107; by-elections, 120; chronic, 2; competiveness- link, 14, 49, 51, 54, 59, 81, 117, 119, 255; cycles of revenge, 8; everyday, 260; ex-militants, 136; geographical control, 130; governmental, 147, 200; historically created patterns, 52; increase in, 250; institutionalised constraints, 49; Kenya history, 176; land-related, 68, 78; local grievances geography, 109; multi-layered, 6, 9; Mungiki reputation, 181, 200; neopatrimonialism, 135; Niger Delta, 137; Nigeria 2015, 141; past politics fed, 191; political conflict context, 254; Rivers State, 150; spatial variations, 28; temporal factor, 18, 251; Ugandan state, 47-8; variations, 258; Zimbabwe, 198
elites, political: chieftain alliances, 127; election lessons learning, 51, 258; electoral violence instrumentalised, 6; ethnicity, 41; ex-combatant use, 168-9; exclusionary rhetoric, 71; Kikuyu, 34; land question manipulation, 72, 76; national-local link, 10, 115, 255; Nigeria, 135, 143; northern Ghana, 238; violence temptation, 14 elites-local actors relation, 115
employment, informal sector Liberia, 171
Equatorial Guinea, electoral violence, 2
Eriksson Baaz, M., 6
Esi, Baba, killing of, 224
Ethiopia, electoral violence, 67
ethnic identities: colonial formation legacy, 37; elite strategic use, 27-8, 38; exclusionary politics, 17, 36; loyalty strategy, 96; politicization, 177

Kabbah, Ahmed Tejan, 118; post-war regime, 121
Kalenjin ethnic group, Kenya, 32, 35, 37, 39; -Kikuyu clashes, Kenya, 32
Kallay, diamond miner, 129
Kalo, Orji Uzo, 227
Kalyvas, S.N., 6, 9, 67, 69, 78-80, 255
Kamenge neighbourhood, Bujumbura, 96, 104
KANU (Kenya African National Union), 32, 35-8; -intra violence, 39; leaders, 40; one-party rule, 31; opposition co-opting, 34; state-sponsored violence, 33
Karangi, M.M., 190
Kariobangi estate, Nairobi, massacre, 186-7, 189
Kariuki, G.G., 189
Kelly, B., 239
Kenya: 'alliance of the accused', 185; authoritarian rule, 28; demographic development, 182; elections, *see below*; ethnic exclusionary politicised, 14, 33; Independent Electoral Boundaries Commission, 40; land grievances, 38; Mungiki movement, *see below*; rule of law absence, 17; single party ethnic rule period, 30
Kenya elections: stakes increase, 178; 1992 elections, 27, 29-30; post-2008 violence, 61, 177; 2003 elections, 40; 2007 violence, 39; 2007 lessons from, 56; 2017 elections, results court challenged, 40; violence, 2, 18, 67
Kenya National Youth Alliance, 189
Kenya People's Union (KPU), banned, 35
Kenyan National Democratic Union(KADU), ethnic base, 34
Kenyatta, Jomo, 31, 34, 38, 180, 188; KADY co-opting, 35; single-party rule, 34
Kenyatta, Uhuru, 40, 60, 182-5, 187-8, 190
Kibaki, Mwai, 39-40, 182-3, 187
Kibble, S., 208-9
Kikuyu ethnic group, Kenya, 36; civil service dominance, 35; Kenya heartlands, 182; mythology of, 179, 181, 186; political elite, 187, 189; political elite-Mungiki tensions, 191-2; Rift Valley, 33
Kimathi, Dedan, 183
Kinama, Bujumbura neighbourhood, 104
Knomnanyi, Diana, 129

Kolleh Yumkella, Kandeh, 125
Kono: 'cliques' (youth gangs), 129, 257; chiefs' role, 126-7; cosmopolitan nature of, 120; election officials intimidated, 130; election 'swing' district, 19, 115, 124; ex-combatants, 128; post war grievances, 261; Sierra Leone Progressive Movement, 121; 2015 by-election, 114
Koroma, Ernest, Bai, 1, 121; re-election, 125
Kuhn, P.M., 41
Kunaka, Jim, 201, 204, 207-9; departure and return, 205; ZANU-PF exit, 210

Laakso, I., 5, 236
Lagos, Nigeria: *danfu* (minibus taxis), 216; election-related violence, 215; motor-parks contested, 223-5; patronage politics, 20, 229; political elites, 227; transport public space usurped, 217-18; urban transport, 10, 13, 216, 256
land: chieftaincy weakness, 76; conflicts election role, 67, 262; Kenyan grievances, 27, 38; leasing-selling ambiguity, 75; local grievances instrumentalised, 79; sales disputes, 74; tenure policy Cote d'Ivoire, 69; unequal distribution, 255; urban grab, 100; Zimbabwe reform violence, 200
language, cloaked threats, 8; encoded grievances, 243; politically violent, 21, 236, 238, 251
Lewis, T., 158
Liberia: Americo-Liberian elite, 162; democracy-violence interplay, 158; electoral violence, *see above*; ex-combatants networks, 138, 168, 256; National Police, 160-1, 164; past wars, 173   ; ruling elite, 166; 2005 elections, 159, 168; 2011 elections, 19, 156, 158, 171-2; winner-takes-all elections, 256-7; youth unemployment, 170
Limbas people, Sierra Leone, 118
Limuru rally, 2012, 185
Lindberg, S.I., 50, 116
local elections, importance of, 122
local-national actor dynamics, 9, 77, 254
Lubkemann, S.C., 216
Luo people, delegitimised, 35

Also available in the Africa Now series

The Future of African Peace Operations: From the Janjaweed to Boko Haram
EDITED BY CEDRIC DE CONING, LINNÉA GELOT, AND JOHN KARLSRUD

'Essential for understanding the history and complexity of peacekeeping on the continent and the human dimensions of the problems involved.'

> Lt Gen Carlos Alberto dos Santos Cruz, former force commander of the UN mission in the DRC

'Brings together leading African experts who offer a frank analysis of recent developments in African security institutions and policy responses.'

> Thierry Tardy, senior analyst, EU Institute for Security Studies

Warlord Democrats in Africa: Ex-Military Leaders and Electoral Politics
EDITED BY ANDERS THEMNÉR

'A valuable corrective to broad-brush takes on post-conflict governance on the continent. Through detailed case studies it accomplishes that most rare feat: thinking African politics on its own terms.'

> Danny Hoffman, University of Washington

'A major work. Extremely insightful and clear, it is likely to spur a new research programme in the study of post-conflict politics and state-building. It should be widely read.'

> William Reno, Northwestern University

The Rise of Africa's Middle Class: Myths, Realities and Critical Engagements
EDITED BY HENNING MELBER

'Subjects recent hype about the rise of the middle class in Africa to sceptical and critical analysis. An essential read for all engaging with the middle classes in development debate.'

> Gordon Crawford, Coventry University

'Intellectually ambitious and innovative ... Timely and hugely relevant, it marks a leap forward in our understanding of the middle classes.'

> Uma Kothari, University of Manchester

www.ingramcontent.com/pod-product-compliance
Lightning Source LLC
Chambersburg PA
CBHW071845270326
41929CB00013B/2105